A *Biography* of
THE CONSTITUTION
OF THE UNITED STATES

A Biography of
THE CONSTITUTION
OF THE UNITED STATES

Its Origin, Formation, Adoption, Interpretation

Broadus Mitchell
PROFESSOR OF ECONOMICS, EMERITUS,
RUTGERS UNIVERSITY

Louise Pearson Mitchell
SOMETIME CHAIRMAN SOCIAL SCIENCE DIVISION,
MILLS COLLEGE OF EDUCATION

SECOND EDITION

NEW YORK   OXFORD UNIVERSITY PRESS   1975

To

Orlene and Anatol Murad, old friends;
in the enjoyment of their society
these pages were written

FOREWORD

This book compresses the life story of the Constitution. We hope the reader will be served by finding main features, from inception to the present, in a single handy volume.

Construction of the Constitution has been in two phases—framing and adoption of the document, followed by its interpretation in stat utes and court decisions as the nation progressed.

To be brief and at the same time include enough detail to convey meaning we have been selective. We shall better understand reception of the Constitution by the people if we examine discussion in ratifying conventions of selected states than if we attempt a hasty view of a larger number. In Massachusetts, Virginia, and New York most questions were fully reviewed, pro and con. In each of these important states the issue was doubtful until the final vote registered a close decision for the Constitution.

Similarly for a notion of how the Supreme Court has interpreted the fundamental law we invite the reader to explore a few celebrated cases with some care instead of making a superficial general survey. In each instance we offer not simply the opinions of the justices, but the developments in American life which led to the controversy. This shows how law, which we are apt to think of as hard and fast rule, is in fact a fluid body of doctrine, a reflection of social experience. The most significant decisions are those arriving at policies for the national community. The court pronouncement is apt to be empty unless we grasp the history of the problem.

We do not burden the text with footnotes and citations. It is enough to add a sample list of books for further reading. Included are original materials on which the story is based, and explanatory works of a high order. All volumes with the possible exception of the abbreviated edition of Annals (Debates and Proceedings) of Congress are likely to be found in any good working library. We acknowledge with special gratitude the help received from Carl B. Swisher's *Constitutional Development of the United States* and Charles Warren's *The Supreme Court in United States History*. We thank Hofstra University and Mills College of Education for grants for secretarial assistance.

New York City, May 1963   B.M.
                                                           L.P.M.

CONTENTS

INTRODUCTORY

If in an unhappy distant time the physical monuments of this country should disappear, and mankind still had memory, what achievements of United States civilization would remain to speak in history? We shall not be far wrong if we venture: the Constitution and the assembly line.

Both are triumphs of organization, of social engineering, fitter to endure than reinforced concrete skyscrapers or the treasure pit beneath Fort Knox. Both are solutions of eternal problems—one political, the other economic. Both are contrivances peculiar to the American people.

The Constitution and the assembly line are parts of each other. Without a workable plan of living together as citizens, we could not have industrial mass production for a vast free market. Without government we could not have goods. Without the invention at Philadelphia in 1787 there would have been no invention at Detroit a century and a half later. We are apt to think that economic proficiency, the skill we use to supply our material wants, is fundamental in the prosperity of a community. But here the order of priority was first the charter and afterward the commerce.

We are concerned with the Constitution. Since it is a story of union, it comes to involve all of our progress in wealth and welfare. We shall see how the Constitution has been applied to developments beyond the expectation of the imaginative men who made it. The living Constitution serves a population fifty times as large as that in the beginning, reaching across the continent and beyond, instead of being confined to a string of states along the Atlantic seaboard. And growth in size of the country governed is less remarkable than increase in complexity of our culture. The Constitution, in the beginning competent for the needs of farmers and townsmen, merchants and mariners in simple settlements, is equal to the demands of an intricate social network. For the old similarities are substituted astonishing variety in ways of getting a livelihood and in racial stocks. Activities mostly local have become national, and international. It has been all one to our comprehensive, adaptable Constitution.

Some will say that we should name foremost among American public papers the Declaration of Independence, because that announced the birth of the nation in the cherished principles of human equality and self-government—in a word, democracy. We do not subtract from its celebrity if we remember how it differed, as a political instrument, from the Constitution. The Declaration eloquently recorded what, for America, was already a fact. The military rebellion against Britain had been in progress for more than a year. The Declaration was read to the patriot army, with General Washington at its head, in New York on the eve of the major battle of Long Island. The Declaration, as a document, had precedents in earlier pronouncements in American colonies abroad. It was quickly drafted, mainly by the single hand of Jefferson, was as swiftly adopted by Congress, and proclaimed to the world. It was a flaming defiance to tyranny and a pledge of loyalty to high aspirations.

The Constitution, by contrast, could not complain of the errors of a distant government, but must busy itself with repairing the mistakes of our own earlier Confederation. It must, in effect, confess failure, and prepare for a second start. It is one thing to call Heaven to witness the purity of a people's resolve, and another to translate that purpose into practical ways and means. We could shout in thrilling accents, "We will not live under former masters." It was harder and less exciting to say how we could manage to live with ourselves. The Constitution was drawn, not in the first flush of freedom, but by many men of many minds deliberating over a period of months, and then was submitted to the states for wide-flung debate. The Declaration was a splendid claim in which all patriots determined on independence could join with one voice. The Constitution was a negotiation, an accommodation of conflicting interests. One looked to war, the other to the tougher task of peace. The Declaration was done when it was sent forth. The Constitution, when ratified, must demonstrate its wisdom in the actual trial under unguessed circumstances. The Constitution must realize in practical experience the bright promise of freedom and permanence.

In this praise of the Constitution as a durable bond for a fast-changing society we must not forget that midway of our national history the tie came near being torn in two. The foresight of the Founding Fathers did not prevent the Civil War. We may not say that the states in rebellion failed the Constitution, and thus excuse the instrument that was supposed to hold all together. Four years of military strife between two groups of states—let alone the threatening political contentions that went before—meant that the Constitution did not work. To promote union and keep the peace had been its purpose. That it must be preserved by bloodshed had never been the idea.

This book deals principally with the framing of the Constitution and its later interpretation by the courts. We must remember, in sorrow, that it was interpreted also at Manassas, Gettysburg, and Appomattox. If the convention at Philadelphia took four months to give the Constitution form, twice four years were required, after the Civil War, to reconstruct states that had seceded.

Having survived the ordeal of the Civil War, the United States Constitution is the oldest single-document organic law in existence. Its relatively short span is a poor testimony to the endurance of others. One of your authors knew an old man who as a youth had talked with a veteran of Bunker Hill. A President of the United States, born in the eighteenth century, had a grandson born in the twentieth. For all its claim to be the eldest written constitution, ours is young.

Why do men marvel at its age? Precisely because it is written. England is a democracy with a constitution four times as old. But the English fundamental law is built up of documents widely separated in time and occasion, though woven together by tradition, common law, and statute. The English constitution is custom, public habit, with more spirit to give life than letter to fetter. It is flexible and remains unimpaired so long as new policies are agreed to fit in with a few ancient principles. We may call it a floating constitution, like a floating dice game which changes location, changes players, but in which winners and losers abide by the same rules.

In contrast with this unwritten constitution, a written one, like that of the United States, has disabilities. Words, engrossed on parchment and demanding to be respected as words, may hinder as well as protect where a society is evolving as all societies must. A musical composer follows certain rules of harmony but applies them in a thousand supple variations. The performer of a written piece may be better or worse in his rendition, but he enjoys far less freedom than the creator of it. The broader an accepted principle, the easier for the legislator or judge to respect it faithfully. The members of an individual family live together by certain understandings. Suppose this household, instead, were governed by a contract defining the areas of authority of parents, obedience due from children, obligations of elders, and the rights of brothers and sisters between themselves. The rule book would be in danger of being torn up weekly or daily.

The United States Constitution is a rule book. How has the national family managed to live under it and not make it a constant source of discord? That is what our story is about. We may speak in advance of several sovereign features of the Constitution which have preserved it and enabled it to serve a rapidly and radically changing society.

Most obviously, it provides for amendment in an orderly fashion, and it has received in this way more than a score of additions and corrections. Next it provides courts which among other duties say what the Constitution means. Also the Constitution sets up a counterpoise of forces, referred to as checks and balances, between legislature, executive, and judiciary. This separation of powers, weighting each against the others, could have the effect of stalling the machine. In that event it would be safe only because it was incapable of motion. How does it get off dead center? This is where interpretation comes in. Congress or the President takes action which probably raises no dissent. If these doings are questioned, the people who object may be successful in electing new lawmakers or a new occupant of the White House. Or, more swiftly, decision may be referred to the federal courts. If the majority of electors, the political party in power, comes to feel that the Supreme Court is not serving the needs of the country, the composition of the bench may be changed, generally slowly, because only as sitting judges die or retire.

The effort of the framers was to make each of the three great branches of government independent of the others in its own sphere. Nothing was said in so many words about their relative importance or influence. However, it is apparent in the discussions that they considered most depended on the legislature (Congress). The executive (President) was secondary. True, this office was viewed with some suspicion. The Articles of Confederation, which the framers were "revising"—replacing really—provided for no president of the whole country, only the presiding officer of Congress, elected annually. Framers had vivid recollections of autocratic actions of the king of England, surrounded by friends who did his bidding. They would have no king in this country, nor set up any office in which an ambitious man could come to exercise kingly powers. "Monarchy" was a dirty word in the convention. But most considered that the president was simply to carry out the commands of Congress, enforce laws enacted by the representatives of the people and of the states. The President was given some other functions, but they were deemed minor, or were left vague. Everybody knew that Washington would be the universal choice of the country for the first holder of the presidency. He would never usurp authority. Hopefully he would set a pattern which his successors would follow, and if they did not they could be disciplined when they overstepped their bounds.

The federal courts? This branch got the least attention. The Confederation had no judiciary except for a tribunal that tried maritime cases, so federal judges had not interfered in the affairs of the states. The convention talked mostly about the Supreme Court, though the power was given to establish inferior courts. The number and character of these were not defined. In fact, many supposed that the state courts would serve in the first instance, and from these state courts appeal might be taken in federal cases to the Supreme Court. Some feared that the lower federal courts would intrude into the province of the states. The Supreme Court might do the same if in appeals it could review questions of fact (which had already been determined below) as well as questions of law. But on the whole the powers of the judiciary seemed not to be potentially dangerous.

We shall see that the convention missed its guess. Through the years both the President and the Supreme Court have come forward in our governmental system. A single man, entrusted with an office, has a built-in advantage in swift decision and action. The eyes of the country are focused on the President. As he, an individual, cannot dodge his responsibility, so he may discharge his duties with latitude. The convention talked frequently of providing the President with a council of advisers. This was to prevent him from poaching on the preserves of other branches, and to supplement his information and wisdom. But no such additional body was included in the Constitution. The President could ask the advice of the heads of his executive departments, formally in writing. Thus the secretaries of state, treasury, and war—though never in so many words—came to be the President's "cabinet." But these officers were themselves executives, not legislators or judges, and they owed their places to the President. They were nominated by him, and confirmed by the Senate.

The gate was left open for the President to develop what has been called in modern politics a "cult of personality." That is, a forceful President could accumulate extra-constitutional powers and thus dominate policy. In times of crisis this has happened, from force of circumstances combined with unusual ability and popularity in the chief executive. Washington might have seized this commanding position had he not been scrupulously respectful of the authority of his co-ordinate branches, especially Congress. Also the Constitution was much on trial during the first administrations, and its exact stipulations were jealously regarded. But soon President Jefferson, in spite of his former vehement insistence on "strict construction" of the Constitution, took a giant step off limits by acquiring the Louisiana Territory. This was in response to a manifest magnificent opportunity. Most in the country approved his action, though he took it with no constitutional authority. Lincoln, Cleveland, Theodore Roosevelt, Wilson, and Franklin Roosevelt followed suit in enlarging the powers of the President. As we scan the whole history, the President has come to exercise more sway than the devisers of the system ever expected.

At first the federal courts had little business. Consequently, such able chief justices as John Jay and Oliver Ellsworth were scarcely called into action. The judiciary was a sleeping partner in the triumvirate of government branches. By the time critical decisions were to be made, John Marshall dominated the Supreme Court. He ran to meet his double opportunity, to claim a creative role for the Court and to use its powers to elevate the authority of the federal government. We shall see that the two branches which have been on the make—the presidency and the judiciary—have clashed at times. The President has tried to conform the court to his policy by means not laid down in the Constitution. Or the Court has rebuked the President by disallowing his darling laws. These differences have divided the country temporarily. But the result has been that the Court has grown in the esteem and reliance of the American people. Its independence is looked on as "sacred" beyond the privileges of the legislative and executive branches. The Supreme Court cannot take the initiative as the President can, but by forbidding this and permitting that it has a determining influence in steering the ship of state.

Marshall's use of the Supreme Court, during his third of a century as Chief Justice, to fix and increase the importance of the central government brings us to a last general observation on the Constitution, as it was written and as it has become since. Foreigners, taking a detached view, are accurate in saying that the special merit of the constitutional framers was in reconciling and incorporating in the system the sovereignties of the individual states and of the nation. How to unite powers claimed to be separately supreme was a puzzler. By contrast, suppose the English were to write a constitution out of hand. Their task would be easier because the authority of the one government—except in petty local matters—runs throughout the realm. The framers would not have to watch their step at every turn to be sure they did not tread on the toes of the legislature, executive, and judiciary of Hampshire, Sussex, Northumberland, and the other components of the nation. But here our framers had to embrace the rights and interests of thirteen states (and more in prospect), each jealous of its powers, with the needs common to all.

Our Founding Fathers might not have been obliged to perform such an egg dance if they could have constructed a workable plan of government immediately the Revolutionary War was over and our independence was established. But then (1783) the Articles of Confederation had been in effect only two years. The Confederation had been slow and arduous in adoption, and the states were straining at the leash to enjoy their separate liberties. Under the Articles the states were superior to the central government, which had no commission to compel in the most vital areas. There was no cat, and the mice played. During five years the self-willed states, with little regard for each other, almost brought the country to disaster. Most of them (not Rhode Island, the worst offender), were ready to confess the mischief, but they were quick to contest proposals for reform.

As further impediment to agreement, certain states formed blocs of similar character in one way and another—small states against large, planting states (with slave labor) against mercantile or "carrying" states (with free labor).

What was the solution? How was a competent central government erected, or inserted, without trenching on the prerogatives of the prideful states? Big problems had been settled in advance by sad experience under the Confederation. The national authority must have an independent revenue, which meant, in effect, power to lay taxes not on the states but on individual citizens. There must be national regulation of foreign commerce and of that between the states. There must be some kind of national executive and judiciary. These and other provisions were incorporated by compromises little and big, as we shall see. The principle was a division of functions or responsibilities, giving to the national government what exceeded the capacities of the individual states. Central authority was to be supreme within its scope, state authority within its allotted sphere.

Actually, with expansion and development of the country the areas of federal action increased. The idea that the states, on entering the Union, preserved their separate sovereignties faded. Under what southern states considered sharp provocation they later revived the notion, which had been abandoned elsewhere in the country, that the Constitution was not a binding contract but a treaty which a state was at liberty to denounce. The inspiration for this contention lay not in political science, though that was the pretense. The reason was a roller whose metal teeth revolved through slots in a baffle and tore the lint from the seeds of cotton. But of that more later . . .

A *Biography* of
THE CONSTITUTION
OF THE UNITED STATES

Chapter One

ROPE OF SAND

The Constitution of the United States was framed to correct the short-comings of the Articles of Confederation. A confederation had been proposed in the Continental Congress at the time the Declaration of Independence was adopted, July 1776. After much debate, a plan of government was submitted by delegates from thirteen states at Philadelphia July 9, 1778. Eleven states ratified within a year, but Delaware took longer and Maryland did not bring the Articles into effect until March 1, 1781. This was less than eight months before the fighting war ended with the surrender of Cornwallis at Yorktown. Congress, descended from the first continental body assembled back in 1774, had acted by common consent, not under a constitution. The Articles of Confederation were only a nominal improvement.

The center of gravity in the Confederation was in the individual state. The Articles no sooner established the United States than they declared, "Each state retains its sovereignty, freedom and independence, and every power, jurisdiction and right, which is not expressly delegated to the united states [notice, no caps], in Congress assembled." The states entered into "a firm league of friendship," professed to be "perpetual," but the powers each reserved to itself portended conflicts which boded ill for co-operation. The Articles did not say so, but doubtless each state, in signing, considered that it might withdraw for what it contended was good cause.

Delegates in the one-chamber Congress represented the states. Each state named its delegates in the manner it preferred, paid them, and each state had one vote, whether it sent two delegates (the minimum)

3

or seven (the maximum). Each state could recall its delegates and substitute others at will.

The common treasury for general defense and welfare should be contributed by the states in proportion to the value of the real estate in each as determined by Congress. However, taxes for meeting its share should be laid by the state. This meant that the revenue of Congress was precarious, for Congress could not tax the individual citizen and had no way of compelling a state to contribute its quota of funds. In fact states were generally in arrears in responding to the requests or "requisitions" of Congress for money. Congress could regulate its own coinage and that of the states, borrow money, and emit bills of credit.

Congress alone controlled foreign relations. But each state raised and equipped its troops (at the expense of Congress), appointed the officers from colonel down, and could not be obliged to march more than its quota. Only Congress could conclude treaties, but no treaty of commerce could prevent a state from laying import and export duties as it chose. This reservation hamstrung Congress in attempts to secure uniformity in foreign and domestic trade. A navy was the exclusive responsibility of Congress, which also appointed courts for trials of felonies, captures and the like on the high sea, but otherwise there was no judiciary of the Confederation.

Disputes between states (mostly over boundaries) if one state complained, should be settled in the last resort under the auspices of Congress. The same complicated machinery applied in contests between individuals claiming lands under grants of different states.

In Congress the assent of nine states (more than a two-thirds majority) was necessary to pass all important legislation. The president of Congress was elected by that body for one year. He was little more than a wielder of the gavel, by no means a chief executive of the country. Administration was notably weak, for executive functions were entrusted to committees of Congress. A committee is better suited to deliberation than to enforcement. Legislative and executive duties were hopelessly confused. An interim committee (one delegate from each state) was to sit in the recess of Congress, but its authority was confined to minor matters. The Articles could be amended by consent of Congress followed by confirmation by the legislatures of all of the states.

During seven years the states were held together by the stress of war. Not that they were equally obedient to their moral commitment to each other, or, after formation of the Confederation, observed equally their legal obligations. There were times when the personal steadfastness of George Washington was a force for union superior to any signed document. But while hostilities continued, no state, however faulty in co-operation, surrendered the determination to win joint independence.

It was after the war, when the British had evacuated our soil (except for the frontier military posts), that we were plagued by internal dissension and external weakness. Victory over a powerful military foe was mocked by our inability to govern ourselves and to command respect abroad. We had to endure half a dozen years of anticlimax, indeed of discredit. In part this was reaction from the long-drawn effort that had gone before. We were weary of good works. From common purpose we lapsed into languor and mutual suspicion. Other nations have experienced similar confusion and peevishness following strenuous achievement. In the United States the lassitude and refusal of responsibility were the more to be expected because we had embarked on a project new in the world, that of democratic government. But political immaturity was not the whole explanation. Remember that almost a century and a half later, with Allied victory in World War I, we balked at the further effort of forming a League of Nations designed by our own President Wilson to ensure the fruits of success. We would not be nerved to extra exertion. We were tired of striving, and demanded our ease.

In this emotional state following the Revolution, the political results were melancholy. The Articles of Confederation had been submitted to the states with an apology by Congress for their frailty. They were "the best which could be adapted to the circumstances" of "so many states, differing in habits, produce, commerce, and internal police." With fewer compromises the Articles could not have claimed "any tolerable prospect of general ratification." It was piously hoped that the legislatures of "sovereign and independent communities" would be "capable of rising superior to local attachments, when . . . incompatible with the safety, happiness, and glory, of the general confederacy." The disability from the beginning was that these were "Articles of Confederation . . . between the States" (naming the thirteen). The first concern was for the pride and peculiarity of the individual states, which conceded as little as possible to the common need, no matter how desperate. The unit—political, moral, economic, to a degree military—was the separate state. It was the particular state that was taken for granted, which seemed to be the original and natural political unit. These states were to affiliate for their mutual good, but the Congress of the Confederation was regarded as existing by sufferance of the separate sovereignties. Congress was little more than a meeting of ambassadors. They were maintained by their states, and constantly communicated not with their constituents in the present sense of citizens of their states—but with their governors who were their principals.

Responsibility Without Power

The reluctance of the states to yield power to Congress even in the emergency of war is obvious in the Articles. Congress was responsible for declaring war, making peace, and providing for the common welfare, but this body could not tax. The best it could do was receive revenue from the states in proportions agreed upon, revenues which the states raised in any ways they preferred, or preferred not to raise at all. Congress had little authority over the states, let alone the citizens. Impotence of Congress to control foreign and domestic commerce, as we shall see, helped bring the Confederation to grief.

The smallest state counted in Congress for as much as the largest, since each had one vote. It was frequently difficult or impossible to muster the required votes of nine states to pass the most essential legislation—coin, borrow, and appropriate money, or conclude treaties. Several of the small states, containing a fraction of the total population, joined by one or two larger states, could embarrass operations or bring Congress to a halt. For routine business (except to adjourn), as was mentioned, a majority of votes was required—not a majority present in Congress, but a majority (seven) of the states. Since different states, from time to time, neglected to send their delegates to Congress, often there was no quorum.

For years the Articles of Confederation could not go into effect because some states refused to cede their western lands to Congress. Maryland, which had no such westward extension, was stubborn and refused to ratify until others had surrendered claims which, if retained, would have made some states overwhelmingly large and powerful.

So Congress was inhibited and frustrated. The members, collectively, would have been fit patients for the psychiatrist. They were yanked in fourteen directions, by commands and suspicions of their states, and by their obligations to the general government. We may say that Congress, charged with high responsibilities which it was unable to fulfill, developed an inferiority complex. The Articles of Confederation formed a treaty, not a trust. We must try to understand the localism of the men of that day, in spite of the demand for unity to win the war. The colonies had refused a plan of combined action back in 1754 when Franklin urged it. The Continental Congresses had been got up for the emergency, and at first did not think of separation from England. Patrick Henry, assembled with the other delegates at Philadelphia in 1774 had bravely exclaimed, "I am not a Virginian but an American," but this sentiment did not go deep even with him, as his later opposition to the Constitution was to show. The colonies were differently founded and governed, had different products and habits of life, and, with poor means of travel and transport, were distant from each other. They had little experience of self-government. Their knowledge of jurisprudence was theoretical. They were insistent on "the rights of Englishmen," but did not grasp their responsibilities to themselves. Freed of irksome parental oversight, they rejoiced in liberty without much thought of how to preserve it. They fought a war of independence, but did not trouble to organize a nation as a result of it.

We could call over the woes that beset the Confederation once the dread of a foreign foe was removed. The journals of the Continental Congress from 1781 until remedy was discovered in the Constitution furnish a history of confusion and distress. The cause was state jealousies of one another, jealousies that paralyzed accommodation, let alone co-operation. Jealousy is corroding, never creative. It is mean, never generous. James Wilson of Pennsylvania, in 1788 in pleading for the correction that the Constitution promised, summed up what the Confederation had suffered. His words were impressive, for he knew whereof he spoke. "When we had baffled all the menaces of foreign power, we neglected to establish among ourselves a government that would insure domestic vigor and stability. What was the consequence? The commencement of peace was the commencement of every disgrace and distress that could befall a people in a peaceful state. Devoid of *national power*, we could not prohibit the extravagance of our importations, nor could we derive a revenue from their excess. Devoid of national *importance*, we could not procure, for our exports, a tolerable sale at foreign markets. Devoid of national *credit*, we saw our public securities melt in the hands of the holders, like snow before the sun. Devoid of national *dignity*, we could not, in some instances, perform our treaties, on our part; and, in other instances, we could neither obtain nor compel the performance of them on the part of others. Devoid of national *energy*, we could not carry into execution our own resolutions, decisions, or laws."

Dissatisfaction with the impotence of the Old Congress commenced

early and finally became something like disgust. Already in February
1778 Colonel Alexander Hamilton, on General Washington's staff,
was complaining—not of the Articles, for those were as yet only proposed—but of the inferior quality of delegates sent to "the great council of America. . . Each State, in order to promote its own internal
. . . prosperity, has selected its best members to fill the offices within
itself, and conduct its own affairs. Men have been fonder of the
emoluments and conveniences of being employed at home; and local
attachment, falsely operating, has made them more provident for the
particular interests of the States to which they belonged, than for the
common interests of the confederacy." This lack of ability in its members made the central body "feeble, indecisive, and improvident." As
the years wore on this defect was not cured, and the Congress of the
Confederation lost respectability.

Proposals for Constitutional Convention

Conventions of the New England states, in 1779 and 1780, to protest
against inflation, plainly implied in their memorials the need for more
authority in the central government, and a general convention to re-
model the system. Congress in its response illustrated the wisdom of
the recommendation, for all that this body did was refer the problem
of runaway prices to the states which could exercise no effectual control. About the same time young Hamilton at military headquarters,
tormented by Congress's neglect of the army and the consequent peril
to the war, was urging on influential statesmen imperative reforms: the
degenerated paper currency to be displaced by a foreign loan and a
national bank able to issue sound notes to be established. He progressed
from financial to political remedies. "The fundamental defect," he
declared to James Duane, "is a want of power in Congress." He dismissed the plan of a confederation then pending as "neither fit for
war nor peace." He proposed a constitutional convention (this was
eight years before one was held) empowered "to conclude finally
upon . . . a solid coercive union." Congress could not operate through
administrative committees; instead, each department, such as War and
Finance, should be confided to a single capable, responsible individual.
Robert Morris would be the fittest man for the Treasury post. As soon
as Morris was chosen, Hamilton laid before him the plan of a national
bank such as he had suggested earlier to Duane. This central financial
institution, jointly public and private, would do more than battles to
win the war.

Hamilton followed these private pleas to influential individuals with a series of letters in 1781 and 1782 in the *New-York Packet*, drawing public notice to the need to correct the basic ill, an impotent Congress. We had entered the revolution with "vague and confined notions of the practical business of government." This was not surprising, for many among us, of competence and experience, were Tories and were eliminated. Those who remained generally "possessed ideas adapted to the narrow colonial sphere . . . not of that enlarged kind suited to the government of an independent nation." Unless Congress was given more control, the Confederation was "unequal, either to a vigorous prosecution of the war, or to the preservation of the union in peace." Guarding against encroachment on their rights, the members threatened to be "an over-match for the common head." Instead of "a great Federal Republic, closely linked in the pursuit of a common interest," ours was the prospect of "a number of petty States, with the appearances only of union, jarring, jealous, and perverse . . . fluctuating and unhappy at home . . . insignificant by their dissensions in the eyes of other nations."

He did not urge now, as he had done before, a renovation of the system from the ground up, but begged that Congress should make the most of "the powers implied in its original trust," and that it be given authority to lay and collect taxes. "While Congress continue . . . dependent on the occasional grants of the . . . States, . . . it can neither have dignity, vigor, nor credit." The newly appointed financier, Robert Morris, was skillful and energetic, but if he was to succeed "Congress should have it in their power to support him with unexceptionable funds."

Constantly pressing for forceful government, Hamilton drew resolutions which his father-in-law, General Philip Schuyler, had adopted by the New York legislature. In his frustrated efforts, as Continental Receiver of Taxes for New York, Hamilton had learned painfully the necessity of giving Congress command of revenue. The resolves lamented "That the Situation . . . is . . . critical and affords the strongest Reason to apprehend from the Continuance of the present Constitution of the Continental Government . . . a Subversion of public Credit . . . and Consequences highly dangerous to the Safety and Independence of these States." Victory in the war depended on readiness of the states to "unite in some System . . . for producing Energy, Harmony and Consistency of Measures." The "radical Source of . . . Embarrassments" was (so went the constant complaint) "the Want of sufficient Power in Congress." Partial deliberations of the states separately could never serve national ends, "but . . . there should be . . . a Conference of the Whole." Congress should recommend and each state co-operate in "assembling a general Convention . . . especially authorized to revise and amend the Confederation, reserving a right to the respective Legislatures to ratify their Determinations." When the New York legislature sent these urgent proposals to Congress and the states, it was the first call by a public body for a convention to reform the Confederation. Congress resolved that the recommendation be referred to a grand committee, but we hear nothing of the committee's being appointed.

Shortly afterward Hamilton and Schuyler joined in a further effort for renovation of the existing incapable government. This was by rallying New Yorkers who held government securities to demand a general meeting at Philadelphia that would bolster the public credit.

This was none too soon, for with arrival of the preliminary treaty of peace, in March 1783, the army at Newburgh was verging on mutiny. Officers and troops were straining to be discharged, but feared that, once disbanded, they would never get their arrears of pay. General Henry Knox and others of rank had visited Congress and warned that "The uneasiness of the soldiers, for want of pay, is . . . dangerous; any further experiments on their patience may have fatal effects." This forecast was soon followed by open threat. Letters circulated in the camp urging that the army, if unpaid and the war continued, should refuse to defend the country any further. If peace came, perhaps the quickest way to pry pay from Congress would be with bayonets. Anxious exchanges flew back and forth between Newburgh and Philadelphia. Washington was able, in a calm appeal, to keep the soldiers steady in their loyalty to themselves and to the country, but it was a close thing.

Robert Morris, after exasperating disappointments from refusal of the states to supply funds, notified Congress that he would resign as financier. He was barely persuaded to hold on a little longer to test a new effort to extract revenue.

Congress exerted itself to secure independent and certain funds by appealing to the states to approve an exclusive 5 per cent import duty for support of the war. This should be collected by Congress until all war debts were paid. In its first form this resolve sought to eliminate the mischief of varying trade regulations by the states, but as submitted to the legislatures it was confined to the object of income for the central government.

States Refuse To Give Congress Independent Revenue

After almost two years, during which the other states had finally consented to the impost, the lower house of Rhode Island still refused to go along. The objections which the speaker cited were ably answered by Congress and a special deputation was dispatched to the smallest state to implore its compliance. These emissaries turned their horses after a few hours' travel on learning that the greatest state, Virginia, after having agreed to Congress's plan for rescue of the revenue, had reversed her action. Madison particularly was humiliated, but declared, pluckily and truly, that the project must be renewed.

After harassed debate Congress asked (April 1783) for authority to lay import duties on liquors, wines, tea, and sugar, and the 5 per cent tax on the value of all other imported goods. These taxes were to discharge costs of the war and were to run for twenty-five years only. Collectors were to be appointed by the states, but were then to be under the control of Congress. The states, woefully delinquent in their contributions, were to promise to supply a total of $1,500,000 annually for twenty-five years. Quotas of the different states varied from $16,000 for Georgia, the least, to $256,000 for Virginia, the largest. These amounts were temporary, until new permanent proportions, based on population instead of land values as formerly, could be put into effect. The census, when made, should report for the tax base "the whole number of white and other free citizens and inhabitants, of every age, sex, and condition, including those bound to servitude for a term of years, and three fifths of all other persons not comprehended in the foregoing descriptions, except Indians not paying taxes, in each state."

The quoted words were vehemently debated before they were adopted. The significant feature, which was to reappear in the Constitution, was the inclusion of three-fifths of the Negro slaves. Our ancestors had proclaimed in the Declaration of Independence that they were fighting for the rights of man, so they covered their shame at holding fellow men in bondage by the verbal twist of "all other persons." The northern states, mostly without slaves, felt that if the basis of contribution was to be people, slaves were people and should be included. The southern states preferred the old land base (property) which was being discarded. If slaves were persons, then the planting states, on the new scheme, would bear heavier burdens. If they were not persons but property, chattels, as the slave-owners contended, the

South's contribution to the common treasury would be relatively small, to the injury of the North. Hence the compromise of counting a Negro slave as three-fifths of a man. Something else is to be noted in the anxious description of classes of population to enter into the contribution-quotas. The phrase "white and other free citizens and inhabitants" plainly embraced free Negroes. Seventy-five years later, as we shall see, in deciding the crucial case of Dred Scott, the majority of the Supreme Court found that the Constitutional fathers did not regard Negroes, though free, as citizens. In this proposed amendment to the Articles of Confederation they were, however, classed with persons, with no intimation that they suffered any disability.

This medley of proposals went to the legislatures of the states with an earnest letter from Congress explaining their purpose and exhorting to compliance. As peace loomed, the problem was to provide for the war debt of $42,000,000. The principal could not be paid at once nor within a short period. The only expedient was to provide unfailing income (some $2,416,000) to meet the annual interest. Paying the interest would give value to the principal. Creditors who needed to have their capital sum instanter could then sell their claims without loss. Further, if Congress had revenue to discharge the interest on the debt, the domestic debt bearing the highest interest (6 per cent) could be paid off with proceeds of fresh borrowing at a lower rate. This plan, devised by Alexander Hamilton, who was now in Congress, anticipated what he was to recommend seven years later when he became secretary of the national treasury.

The remainder of the letter to the states reminded them that the debt had bought their freedom and that not to provide for it would bring on the country the reproaches of honorable men everywhere and doom the fairest experiment in republican government. The states were slow in response and in the end New York prevented the necessary unanimous consent by attaching conditions which Congress could not accept.

The impotence, or perhaps better say the insecurity, of Congress was demonstrated in mid-June, 1783, when the body was forced by mutinous Pennsylvania troops to decamp from Philadelphia, which served as the capital. The object of the soldiers, who had broken from their officers, was to force the Executive Council of Pennsylvania to pay their back wages. Congress was meeting in the same building (Independence Hall) and in vain called on the state authorities to furnish them protection. President John Dickinson of Pennsylvania feared that the Philadelphia militia could not be relied upon, and refused to order them out. Surrounded by bayonets in the hands of angry rebels, Congress, for safety's sake, felt compelled to adjourn to Princeton. This sudden undignified removal caused confusion, and Congress reconvened (in Nassau Hall, the building of the College of New Jersey) after a week's interruption, with thin attendance. The mood of the members was resentful at the humiliation put upon them.

After futile attempts to supplement the powers of Congress, under the Articles of Confederation, Hamilton determined on another effort for a constitutional convention to bestow adequate remedies. The spectacle of the national legislature expelled from its seat was an immediate spur. He framed a dozen resolves stressing the defects of the existing system. The prime error was "confining the power of the Federal Government within too narrow limits; withholding from it . . . efficacious authority . . . in all matters of general concern . . ." Congress was expected both to legislate and execute; judiciary there was none. Trade went unregulated, treaties could not be supported, and taxes essential for revenue and credit could not be levied. The army was unpaid. Where nine states must assent to every important measure, energy was forfeited. He begged for a convention "with full powers to revise the Confederation."

This proposal was not offered to Congress because Hamilton judged that the members were in no mood to consider such a change in the organization of government. He wrote Washington of his disappointment. He had hoped that Congress might be induced to tell the people that it was impossible to conduct the public business with feeble powers. Congress should adjourn the instant the peace treaty was ratified. Washington retiring at the same moment, with his plea to citizens "to give such a tone to our Federal Government, as will enable it to answer the ends of its institution," might produce a decisive reform. This was not to be, but Hamilton was unwearied. In newspaper pieces and letters to men influential in public life he decried "the want of an efficient general government . . . capable of drawing forth the resources of the country." Madison similarly was devoting himself to "the cause of reform in our federal system, then in the paroxism of its infirmities, and filling every well informed patriot with the most acute anxieties."

Letters exchanged by other leaders—Washington, Schuyler, Sullivan, Gouverneur Morris, Henry Knox, and more—witness their purpose to have "congress . . . vested with greater powers than they exert at present." Several in that body were disappointed in their hopes of securing, as Duane said, additional articles to "give vigor and authority to government."

An anonymous "Dissertation on the Political Union and Constitution of the Thirteen States . . ." published at Philadelphia in 1783 and often attributed to Pelatiah Webster urged a reorganization of government. "A number of sovereign states uniting into one commonwealth and appointing a supreme power to manage the affairs of the union do . . . unavoidably part with and transfer over to such supreme power so much of their own sovereignty as is necessary to render the ends of the union effectual." A congress of two houses should be authorized to tax and to regulate trade. In important respects the scheme outlined approximated the later Constitution.

In 1785 the Massachusetts legislature, in response to Governor Bowdoin's message, resolved that the states should send delegates to a convention to give Congress power over commerce. But the Massachusetts representatives declined to present the proposal to Congress; they seem to have feared that serious change in the Articles at that time would endanger democracy. As we shall now see, a movement commenced in Virginia produced results.

Abortive Commercial Convention

Trade jealousies among the states and their unwillingness to grant an independent revenue to Congress at length produced a surprising end to the distractions of the Confederation. If the states had yielded the little that Congress asked, they might have retained much of the autonomy which they perversely treasured. But refusing a mild corrective, they invited a thorough-going cure. Not that the solution heralded itself in the approach. The steps that were taken seemed limited enough. But behind them was cumulative force demanding genuine union, political as well as economic.

Few in this period of the 1780's were so national in outlook and purpose as James Madison of Virginia. Clear-headed and persevering, he pressed steadily to invest independence with governmental strength. The prize of victory was incomplete so long as each state appropriated freedom to itself and rejected concessions to the common benefit. This produced distrust and selfish rivalries. States with good ports levied duties on foreign commodities going to their neighbors less fortunate. New Jersey was the victim of the importing states on each side of her, Pennsylvania and New York. Connecticut and New Hampshire were in fealty to Rhode Island, Massachusetts, and New York. North Carolina fed the revenues of Virginia and South Carolina. Congress could make no foreign trade treaty which willful states were not free to violate.

If the states as a whole would not respond to supplications of Congress for uniform control of commerce, perhaps something might be done through agreement of individual states to desist from mutual injury. In the summer of 1784 Madison induced the Virginia legislature to invite Maryland to join her in reducing duties on the Potomac River. Such a compact between states was forbidden by the Articles of Confederation, but in the plight to which commerce and currency had come nobody objected. Governor Patrick Henry of Virginia was so unmindful that he forgot to notify his commissioners of the date set by Maryland for the meeting. However, two of them were picked up by the Marylanders, who were resolved not to have their horseback journey in the March mud for nothing. After dawdling several days at Alexandria in the vain hope that Madison and Randolph would turn up, they were glad to accept Washington's invitation to confer at nearby Mount Vernon. They could not have had a host more eager for success of their assignment, and doubtless in ways unrecorded he contributed to the favorable result. Not only was trade in and across the Potomac freed of rival tolls, but similar consent was extended to the Chesapeake Bay, which had not been on the agenda.

This agreement ratified, Madison in the Virginia legislature fought for a resolve to give Congress authority to regulate foreign and interstate commerce. The near-monopoly of America's carrying trade enjoyed by British shipping, and the exclusion of our vessels from the British West Indies caused resentment. Thus the proposal to vest Congress with power to retaliate might claim support from indignation. But this broad effort was defeated, and Madison planned to accomplish the same thing by a roundabout method. He got the Virginia legislature to call a convention of the states "to consider how far a uniform system in their commercial relations may be necessary to their common interest and their permanent harmony." If the states ratified an act with this object, then Congress could supervise trade.

Madison and Edmund Randolph were among the four Virginia delegates who named Annapolis, the first Monday in September 1786, for the meeting. Before this time arrived the situation, economic and political, worsened. The appeal of Congress for power over commerce (which if successful would have made the Annapolis parley unnecessary) was finally approved by every state, even by Rhode Island, which had been recalcitrant before. However, New York insisted on conditions that made the remedy useless—the collectors should be under control of the states, not of Congress, and the duties should be paid in depreciated state currencies. Congress refused to accept these ruinous amendments, but Governor Clinton would not call the legislature in special session to bring New York into line with the other states. For the second time an imperative reform had been blocked by a single objector. The states had their knives into each other in fresh commercial fighting. Connecticut, New Jersey, and Delaware, since their import duties yielded little anyhow, abolished them in order to get back at New York, Massachusetts, and Pennsylvania, from whom they had been buying dutied goods. The treasury of Congress was empty, states were issuing paper money or permitting debts to be paid in land, horses, and cattle. Depression settled on the country. Cash was scarce, unemployment plentiful. But it is an ill wind that blows nobody good; the hard times were to spur America to seek a remedy in genuine reform of the government.

Annapolis was a sufficiently central place for the meeting intended to abolish trade conflicts. It was selected because it was not in the shadow of Congress or of big commercial towns. Ten states appointed delegates. Connecticut was allergic to conventions. Nothing was known of Georgia. Maryland, the host state in this comedy of errors, got the notion that the purpose was to reduce the power of Congress and would have none of it. On the other hand, some critics of the project professed to see in it no commercial design, but rather a subtle scheme to bring into being a stronger central government. Madison approved such an object, but thought it beyond hope for the present; he said, "I do not extend my views beyond a commercial Reform." He attended promptly, but found only two other commissioners there, and as he waited day after day for more to arrive he must have wondered whether the states were enough aroused to accomplish trade agreement, let alone tighten the Articles of Confederation. Delegates from some states never budged from their homes, others set out late and never arrived. Only three states had full representations—Delaware, New Jersey, and Virginia. Two delegates came from New York, Hamilton and Egbert Benson. Only one, Tench Coxe, was present from Pennsylvania.

The thin attendance, a dozen men in all, was a blessing in disguise. After more than a week's delay, during which there must have been exasperated talk, those who had gathered named a steering committee (one from each state present) to recommend what should be done. Since his name stands first on the list, Benson of New York must have been chairman. The report was "That . . . it will be inexpedient for this Convention, in which so few States are represented, to proceed to the business committed to them." Never was a negative conclusion so fortunate. For then came words that led on to salvation: "That nevertheless the Object of the present meeting appears . . . of too much Importance . . . not to be pursued, and . . . the Committee think it will be proper to recommend in strong Terms a future meeting of Commissioners from all the States." The commercial matters to be considered "would essentially affect the whole System of Federal Government, and the exigencies of the United States, in other respects . . . render it advisable that the Commissioners, who may be appointed . . . should be authorized to deliberate on all . . . measures . . . necessary to cement the Union of the States" and promote their permanent tranquillity and security. A committee should address the states to this end. The language recommended for cementing the Union seemed to some of the delegates strong, or perhaps presumptuous. It was toned down but still unmistakably urged "the Propriety of extending the Powers to be given to the future Commissioners to every other matter respecting the Confederation."

Success from Failure

Doubtless all in the little company at Annapolis felt that the new convention should not stop at smoothing commercial frictions, but must revise the Confederation itself. Madison remembered, years afterward, that it was Abraham Clark from New Jersey "who first proposed the second convention." He had come with fuller powers than the others, "to consider how an uniform System of . . . Commercial Regulations and *other important matters* might be necessary to the . . . permanent harmony of the several States." Congress should be enabled, by reform of the Articles of Confederation, "effectually to provide *for the exigencies of the union.*"

Here was the opportunity to confront the country with the necessity of reorganizing the system of government. Alexander Hamilton eagerly seized this chance by drawing up the report of the convention in the form of an address to the states. A new fundamental law to replace the feeble Articles had been his purpose for years. We do not have Hamilton's original draft; it was mulled over by the other commissioners for a couple of days, and seems to have been toned down particularly by Edmund Randolph, who was always cautious when it came to the point of doing something. Nevertheless, it was startling in its frank demand for a cure of the country's depressed, distracted condition.

After first explaining that too few states were present to permit commercial agreement the report came to its real business. All of the states should meet not only to harmonize trade relations but for "such other purposes as the situation of public affairs may be found to require . . . That there are important defects in the system of the federal government" was "probable, from the embarrassments which characterize the present state of our national affairs, foreign and domestic." The best remedy would be through "a convention . . . for the special and sole purpose of . . . digesting a plan for supplying such defects as may be discovered to exist." The report need not enumerate the problems facing the country. "They are . . . so serious, as . . . to render the situation of the United States . . . critical, calling for an exertion of the united virtue and wisdom of all the members of the confederacy." Delegates acting in this emergency should "devise such further provisions as shall appear to them necessary to render the constitution of the federal government adequate to the exigencies of the Union." They should report to Congress a proper act which would then be given effect by the legislatures of the states.

The proposal of a convention to construct a workable constitution would have been incomplete without a final feature. The report named the place and day, "Philadelphia on the second Monday in May next." There and then the delegates should assemble. This brought men's minds to the immediacy of the peril and made the project concrete. If you say to a friend, "We must get together sometime" neither does anything about it; if you are to meet, a date must be set. The crisp call from Annapolis went to Congress and to all of the states, May 14, 1786, signed by John Dickinson of Delaware as chairman.

It is likely that Madison, Hamilton, and Tench Coxe rode northward together as far as Philadelphia. The chief topic of close conversation during several days must have been their resolve at Annapolis to conquer the sickness of the government. Further strategy would be fully discussed. The knitting of the friendship and the firm agreement of Madison and Hamilton were to have momentous results for America. They came from Virginia and New York, states essential to the success of their plans.

When Madison returned to Richmond he found his legislature in a mood to appoint delegates to a constitutional convention. Two events had conspicuously proved the incompetence of the Confederation. One was the insurrection of debt-harassed farmers in Massachusetts under Daniel Shays. They defied the courts, demanded paper money, attacked the arsenal at Springfield. For months the state could not suppress warfare among its own people. Virginia was warned not to let that happen in her own limits or elsewhere again. Further, Foreign Secretary John Jay had recommended that Congress surrender the right of navigation of the lower Mississippi. This commerce was important to Virginia. She suspected that Jay had yielded to the rival demands of New England, which was angling for trade favors from Spain. Congress seemed inclined to consent. Should Virginia spend her energies in a fight within the shambling Confederation? The better choice was to join in the effort to reform our national government.

Madison's hopes were rewarded by the legislature's swift, unanimous approval of the Annapolis proposal. He wrote triumphantly to Washington that "to give this subject a very solemn dress, and all the weight that could be derived from a single state," distinguished delegates would be appointed with "your name at the head of them."

Quickly five other states responded similarly. Congress dawdled some months before, on February 21, 1787, prodded by New York and Massachusetts, that body sanctioned the calling of the convention. Congress could not refuse for, penniless and powerless, the federal government threatened to expire. However, approval by Congress made the project regular. The other states fell into line, except rebellious Rhode Island. New Hampshire was favorable, but lacked money to send delegates until later.

Chapter Two

FOUNDING FATHERS

What can explain such a cluster of men of first-rate abilities in the period of the Revolution, Constitution, and new nation? Were they called out by perilous times, or did they create noble projects? They were both products and makers of history. Had there been no individuals named Washington, Patrick Henry, Jefferson, Sam and John Adams, Tom Paine, Nathanael Greene, Madison, Hamilton, and many more, others would have appeared to play similar parts. The American colonies were prepared for independence. British dominance on this continent was ready to be relaxed or destroyed. Mercantilism—a feature of which was exploitation of distant colonies to the advantage of the mother country—was reaching the limit of endurance. Trade restriction was giving way to freedom. Protests in America were matched in Britain. Adam Smith's *Wealth of Nations*, proclaiming economic liberty, and the Declaration of Independence, demanding political democracy, appeared in the same year—1776. A decade and more before either of these documents broke on the world, French philosophers—the Physiocrats—had celebrated the claims of the individual against king and autocratic government. The end of an era approached.

The Founding Fathers in America were symptoms or tokens of a development. They were vigorous shoots from a plant of deep and spreading roots. This does not diminish their qualities of imagination, courage, and wisdom. The accomplishments of lesser men would have been tardier, or fewer, or both. Granted that the curtain was about to be lifted on a new play, how account for the excellence of our actors

in the momentous drama? We may give several answers. Remember
that most of them were born Englishmen, inheritors of a long tradition of responsible government and civil rights extending from Magna
Carta. They grew up in the oldest, most advanced school of political
thought and practice. Consider that it was to be almost two centuries
before Asians and Africans established self-determining nations. More
specifically, many American leaders had been educated in England,
in letters and in law. Among these were Dickinson, the Rutledges, the
Pinckneys. Others had attended colonial colleges—Harvard, William
and Mary, King's (Columbia), Nassau (Princeton)— which, like their
older British counterparts, fitted for public life. Such were the Ad-
amses, Otis, Jefferson, Jay, Hamilton, Marshall. Still others, self-taught,
were no less partakers of British attitudes—Washington, Franklin,
Wythe, Mason, Knox, for example.

It was a homogeneous society, not only in blood and background
but in pursuits. The country was primarily agricultural, with wholesale
merchants at the principal ports. Manufactures were few, simple, and
for home consumption. With little variety in economic life it was
easy for public men to concentrate on obvious problems. Cleavage
there was between small farmers of the North and slave-owning planters of the southern seaboard, but, as the Constitution itself illustrated,
they found a compromise for their differences.

Edmund Randolph exclaimed in the Virginia convention, "I am a
child of the revolution . . . I feel the highest . . . attachment to
my country; her felicity is the most fervent prayer of my heart . . .
The unwearied study of my life shall be to promote her happiness."
The war for independence, in which nearly all of these men had part
as soldiers or in civil posts, was a cement. They were committed to
each other to reap the rewards of sacrifice and danger and not to let
the national effort dissolve in weakness and bickering. Even those
who opposed the Constitution as coercive professed concern for continued union; many of these acknowledged that bonds of the Confederation should be tightened. During the quarter-century from Lexington through the administrations of Washington and John Adams
men were constantly confronted by the project of winning and establishing independence.

Spokesmen for American society were few in number. Democracy
and popular government were the watchwords, but actually policies
were made by an aristocracy of learning and relative wealth. Tillers of
the soil and small tradesmen sat in the legislatures and state conventions, but they were content to vote upon rather than to formulate

designs. Lawyers, clergymen, men of fortune, and some who even in that day could be described as politicians carried disproportionate influence.

American newspapers were vehicles of opinion more than of news. Readers were treated almost exclusively to a diet of views on public questions. Letters to the printer and essays in his columns offered serious discussion of the political scene. Literary talents were confined to a select company. Ability to impress public meetings was limited to men of position and of oratorical gifts. A poor speaker was at hopeless disadvantage in the forum. Proof of this appears repeatedly in the records, where shorthand reporters explained that a delegate could not be heard and hence what he had to say was lost. A "plain, honest man" was attended to if he gave his sentiments briefly, but an audience demanded skill in argument and art in presentation.

Public men, being few, knew one another in camp and council chamber. In the Constitutional Convention at Philadelphia not many were strangers to the company. Personal familiarity made for political influence. Leaders formed a sort of "School of Athens." Adam Smith, the Scottish philosopher, at just this time said of such a collection of men, "their situation . . . seems to have formed in them all at once the great qualities which it required, and to have inspired them both with abilities and virtues which they themselves could not well know that they possessed."

We need to know the careers and personalities of the principal actors in the stressful scenes we are to picture. The Founding Fathers are apt to be disembodied by their very celebrity. They become graven images on banknotes and postage stamps, honored names symbolizing faith, loyalty, courage, and wisdom, lacking flesh and blood. Actually, of course, they possessed among them mortal merits and defects. They were passionate and profound, vain and modest, decided and wavering, generous and jealous, deliberate and hasty. The spotlight in which they stood reveals not only shining integrity but some actions unworthy of the man's better moments. We may not understand their principles and policies unless we have in mind the training, ambitions, occupations, and local biases of the different ones. They were not born Patriots with a capital P, but became such by their own wills or accidents of fate. The ideas and ideals of the learned ones were partly formed or strongly tinctured by the books they knew—Greek and Roman classics, Locke, Hobbes, Grotius, Machiavelli, Blackstone, Montesquieu, Hume, Adam Smith, and others of similar influence. The less academic had been taught by observation and by experience of responsibility. In any event their lives, the niches into which they fitted in society, do most to explain their views.

They formed such a constellation as never again appeared in the American skies. We may venture the judgment that as a company they were superior in stature to the next group of leaders that occupied our public stage. Comparison may be idle because the times changed. And yet, Clay, Webster, Calhoun, Jackson, Van Buren do not belong in the Pantheon with a similar number of the first period and the same may be said of the *dramatis personae* of later epochs.

In scanning the brief sketches that follow, any knowing reader has a right to say, as he is apt to, that this or that man might have been omitted in favor of others. We have aimed to make the roster fairly illustrative. Many advocates, here nameless, bore their parts. For convenience, and to recall figures as they may have appeared to contemporaries, we have grouped them as (1) friends of a strong central government; (2) those more attached to state authority; and (3) those who were now in one camp, now in the other. The divisions are rough; reasons could be given for changing alignment. By definition our Founding Fathers proper made themselves felt in the crises of the Revolution, Constitution, and new national government. But some of these continued to be influential in later years. Anyhow, in reciting their careers we have not cut them off once they have played their public roles; since we treat them as people, we allow them a few extra lines to complete their lives! Also included are some who contributed to limit or enlarge the Constitution long after the makers of it had passed from the scene.

Advocates of Central Authority

The following statesmen favored a vigorous national government. Some may think Madison belongs in the off-and-on group, but, whatever his later policies, his services in construction and adoption of the Constitution place him with its firmest friends. Daniel Shays is here because—without meaning to do it—he stiffened the authority of the Constitution.

OLIVER ELLSWORTH (1745-1807) was born and lived all of his life in his beautiful house, yet standing, in Windsor, Connecticut. He studied at Yale and Princeton, was tutored in theology, but switched to law. Briefless for three years, when he began to practice in nearby Hartford he was quickly and conspicuously successful, laying the foundation of his large fortune. Noah Webster read law in his office. During the Revolution he was active in administrative and judicial posts in his state, and was a member of the Continental Congress. In the Constitutional Convention he may have given us the figure of "Uncle Sam," since he was known for substituting "United States" for the word "nation" in a resolution. He helped engineer the principal compromise (between larger and smaller states); he offered the motion that each state have equal representation in the Senate. He was effective, by tongue and pen, in persuading Connecticut to ratify the Constitution.

In the Senate he heartily forwarded Hamilton's fiscal proposals and is credited with having drafted the influential Judiciary Act of 1789. ("This vile bill," said the ultra-democratic Maclay, "is a child of his, and he defends it with the care of a parent.") He left the Senate to become the second Chief Justice of the United States. In this place he was acceptable but not distinguished, for his talents were those of the bar rather than the bench. In 1799-1800 he was one of our three commissioners to France who composed differences that otherwise might have led to war.

In person he was tall, impressive, and preoccupied in manner, often talking to himself even in the presence of others. An inveterate user of snuff, when absorbed in writing he would take pinches from his box but forget to convey them to his nose; instead he would drop the powder in little piles encircling his chair. He was in all respects a competent, faithful public servant, a notable prop to the administrations of Washington and John Adams.

ALEXANDER HAMILTON (1755-1804) was born in the British West Indies, spent his youth as clerk in a trading post in the Danish (now United States) island of St. Croix. His talents, early demonstrated, prompted relatives and friends to send him to the continent for education. At King's College he championed the cause of the colonies in anonymous pamphlets which were attributed to patriots twice his age. He left King's to command an artillery company and a year later (spring of 1777) was invited to join Washington's staff as aide de camp. In the course of four years, at headquarters and in the field, he was painfully conscious of the feebleness of the Old Congress, which crippled prosecution of the war. In camp he framed plans for a more effective government. At Yorktown he commanded the force that captured one of the last British redoubts before the surrender of Cornwallis. Back in civil life as lawyer, legislator, and newspaper contributor he seized every chance to promote the project of a convention to construct a muscular nation in place of the flabby Confederation of states. When an attempt at trade agreements failed at Annapolis, Hamilton penned the call for the meeting at Philadelphia that produced the Constitution.

In this convention he would make the central government a giant, leaving the states with minor local functions. When this extreme position (as he guessed) proved unacceptable to most delegates, he moderated his pleas, worked diligently for unanimous consent to a Constitution which did not meet his own wishes, and was the only member from New York to sign the document. He had a way of following through on his purposes. He projected publication of the *Federalist* papers designed to bring New York into the Union, and labored ceaselessly in the Poughkeepsie convention which accomplished this end.

He was by no means through. The Constitution was a resolve, but the new nation had to be brought to realization. Brave words were one thing, but successful operation was another. As first secretary of the treasury, Hamilton promptly reported to Congress a program to rescue the credit and develop the economy of the country. Afterward he continued as a chief adviser to Washington (notably in preparation of the Farewell Address), and was leader of the Federalists until his death at the hands of his political foe, Aaron Burr.

Hamilton was below middle height, slender but erect, with reddish-brown hair, deep blue eyes, and handsome features. He was a dynamo of nervous energy. The first decade of our nation's history cannot be understood unless we appreciate his eager contribution.

JOHN HANCOCK (1736-1793), merchant and patriot, inherited a middling mind which he improved by study at Harvard, and a munificent fortune which he did not improve by his generous gifts to public objects. His signature on the Declaration of Independence, which is almost as well known as the sentiments of the document, tells us much of the man's vanity but also of his unquestioned commitment to his chosen cause. In early years of the Continental Congress and of the war, Hancock and Sam Adams were fast friends. Hancock's velvet and lace presented a contrast to Adams's plain garb, Hancock's showiness to Adams's deceptive simplicity. But it takes all kinds to make a revolution, and it must be said for Hancock that whatever he had of talents and treasure he pledged to the popular side in the contest with Britain.

Born at Braintree, Massachusetts, the son of a clergyman, and orphaned early, he was rescued by his rich uncle Thomas Hancock of Boston. In the latter's counting house and then in London he learned the shipping business. In 1768 he was prosecuted on the charge of landing Madeira wine sans duty, from his sloop, well named the *Liberty*. His lawyer, John Adams, got him off, but the *Liberty*, towed under the guns of the warship *Romney* in Boston harbor, then was used—a galling piece of poetic justice—to guard the coast against smugglers. Though he lost his vessel, Hancock was acclaimed a hero of resistance. The next year he was elected to the General Court (Massachusetts legislature). Shortly afterward, in 1774, he was the popular choice to give the oration on the anniversary of the Boston Massacre, was elected president of what was now the Provincial Congress, and was chairman of the committee of safety. Thence he went to the Continental Congress. Here, to the prestige of the presidency, he was eager to add appointment as commander in chief of the colonial forces, but the choice wisely fell on George Washington. Hancock did command Massachusetts troops in the attempt to oust the British from Rhode Island; his military ineptitude was only a minor item in the failure of that venture.

In 1780 he became governor of his state. Five years later high living brought him low with the fashionable gout. The suspicious have supposed that he resigned the chief magistracy in 1785 not because he had to rest his swollen foot on a cushion, but because he guessed that Shays's insurrection—unlikely to add to the governor's comfort—was imminent. Hardly had his successor, Bowdoin, put down the rising, than Hancock was back in the executive chair, conferring pardons that boosted his popularity.

The Massachusetts convention to pass on the Constitution elected Hancock its president. He accepted, but the position was ticklish because the state was sharply divided. Again Hancock had the gout, and preferred to keep his chair at home rather than attend and occupy the chair in the convention. Federalists relieved his perplexity by furnishing him with a speech and a list of amendments which he should propose. This therapy routed his gout and hastened him to the hall, where he spoke his lines with such effect that he was proclaimed peacemaker and savior of the commonwealth.

He died at the age of fifty-six while serving his ninth term as governor. His fine mansion, which was removed from Boston's Beacon Hill and duplicated at Ticonderoga, is open to the public as a memorial to a patriot with some foibles but more faith.

RUFUS KING (1755-1827) was what the British would call a "stout fellow." He was a New Englander (born in Maine, then part of Massachusetts) who removed to New York, thus combining two areas for federalism. In the Massachusetts legislature and in the Old Congress he was on the side of strengthening the central government. He supplied a phrase to national law when he moved that in the Northwest Territory there should be neither "slavery nor involuntary servitude." In the Constitutional Convention he was perhaps the most eloquent speaker, always for genuine revision of the political system. Having a turn for words, he was a member of the committee on style. He kept notes of the debates, briefer than Madison's but revealing. He worked effectively for adoption of the Constitution by Massachusetts.

Once settled in New York, he was chosen (with Philip Schuyler) one of the state's first United States senators. He supported Hamilton's fiscal proposals, and heartily promoted Jay's Treaty, not only by his influence as legislator but by contributing (with his friend Hamilton) to the *Camillus* papers defending the agreement with Britain. He followed this with seven years as minister to the Court of St. James. He believed that had he remained there longer he could have persuaded that government to abandon the impressment of American seamen. He was three times a candidate in presidential elections, against Jefferson and Monroe. Always against slavery, in the Senate he opposed the Missouri Compromise of 1820. He spent his later years on his estate at Jamaica on Long Island. His splendid mansion is standing, though his meadows are undermined by subways. A forceful, florid man, he fought his political foes better than he contended against a worse enemy, the gout.

JAMES MADISON (1750-1836), in the estimate of many, contributed more than any other single man to the creation of the Constitution. Service from the first in Virginia legislative and constitutional bodies, plus systematic reading in the history of previous confederacies, and concern over defects of that of America, prepared him for his role. He prepared others by his correspondence, by promoting a trade agreement between Virginia and Maryland, then the Annapolis convention (which he attended). He promptly secured Virginia's endorsement of the call for the Constitutional Convention at Philadelphia. Madison's ideas of a national government "with positive and compleat authority in all cases which require uniformity" inspired the "Virginia Plan" on which the Constitution was framed. He was prominent in guiding discussion, and industriously recorded debates. Afterward he led Virginia, in an arduous contest against Patrick Henry and George Mason, to ratify the Constitution. With Hamilton and Jay he collaborated in the *Federalist* papers, which helped secure similar adherence by New York and other states.

In the First Congress he continued as a nationalist until, in the second session, he opposed the fiscal policies of Hamilton. From that time he was in political alliance with Jefferson. His extreme demand for states' rights was set forth in the Virginia Resolutions, 1798. These declared that a state might disregard an act of Congress which, in belief of the state, violated the Constitution. These resolutions were echoed in later divisive movements—the Hartford convention, South Carolina nullification, and secession.

Madison was studious, thoughtful, and influential because he was informed and manifestly devoted to the country's good. He was small in stature, amiable in manner rather than animated, and spoke in public with logical reasoning but in a low voice without flourishes. In addition to the events already mentioned, he appears in our story as defendant in the suit of *Marbury v. Madison*. As President he approved the charter of the second Bank of the United States which led to the case of *McCulloch v. Maryland*.

JOHN MARSHALL (1755-1835) was a "child of the wilderness," his early life being not unlike that of Abraham Lincoln, whom he resembled in rangy frame, physical strength, rugged countenance, love of fun, and devotion to the union. His father, to whom he owed much in precept, was a local worthy on the then frontier of Virginia, Fauquier County. John Marshall fought through most of the Revolution, endured the rigors of Valley Forge, and shared in the capture of Stony Point. His self-education featured repeated reading of the poetry of Alexander Pope. Later he battened on Blackstone and had a single month of attendance at the law lectures of George Wythe at the College of William and Mary. One must have a strong mind and self-confidence to offer himself for the bar with this slender preparation, but he was admitted (1780), and in three years moved his practice from the backwoods to the Virginia capital at Richmond. He entered the Assembly for the second time (1787) in order to speed the Constitution, and had his wish of seeing it sent to the Virginia convention of 1788 without crippling instructions. In the ratifying meeting he was a vigorous support to Madison and other champions; especially (of importance in his later career) he pleaded for the principle of judicial review.

As a leader among Virginia Federalists he defended Jay's Treaty, and President Washington offered him cabinet posts, which he declined. President Adams sent him as one of the famous "X.Y.Z." commissioners to France in 1797. A relaxed man, he could put up with the delays, but resented the affront from Talleyrand as much as either of his colleagues. He became secretary of state and while still in that office he was named chief justice by Adams.

Presiding over the Supreme Court for a full generation, he did more than anyone else in that period to translate constitutional powers of the national government into operating force. Few had supposed that the judiciary was competent to such achievement, but from his high, though not always secure, position he beat back opposition. Some of his most significant decisions are reviewed elsewhere in these pages. They reveal his bias in favor of central government. Long after the Federalists as a party had been eclipsed, Marshall carried forward their policies.

GOUVERNEUR MORRIS (1752-1816), except that he held the nationalist principles of Madison, differed from the latter in most respects. He was vehement where Madison was moderate, he practiced the arts of oratory where Madison spoke in a matter-of-fact style. Morris was brilliant where Madison was thorough. Morris, long a bachelor, was a sport (maybe a libertine), where Madison was a conventional family man. Madison was friendly, but Morris, an extrovert, relished society and shone in it. Morris was a notable wit, with striking gifts for conversation and literary composition. Whereas Madison was anything but conspicuous in a crowd, Gouverneur Morris was large, had a Roman nose, carried himself with an air, was a man of style.

He was born on his father's country estate, Morrisania, New York (in what is now the East Bronx). Graduating from King's College (then known for its Loyalist sentiment, while the College of New Jersey, where Madison studied, was more "republican"), he was admitted to the bar at the age of nineteen. His successful law practice was interrupted for long periods by public engagements and business errands, the last adding to his patrimony, so that he became rich. His fancy for fast horses got him into an accident in which he lost a leg; the replacement was the only wooden thing about him.

His experience with constitutions began in 1776 when he helped draft that of New York. In it he tried to rule out slavery, but colleagues would not agree. Defeated for re-election to the Continental Congress in 1779, he transferred his citizenship to Pennsylvania, and was a delegate to the Constitutional Convention from that state. In spite of a long absence, he spoke oftener than any other member of the convention. Morris was for a vigorous central government, with the executive elected by the people. While he was himself an aristocrat, he uttered some of the most democratic sentiments heard in the debates.

About the time the national government commenced, Morris went to Europe, where he remained for a decade, first in trade and speculation, afterward as United States Minister to France. He had no sympathy with the French Revolution, and did not remain long in his diplomatic post. In later years he devoted energy to development of what became the Erie Canal. He was always the firm friend of Washington, Schuyler, and Hamilton. He might have been a candidate for the title "Mr. Federalist."

DANIEL SHAYS (1747?-1825). The place and date of his birth are not certainly known. Hopkinton, Massachusetts, has been put forward, and Shays may have been as much as six years older than is indicated above. The doorstone of a house in which he lived at Prescott (one of the towns obliterated for the Quabbin Reservoir) has been placed on the common of New Salem, Massachusetts. The great new highway running through the portion of the state best known to him is named for Daniel Shays.

He was not the only leader in the insurrection of farmers in the western parts of Massachusetts in 1786-87, but the rebellion has come to be identified with him chiefly. In a backhanded sort of way he contributed mightily to the formation of the Constitution. His followers, reaching through most of the country between Worcester on the east and Great Barrington on the west, were victims of the economic depression after the Revolutionary War. They had incurred debts, especially for land, at inflated prices, and later, when values collapsed, were unable to meet their obligations. They repeatedly petitioned the legislature for relief, to postpone their payments, or issue paper money. But the lawmakers, controlled by business people and meeting in Boston, far from the scenes of agricultural and frontier distress, were obstinate in their refusals. The little country jails were jammed with helpless debtors. In these circumstances those threatened with foreclosures on their farms left off supplication and began to gather at the county towns to prevent the sitting of the courts. This was physical coercion, but worse violence followed when the militia were called out against the mobs.

Shays figured as both spokesman and captain of the insurgents. He had had a creditable record in the war. He was promoted for gallantry in the battle of Bunker Hill, and fought at Ticonderoga, Saratoga, and Stony Point. In 1777 he was commissioned a captain in the Fifth Massachusetts Regiment, where he bore a reputation for bravery and kindness to his men. Lafayette presented him with a handsome sword. He resigned from the army in 1780, settled at Pelham, served on the committee of safety, and held town offices. Sincerely in sympathy with his protesting neighbors, he was the one who declared the terms on which the court would be allowed to sit at Springfield in September 1786, namely, that no debt cases should be heard and no one should be indicted for actions against the government.

Four months later the frustrated farmers, by now guilty of further violence, resolved to attack the federal arsenal at Springfield. Plans for a union of their forces miscarried, and the body under command of Shays was dispersed by the militia. Nevertheless, they collected, were joined by others, and fell back to Amherst. Finally the legislature had roused itself to a determination to restore order and sent General Benjamin Lincoln with competent troops in pursuit of Shays. The insurgents were forced from town to town in the vicinity. General Lincoln offered the pardon of the legislature if the rebels would lay down their arms and take an oath of allegiance. Shays was not ready to accept this unless the legislature promised redress of grievances. But Lincoln had no authority to grant delay. On the night of February 2, 1787, Lincoln made a surprise march through heavy snow against Shays's men at Petersham. After ragged resistance the insurgents were defeated. Daniel Shays fled northward to Vermont. This was practically the end of the rebellion. Though a general pardon was issued, Shays was not covered by it. Instead, he was condemned to death by the Supreme Court of Massachusetts. Still taking refuge in the independent government of Vermont, he petitioned Massachusetts for forgiveness and was pardoned a year after the action at Petersham. Shays moved westward in New York, and so far reinstated himself as to collect his Revolutionary pension.

Citizens who rise in arms against their government are manifestly at fault. The authorities of Massachusetts were not without their mistakes, but they were unable to remove the causes of the Shaysites' discontent. We still do not know how to prevent, though we can modify business depression and administer relief. The rebellion in Massachusetts convinced leaders throughout the country that a state, acting alone, was unable to prevent violent uprising. Obviously a stronger national government was imperative. A new constitution of union must provide against internal insurrection. Further, as a lesson from what happened in Massachusetts, no state must be permitted to issue paper money, or pass laws deferring payment of debts, or otherwise violate the sanctity of private contracts. Daniel Shays was damned up and down before he was forgiven, and he still bears an evil reputation in historical accounts. But if he is to be thanked for nothing else, he firmed the resolve of the delegates at Philadelphia to close the loopholes in the Confederation.

GEORGE WASHINGTON (1732-1799) was the most prominent member of the Constitutional Convention, and consequently was its presiding officer. Although past his physical prime, Washington had not yet reached the height of his reputation. He had earned the praise for being "first in war," but now he was entering upon his civil services which made him also "first in peace." As we shall see, he had been reluctant, for several reasons, to attend the convention. Not least among his remarkable traits was his ardent wish to retire to private life as soon as his imperative public duties were discharged. So many times in history a victorious general has used his power to make himself a monarch or other political ruler. Washington provoked universal admiration for the promptness with which he returned to his farms from which he had come to lead the country's armies. This was no false modesty in him. Nobody can read his words, often repeated, without knowing that his yearning for private life was among the deepest demands of his nature. Doubtless he guessed, when he went to Philadelphia, that if the convention moulded and the people accepted an effective new government, he would be called upon to head it. He would not be found refusing this high responsibility, but he would surely be happier if the obligation were not put upon him. Afterward, when he did become President and unprincipled newspaper editors accused him of having kingly designs, he replied, with perfect truth, "I would rather be on my farm than be emperor of the universe."

Nobody in America, by his sponsorship, could have so powerfully recommended the Constitution to the citizens. In the state conventions called to pass on the new plan, discussion was anxious, and many political leaders honestly fought adoption. But champions of the Constitution had always majestic support in everyone's knowledge that Washington had helped write the document and urged that it would be good for the country. Moreover, he would surely be the first President and establish precedents for just administration. Nor did the experiment of a solid Union benefit simply from Washington's fame. He gave the national government an energetic yet prudent direction which lists him among the most successful of American Presidents. Washington contributed to the respect in which the Constitution is held by referring his every action as chief executive to the permissions and limitations set forth in the fundamental law of the Republic.

JAMES WILSON (1742-1798) was a jurist of the first order of ability, and was among those who left an unmistakable impress on the Constitution. Strangely for a justice of the Supreme Court, and a Scotsman besides, he was anything but wise in large land speculations, his passion, which detracted from his public reputation and ruined him financially. His excellent education at the universities of St. Andrews and Edinburgh, supplemented in this country by law studies with John Dickinson, was early reflected in essays vindicating the colonies' action against Parliament. In the Continental Congress he strove to strengthen the central government. As a "Philadelphia lawyer" with many Loyalists for clients he attracted popular hostility and once was forced to barricade his house against mob attack.

In the Constitutional Convention he illustrated his conviction that sovereignty was in the people, and consequently he wanted them to elect the President and members of both legislative houses. He was a knowledgeable member of the committee of detail, as is proved by his drafts of the Constitution. He made forceful and illuminating speeches in the Pennsylvania state convention that ratified the document. His addresses were quite equal to the *Federalist* papers of Hamilton and Madison.

President Washington appointed Wilson an associate justice of the Supreme Court, and the same year (1789) he delivered the first law lectures at the College (now University) of Pennsylvania. His grandiose speculations, including a project to induce large numbers of European immigrants to settle western lands, brought him to grief. He moved from Pennsylvania to Burlington, New Jersey, to avoid arrest for debt, but continued to sit on the Supreme Court, which action subjected him to criticism. He died, mentally deranged, in Edenton, North Carolina, where he had gone seeking health.

The States Were Their First Love

The worthies sketched next opposed the Constitution on various grounds. Patrick Henry was later mollified, but his shrill denunciations silence his whispered retractions. Luther Martin came round also, but in the eyes of history did not change his earlier page.

GEORGE CLINTON (1739-1812) was an early example of men of Irish blood who have shown a turn for politics in New York. He was governor seven times and twice Vice President of the United States. Except that his attachment to state rights was practical more than philosophical, we might call Clinton a northern political counterpart of Jefferson. He comes into the story of the Constitution at several points.

He had early military experience in the expedition against Fort Frontenac, later was brigadier general of the New York militia, and soon afterward held the same rank in the Continental army. Though no man loved New York more than Clinton did, he was unable to keep the British from ascending the Hudson; they took Fort Montgomery, near West Point, from him, and burned the then capital, Esopus (Kingston). That same year, 1777, the people showed their undiminished trust by electing him both governor and lieutenant governor. He resigned the second office but was re-elected to the governorship five times in a row.

Clinton gave the Loyalists a hard time; after the war he approved legislation which obstructed the payment of debts to them though this was against the terms of the treaty of peace. Wanting to remain a big fish in a little pond, he antagonized growth of federal power. He helped to block an independent revenue for the Old Congress, he published newspaper pieces against the Constitution, and at the Poughkeepsie convention he did all in his power to prevent New York from ratifying the instrument. He was an adroit politician, but he offended many when in 1792 he accepted an election to the governorship which John Jay undoubtedly would have won had the votes for him been counted. After that Clinton retired briefly. In 1800 he was again made governor, and in 1804 and 1808 Vice President. In this last office he cast the deciding vote in the Senate against re-charter of the first Bank of the United States.

PATRICK HENRY (1736-1799). Some leaders opposed the Constitution with strong reasoning (George Mason), others from jealousy of superior

power (Clinton) or with obstinate truculence (Luther Martin). Patrick
Henry combined all three promptings but added his own gifts of persuasion. He had refused to go to Philadelphia as a delegate to make the
Constitution, and when the document came before the Virginia convention he was its loudest antagonist.

He was born in Hanover County, Virginia, then an impoverished
frontier. His father was a Scotsman of education and local prominence,
his mother the daughter of a settler from Yorkshire. His youth was a
disappointment to his family and friends. A fiddler and idler, he twice
failed at storekeeping. He married with no prospect of supporting his
family, which rapidly accumulated. However, after the briefest study of
law, successes for his clients spread his reputation and his services
were in brisk demand; in fact he often collected his fees in advance.

Patrick Henry's debut, or discovery, as an orator and advocate came
in the celebrated Parson's Cause in 1763. He defended a country vestry
against a claim for damages preferred by the rector. Henry took the
case when it had been abandoned by another lawyer because it looked
hopeless. Tobacco being scarce and dear, the vestry wished to commute
the rector's pay into money at two pence a pound, according to the Virginia Colony's law, when the weed was worth three times that. The
court had found for the rector and when Henry rose seemingly all
that remained was for the jury to fix the amount of the award. Henry
had a genius for seizing the precise moment for a surprise, or he created the moment. Now he astonished the court (and soon all that
part of the country) by pleading that the cheating statute of the Virginia Burgesses and not the statute passed in Parliament and upheld
by the King in Council was the law. The oppressive ruling overseas
had dissolved the social compact, declared Patrick, and the Virginia
Colony was right to protect its people.

In 1765, when the Virginia tidewater aristocracy was willing to accept the Stamp Act, Henry invoked against it the same principle of
exclusive validity of colonial taxation. As a new, up-country member
of the Burgesses, he drafted and pressed through resolutions declaring
the colonials had all the rights of Englishmen and that impositions laid
on them in Westminster destroyed British and American freedom. His
bold resolves sped northward and like a flaming brand carried through
dry fields lighted fires all the way to New England.

He was similarly nationalist in the Continental Congresses. At the
head of hastily gathered troops he compelled the royal governor of Virginia to return the colony's powder from a warship to the magazine
at Williamsburg. If the battles of Lexington and Concord began the

Revolution, Patrick Henry anticipated the sound of those shots with his "liberty or death" speech in the Virginia assembly in March 1775. His other chief contribution to the war was as governor of Virginia when he dispatched George Rogers Clark to seize the British posts on the northwest frontier in 1778, thus winning an empire in a single bold stroke.

He was five times governor of Virginia. His strength lay with the votes of the plain people, of dissenting religious sects, who were pushing westward. He himself acquired large land holdings on the Ohio and Mississippi. He stimulated the belief that New Englanders, for their own commercial advantage, were willing to see the mouth of the Mississippi closed to exports of the southwestern settlers. Thus he abandoned his early national advocacies, and joined ardently with Jefferson and Madison in urging states' rights. However, President Washington wooed him back to support of the national administration, though Henry declined to be appointed secretary of state or chief justice.

Patrick Henry was more the artist or the actor than he was a thinker or statesman. With a matchless gift of swaying others, he also swayed himself. He had about him more than a touch of the high-class charlatan. As an audacious arouser of popular emotions he had no equal.

LUTHER MARTIN (1748?-1826) was usually known as the Attorney General of Maryland, because he held that post for thirty-one years. In the Constitutional Convention he was the most insistent opponent of giving power to the national government, since he believed more dogmatically than others in state sovereignty. He left the convention (with his Maryland colleague, James F. Mercer) in disgust before the meetings adjourned, berated the Constitution to the Maryland legislature, and did his best to prevent his state from ratifying it. Yet such are the changes in men's opinions that he later became a determined foe of Thomas Jefferson, whose attachment to states' rights was notorious. Martin was born in New Jersey, graduated from Princeton, then spent some years on the eastern shore of Maryland and in Virginia as school teacher and lawyer. He wrote patriotic pamphlets, and Samuel Chase recommended him to Governor Thomas Johnson of Maryland for attorney general.

Martin was a good deal of a nuisance in the Philadelphia convention because his speeches were rambling and interminable, and he offered over and over again the same "no" to most constructive proposals. Fortunately Maryland had other delegates who signed the Constitution— McHenry, Jenifer, and Carroll.

For all the fact that Luther Martin was a good-natured, friendly man, he had a sad life. His wife, a daughter of a Maryland frontiersman, Michael Cresap, died young, leaving him two daughters. These married against his will; one went insane, and Martin had a pamphlet war with the husband of the other. He courted another wife, but was refused; he fell in love with Theodosia, the daughter of Aaron Burr, but this was hopeless because she had an excellent husband already.

Martin defended his old friend Samuel Chase in his impeachment trial over which Aaron Burr presided, and later defended Burr himself in his treason trial. Martin's last celebrated appearance was for his state in *McCulloch v. Maryland*. Both the Chase and McCulloch cases are treated elsewhere in these pages. Martin's unusual physical strength at length gave way under hard work and hard liquor. He spent his last years as a guest in the home of Burr.

GEORGE MASON (1725-1792) was a "lord of the Potomac" (owning a plantation of 5000 acres, with distinguished mansion and garden), a close neighbor of George Washington. He was, properly, one of the loudest in the Constitutional Convention in excoriating the evils of slavery. But, like many others who publicly condemned the practice, he continued to hold his many slaves who toiled on his broad acres for mere subsistence to make Mason rich. True, he had a scheme for freeing and resettling elsewhere all slaves, who were to be purchased from their owners with proceeds of sales of western lands. But this was in the problematic future; meantime he contented himself with penning the Virginia Declaration of Rights, which was echoed in the Declaration of Independence and was the model for the first ten amendments to the Constitution ("Bill of Rights").

We must not be too hard on Mason. Few who detested slavery, besides Quakers, had the consistency to free Negroes belonging to them. Mason, Jefferson, Washington, and so many more doubtless felt that it would be quixotic for them, as individuals, to manumit their slaves until some feasible general plan was worked out. The moral wrongs and social injuries of slavery were greater than are those involved in any modern human exploitation, yet we also have persons who condemn the evils of private capitalism but themselves continue to profit by its privileges.

Except for service in the House of Burgesses and other Virginia bodies, Mason's earlier life was devoted to legal studies, plantation management, and speculation in western lands. He was active in preparing the military expedition of George Rogers Clark that won the

Northwest Territory. He was one of those who conferred at Mount Vernon, 1785, to abolish trade restrictions between Virginia and Maryland. For whatever reason, he did not attend the Annapolis convention the next year, to which he was named a delegate.

In the Constitutional Convention he was among the most frequent speakers. Until the last weeks he was favorable to what was being worked out for vital reform of the Confederation, but then opposed it. He refused to sign the Constitution because it did not contain sufficient protections for civil liberties, and did contain the compromise guaranteeing further life to the slave trade. Then, with Patrick Henry, he fought approval of the Constitution by Virginia. He would have done better to join his colleague, Edmund Randolph, who repented of his original rejection of the document and urged its approval at Richmond. Others of the framers were dissatisfied with the Constitution, but wisely trusted to actual experiment to remove or lessen its defects. Unhappily, Mason died before he could see how successfully the new fundamental law would operate.

MELANCTON SMITH (1744-1798) was the floor leader for Governor Clinton against ratification of the Constitution by the New York convention at Poughkeepsie. He was as ardent a Presbyterian as he was tenacious in his political beliefs. Born at Jamaica, Long Island, he was taught chiefly at home before, still a boy, he was put to work in a retail store at Poughkeepsie. He kept to his duties, invested what he could in land in Dutchess County, and commended himself for his intelligence and honesty. His early public service was as commander of rangers or home guards to prevent depredations by Loyalists during the Revolution. He was also on the commission of the New York legislature for "inquiring into, detecting and defeating conspiracies . . . against the liberties of America." This was the civil counterpart of his military action against Loyalists. The two together gave him power which makes us wonder whether he should have bought confiscated estates, as he did to his profit. At any rate, Washington trusted and used him in the commissary department of the army.

After the war he moved to New York City where he won success as both merchant and lawyer. It is not known how he fitted himself for the bar; this was often a quick and informal process in those days, but anyhow his habits of accurate reasoning had been developed early. He was in the Old Congress, 1785-88. With his record of prosecution of Loyalists he could not be elected a delegate to the Poughkeepsie convention from New York County, but had no difficulty in being chosen from Dutchess as an Anti-Federalist. In the historic meeting to decide whether New York would come into the new Union he gave Hamilton, Livingston, and other friends of the Constitution their most implacable opposition. However, once persuaded that he was mistaken he said so, and enough of his followers changed sides with him to turn the tide in favor of approval. He was one of numbers of men whose chief distinction was in a brave surrender. While still in middle life he unhappily fell victim to a yellow fever epidemic.

ROGER BROOKE TANEY (1777-1864), included here because of his decision in the Dred Scott case, was a political schizoid, maybe because he was a native of the Border state of Maryland where sentiment came to be sharply divided between northern and southern, national and sectional loyalty. He began as a firm Federalist, practiced law in the prosperous interior town of Frederick, and married the sister of Francis Scott Key whose "Star Spangled Banner" was to be the national anthem. He manumitted his slaves and was active in colonizing freed Negroes in Africa. He denounced the New Englanders of his party who opposed the war of 1812. He deplored loose banking practices that resulted in currency inflation. In the Maryland legislature he voted with the minority against the law taxing the notes of the Baltimore branch of the Bank of the United States.

Then he began to change sides. He had served as director of two state banks in Frederick, and in pressing the case of a client against the national bank he was persuaded that the officers of that institution were corrupt. Many in Maryland agreed, for the Baltimore branch had been notoriously mismanaged. When the Federalist party expired, he did not join the Whigs (Webster, Clay, etc.), who inherited the nationalist tradition, but supported Jackson for the presidency in 1824. Defeat made Taney more vehement than before. He was Maryland manager of Jackson's second try, 1828, which was successful.

Jackson rewarded Taney with a recess appointment as United States Attorney General. He advised the President to reject recharter of the Bank of the United States and helped draft the veto message which figured prominently in Jackson's 1832 campaign. Re-elected, Jackson did not need to be convinced that the Bank, his political foe, was by the same token a menace to the country. How destroy this "monster"? The charter had four years to run. Taney urged the President to bleed it by withdrawing the government deposits. Jackson removed his Secretary of the Treasury, Louis McLane, who refused to go along. Suppose the new Secretary, William J. Duane, had proved obstinate, would

Taney take the post and do the deed? Jackson dismissed Duane and installed Taney, who at once announced that in future government funds would be kept in certain state banks.

The Senate would not confirm Taney's appointment in the Treasury, nor, the next year, agree when Jackson named him an associate justice of the Supreme Court. Shortly thereafter John Marshall died and Jackson succeeded in making Taney chief justice. In contrast to Marshall, Taney construed the Constitution strictly, to curb the pretensions of the national government which he felt had come under the sway of northern business interests threatening the agrarian culture of the South. The supreme illustration of his attitude was in the majority decision in the case of Dred Scott (1857). This case is treated at length elsewhere in these pages. It is sufficient to remind here that Taney might have contented himself with finding that Scott, a slave, was not a citizen, and could not sue in a federal court. But, urged on by his bias in favor of the South and states' rights, he declared that the Missouri Compromise was illegal, for the national government had no constitutional power to forbid slavery in the territories. The permission Taney and the majority on the court gave to slavery to extend westward helped precipitate the Civil War.

Taney was a tall but stoop-shouldered man with a long, lined, worried face. Those who have studied his career most closely have admiration for him as a man and jurist. We may call him sincere but he was a poor forecaster of American history.

Some Who Changed Sides

There is no doubt that each of the following characters belongs in the for-and-against classification on the issue of the Constitution and new national government. For instance, Sam Adams's unequaled exploit was in rousing the colonies to demand independence of Britain, and in that he was a nationalist. Later his inclination was against the Constitution; true, he voted for it, but that was because he was manipulated by Massachusetts Federalists.

SAMUEL ADAMS (1722-1803), a Tory warned, was "as equal to the task of forwarding a rebellion as most men." General Gage in 1775 offered pardon to all who had sinned against the Crown if they would "return to the Duties of peaceable Subjects, excepting only from the Benefit of such Pardon Samuel Adams and John Hancock, whose Offences are of too flagitious a Nature to admit of any other Considera-

tion than that of condign punishment." Governor Hutchinson's description was, "I doubt whether there is a greater incendiary in the
King's dominion or a man of greater malignity of heart." That he was
shabby in his dress and chronically out of pocket made no difference,
Adams told a friend, "so that his poor abilities was of any service to
the publick."

Other men, like Patrick Henry and Christopher Gadsden, stirred
America to revolt against Britain, but for talents in this direction Sam
Adams takes the palm. His was not an occasional eloquent outburst,
but a campaign of a dozen years of resolves, correspondence, organizing, and action. He did more than others to create a climate of opinion,
sulphurous against the tyrants overseas. When the indignation of his
neighbors subsided he kept up a rat-tat of complaints, not to let silence imply assent. When the throng was aroused, not a little by his
own arts, he left off protesting against particulars and denounced violations of the colonists' natural rights. It was as though the ardor of a
hundred men had been collected in this single unpretentious citizen.

Sam Adams was born in Boston, whose boast he will ever be. His
father bequeathed him an excellent fortune which Sam steadily diminished until he had scarcely a roof over his head. As he omitted to provide income for himself, so, when named tax collector, he neglected to
supply the town treasury. He had foresight for nothing—except an independent nation.

It is supposed that at the end of a day-long meeting in Faneuil Hall
to protest against landing the tea from the ship *Dartmouth* (December
1773) it was chairman Adams who gave the nod to the "Mohawks"
who swiftly repaired to the dockside and dumped the cargo. Then he
led resistance to the British acts that would punish Boston for the
town's contumacy. The response of other colonies with food for their
Massachusetts brethren did much to encourage the unity of sentiment
and action which was Adams's constant hope. It must have been
Adams who urged in 1773 that "a congress of American States be assembled as soon as possible."

When he had rallied his own and other colonies for the first Continental Congress in 1774, he was fitted out for Philadelphia by friends
—wig, silk suit, pumps, and purse. He needed nobody to supply him
with purpose. He knew when not to be conspicuous. At first he remained in the background among the delegates because, notoriously
radical, he wanted no action of his to discredit the movement he had
at heart.

Sam Adams signed the Declaration of Independence, the argument of which he had anticipated in demanding for Americans the rights of Englishmen, especially no taxation without representation. He was twice governor of Massachusetts, and continued to figure dutifully in local affairs, but his last years were spent in eclipse. He did not like the Constitution, and was persuaded by a trick to give it his blessing. His forte was rebellion, not construction of a constitution. His statue stands in front of Faneuil Hall in Boston, the forum of his most fruitful exertions.

ELBRIDGE GERRY (1744-1814). This member of the Constitutional Convention during the Revolution once fled from a search party of enemy soldiers into a corn field in his nightshirt. As this was mid-April, the corn field must have been bleak, and if poor thin Gerry had on no more clothes than the historian allows the breeze must have been as bad as the British. This man's career presents a gallery of contradictions; he was constantly at war with himself. He was against a federal import duty, then for it. He was against federal regulation of commerce, then believed it imperative, but in the end refused to attend the Annapolis commercial convention. In early debates on the Constitution he pressed for a strong central government, but later had such qualms that he refused to sign the document. He demanded a bill of rights, later would have the Constitution take effect without amendment. He approved the administration of John Adams, but shed a tear for recall of Monroe as minister to France. At one period he was the boast of the Federalists, only later to condemn them as treasonable.

Gerry was born in Marblehead, Massachusetts, where he followed his father as well-to-do shipowner and merchant. His most consistent services were in preparation for the Revolution and in seeing that the army was supplied with munitions and all sorts of equipment. In this he was unswerving and indefatigable. He was often a member of the board of treasury of the Old Congress. This sorry experience should have dissuaded him, in the new national Congress, 1789, from urging a commission rather than single official to manage the finances. Nonetheless, he defended Hamilton's policies, including assumption of the state debts. Earlier he had deplored the implied power of Congress to charter corporations, but he endorsed the Bank of the United States and bought thirty shares of its stock.

Though easily offended, when his colleagues on the "X.Y.Z." commission to France, 1797-8, were insulted by Talleyrand and had returned to rouse the indignation of the people at home, Gerry remained in Paris. He persuaded himself that his patient further efforts formed the prelude to peace. As Republican governor of Massachusetts he fulminated against Federalist slanderers of public officials as earlier the Federalists had done. Only once in his career was he up to mischief. This was in 1812 when he engineered a redistricting of Massachusetts counties in order to give the Republicans more senators than their voting strength warranted. The result was queerly shaped electoral districts, concentrating the Republican votes and diluting the Federalist votes. This trick was called Gerrymandering, and it has been used repeatedly since in American politics. He became Vice President of the United States under Madison, but died in office.

GEORGE NICHOLAS (1755?-1799) was among those most effective in persuading the significant Virginia convention to ratify the Constitution. In his short lifetime he had two political careers, or played two political roles, corresponding to his move from eastern Virginia (Hanover County) to Charlottesville, and (about 1790) thence to the new state of Kentucky. An officer in the Revolution, he proposed in the Virginia Assembly an investigation into the conduct of Governor Jefferson in fleeing when the legislature was threatened by a squadron of British dragoons. A successful lawyer and frequently a member of the Virginia House of Delegates, he devised statutes concerning the District of Kentucky and bought lands there. When he moved his home and practice to that state he remained in the beginning a firm Federalist. He drafted the first constitution of Kentucky; he made it so much an imitation of the national Constitution that it even provided a clumsy electoral college for choice of the governor.

Though he had been a stout advocate of central authority, he could not stomach features of John Adams's administration. He was particularly vocal against the Alien and Sedition Acts. Though President Adams was provoked and made informal inquiries into these attacks, Nicholas was not proceeded against as many others were. It was to Nicholas that Jefferson sent the Kentucky Resolutions for adoption by the legislature. Thus at the end of his life he became closely allied with the leader whom he had earlier assailed. Had he not died so early (at the age of about 45) he would have taken high place in national affairs, though in which party, Federalist or Republican, it is impossible to say.

ROBERT R. LIVINGSTON (1746-1813) was the chief colleague of Hamilton in persuading the New York convention to approve the Constitution. He was an aristocrat—tall, graceful in deportment, eloquent in public speech, endowed with many talents in law, science, and diplomacy, and slightly contemptuous of those who disagreed with him. He was the most prominent member of a large clan on the Hudson and in New York City. A brother was Edward Livingston, a brother-in-law General Richard Montgomery, who fell at Quebec. He graduated at King's, studied law with his cousin William, was for a time a partner of Jay. In Congress he was on the committee to draft the Declaration of Independence, and helped write the first New York constitution of 1777. He was secretary for foreign affairs under the Confederation. Though ratification of the Constitution by New York encountered dreary prospects because of the opposition of Governor George Clinton and his upstate following, Livingston, undismayed and resourceful, worked hand in hand with Hamilton, as well as with his connections James Duane and John Jay, to achieve success. In the new national government the Federalists, unhappily, ignored him; he joined the Republicans, opposed Hamilton's fiscal proposals, and fought the Jay Treaty.

As Jefferson's minister to France he negotiated the Louisiana Purchase, which was sufficient claim to fame. Thereafter he retired to his estate, "Clermont on the Hudson," where he introduced Merino sheep. More important, he continued his patronage of Robert Fulton, begun in France, and was second only to Fulton in the development of steamboat navigation. He is generally known as "Chancellor" because he headed the New York judiciary for nearly a quarter-century.

EDMUND RANDOLPH (1753-1813) presented to the Constitutional Convention the Virginia or Randolph plan which the final document most nearly resembled. He was proud of his Indian blood, which showed in his complexion, but he was not bold or fierce. Instead he was hesitant, found it difficult to make up his mind. He was briefly on Washington's military staff at Cambridge, Massachusetts, but returned to Virginia to become a member of the convention that adopted the first constitution for the state. While hardly more than a youth he became attorney general, then represented Virginia in the Old Congress. When he attended the Annapolis convention he had been elected governor of his state. We are told that at his demand the report of this convention, which condemned the shortcomings of the Confederation, was toned down.

In the Constitutional Convention at Philadelphia he was the champion of an effective central authority, but he flinched from the proposal of a single executive (wanted three men to perform the executive function), and hoped there might be a second convention to repair mistakes of the first. Though he had submitted the plan which was the model for the Constitution, he refused to sign the document, and criticized it in print. Then, changing back to a previous viewpoint, he supported ratification in the Virginia convention.

Randolph, as United States attorney general, was consulted on the more important policies of Washington's first administration and when Jefferson resigned as secretary of state, Randolph was given that office. He quit this post suddenly when he felt that President Washington and colleagues in the cabinet unjustly suspected him of soliciting a bribe from the French minister. He successfully refuted all charges in his essay of *Vindication*, returned to the private practice of law, and was chief defense counsel of Aaron Burr in the latter's trial for treason.

Chapter Three

THE CONSTITUTION IS CONSTRUCTED

I FRAMEWORK

Fifty-five delegates attended the Constitutional Convention for part or all of the sessions. Ten more were appointed but never came. Sixteen took part in the deliberations but for one reason or another did not sign the document; of these Edmund Randolph and George Mason of Virginia, and Elbridge Gerry of Massachusetts were present at the signing ceremony but refused to put their names to the Constitution. Three who would not sanction it—Luther Martin of Maryland, and Robert Yates and John Lansing of New York—gave their reasons to their legislatures. All the states were represented except Rhode Island, which refused to send delegates. Of those elected but who declined their appointments two were of special distinction, Charles Carroll of Carrollton (Maryland), and Patrick Henry of Virginia. One attendant who would have made a contribution to the convention, George Wythe of Virginia, was recalled home almost immediately by the illness of his wife.

Of the members George Mason said, "America has certainly, upon this occasion, drawn forth her first characters; there are upon this Convention many gentlemen of the most respectable abilities, and so far as I can discover, of the purest intentions. The eyes of the United States are turned upon this assembly, and their expectations raised to a very anxious degree." Benjamin Rush of Philadelphia gave the testimony of his fellow-townsman, Benjamin Franklin: "It is the most august and respectable Assembly he was in in his life." Franklin in a letter said it was "what the French call *une assemblée des notables*." Without invidious comparison, we may divide the participants into three groups. Of the first order in ability were Alexander Hamilton, Benjamin Franklin, James Madison, George Mason, Gouverneur and Robert Morris, George Washington, and James Wilson. Men of character and parts who would have graced any deliberative assembly were John Dickinson, Ellsworth, FitzSimons, Gerry, William Samuel Johnson, King, Langdon, William Livingston, Luther Martin, Paterson, Charles and Charles Cotesworth Pinckney, Randolph, John Rutledge, and Roger Sherman. Others were sincere, esteemed, and able, but made less impress on the gathering.

As we look back, it was a convention of young men—the average age was about forty-two years. This was not then surprising, for the life span was less than now, and those thought eligible for assignment were mostly active participants in public affairs. Franklin at eighty-two was the oldest member; Charles Pinckney at thirty was the youngest. Washington was fifty-five. At the average session about thirty members attended, so that it was more like a large committee in which anyone present could take part, than a convention in which only a few could be heard. Not that all of the members offered their views on the floor. Some, including Robert Morris, sat silent throughout, except to give their votes. Franklin, since it tired him to stand, usually wrote out his remarks to be read to the company by his colleague James Wilson. Washington, in the chair of the convention (but not presiding over the committee of the whole), spoke from the floor only once, but his manner did not conceal his feelings. Frequent speakers, on their feet a hundred times and more, included Hamilton, Gouverneur Morris, and Madison. The longest speeches were by Hamilton (five hours on one day) and Luther Martin (not quite so long, but continued on a second day). Though the group was small, hardly composing what we would call an audience, members who had talents for public speaking did not turn off their oratory. It was the day when a public man was expected to reinforce his reasoning with whatever elocutionary powers he possessed.

Were They Feathering Their Own Nest?

Professor Charles A. Beard put forward, a century and a quarter after the event, the most famous theory of the convention in his *Economic Interpretation of the Constitution*. This was that the dominant motive of the men who constructed the new instrument of government was that of rescuing their own property interests. Beard rummaged theretofore unexplored Treasury records to discover the holdings of many members of the convention in public securities and western lands. If the Confederation went to pot, these claims on Congress and the states and hopes of rising value of lands would be blasted. The only chance of saving their property prospects was in throwing more power to the central government to ensure unity and stability. Thus the framers of the Constitution were inspired, on the whole, by pocketbook patriotism. Instead of being demigods, our constitutional fathers were shrewd husbandmen of their material fortunes. They were moved less by devotion to the public good than by determination to forestall the wreck of their estates. As representative of the owning class, they acted in the nick of time before the American experiment in self-government fell apart. Washington wrote to Jefferson from Philadelphia a week after the delegates assembled: "The business of the convention is as yet too much in embryo to form any opinion of the conclusion . . . That something is necessary, none will deny; for the situation of the general government, if it can be called a government, is shaken to its foundation, and liable to be overturned by every blast. In a word, it is at an end; and, unless a remedy is soon applied, anarchy and confusion will inevitably ensue."

Beard cautioned that his thesis was tentative, and that further enquiry would be necessary to establish it. With this apology, however, he went ahead to draw conclusions as though his data were complete and dependable. For many years others accepted his view with few misgivings. What he had done was bold and original. It had the merit of substituting realism for emotional reverence. He ripped haloes from heads that were merely bewigged. The forefathers were human, stirred by prudence in their own behalf.

This sally performed a service for historical study in America by highlighting the economic forces in political development. Beard brought discussion down from the clouds of mystical veneration. The Constitution was not a miracle, but a clever—in fact, disingenuous—remedy for dangers which had beset the country and by the same token threatened the private expectations of the wealthy. Beard imported into American inquiry the materialist—as against the idealistic—explanation of social development which we associate especially with the work of Karl Marx.

Beard's hypothesis was an enrichment of our scholarship rather than an illumination of the crucial episode of the Constitution. From the first, certain reflections stood against the generalization that the new plan of government was really a defense against impending private losses. It is true that many in the convention were possessed of public paper and were speculators in wild lands or were otherwise men of property. But these were the men who all along had felt responsibility for government. It was these who had served in Congress, in state legislatures, in executive posts, and as judges. They had the education and the leisure, and they enjoyed the public esteem which enabled them to be guardians and promoters of the general welfare. It was these men who had supported the Revolution with their arms and their means and their influence. Some of slender fortunes had risen to places of political trust, but a degree of wealth was commonly a recommendation for office. Did these characters, with reputation for good conduct in the public behalf, suddenly turn canny for their individual advantage? Did they come together in the convention because mental telepathy told each man, "You had best band together with your fellows who have something to lose and construct and impose a radically corrective system of government ere it is too late." From patriots did these prominent figures, as by common consent, become plotters? Did they abandon sincerity, and conceal their self-interest behind a façade of altruistic duty?

Further, as Beard was bound to admit, some in the convention who answered his description of men with a substantial stake in stability and security were opposed to the plans for more consolidation in the political system, among them, George Mason, one of the lords of the Potomac in Virginia. By contrast, some who were most ardent for reform of the Confederation in the direction of a cemented nation possessed no private fortunes. A conspicuous example was young Alexander Hamilton, who had been working for this object for almost a decade since the time he was a penniless subaltern in Washington's camp. It is true that Hamilton and some others of his description had wealthy connections, or, like him, had aristocratic leanings, but this was a point removed from private designs.

Also much of the contest in the convention disregarded property claims as such, being between the few larger states and the more numerous small ones who feared they would lose their self-direction or even their identity. Another tug of war, not quite so prominent at the time, was that between the planting states to the south and the small-farming and commercial states to the north. To the extent that property figured, slaveholders were at odds with merchants and shipowners. The line of cleavage was geographic, not between haves and have-nots. Every feature of possessions and opinions of delegates, and of economic and suffrage divisions in the country at the time, has been re-examined by careful students, notably Robert E. Brown in *Charles Beard and the Constitution* (1956). The conclusion is that Beard's proposition was hasty and, in the sweeping fashion in which he presented it, invalid.

Meticulous revision of the contention that the constitution was a cunning contrivance to salvage personalty has been rewarding. It was necessary to persuade the cynically-minded to restore the Founding Fathers to their pedestal. But it may be that an attentive reading of the records of the convention, plus some knowledge of the earlier and subsequent careers of influential members, was always sufficient to discredit suspicion of their motives. Generally men's personal interests cannot help but form an ingredient in their public advocacies. But we are warranted in believing that at a time of social crisis, when men offer themselves as saviors of the community, their selfish concerns are a tincture, but subordinated to their obligation to their fellows. One is not being sentimental or credulous in ascribing sincerity to those in the convention anxious to redeem America from imbecile government. They had invested more than money in the independence and prosperity of their country. They were men of integrity, incapable of playing a solemn farce in which they mouthed solicitude for the public while they were consciously animated by private purpose. From our ample knowledge of the architects of the new nation we are impelled to judge them men of good will, in fact of noble impulse. Of course they differed in commitment. Some sought places in the convention from ambition, but these were in the minority. More came from a conviction of duty, which may be measured against the refusal of others, in some cases, to be bothered.

It is surprising to find that Washington, elected by the Virginia legislature to head her delegation to Philadelphia, was long reluctant to be thus associated with the project of reforming the government. For once in his life he thought more of his own personal comfort and reputation than of his public responsibility. He was afraid that the convention might be poorly attended, by representatives limited by their states in what they might do. If the attempt was feeble and failed, Washington told himself he would be discredited for his pains. He gave himself different excuses for delaying his acceptance, and only after important states named strong deputations, and his advisers urged him, did he consent to throw in his fortunes with the rest. The joyous receptions given him along the route and by the people of Philadelphia must have assured him that disappointing results of the gathering would not damage the esteem in which he was held.

The convention was to open May 14, 1787, but as had become habitual, delegates drifted in tardily. Washington was prompt, but found only his own state and Pennsylvania represented, and for days had to record in his diary slow progress toward a quorum. Madison, after the convention was organized May 25, was still disturbed by recent "daily disappointment from the failure of the deputies to assemble," and concluded, "It is impossible as yet to form a judgment of the result of this experiment. Every reflecting man becomes daily more alarmed at our situation."

Behind Closed Doors Through Hot Summer

Eleven days behind schedule, seven states were represented in the east hall on the second floor of the State House. The rumble of cart-wheels over the cobbles about the building was muffled by earth spread for that purpose. Franklin, president of the host state, was to have nominated Washington chairman of the convention, but he was kept away by stormy weather, and his colleague Robert Morris performed this office. Washington was unanimously elected, and Morris and John Rutledge of South Carolina conducted him to the dais. William Jackson of Georgia, who had been a gallant soldier in the Revolution and who had sought the place, was chosen secretary. In the large, dramatic painting by Howard Chandler Christy of the closing scene of the convention (in the national Capitol), Major Jackson, in a scarlet coat, is calling up the delegates to sign the Constitution; next to Washington, the artist makes him most conspicuous. Unexpectedly, he kept the records in careless fashion, which has diminished our knowledge of what went forward.

The committee on rules—Wythe, Hamilton, and Charles Pinckney—reported three days later. Two orders on procedure were of more than formal sort. First, voting was to be by states, one vote for each; seven states made a quorum, and a majority of states present could decide all matters. Second, deliberations of the convention were to be secret. Care was taken to ensure that no information of the proceedings passed outside the hall. This was generally approved by the delegates, though a few objected. George Mason's view was typical: "our doors will be shut, and communications upon the business of the Convention [will] be forbidden during its sitting. This I think myself a proper precaution to prevent mistakes and misrepresentations until the business shall have been completed, when the whole may have a very different complexion from that in which the several crude and undigested parts might in their first shape appear if submitted to the public eye." This was a wise provision for other reasons too. Members would not express themselves so freely in the meetings if later they were to be accused of inconsistency in their positions. If their doings were broadcast they would be bombarded by editors and other controversialists, correcting and urging. Features were discussed which in the end formed no part of the document submitted. If remarks in convention were to be reported out of doors, delegates would have been more than ever prone to make speeches. Better consult together in peace and security, then submit a considered scheme which must be taken up or rejected on its merits.

It was principally after the convention adjourned, when the Constitution was published to the country, that hostile critics became vocal against the policy of secrecy that had been imposed while the document was taking shape. The proposed Constitution was sinister, hatched in darkness, etc. However, while the sessions were in progress, most of those who eagerly awaited the result credited the members of the convention with sincerity and earnestness. The fact that all was being done under Washington's eye was in itself enough to confer confidence.

A further general comment on the conduct of the convention must not be omitted. Not only were the members addressing themselves to George Washington when he was in the chair, but all knew if a different form of government emerged, Washington would unmistakably be called to head it. This foregone conclusion tempered misgivings in nameless ways.

Of course when published the document spoke for itself. Numbers among the public would have liked to know the process of its construction, but their curiosity had to go unsatisfied except for a few revelations by such vehement critics as Mason and Martin. Other members considered that they were sworn to secrecy for life. It was not until 1818 that Congress ordered the printing of the official records of the convention. These proved to be few and fragmentary; the poorly kept minutes had not been worked into a regular journal, and jottings of votes were without sufficient identification. John Quincy Adams, then secretary of state, made what he could of these materials (Jackson himself could give no assistance) and published them in 1819. Two years later the notes taken by Robert Yates (present only during the first half of the convention) were brought out. At different times later memoranda made by other delegates—King, McHenry, Pierce, Paterson, and Hamilton—added in minor ways to the record.

By far the most jointed and illuminating account of the debates and proceedings, however, was that of James Madison. He was present every day the convention met, and having taken a seat where he could hear all that transpired, he industriously put it on paper in his own abbreviations. These notes he wrote out each evening, taxing his health by his incessant application. After the official records and Yates's summaries were published, Madison revised his own manuscript in places (not always for the better) and, at his direction in his will, it was published in 1840. This offers us the *open sesame* to the doings of the convention.

This was a hard-working body, sitting through the sweltering Philadelphia summer from May 25 to September 17, from ten in the morning till three or four in the afternoon, with only two breaks—two days for the fourth of July and ten days three weeks later to allow time for a committee to put the decisions of the convention together in usable form. Members had special assignments besides, caucused on occasion, and did much of the work in informal discussions out of hours. The delegates deserved the relaxing entertainment they enjoyed from Philadelphia hosts. The night of adjournment Washington "retired to meditate on the momentous wk. which had been executed, after not less than five, for a large part of the time six, and sometimes 7 hours sitting every day," Sundays and the brief adjournments excepted, "for more than four months."

The convention began by considering two plans that were offered for reforming the government. The first was framed by the Virginia delegates, principally Madison, while they waited for others to assemble, and was presented by Governor Edmund Randolph. In an elaborate speech he outlined over-all objects, enumerated the failures of the Confederation, declared the peril in which the country stood, and offered the remedies. His method was at once tactful and forceful. He was unsparing in showing "that the confederation fulfilled *none* of the objects for which it was framed." It provided neither external security nor internal harmony. Congress was at the mercy of the pride and jealousy of the states, was starved for revenue, and could not produce the benefits to agriculture, manufactures, and commerce which only the central organ could furnish. Knowing that he had before him delegates who were lenient toward the existing system, or strongly attached to state domination which it embodied, Randolph followed blame of the Articles by excuses for those who devised them. The authors were concerned with redressing the tyranny of Britain, not with a workable plan for using the rights which we claimed. Only actual experience of public debt, "the havoc of paper money," state dissensions, insurrection, and violation of treaties could discover fatal lacks in the scheme they projected.

Confederation To Be Replaced, Not Revised

Then Randolph submitted the Virginia plan of remedies, "leading principles whereon to form a new government. He candidly confessed that they were not intended for a federal government—he meant a strong *consolidated* union, in which the idea of states should be nearly annihilated." This last sentence was the interpretation of Randolph's purpose by Robert Yates of New York, whose bias against central authority would make the most of any threat in that direction. However, the particulars of a new constitution which Randolph offered bore out his contention, as he himself put it next day: "Resolved that a union of the States, merely foederal, will not accomplish the objects proposed by the articles of confederation, namely 'common defence, security of liberty, and general welfare' . . . Resolved that a national government ought to be established consisting of a supreme legislative, judiciary and executive." Further, "the National Legislature ought to be impowered . . . to legislate in all cases to which the separate States are incompetent, or in which the harmony of the United States may be interrupted by individual Legislation; to negative all laws passed by the several States, contravening . . . the articles of Union; and to call forth the force of the Union agst. any member of the Union failing to fulfill its duty under the articles."

The members of the national legislature should be "proportioned to the Quotas of contribution, or to the number of free inhabitants [of the several states], as the one or the other rule may seem best in different cases." There should be two houses, the lower elected by the people of the states, the upper by the members of the popular branch from nominations made by the state legislatures.

These proposals were enough to provoke two objections which for the moment embarrassed proceedings. The convention, for freer discussion, had gone into committee of the whole, with Gorham of Massachusetts as chairman. Charles Cotesworth Pinckney observed, logically, that such resolves went beyond Congress's call for the convention "for the sole and express purpose of *revising the articles of confederation*." Pinckney "expressed a doubt whether the act of Congs. recommending the Convention, or the Commissions of the deputies . . . could authorize a discussion of a System founded on different principles from the federal Constitution." As another quoted him, if they agreed to Randolph's plan "their business was at an end," for if it was held that the Articles were incapable of improvement and required to be supplanted, the powers of the convention were dissolved. Elbridge Gerry shared Pinckney's view.

This poser, right at the start, brought Gouverneur Morris to his feet. He eagerly agreed that the convention, in receiving Virginia's proposition for "a *national* Government . . . consisting of a *supreme* Legislative, Executive & Judiciary," was on a different course from that which Congress had assigned. A federal government was "a mere compact resting on the good faith of the parties," whereas a national one had "a compleat and *compulsive* operation. He contended that in all communities there must be one supreme power, and one only." George Mason reinforced this. The present confederation was deficient not only because it provided no coercion of delinquent states; "such a Govt. was necessary as could directly operate on individuals . . ."

Roger Sherman of Connecticut, who had taken his seat that day, smoothed over the difficulty. He was "not . . . disposed to Make too great inroads on the existing system," but "admitted that . . . additional powers were necessary" for Congress, "particularly that of raising money which . . . would involve many other powers." Pinckney and Gerry were really injecting a technical point before the convention squared away. They wanted a competent system. Pinckney immediately took the opening others had given; he would omit Randolph's use of the word "supreme" and resolve simply that "to accomplish the objects proposed by the Confederation a more effective Government consisting of a Legislative, Executive and Judiciary ought to be established." Pretty much this was accepted thenceforth as a working assumption.

The other snag was similar. Delegates "generally relished" the premise that equal representation of states "established by the . . . Confederation ought not to prevail in the national Legislature, and that an equitable ratio of representation ought to be substituted." Immediately George Read of Delaware reminded that the deputies from his state "were restrained by their commission from assenting to any change of the rule of suffrage, and in case such a change should be fixed on, it might become their duty to retire from the Convention." (Delaware, favorable to revision, yet refused any alteration in the rule of the Confederation that "in Congress . . . each state shall have one vote.") Again Gouverneur Morris replied to the objection. The change in the rule of representation "was . . . so fundamental an article in a national Govt. that it could not be dispensed with." He hoped services of the Delaware delegates would not be lost, and their secession would be unwelcome proof of discord at the very outset. After some other

expedients failed to satisfy Read, the thorny question was postponed in
order to keep Delaware in the convention. This was altogether wise,
for time produced a solution, as we shall see.

Randolph's resolutions, forming the "Virginia Plan," were sent to
the committee of the whole for detailed examination and debate, and
at the same time "the draught of a foedceral government" offered by
Charles Pinckney of South Carolina was similarly referred. Pinckney
confessed that his scheme "was grounded on the same principle as
. . . the . . . resolutions" of Randolph. During the next two weeks
discussion revolved around Randolph's proposals, but those of Pinckney, less noted in the accounts, were not lost to sight; indeed, they
may have had superior influence.

"Legislation over Individuals"

After a fortnight of discussion the committee of the whole reported to
the convention a score of resolutions substantially embodying the Virginia plan. Those insistent on replacing the shambling Confederation
with a firm national government had won. Indeed practically all members agreed that a decided change, giving adequate power to central
organs, was necessary. Decisions in this direction would have been
more readily reached had not Hamilton, most of all intent on a consolidated union, been canceled by the votes of his New York colleagues. Contrary to the state's size and economic interests, the New
York delegates regularly aligned it with the small states fearful of
domination by the larger. Hamilton from time to time made his own
position clear, but his vote could not count.

The tentative proposals were for a two-house legislature with proportional representation in both branches, a single executive, and a national
judiciary (a supreme court with power in the legislature to create inferior ones); the legislature could veto state laws in conflict with the
constitution and treaties; the constitution, when formed, was to be
submitted to conventions in the states chosen directly by the people.
This last was decisive of the national character of the scheme. Against
a contingent who wanted approval to lie with the state legislatures, the
majority was resolved that the fundamental law must be sanctioned by
the citizens, carry none of the disabilities of a treaty between sovereign
commonwealths.

These provisions, endorsed by the committee of the whole, roughed
in the document, but they left much detail to be added and would not
be accepted by the convention proper until critical conflicts were

settled. The chief of these differences—between the large states (nationally-minded) and the small ones (anxiously clinging to separate rights)—was immediately brought forward in a rival plan. Paterson of New Jersey was the spokesman of his own state and of Connecticut, Delaware, New York, and maybe Maryland in asking a day's adjournment until they could mature a scheme "purely federal, and contradistinguished from the reported plan." This request was granted; the plan was offered, referred to the committee of the whole, and the Virginia plan was referred back so the two could be considered together.

In one version, in Paterson's hand, the opening proposition was, "Resolved, That a union of the States merely federal ought to be the sole Object of the Exercise of the Powers vested in this Convention." Certain concessions, by now commonplace, were made. The Articles should be revised to make them adequate to the exigencies of government. There should be a supreme legislative, executive, and judiciary. Congress could lay and collect an import duty and regulate foreign and interstate commerce. Acts and treaties of Congress should be supreme over the states, and the state courts should be bound thereby in their decisions. If requisitions for revenue were not filled, Congress could "direct the collection thereof in the non complying States" if the requisite number of states authorized this coercion, though the method of enforcement was not described. However, since "every State . . . possesses an equal . . . Share of Sovereignty, Freedom, and Independence . . . the Representation in the Legislature ought to be by States." These amendments to the Articles should be sent to Congress and the states for approval.

Lansing of New York was quick to justify Paterson's minimal program, for it "sustains the sovereignty of the respective States" while "that of Mr. Randolph destroys it." The convention was "restrained to amendments of a federal nature, and having for their basis the Confederacy in being." The states would ratify nothing more than this. "N. York would never have concurred in sending deputies to the convention, if she had supposed that the deliberations were to turn on a consolidation of the States, and a National Government."

Wilson, of Pennsylvania, steadily nationalist, contrasted the shortcomings of the New Jersey plan with the competence of that of Virginia. In masterful fashion he briskly ticked off a dozen points on which the small-state intentions would not answer. Instead of two branches of the legislature, Paterson preserved one; instead of representation of the people at large, he made "the States Legislatures the pillars," with equal, not proportional suffrage; "a single Executive

Magistrate is at the head of the one, a plurality . . . in the other."
And so on for additional features. Most of all, under the Virginia plan,
"the Natl. Legislature is to make laws in all cases to which the separate
States are incompetent," but the small states proposed "Congs. are to
have additional power in a few cases only." Instead of the people ratifying, the states would have this decision.

This launched Wilson on a refutation of the timid supposition that
the country would not accept a true reform. "He could not persuade
himself that the State Govts. & sovereignties were so much the idols
of the people, nor a Natnl. Govt. so obnoxious to them. Why s[houl]d
a Natl. Govt. be unpopular? Has it less dignity? Will each Citizen
enjoy under it less liberty or protection? Will a Citizen of *Delaware*
be degraded by becoming a Citizen of the United States? Where must
the people look at present for relief from the evils of which they complain? Is it from an internal reform of their Govt.? No. Sir, It is from
the Natl. Councils that relief is expected . . . he did not fear, that the
people should not follow us into a national Govt. and it will be a
further recommendation of Mr. R's [Randolph's] plan that it is to be
submitted to *them* and not to the *Legislatures*, for ratification."

Randolph was forthright in defense of his national system. "He
painted in strong colours, the imbecility of the existing confederacy, &
the danger of delaying a substantial reform." He "was not scrupulous
on the point of power. When the salvation of the Republic was at
stake, it would be treason to our trust, not to propose what we found
necessary." He explained, accurately, how a state in sending delegates
to the convention did not presume to disparage the Confederation, but
becomingly contented itself with authorizing amendments. But now
that delegates were together they could accept "reasons of a peculiar
nature where the ordinary cautions must be dispensed with. . . The
present moment is favorable, and is probably the last that will offer."
States might not be safely coerced as Paterson contemplated. "We
must resort therefore to a national *Legislation over individuals*" for
which the Old Congress was unfit, since it had no will of its own, was
"a mere diplomatic body." If the convention did not provide a rescue
in a national government the people, so far from being content with
weak remedies, "will yield to despair." Madison's feeling summary in
his notes of Randolph's rebuttal of Paterson and Lansing had the
speaker's approval, so we are doubly sure of what was said.

Young Charles Pinckney of South Carolina, who had urged an integrated nation, not a league of sovereign states, could not take Paterson's grudging adjustments seriously. The scheme was a pretense, a

façade that hid a lesser demand. "Give N. Jersey an equal vote," said Pinckney, "and she will dismiss her scruples, and concur in the Natil. system." He thought the delegates were authorized to go to any length in recommending what "they found necessary to remedy the evils which produced this Convention." This proved to be true, for, as we shall see, the small states were soon satisfied by a single concession in a sensible compromise. Paterson was a man too intelligent to believe in minor doctoring of a government that threatened to collapse. When, soon, the convention removed the fear that the small states would be expunged, he became and ever remained a firm friend of central authority.

An Imitation of British Monarchy

The convention (or committee of the whole) now had before it three plans, the last, of New Jersey, the most timid. At this point Alexander Hamilton boldly urged "The forming a new government to pervade the whole with decisive powers[,] in short with complete sovereignty. . . The general government must . . . not only have a strong soul, but *strong organs* by which that soul is to operate. . . 'Tis essential there should be a permanent will in a community." He had not given his ideas earlier because men of more years and experience were to be heard, and because he was in the minority in his own New York delegation. "The great question is what provision shall we make for the happiness of our Country?" Sure that neither the Virginia nor the New Jersey plan would serve, he would "point out such changes as might render a *national one*, efficacious." He did not offer his as a rival scheme for debate, did not lay it before the committee. Rather, he begged to declare his own views and thereby indicate what changes he would later recommend in the plans of others. He did not doubt the extent of delegates' powers "to form such a national government as we think best adapted for the good of the whole . . . we must establish a general and national government, completely sovereign, and annihilate the state distinctions and state operations; and unless we do this, no good purpose can be answered."

In a speech of more than five hours, topped by reading and commenting on his outline of a sufficient government, Hamilton went to the other extreme from the faint-heartedness of Paterson. Feeling himself alone in the convention, he indulged too far his audacity. His own preference, to cure the "weak and distracted" state of the federal government, was an adaptation of the British limited monarchy. This combined *"public strength* and *individual security."* He explained at once that he would not propose this for America because here attachment to the republican form was ingrained. However, with the Confederation toppling, men were becoming disillusioned with the dangers of democracy, and public opinion was progressing to the point where the principles of the British constitution might be approved.

He got below the surface of political forms. In the genes of society was a conflict between the few of wealth and position and the unpropertied many. Put government in the hands of the first citizens and they will tyrannize over the mass; make the many masters and they will dominate the minority. Government should be in the hands of both, but they should be separated, and have a mutual check. "This check is a monarch." The people—turbulent, demagogue-ridden, seldom judging right—should be offset and steadied by a permanent aristocracy which, standing to gain nothing from change, would resist precipitate popular proposals. To create an enduring union, with vigorous centralized administration, the interests and therefore the affections of citizens must be diverted from the states, and "Passions must be turned towards general government."

What structure of government would produce this result? A "Legislature of the United States with power to pass all laws whatsoever" should consist of a more numerous house elected directly by the people and an upper house chosen at one remove, by electors chosen by the general suffrage. Members of the Assembly (lower house) would serve for three years, those in the Senate during good behavior. (Here were counterparts of the English Commons and Lords.) The supreme executive should be an individual chosen by electors representing the people and continuing during good behavior. He should have a veto on all laws of the national legislature, appoint department heads, and, with advice of the Senate, all ambassadors. When the Senate declared war, the executive should direct the military forces. "All laws of the particular States contrary to the Constitution or laws of the United States to be utterly void; and the better to prevent such laws being passed, the Gouvernour . . . of each state shall be appointed by the General Government" and have a negative on laws about to be passed in his state. (Hamilton's supreme executive was practically an elected king. However, he, the senators, and all officers of the United States were subject to removal by conviction on impeachment).

The national government would set up a supreme court and lower courts in the states to determine all matters of general concern.

Hamilton's speech—it was June 18—unveiling this highly centralized government, as a friendly delegate reported, "has been praised by every body, [but] he has been supported by none." Yes, Read of Delaware approved "the plan of Mr. Hamilton, & wished it to be substituted for that on the table" (Randolph's). Several in the convention went as far or farther than Hamilton in willingness to extinguish state authority. Read foresaw disappearance of the states; "A national Govt. must soon of necessity swallow all of them up." And Gouverneur Morris exclaimed in one of his flights, "What if all the Charters and Constitutions of the States were thrown into the fire, and all their demegogues [sic] into the ocean. What would it be to the happiness of America." Madison, in no passion, pronounced that the states, which never had possessed the rights of sovereignty, "ought to be placed under the control of the general government. . ."

Hamilton's extreme plan, which he knew did not meet the wishes of the members of the convention, yet had a nuisance value. He had dared to go to the limit in the service of national solidity and efficiency. He had held up the British monarchy, not as a model which democratic America would imitate, but as the form which had his personal approval. (Later on, he was obliged to defend himself against the charge of enemies that in the convention he advocated a Commons, Lords, and King for this country. This was not true, for he knew it would be foolish.) Hamilton's plea could not be put down to caprice, for there was sincerity in his very indiscretion. Members more inhibited had now heard the worst, and doubtless were emboldened to listen to promising remedies without their former shuddering. Further, at a later stage of the convention Hamilton moderated his advocacies. He drew up a new and more detailed plan of a constitution much closer to the general idea. On the floor and circulating among the delegates he aided compromises to secure something workable. This useful behavior commended him, so that numbers of his earlier forthright proposals found their way into the finished document.

Fears of Small States

The committee of the whole did not tarry over Paterson's plan for keeping the Confederation, only adding a few necessary powers for Congress. It was promptly dismissed and the Virginia framework of a more national government was again reported to the convention. But the small-state advocates were by no means done. Their disappointment expressed itself in persistent objection to each feature of Randolph's scheme as it came up for discussion. The leaders in this were Lansing of New York, who was argumentative but delivered no ultimatums; Luther Martin of Maryland, stubborn and surly; and, far more moderate in attachment to the claims of state sovereignty, two from Connecticut. These were Roger Sherman, hard-bitten but wise and patriotic, and Oliver Ellsworth, a mellow man eager to compose difficulties. There were others in this camp, in differing degrees—Johnson of Connecticut, Dayton of New Jersey, Baldwin of Georgia.

The national side was supported principally by Madison, Wilson of Pennsylvania, King of Massachusetts, Charles Pinckney of South Carolina, Read of Delaware, and Hamilton. Few others spoke. In fact, much of the debate in the convention was by a minority of the delegates, who through study, earnestness, and early commitment to one or another position were prepared to explore problems as they arose. In this sense a dozen delegates hammered out the Constitution, though we must not forget that all were dependent on the votes of colleagues who were more reticent in voicing their views on the floor.

Two questions were the focus of controversy. The first was general—should the government being formed be described as "national" or simply as that "of the United States?" The second was specific—how should the legislature be constituted? Particularly if the lower house was to represent the people in proportion to numbers, should members of the upper house be chosen by the states with equality in votes? As one reads the record of debates and votes, day after day, he finds three grounds of objection to reducing the importance of the states, or, worse, obliterating the states except as administrative sub-districts. The most rational champions of retaining the states considered that the large area of the country—say 1500 miles one way and 400 the other—made centralized control impossible; in view of marked differences in ways of life, state governments were vital not only locally but for the good of the nation. The plea of another group was technical or historical; the Confederation was the creature of the states, the states sent delegates to amend it, and no proposals issuing from the convention, if they hoped for approval, should omit the states as an integral part of the whole. Last there were those (e.g. Lansing and Martin) whose first loyalty was to their states, who were possessed by fears that state sovereignty would be canceled, their rights taken from them by the major commonwealths of Virginia, Pennsylvania, and Massachusetts. Numbers of these were from small states; Lansing and Yates of New York were in a different case, obedient as they were to the refusal of Governor George Clinton to sacrifice any of his power or pride. It is fair to say that those who clung emotionally to state autonomy were obstructing progress. They failed to see the desperate pass to which the country had come, and in extreme instances were willing to contemplate disdisunion rather than make concessions to national demand.

Those who urged a more integrated government showed patience in arguing away the fears of the states' rights delegates. The states would retain their identities, keep authority over local concerns, be vital as administrative units in the large scheme. They assured the small states, "Your anxieties are misplaced. The three largest states (Massachusetts, Pennsylvania, Virginia) are geographically separated, have different products (fish, flour, tobacco), are more apt to contend against each other than to combine against their smaller neighbors."

Further (this was Hamilton's earnest plea) "as States are a collection of individual men which ought we to respect most, the rights of the people composing them, or of the artificial beings resulting from the composition? Nothing could be more preposterous . . . than to sacrifice the former to the latter. It has been s[ai]d that if the smaller States renounce their *equality*, they renounce at the same time their *liberty*. The truth is it is a contest for power, not for liberty. Will the men composing the small States be less free than those composing the larger." Would one of Delaware's 40,000 be less free than one of Pennsylvania's 400,000, so long as every citizen had an equal vote? The protection of the people of the little states was in a national government able to discharge our responsibilities at home, and command respect abroad. If small states flung off in independence, they would invite foreign alliances which would soon destroy them with the rest of the country. If complaint there was, it should be from the large states against the small, as the small states demanded an equality that would permit a minority of the people to dominate the majority. The small states must recognize that this the large states could not reasonably allow.

Luther Martin, in tirades on successive days against surrender of state sovereignty, was a trial to other delegates. In spite of a reputation as a hard-hitting lawyer, his performance was diffuse and dogmatic. He contended that "the General Govt. was meant merely to preserve the State Governts: not to govern individuals: that its powers ought to be kept within narrow limits . . . he had rather see partial Confederacies take place, than the plan on the table." Madison, Gerry, and others answered that the states were not, indeed had never been sovereign, so Martin and those of his mind were defending a fiction.

Stalemate Threatened

With the convention in a wrangle, and Martin menacing, Dr. Franklin sought to relax tensions and bring disputants to a more conciliatory mood. If anyone could have prevailed it was this Nestor of the meeting. He recommended that as delegates could not understand each other, they should every morning hear prayers to God for guidance. If a sparrow could not fall without God's notice, "is it probable that an empire can rise without his aid?" But objections were offered to this best intentioned expedient. To begin supplication so late in the sessions would notify the public that the convention was beset by dissensions, and diminish confidence in its deliberations. Franklin, Sherman, and others said, sensibly, that it was never too late to mend, and that refusal to invite a clergyman to offer prayers would induce suspicion; moreover, if the public got wind of divided counsels, this might do good as well as ill. Hugh Williamson, who was a clergyman, flatly remarked that no minister had been invited because the convention "had no funds."

Almost forty years later a tale, said to have originated with Jonathan Dayton, was that Hamilton, satisfied with the competence of the delegates, "did not see the necessity of calling in *foreign aid!*" But this specious story was discredited by Madison, who, however, recalled vividly the stalemate between smaller and larger states over equal representation in the senate. "Great zeal and pertinacity had been shown on both sides, and an equal division of votes on the question had been reiterated and prolonged, till it had become not only distressing, but seriously alarming. It was during that period of gloom, that Dr. Franklin made the proposition for a religious service in the Convention . . ."

The convention was cloaked in secrecy, and the notes of its proceedings record only a fraction of what went on. But we are at no loss to picture the anxiety at this stage (end of June) when states' rights men, repeatedly saying "No," blocked advance toward an effective general government. The committee of the whole, on the critical question of make-up of the legislature, had recommended that in the lower house the rule of representation of the Confederation be abandoned—that is, members of the lower house should be elected by citizens, not by the states. The same was to apply to the upper house. This meant that the states as such were knocked out. Lansing of New York, seconded by Dayton of New Jersey, moved to reject this popular representation in the lower house and restore it to the states. As the committee had proposed that both houses be constituted alike, this meant that, if Lansing and Dayon had their way, both houses would be composed of delegates sent by the states. Here was a complete opposition of demands. Would the legislature, in both branches, belong to the people, or to the states?

Washington was as worried as anyone. Writing to a friend, he could not reveal particulars, but the crisis was painfully clear. "Happy . . . would it be," he declared, "if the Convention shall be able to recommend such a firm and permanent Government for this Union, as all who live under it may be secure in their lives, liberty and property, and thrice happy would it be, if such a recommendation should obtain. Every body wishes . . . some thing from the Convention—but what will be the final result of its deliberation, the book of fate must disclose. Persuaded I am that the primary cause of all our disorders lies in the different State Governments. . . Whilst independent sovereignty is so ardently contended for, whilst local views . . . will not yield to a more enlarged scale of politicks . . . disrespect to . . . the general government must render the situation of this great Country weak, inefficient and disgraceful. It has already done so,—almost to the final dissolution of it—weak at home and disregarded abroad is our present condition, and contemptible enough it is."

He hoped that men of good will would prevail to present a serviceable reform, "and trust . . . to the patriotism of the people to carry it into effect." And George Mason said with similar restraint: "Things . . . are now drawing to that point on which . . . fundamental principles must be decided, and two or three days will . . . enable us to judge—which is at present very doubtful—whether any sound and effectual system can be established or not." Johnson of Connecticut lamented "great diversity of sentiment, which renders it impossible to determine what will be the result of our deliberations." Madison and Hamilton on the floor entreated that this precious moment for salvation be utilized; if the convention broke up without proposing a workable government, no similar chance would offer again, and the people would despair.

Elbridge Gerry was not a man to give up easily, as his later history showed. A way had to be found through the impasse. Advocates of the states, he thought, were "intoxicated with the idea of their *sovereignty*," which in fact never existed. "The present confederation he considered as dissolving. The fate of the union will be decided by the Convention. . . He lamented that instead of coming here like a band of brothers . . . we seemed to have brought with us the spirit of political negociators."

The way to secure a capable general government while satisfying demands of the states as entities had been hinted at weeks earlier, by Dickinson and others, and it is surprising that the simple formula was not made prominent before the delegates had got into a snarl. As it was, June 29 two Connecticut members came forward with a saving compromise. William Samuel Johnson, known for his learning and prudence, observed that "in some respects the States are to be considered in their political capacity, and in others as districts of individual citizens." These "two ideas embraced on different sides, instead of being opposed to each other, ought to be combined; that in *one* branch [of the United States legislature] the *people*, ought to be represented; in the *other*, the *States*." But other speakers continued the conflict. Read, though of Delaware, which had been jealous of its sovereignty, insisted "the States . . . must be done away."

Lansing called up his motion for states to compose the lower house. If this had passed, the upper house also would represent the states, according to the proposal before the convention. Lansing's motion was voted down. The six states against it were Massachusetts, Pennsylvania, Virginia, North Carolina, South Carolina, and Georgia. Four states supported Lansing (his own New York and Connecticut, New Jersey, and Delaware). One state was divided (Maryland). If this decision held, both houses would be popularly elected. The temptation of the large state men was to clinch their victory by going on to adopt the rule of representation which had been recommended (all whites and three-fifths of the slaves).

Had this been pushed at that moment, plainly many in the convention feared that the small state delegates would walk out. Something had to be done to keep the losers in their seats, and quickly.

Peacemakers

Johnson and Ellsworth rose to the occasion. They had voted with the others from small states. Their disappointed colleagues would listen to them. They proposed a postponement in the discussion of just how the people's representatives should be elected. The knife that had been put into the small-state men was not to be turned in the wound. The convention should proceed at once to consider the make-up of the upper house, on its merits. A sigh of relief must have passed through the members, for nine states said yes. Massachusetts voted no, evidently determined to press the large states' advantage, and have the people elect both houses. Delaware also voted no; this seems perverse, as that little state had everything to gain by a change of temper in the convention.

Then Ellsworth at once carved a niche for himself in history when he moved "that in the second branch of the Legislature of the United States [Senate] each State shall have an equal vote." This is the wording of the official journal. Madison in his notes put it "that the rule of suffrage in the 2d. branch [Senate] be the same with that established by the articles of confederation" [that is, equal representation of the states]. And Madison went on to quote Ellsworth's speech. The Connecticut man was not sorry on the whole that the lower house was to be popularly elected. "He hoped it would become a ground of compromise with regard to" the upper house. "We were partly national, partly federal. The proportional representation in the first branch was conformable to the national principle and would secure the large States agst. the small. An equality of voices was conformable to the federal principle and was necessary to secure the Small States agst. the large. He trusted that on this middle ground a compromise would take place. He did not see that it could on any other. And if no compromise should take place, our meeting would not only be in vain but worse than in vain." Without this deal the country would be cut in two, for the states north of Pennsylvania (all but Massachusetts) "would risk every consequence" rather than part with the "dear . . . right" of equal representation.

The bargain he urged was fair to both sides. The large states would have superiority in the lower house. There was some danger that the large states might combine against the small. Therefore, "The power of self-defense was essential to the small States. Nature had given it to the smallest insect of creation." Equal voice in the Senate would protect the small states. Furthermore, the Confederation was founded on equal votes of the states. This precedent, "this antecedent plighted faith" should not be completely discarded. He illustrated the saying that "enough is enough." "Let a strong Executive, a Judiciary & Legislative power be created," he begged, "but Let not too much be attempted; by which all may be lost. He was not in general a halfway man, yet he preferred doing half the good we could, rather than do nothing at all." If his scheme did not work it could be changed later.

This was the end of the day and no action had been taken on Ellsworth's compromise. Doubtless it was fortunate that the convention adjourned, for the lathered delegates could cool off over night. Next morning they went at it again. Ellsworth declared that his expedient would produce tranquillity, efficiency, "and it will meet the objections of the larger states." Though acting in good faith, he deceived himself, for now it was the turn of the spokesmen for a national government to be reluctant and make difficulties. Thus Madison, Wilson, and King found reasons for rejecting the Connecticut solution. Ellsworth had gone far to conciliate them, begging that the delegates of the larger states accept the bargain to begin with and rely on future amendment if their complaints were justified. But Madison cited historical examples of various leagues in which correction of wrong principles had proved impossible. Ellsworth's scheme was condemned because it retained "the old fabric of the confederation." Ellsworth believed that if his proposal was not adopted, only Massachusetts of the northeastern states, would consent to a general government. Wilson "entertained more favorable hopes of Connt. and of the other Northern States." But should they abandon the country, "it would neither stagger his sentiments nor his duty. If the minority of the people of America refuse to coalesce with the majority on just . . . principles, if a separation must take place, it could never happen on better grounds." Should three-fourths of the people "renounce the inherent, indisputable, and unalienable rights of men in favor of the artificial systems of States? . . . The rule of suffrage ought . . . to be the same in the 2d. [Senate] as in the 1st branch [House] . . . any other principle will be local, confined & temporary."

King was worked up to declare that if opponents clung to "the phantom of *State* sovereignty," if "this wonderful illusion continue to prevail, his mind was prepared for every event, rather than sit down under a Govt. founded in a vicious principle. . ." Old obstructions of which small states had been guilty were flung in their faces. Delaware during the war had refused to consent to an embargo, and had supplied the enemy. Connecticut had paid nothing into the common treasury for the past two years. Of course such recriminations produced retorts that did nothing for harmony.

A request by a New Jersey delegate that the presiding officer write to New Hampshire to hasten attendance of her delegates was viewed by the big-state men as an effort to recruit the ranks of the little states, and was rejected.

Gunning Bedford of Delaware was stung to retaliation. If the small states were threatened that they must subordinate themselves to the big states or all deliberations were at an end, then so be it. The small states would never be trapped. "Sooner than be ruined, there are *foreign powers who will take us by the hand*. I say not this to . . . intimidate, but that we should reflect seriously before we act." This was the most shocking menace thrown out in the convention, one for which other delegates scolded Bedford roundly. But it showed how brittle the situation had become. The big-state men may have reflected that their objection to compromise had produced the Delaware passion.

II GIVE AND TAKE

Dr. Franklin recommended the method of a skilled joiner fitting boards with rough edges, that is, shaving off some from each. His formula was a compromise within a compromise; in the Senate equal votes of the states on all matters touching their sovereignty, but on appropriations states would vote in proportion to their contributions to the treasury. This did not commend itself. Then on Ellsworth's motion for the equality of states in the Senate the vote was even—Connecticut, New York, New Jersey, Delaware, and Maryland, aye; Massachusetts, Pennsylvania, Virginia, and the two Carolinas no; Georgia ("though a small State at present, she is actuated by the prospect of soon being a great one") divided.

The delegates were facing a blank wall when the two Pinckneys came forward. Young Charles was "extremely anxious that something should be done. . . Nothing has prevented a dissolution of [the federal government] but the appointment of this Convention," and its failure would be fatal. His elder cousin, Charles Cotesworth, moved for a committee of a member from each state "to devise & report some compromise." It was another of those times when a wise man used moral force. Numbers of decisions in the convention were not political, dealt not at all with devising machinery of government, but proceeded from patriotic purpose to promote harmony. Sherman, a dependable member and from a smaller state, Connecticut, endorsed Pinckney's proposal, for a committee was "most likely to hit on some expedient." Luther Martin of Maryland, stubborn as ever, said all right, set up the committee, "but no modifications whatever could reconcile the Smaller States to the least diminution of their equal Sovereignty."

Gouverneur Morris applauded the idea of a grand committee to break the deadlock. By way of pointer to what should be done, he outlined what the second branch or upper house should be. Not the agency of the states, for then it would fall victim to demagogues. It should represent wealth, aristocracy. The members of the Senate should be appointed by the national executive, and serve for life without salaries. They should be eligible to hold other offices, civil or military, at the same time. They would be conservative, selfish in their own economic interest, anti-democratic. This was inevitable from their nature. The need was to identify, indeed to distinguish this powerful group, to license them as a counter-force to the turbulent popular branch, a check on all precipitate action. Incidentally, in this frank speech Morris undercut the later contention that the Constitution was devised by designing men to salvage claims of wealth and privilege. Morris was rich and as far to the right as any delegate. "The Rich will strive to establish their dominion & enslave the rest. They always did. They always will. The proper security agst them is to form them into a separate interest. The two forces will then controul each other."

Others endorsed the appeal to a committee to contrive an exit—Gerry and Strong of Massachusetts and Williamson of North Carolina, all spokesmen of bigger states. The world expected the convention to accomplish something positive. If the delegates defaulted, war and confusion, broken treaties and repudiated debts would be the consequence. The convention had not come about spontaneously, but was the product of crying evils of which the country had become cumulatively conscious. The members were thoroughly aware of their duty not only to rescue America but to establish the principle and practice of democracy.

One would suppose that at this juncture men with the wits and commitment of Madison and Wilson would have approved this further effort at compromise. But no, they quarrelled with it on several grounds. Unfortunately, some who had spoken often, taken positions known to all, were to a degree disqualified from volunteering concessions. The successful issue of the convention owed much, at critical points, to the work of men who listened more than they talked.

In the end the committee was named, all states for it except Pennsylvania. On it were both bitter-enders like Martin and Bedford, and also those of different sort, such as Gerry (chairman), Franklin, Ellsworth, and Mason. The convention adjourned over Independence Day partly to allow the committee to do its work. It recommended that two propositions be adopted together. The first concerned the lower house of the legislature. It should consist of one representative for every 40,000 people (counting three-fifths of the slaves), but each state should have at least one delegate. Money bills should originate here and could not be changed in the Senate. The second proposal was the flat one that in the upper house "*each state shall have an equal vote.*" As debate brought out, the idea in coupling these provisions was to give something valuable to each group in the convention. The big states, furnishing most of the revenue, received control over appropriations. The small states got equal voice with their larger neighbors in the upper house, which had important powers in appointment and treaty-making.

This attempted compromise left delegates as jarring as before. Indeed the particular provisions threw in new bones of contention. Martin, of the committee, wanted to consider all together. Wilson claimed the right to decide on parts of the report separately. Madison led by calling the right of appropriation in the popular house no concession on the part of the small-state people. If seven states wanted a money measure introduced, they could get their friends in the lower house to do it. (This was being too suspicious, and belittled an important principle that the people who paid the revenue should in the first instance have the say in its spending.)

Madison, and Gouverneur Morris more picturesquely, defied those who demanded unjustified privileges for the states as such. The convention must present a national plan, free of the bane of local attachments. The people as a whole would approve. If small states rebelled it would be for a moment, followed by accommodation to the general wishes. If they persisted in rejection, civil war would force them into the common union. Morris did not spare the feelings of his opponents. "The stronger party will . . . make traytors of the weaker; and the Gallows & Halter will finish the work of the sword." Perhaps foreign powers would intrude. Under Morris's fire, Bedford of Delaware apologized for his heated threat to court foreign assistance, but ended by repeating his offensive expressions. The meeting hall rang with angry exchanges. At this point Ellsworth, Williamson, Mason, and Gerry had the merit of pleading that the antagonists sink their differences. Compromise was essential to avoid secession, violence, disgrace before the world. Said Gerry the business man, "It could not be more inconvenient to any gentleman to remain absent from his private affairs, than it was for him: but he would bury his bones in this city rather than expose his Country to the Consequences of a dissolution of the Convention without any thing being done."

Discussion then centered on the rule of representation in the lower house. Several members—Gouverneur Morris (who had recently returned to the convention and was on a talking spree), Butler of South Carolina, King of Massachusetts—objected to the count of population and wanted property to be the basis of representation in the lower house. Protection of property was the object of government. Morris particularly was worried because new states to the west would be admitted to the Union; these would have more people than the older Atlantic states, but less wealth, and would squander the substance of the richer parts. The original states should be given, arbitrarily, more representation than the newer ones to be formed. But others opposed these views. It was not feasible to value property, and population was a good enough index of wealth. Nor was it fair to discriminate against the new states expected to enter the national family. In the end the question was referred to a committee of five. The business was being complicated, for here was a small committee to revise a part of what was pending from a larger committee.

Arithmetic of Representation

However, some progress was made forthwith. The small committee reported a distribution of fifty-six representatives among the states, as a beginning. The grounds were supposed population but "with some regard to supposed wealth." Virginia had the largest number, nine; Rhode Island and Delaware were assigned one each. Dissatisfaction was expressed, especially by Paterson, with "the . . . estimate for the future according to the Combined rule of numbers and wealth, as too vague." He reopened the question of including slaves in the population. "He could regard negro slaves in no light but as property. They are no free agents, have no personal liberty, no faculty of acquiring property, but on the contrary are themselves property, & like other property entirely at the will of the Master." If slaves were not represented in the states, why in the general government? In principle this could not be disputed. Others thought some inclusion of slaves—call them persons or property as you wish—was necessary to persuade the southern states to remain in the Union. Representation and taxation must go together, and slaves were to be taxed. This vexed question was taken from the small committee and referred to a larger one, with a member from each state.

Rufus King as chairman of this grand committee reported next day (July 10). The total of members was now to be 65—Virginia 10, Massachusetts and Pennsylvania 8 each, Delaware and Rhode Island, as before, 1 apiece. On a South Carolina move to reduce New Hampshire from three to two representatives, King explained the policy of the apportionment. It had little to do with fact. The genuine division of interest, as Madison had said earlier, was not between small and large states, but between eastern and southern (slave and free). The four New England states had 800,000 people, but one-third fewer representatives than the four southern states with 700,000 people, counting three-fifths of their slaves. The New England states would complain as it was, but would accept the inequality for the sake of keeping the South in the Union. Certainly New Hampshire must not be reduced. General Pinckney, comparing southern with northern (not just New England) states, said the planting states would suffer an inequality. The northern states would regulate commerce and the southerners would become mere overseers for them, raising staples which the northerners would ship. Gouverneur Morris, still deploring local or regional bias, agreed that southern wealth in slaves should weigh, but not beyond what was allowed in the scheme reported. After various counter-proposals, the rating for representation as drawn up by King's committee was accepted.

This was to be the temporary apportionment of representatives in the lower house. But soon a true count of population must be made. After discussion, willingness to trust to discretion of the state legislatures was voted down; rather, the national legislature was to conduct a census within six years and every ten years thereafter. The issue was joined on how slaves were to be counted—all of them, or none of them, or three-fifths of them as proposed by the existing Congress for tax purposes? C. C. Pinckney and Pierce Butler of South Carolina wanted all the slaves included. Slaves added as much to the wealth of the country as did free laborers in the North. This was in itself a questionable proposition, but it neglected the fact that other wealth, not in the form of slaves, was to be omitted in the census, and so the South, with this peculiar sort of property, would be favored in representation.

Gouverneur Morris said, accurately, that southern delegates were determined to used their slaves for "gaining a majority in the public Councils" in spite of the fact that the South had a minority of citizens. A "transfer of power from the maritime to the interior & landed interest will . . . be . . . an oppression of commerce." He was against equal representation of the states in the Senate, but might have to swing over to that as some protection of the North against the South's design. Davie of North Carolina, and South Carolinians less explicitly, declared that unless their slaves were included (at least to the extent of three-fifths) for purposes of representation, their states would leave the Union. Further, Southerners wanted slaves included in the census as a guarantee that the North would not put an end to the slave trade.

On the other hand, Morris was sure that the people of Pennsylvania would revolt at the idea of being put on a footing with slaves. "Morris was compelled to declare himself reduced to the dilemma of doing injustice to the Southern States or to human nature, and he must therefore do it to the former. For he could never agree to give . . . encouragement to the slave trade . . . by allowing them a representation for their negroes." Morris spoke plainly. If the antagonism was as real as he supposed, "instead of attempting to blend incompatible things, let us at once take a friendly leave of each other." The Middle States could then join with New England and let the South go its own way.

The whole mischief was made by the Southerners' attachment to slavery. Here were leading men, from all of America, striving to form a firmer constitution for a society in which power rested on the consent of the governed. This was the boasted political premise. But, concentrated in the South, were black men, chattels, denied all rights, economic or political. The institution of slavery did not belong in the kind of society for which the delegates were framing a fundamental law. But the Southerners, rather than relinquish slavery, committed themselves to a contradiction. They were determined to keep their slaves as property. How do so unless southern whites had sufficient voice in the national legislature? How secure that voice unless the slaves, at least in part, were counted for purposes of representation? The South denied that the slaves were citizens, but demanded that they be included in the census as such. The convention, after contests, had worked around to agreement that population fairly stood for wealth. People could be counted in a census, whereas an inventory of property would be impracticable. Taxation must be according to representation. The wealth of the North—farms, ships, stores, shops—on which taxes were to rest, was represented by the people. But the wealth of the South, consisting in great part of slaves, was only partially represented unless slaves were counted as people. But in the same breath, the South said they were not people, or at least they were not political persons, or citizens. In short, the South wanted to have it both ways—to keep their slaves as property, but have them counted as persons.

A Bargain Is Struck

In order to hold the convention together, the Southerners had to be satisfied in some degree. The conclusion was to count not all of the slaves, but three-fifths of them. There was no logic in this fraction. It was a compromise pure and simple—an arithmetical compromise that expressed a social and moral compromise. This ratio was familiar, not a fresh invention to meet the present emergency. Soon Rufus King, in the Massachusetts ratifying convention, was explaining that "this rule . . . was adopted, because it was the language of all America." The Continental Congress had used it in the revenue recommendation of 1783, the committee of the whole inserted it in the Virginia plan, and it figured in the New Jersey scheme for a constitution. The three-fifths formula was at hand to be fitted into the agreement that representation should be proportioned to direct taxation.

Before we paint the inconsistency of the Southerners in colors too glaring, we must be historically mindful of their attitude toward slavery. Many years must pass before it was generally recognized, in Russia, Britain, Spain, and in America, that slavery was a mistake economically and morally. We have to take men in their time. Some there were in the South, and in the Constitutional Convention, who deplored slavery, and fewer who condemned it. But most were persuaded by their selfish interest, by acceptance all around them, and by fears of the results of emancipation, to take a tolerant view of the institution, or actually to defend it. Numbers of states to the north had slaves, and northern shipowners and ports were heavily engaged in the slave trade. In picturing the case to ourselves today we are helped by remembering that George Washington, the president of the convention, was the owner of many slaves. We know his integrity, but we are compelled to include, in his noble nature and correct conduct, his steady practice of holding human beings in bondage, profiting by their unrequited labor, buying and selling them at will.

July 16 the principal compromise of the Constitution was agreed to by a narrow margin, 5 to 4 and one state divided. Those favorable were New Jersey, Maryland, Delaware, Connecticut, and North Carolina. The divided state was Massachusetts, with Gerry and Strong for, and King and Gorham against. No delegate from New York was present, those from New Hampshire had not arrived. The terms were those long discussed. The lower house in the beginning should have sixty-five members, distributed between the states as agreed. As direct taxation was to be in proportion to representation, the legislature should take a census within six years and every decade thereafter, counting three-fifths of the slaves. Money bills should originate in the lower house and not be altered in the upper house. Finally (what had caused all the trouble) "in the second Branch of the Legislature of the United States each State shall have an equal vote."

Spokesmen of the big states, Randolph taking the lead, died hard.

The Virginian wanted an adjournment "that the large States might consider the steps proper to be taken in the present solemn crisis of the business, and that the small States might also deliberate on the means of conciliation." Paterson of New Jersey, for the little states, went one better. It was "high time" for the convention to adjourn *sine die*, rescind the rule of secrecy, and have delegates consult their constituents. If Randolph would put his motion, Paterson would "second it with all his heart." Paterson was plainly angry. After long conflict the small states had won equal votes with the large in the upper house, and they would concede none of what they had gained. Others protested against a long adjournment. They were not prepared to go back to their states for fruitless consultation, and return to a convention no farther forward than at present. Randolph explained that he wanted an adjournment only till tomorrow, to allow the large states, if the small proved obdurate, to "take such measures, he would not say what, as might be necessary."

The adjournment was turned down by an even vote, 5 to 5, but then Gerry shifted over, and the convention quit till next day. Nothing was accomplished by this. When delegates, mostly from the big states, gathered before the next morning's session, the "time was wasted in vague conversation" because the men from the large states were divided among themselves on how to take the victory of the little states in the upper house. Some thought "that the side comprising the principal States, and a majority of the people of America, should propose [their own] scheme of Govt." Others said better yield to the little states than come out with two constitutions. The little states, from these divided counsels of their large neighbors, concluded that they had finally won their point. And so it proved. When the convention resumed July 17 the compromise stood, and discussion was on the powers of the legislature, not on its composition.

To call this the "Great Compromise" of the Constitutional Convention also is to recognize lesser adjustments which contributed to final substantial agreement. Some of these episodes of give and take were prominent. One was when the plantation states, with little shipping of their own, gave Congress control over commerce, but with the provisos that no tax should be placed on exports and that the foreign slave trade should not be forbidden for twenty years. Other mutual concessions of frequent occurrence were incidental nuances in debate. The longer the delegates worked together, the easier these solutions became. Major conflicts had been composed, so all could see the new government taking form. The farther they advanced beyond the Articles of

Confederation the plainer became the choice between genuine reform and relapse into political distraction. True, at the very end three recalcitrants refused to sign, but the entreaties addressed to them to make the endorsement unanimous showed the progress of harmony in the convention.

Too Little Trust in the Future

The tussle over votes in the upper house, whether proportional to population or wealth, or with all states as such enjoying equality, though it twice threatened to destroy the effort for a correction of the dismal condition of the country, need not have aroused such passionate demands on either side. Many fears of delegates, which were erected into formidable obstacles in the convention, were groundless. Men on both sides started back from words, were unwilling to trust to the working out of relations in the actual experience of government. We must remember that they had had two governments within a few years—that of Britain which was too forceful, that of the Confederation which was too faint. In making a third, every specification seemed critical. Further, by the time of which we speak the convention had been in session seven hot weeks. Delegates, especially those who took chief part in devising and debating expedients, were fatigued and fractious. It was here that the back benches performed a service. Men who had been on their feet less often, and were less committed to positions, were more relaxed and counseled conciliation. Better the convention should compose differences and come out with something hopeful, though not perfect in every man's eyes, than break up in bitterness and confusion, champions of opposed views going to the country with recriminations against their erstwhile colleagues.

Actually, with the wisdom of hindsight, we can say that the delegates when most at loggerheads neglected a prime consideration. It was that any substantial reform of the government, supported on all sides by men of good will, promised well. Evils that loomed beforehand disappeared in the practical trial. All yielded to adjustment as a result of experience. This the delegates might have known from the example of the British system, which they constantly cited, for that ancient and triumphant government was full of glaring contradictions and anomalies. Somehow in the process of time all but outrageous wrongs could be borne with, even turned to workable account.

The members of the convention were to discover what every marine architect, shipwright, and sailorman knows. A vessel, however cleverly designed and constructed, on her first voyage creaks, groans, whines in all its parts. These painful sounds are not alarming. The ship is merely "finding herself," the trees, planking, keel, spars, rigging tightening or giving in response to wind and wave until a mutual fit has been accomplished. The Constitution the delegates at Philadelphia put together with misgivings was a sound vessel, needing only to voyage to demonstrate her seaworthiness. Several in the convention said that the test must come in the actual operation of government, that satisfaction or disappointment would depend on the success of administration. So it was.

The validity of this principle of trusting much to the future, given the desire for accomplishment, is illustrated in the history of the Senate which was the subject of such controversy and twice nearly broke up the convention. Giving the states, little as well as big, equal votes in that body appeared to mean to the delegates a hybrid creature, partly national (a union of citizens), partly federal (a union of sovereign states). The national men, acutely resentful of the selfish refusals of states under the old government, were sure this mixed bag could never serve. True, representation in the Senate is grossly disproportioned to population of the United States; Nevada and New York have the same number of votes. But the Senate, contrary to expectation, has become in practice a national body, a senior branch of the legislature, and not more dominated by local prejudice than is, for example, the rules committee of the House.

The composition of the national legislature having been settled, discussion turned to its powers. Here Luther Martin, for once, expedited business by moving that statutes and treaties of the United States should be the supreme law of the several states, and that state courts should be bound by them. This was unanimously agreed to. However, the convention refused to give the national legislature authority to veto acts of the states.

A Single Executive, with What Powers?

It was promptly decided that the national executive be a single person, but the manner of choosing him, the extent of his tenure and powers, and how he should be removed if that were necessary, produced sharp differences of opinion. This was an office that had not existed before, as the President of Congress was annually elected by that body as its chairman, and he did not constitute a distinct branch of government. Gouverneur Morris made a vigorous, prophetic argument for election of the chief executive by the people at large, for "they will never fail to prefer some man of distinguished character, or services; some man . . . of continental reputation." Immediately objections came in rapid fire from those who thought the choice should be made by the national legislature or some other select body. The people in such a vast country would be uninformed of eligible figures, they would select from their own states, which, especially in combination, would give the large states the advantage. Or, contrariwise, the votes of the people would be scattered, giving nobody a majority. Or the people would be manipulated by demagogues. The examples of Poland and Holland were cited against a popular election. George Mason "conceived it would be as unnatural to refer the choice of a proper character for chief Magistrate to the people, as it would, to refer a trial of colours to a blind man."

Morris continued on his theme that the people could not fail to know "those great & illustrious characters which have merited their esteem & confidence." The legislature, on the other hand, if it selected, would be governed by cabal; it was here, and not in the broad electorate, that deals could be consummated. Morris's proposal to trust choice of the chief executive to the people derived force from recognition of all in the convention that if the new Constitution became a fact, George Washington would be elected by one voice. Williamson countered this by reminding that there would not always be candidates of whose fitness all the people of America could judge. Wilson had a compromise. If a majority of the people (if a majority was deemed necessary) failed to hit on the same man, let the legislature decide between the candidates. But the method of popular election was voted down, and attention was centered on a selection by a smaller and supposedly more discreet group.

Luther Martin, jealous as usual for the authority of the states, suggested that the executive be chosen by electors appointed by the legislatures of the states. This was rejected in favor of selection of the chief magistrate by the national legislature. The problem was to keep him from being dependent on the legislature, and therefore apt to do its bidding. If the term was seven years, it was suggested that he be ineligible for a second election. Immediately several influential delegates objected that restricting the executive to a single term "tended to destroy the great motive to good behavior. . . It was saying to him, make hay while the sun shines." This reasoning was accepted, and the chief executive was made eligible for reappointment. If that was to be the case, then perhaps his term should be shorter than seven years.

Dr. McClurg of Virginia, who spoke with diffidence but was listened to with respect, wished the executive to hold office during good behavior. This was the best way to free him from control by the legislature. Gouverneur Morris, and Broome of Delaware, agreed; this was "the way to get a good Government." Madison did not condemn indefinite tenure, since it would at least preserve the executive from being engulfed in "the Legislative vortex."

George Mason took alarm. "He considered an Executive during good behavior as a softer name for . . . an Executive for life," after which an easy step would be "to hereditary Monarchy." Were the delegates forgetting their commitment to republican principles? Madison, Morris, and McClurg replied that they could not be accused of favoring monarchy; rather, they wanted a republican system that would make the people happy and prevent a desire of change." But tenure during good behavior did not commend itself to most, and the provisional decision was for seven years, with possibility of reappointment. The President could negative acts of the legislature if they were not reaffirmed by two-thirds of each house. So the position of the executive was left for the time being. Delegates were sure the branches of government should be kept separate, should be checks on each other. They wanted the executive to be independent of the legislature, but not so free that he could not be disciplined for cause.

As often, the convention attempted to get out of a tangle by turning to a new topic, namely, how to select federal judges and what powers to give them. It was readily agreed that there should be "one supreme tribunal." But at once the executive was back in the picture. For if he appointed the judges, as some wished, and these judges were to try the executive on impeachment, they would favor him. Further, the executive would not know eligible characters throughout the country, but would appoint judges from the state that was the seat of government.

Earlier, in committee of the whole, Rutledge had been unwilling "to grant so great a power to any single person. The people will think we are leaning too much towards Monarchy." Before deciding whether the national judges should be named by the legislature or the executive, Franklin wanted to hear other ways discussed. ". . . he would mention [one which] he had understood was practiced in Scotland." He entertained by relating the "Scotch mode, in which the nomination proceeded from the Lawyers, who always selected the ablest of the profession in order to get rid of him, and share his practice (among themselves). It was here the interest of the electors to make the best choice. . ." Hamilton suggested the idea—which later on prevailed—

that the executive should nominate judges to the Senate, "which should have the right of rejecting or approving."

Federal Judicial Network

But Rutledge was less concerned about how the judges were chosen than he was anxious to limit the federal judicial authority to one supreme court. He moved to eliminate from the Virginia plan the establishment by the national legislature of "inferior tribunals." Operating throughout the country, these would make "an unnecessary encroachment on the jurisdiction of the States." Cases could be determined in the first instance in the existing state courts, "the right of appeal to the supreme national tribunal being sufficient to secure the national rights & uniformity of Judgmts." The states would recoil from any invasion of their function; why create an unnecessary obstacle to their adoption of the new government? The South Carolinian's rejection of lower federal courts was strengthened when his move to dispense with them was seconded by Sherman from Connecticut.

Madison arraigned this effort to shorten the tether of the national judiciary. ". . . unless inferior tribunals were dispersed throughout the Republic with *final* jurisidiction in *many* cases, appeals would be multiplied to a most oppressive degree." Verdicts in state courts might be biased by local prejudices. "To order a new trial at the supreme bar would oblige the parties to bring up their witnesses, tho' ever so distant from the seat of the Court." Madison struck at the states' jealousy of conferring independent national powers. "An effective Judiciary establishment commensurate to the legislative authority, was essential. A government without a proper Executive & Judiciary would be the mere trunk of a body without arms or legs to act or move." Wilson and Dickinson used additional arguments in support of this position.

However, the motion to omit the mandate to establish inferior federal courts was passed, 5 to 4, and two states (Massachusetts and New York) divided in their votes. Immediately Madison and Wilson came to the rescue with a motion to make lower courts permissive. "They observed that there was a distinction between establishing such tribunals absolutely, and giving a discretion to the Legislature to establish or not establish them." After debate this was decisively accepted.

We return now to debates in the convention proper on recommendations of committee of the whole. It was proposed that the salary of a judge be neither increased nor diminished while he was in office. But

Franklin, who always had an eye to the economic, pointed out that judges' salaries might be raised because "money may not only become plentier, but the business of the Department may increase as the Country becomes more populous." Madison, against any increase, was not so clear-headed. "The variations in the value of money," he thought, "may be guarded agst. by taking for a standard wheat or some other thing of permanent value." (Of course wheat might become more or less valuable quite apart from changes in the value of money.) Though there was no objection to a national supreme court, men of local attachment, as earlier, did not want federal judges sitting in the states, where state courts could handle national cases as well. But again weightier sentiment bore them down, and "inferior tribunals" appointed by the central legislature were agreed to.

The character and functions of federal courts emerged in various stages of the debates. Johnson of Connecticut suggested that jurisdiction should extend to equity as well as law cases. Read objected to vesting both powers in the same court, but Johnson's motion was accepted. Dickinson moved that the judges could be removed by the executive on application of Senate and House. Gerry and Sherman favored this, but Gouverneur Morris pointed out that it was a contradiction in terms to say judges should continue during good behavior and yet be removable without a trial. Judges should not be subjected to arbitrary authority. Rutledge, Wilson, and Randolph were sure that if the Supreme Court was to decide controversies between the United States and particular states, this alone was an insuperable obstacle to the motion. "The Judges would be in a bad situation if made to depend on every gust of faction which might prevail in the two branches of our Govt." Dickinson's motion for summary removal received only one vote.

Gouverneur Morris raised the thorny question whether the appellate jurisdiction of the federal courts reached to matters of fact as well as of law, and to cases of common law as well as civil law. It was unanimously agreed to add "both as to law and fact" in the appellate jurisdiction. The committee on style reported similarly, though it blurred the authority; while the appellate jurisdiction of the Supreme Court extended "generally" to law and fact, Congress might make exceptions. After the convention, George Mason complained, "The Judiciary of the United States is so constructed and extended, as to absorb and destroy the judiciaries of the several States; thereby rendering law as tedious, intricate and expensive, and justice as unattainable, by a great part of the community, as in England, and enabling the rich to oppress and ruin the poor."

Luther Martin, in his dissents from the Constitution, was more explicit on latitude of the federal courts. ". . . as the clause now stands, an appeal being given in general terms from the inferior courts, both as to law and fact, it . . . is avowedly intended, to give . . . a power of the most dangerous and alarming nature, that of setting at nought the verdict of a jury, and having the same facts which [a jury] had determined . . . examined and ultimately decided by . . . judges immediately appointed by the government." The point was that if the Constitution had not allowed appeal to the Supreme Court, "for correction of all errors both in law and fact," the Court "could not in any respect intermeddle with any fact decided by a jury." As it was, appeal was left in general terms as to both law and fact.

In view of differences in the convention, later heated debate in Congress over the Judiciary Act of 1789, and the subsequent Eleventh Amendment, the testimony of Gouverneur Morris on wording in the Constitution is of peculiar pertinence. He described, to Timothy Pickering in 1814, how, for the committee on style, he cast the document in final form. "Having rejected roundabout and equivocal terms, I believed it to be as clear as our language would permit; excepting, nevertheless, a part of what relates to the judiciary. On that subject, conflicting opinions had been maintained with so much professional astuteness, that it became necessary to select phrases, which expressing my own notions would not alarm others, nor shock their selflove, and to the best of my recollection, this was the only part which passed without cavil."

Aside from this disputed matter of the scope of appeals, the convention proposed that the jurisdiction of the Supreme Court should embrace laws passed by the national legislature "and . . . such other Questions as involve the national Peace and Harmony." The committee of detail spelled out the jurisdiction to "extend to all Cases affecting Ambassadors, other public ministers & Consuls to the Trial of Impeachments of Officers of the United States; to all Cases of Admiralty and Maritime Jurisdiction; to Controversies between States . . . between a State and a Citizen or Citizens of another State, between Citizens of different States, and between a State or the Citizens thereof and foreign States, Citizens or Subjects. In Cases of Impeachment, Cases affecting Ambassadors and . . . those in which a State shall be a Party, this Jurisdiction shall be original. In all the other

Cases . . . it shall be appellate . . . Crimes shall be tried in the State where they shall be committed, and The Trial of all Criminal Offences shall be by Jury."

Conflict of Courts

Disagreements in the Constitutional Convention were revived two years later when Congress discussed the bill to organize the judiciary as a branch of the national government. We may run forward to glance at these exchanges because they resolve unfinished business of the convention. The Senate took five weeks to contrive a comprehensive, detailed measure, but care bestowed on this endeavor did not deter complaints in the House such as had been heard in the convention. Tucker and Sumter of South Carolina would strike the whole provision for thirteen district and three circuit courts, as state courts were fully competent to discharge the duties designed for the inferior federal tribunals. The federal judicial system, said Livermore, "will . . . fill every State in the Union with two kinds of courts for the trial of many causes. A thing so heterogeneous must give great disgust. Sir, it will be establishing a Government within a Government and one must prevail upon the ruin of the other." The Constitution could be perfectly administered without duplicating judges, attorneys general, marshals, clerks, constables, court houses, jails, and gibbets.

Since the Confederation had no separate judiciary, "the State courts have hitherto decided all cases of a national or local import." He could conceive no reason for a superfluous federal network "unless it be to plague mankind." He contemplated "with horror the effects of the plan. I . . . see a foundation laid for discord, civil wars, and all its [sic] concomitants. To avert these evils, I hope the House will reject the proposed system." His imagination played on the clashes resulting from concurrent jurisdiction of federal district courts and state courts. If a debtor was held by a state court and a federal court demanded him, "what is to be done with the unfortunate person? Is the man to be divided that one half may appear in one court, the other in another?"

Smith of South Carolina, and Benson of New York, both stout Federalists, sought to refute these fanciful fears. The Constitution demanded inferior federal courts, and Congress was bound to create them. Not so, replied Jackson of Georgia. The language was, "Congress may from time to time . . . establish" inferior tribunals. It might choose to establish none. Ames repudiated "the expedient of hiring out our judicial power . . . it would not be more strange to get the laws made for this body, than . . . to get them interpreted and executed by those whom we do not appoint, and cannot control." Sedgwick reminded that state after state had flown in the face of national commitment in the peace treaty, had blocked payment of debts of our citizens to British subjects, and state judges had upheld these acts. Madison reinforced this complaint of parochial state courts by declaring that those of Connecticut, Rhode Island, Georgia, and Pennsylvania were not independent of their legislatures.

Stone was for no subordinate federal courts. He agreed with Livermore's extravagant forecasts. The execution of rival orders of federal and state courts might necessitate calling out the posse comitatus by both sides; "murder may be the consequence . . . and all the officers in the different courts must be hanged for acting legally." If Congress angered by establishing inferior courts, the people might curtail legislative and executive powers, "to the total . . . destruction of the whole system of Government. I am . . . for . . . moving as silently as death, that the people should not perceive the least alteration for the worse in their situation." Sumter's poor constituents did not require "the rein of despotism . . . to curb them." Livermore's motion to eliminate federal district courts was finally put and lost, 31 to 11.

The fate of a few House amendments to the Senate bill is not recorded. The Judiciary Act became law on September 23, 1789.

We return to discussion in the Philadelphia Constitutional Convention. Federal judges throughout the country were one thing, but could the national government suppress rebellion within a state? The recently quelled insurrection of Shays in Massachusetts was in everybody's mind. Luther Martin of Maryland was for leaving such risings to be coped with by the states themselves, but his colleague Daniel Carroll thought the states incompetent to do this. Gorham of Massachusetts, from sad local experience, enlarged on the necessity for national intervention to preserve orderly processes. Wilson put this in words since familiar ("a Republican form of Governmt. shall be guarantied to each State & . . . each State shall be protected agst. foreign & domestic violence"), and this important feature of the Constitution was fixed.

Who Should Choose the President?

The convention reverted to the subject of the executive. The dominant idea of many was to render him an effective check on the legislature, which would be prone to engross too much power. How should the executive be chosen, for what term, should he be eligible for re-election, should he be impeachable for abuse of his office? Gouverneur Morris again delivered himself of surprisingly democratic beliefs. "It is necessary that the Executive Magistrate should be the guardian of the people . . . agst. Legislative tyranny, against the Great & the wealthy who in the course of things will . . . compose the Legislative body. Wealth tends to corrupt the mind & to nourish the love of power, and to stimulate it to oppression. History proves this to be the spirit of the opulent." The executive should have a short term but be eligible to reappointment. This would incite him to his best efforts, and make impeachment unnecessary, for if he did wrong he would lose his place. He should be named by the people, who would surely have knowledge of sufficiently eminent characters. Randolph was afraid to give a free hand to the people, preferred election of the executive by the national legislature for one term only. Gerry agreed that "the popular mode of electing the chief Magistrate would . . . be the worst of all." If he did his duty he would be turned out of office, like Governor Bowdoin of Massachusetts because he suppressed Shays's insurrection. But respected delegates like King, Paterson, Wilson, and Madison supported the plea of Morris for election by the people, either directly or indirectly. These men have been vindicated by history, for theirs is the method of choosing the President which the country later adopted.

At this time, however, the preference of most of the delegates was for giving selection of the President to the state legislatures through electors whom the legislatures should name. Reasons were that the executive should not be beholden to the national legislature (even with the safeguard of a long term), and also the desire was strong to keep significant power in the hands of the states. It was now judged that the President should be elected for a term of six years and be eligible for re-election. The question of how many electors each state should be allowed naturally caused debate. Before there was a census of population the allocation must be by approximation. Gerry offered a formula which was accepted by a close vote. Massachusetts, Pennsylvania, and Virginia were given three electors each, New Hampshire, Delaware, and Georgia one each, and the others two each.

Most of a day was given to the pros and cons of impeachment of the executive. Would this means of removing him from office put him too much in the power of the legislature? If his term was short, he could be got rid of without impeachment. Many delegates were suspicious of the future executive's motives and behavior. He might corrupt the electors, take bribes from foreign powers, abuse his control of the military and of money in time of war. Rufus King warned, however, that "extreme caution in favor of liberty might enervate the Government" being formed. He evidently relied on the support of Gouverneur Morris, who had wanted no impeachment except for a few stated crimes, but Morris was converted by the counter-arguments of Madison, Wilson, Mason, Franklin, and Randolph. In the end all of the states except Massachusetts and South Carolina agreed that the chief executive could be impeached and if convicted be displaced from office.

Grounds for Impeachment

The final wording of Article II, Section 4 was "The President, Vice President and all civil Officers of the United States, shall be removed from Office on Impeachment for, and Conviction of, Treason, Bribery, or other high Crimes and Misdemeanors."

As with some other provisions of the Constitution, the grounds of impeachment, aside from treason and bribery, were left uncertain. In discussions in the Constitutional Convention of impeachable offenses most of the expressions used admitted of meaning other than violations of law. The cause or causes for impeachment hung partly upon how the chief executive was to be elected and how long he was to serve. Sherman was for appointment by Congress "and for making him absolutely dependent on that body, as it was the will of that which was to be executed. An independence of the Executive on the supreme Legislative, was . . . the very essence of tyranny." Sherman was understood to contend that the legislature should have power "to remove the Executive at pleasure." Wilson, on the other hand, wanted an independent executive, but with a short term, three years, though thereafter he might be re-eligible. Wilson said that if a single executive appointed officers "he is responsible for the propriety of the same." Gerry wished a council to advise the executive on "the persons proper for offices"; their recommendations should be recorded, and in case of misconduct of those recommended the members of the council could be "called to acct. for yr. [their] Opinions & impeached." This was far from a statutory offense.

According to Pierce, "Mr. Maddison observed that to prevent a Man from holding an Office longer than he ought, he may for malpractice be impeached and removed; he is not for any ineligibility." Williamson and Davie cautioned that if the executive was to be chosen for a seven-year term he should "be removable on impeachment and conviction of mal-practice or neglect of duty." This wording was temporarily adopted. In Dickinson's view the executive should be removed by the legislature on petition of a majority of the states. Madison and Wilson opposed this because, population of the states being unequal, a minority of the people could "prevent ye removal of an officer who had rendered himself justly criminal in the eyes of a majority." Such a plan would open the door "for intrigues agst. him [the officer] in States where his administration tho' just might be unpopular. . . ."

At different times in the debates vague terms were employed. The President and cabinet officers should be liable to impeachment "for neglect of duty, malversation, or corruption." Rutledge and Gouverneur Morris moved that persons impeached be suspended from office until tried and acquitted. Madison objected that this would put the executive in the power of one branch of the legislature, which could at any moment temporarily remove him "to make way for . . . another who will be more favorable to their views." This proposal was voted down as allowing too much latitude of accusation. James McHenry reported to the Maryland legislature that the trial of impeachments was lodged with the Senate "as more likely to be governed by cool and candid investigation, than by those heats that too often inflame . . . more populous Assemblys."

At a late stage Mason demanded to know why impeachment should be confined to treason and bribery. "Treason as defined in the Constitution will not reach many great and dangerous offences. Hastings is not guilty of Treason [Warren Hastings, late governor-general of India, was tried in 1787 after impeachment for 'high crimes and misdemeanors']. Attempts to subvert the Constitution may not be Treason as above defined." He moved to add after bribery "or maladministration." Madison rejoined that so vague a term would be "equivalent to a tenure during pleasure of the Senate." Mason then withdrew "maladministration" and substituted "other high crimes & misdemeanors." This wording was adopted, eight to three. Madison feared that the House might impeach the President "for an act which might be called a misdemeanor." Rather than trial by the Senate he would prefer judgment by the Supreme Court or by a tribunal of which that should form a part. Charles Pinckney also disapproved the Senate as the court of impeachments. "If [the President] opposes a favorite law, the two Houses will combine agst him, and under the influence of heat and faction throw him out of office." Gouverneur Morris replied that the small number of Supreme Court judges might be warped or corrupted. There was "no danger that the Senate would say untruly on their oaths that the President was guilty of crimes or facts."

Madison insisted that the community should be defended against "the incapacity, negligence and perfidy of the chief Magistrate. The limitation of the period of his service was not a sufficient security . . . He might pervert his administration with a scheme of peculation or oppression." Gouverneur Morris admitted that corruption "& some few other offences" should be impeachable, but thought "the cases ought to be enumerated and defined." They were not specified, and the general terms "high crimes and misdemeanors" stood.

The framers of the American Constitution were aware of British practice of impeachments which reached back four centuries. That history showed that while indictable crimes such as treason and bribery were grounds of impeachment and conviction, political offences were also included. Of these subversion of the Constitution was the chief. This might consist in abuse of power or usurping authority lodged elsewhere. The obnoxious acts might be those of the accused himself or of others for whose conduct he was responsible. The ruler or other executive or judge could be impeached for unfit behavior in office. The American framers, it is clear from their debates, adopted this cause for impeachment and at the same time made an advance over British procedure. In Britain, conviction on impeachment could carry the death penalty or imprisonment. In the United States Constitution, conviction means removal from office. If the offence is a criminal one, triable in the courts, that may follow, but the two prosecutions are separated.

That trial by the Senate on impeachment is not an ordinary criminal proceeding is plain from two precautions in the Constitution. An accused person may not be placed twice in jeopardy for the same offence, which would be the case if he was tried by the Senate on a criminal charge involving punishment other than removal from office, and then were liable to indictment and trial according to law. In the second place, if trial on impeachment was a criminal prosecution the accused would enjoy the right of judgment by a jury, which the Senate is not.

In a period (1868) of passion and prejudice the impeachment and trial of President Andrew Johnson were emphatically political. Technically he was charged with breaking the law (Tenure of Office Act) which forbade him to remove an officer without consent of the Senate. But that law had been passed to keep Stanton in the cabinet, was really a dare to the President to remove him and thereby make himself subject to impeachment. All of the counts in the impeachment resolution were political in character. In fact they were not spelled out until after the resolution was adopted by the vote of 168 to 47. In the trial before the Senate, with Chief Justice Salmon P. Chase presiding, the political motive to convict Johnson was at once evident in the demagogic attack by Benjamin F. Butler, one of the House managers of the prosecution. The same hostility continued, with unseemly effort to corral votes against the President. After intensive struggles the votes on three articles, taken ten days apart, stood at 35 to 19, one vote short of the two-thirds required for removal.

Thereafter the other charges were dropped. The failure of the attempt to oust Johnson was fortunate because had it succeeded the proper function of the President in the constitutional system would have suffered. Fear of incurring the antagonism of Congress would have numbed the President's initiative. As it was, the design of the radical Republicans to punish the President for his independence was discredited. When Johnson was upheld Stanton resigned; Johnson's successor, Grant, appointed Stanton to the Supreme Court, but he died before ascending the bench. A score of years after Johnson's impeachment the Tenure of Office Act was repealed, and in 1926 was declared unconstitutional.

IMPENDING IMPEACHMENT AND RESIGNATION OF PRESIDENT NIXON

The Civil War represented a complete breakdown of the Constitution. The impeachment of President Andrew Johnson, as we have seen, resulted from war bitterness and was political in animus. In contrast, the Constitution triumphed in the resignation of President Richard M. Nixon in 1974, in the face of impending impeachment and almost certain conviction. The success of legal process was the more conspicuous because Nixon had been overwhelmingly elected to a second term less than two years before his voluntary exit from office.

The background for this unprecedented action was the criminal behavior of some persons employed by the Committee to Re-elect the President ("CREEP") and some of the White House staff. A burglary and "bugging" (for reasons still not clear) in June 1972 of the Democratic National Headquarters in Watergate, a well-known apartment complex, gave the scandal its name. But as the tale unfolded many other unscrupulous if not illegal acts were uncovered, from political "dirty tricks" to misuse of campaign money, perversion of government agencies for political purposes, perjury, possible bribery, payment of hush money, evasion of income taxes, and a pervasive and elaborate cover-up of all the misdeeds. The executive branch of the government was demoralized; at the heart of the scandal, finally, was the guilty secrecy of the President himself.

Initially the cover-up was so successful that the burglary had no effect on the 1972 election. Subsequently, diligent investigation by Washington newspaper reporters, plus the suspicions of a Federal judge and the decision of one defendant to turn informer led to unraveling the whole sorry mess. Investigation by a select committee of the Senate in 1973-74 and indictments by federal grand juries of two former cabinet members and numerous other presidential appointees followed. By mid-1974 more than a dozen presidential associates had been convicted, or had pleaded guilty to reduced charges in return for partial immunity. Meantime Vice President Spiro T. Agnew pleaded guilty to income tax evasion and was allowed to resign in October 1973, the federal prosecutors releasing simultaneously a 40-page account of other wrongdoing centering on bribe-taking. For the first time, the Twenty-fifth Amendment to the Constitution was used; the President nominated Gerald R. Ford, the minority leader in the House, to be Vice President. After extensive investigation, Congress confirmed the nomination by majority votes in both houses.

Though professing cooperation with official probes, President Nixon in fact long resisted the furnishing of evidence, on grounds of executive privilege and national security. He allowed a special prosecutor for the Watergate cases to be appointed, but had him discharged in six months, in the process losing two attorneys-general who refused to obey the President's demand. This set off a nation-wide storm of protests, forcing the appointment of another special prosecutor. The Senate inquiry revealed that a recording system in the White House made tape recordings of most conversations involving the President and his associates. First refused to the Senate committee and the special prosecutor, some of these tapes were finally given piecemeal to the federal judiciary, and others, in edited form, were made public by the White House.

The House Judiciary Committee, though lacking a substantial number of tapes which the President still refused to surrender, voted three resolutions of impeachment by bipartisan majorities in late July 1974. The resolutions concerned themselves with obstruction of justice, failure to see that the laws were faithfully executed, and defiance of the subpoenas of Congress, all with supporting evidence. At the same time, the Supreme Court decided unanimously that 64 tapes must be surrendered to the special prosecutor.

While preparations were going forward for impeachment debate in the House and trial in the Senate, if necessary, the President released transcripts of three conversations held a few days after the Watergate break-in. The evidence so startlingly confirmed the Judiciary Committee's charges that all of the ten Republican members who had voted consistently against impeachment made public statements supporting the charge of obstructing justice. Nixon's statement accompanying release of the evidence acknowledged that he had lied, deceiving the public and his own lawyers as well as official investigators.

The President wavered only briefly between facing impeachment and trial and resigning, before taking the latter course on August 8, 1974. In a television speech he gave as his reason only "erosion of his political support" in Congress, and made no further confession of complicity. Vice President Ford at once became President. This orderly transition did something to counterbalance the disgrace of the outgoing administration.

Left unresolved by resignation were questions of procedure against the former President, now a private citizen. Several former associates were scheduled for trial for conspiracy in the cover-up in September 1974, and on August 15 Nixon was subpoenaed as a witness by one of the defendants.

On September 8, 1974 President Ford surprised the nation by issuing an unconditional pardon to his predecessor for any acts which he had (or might have) committed from January 20, 1969, to August 9, 1974. Former President Nixon accepted the pardon, but acknowledged only "mistakes," not guilt. Constitutionalists differed as to whether pardon could thus be granted in advance of formal accusation or trial, but there seemed no likelihood that Ford's action could successfully be challenged. It was clear that the former President had lost his Fifth Amendment protection, if he appeared as a witness in judicial proceedings.

Constitution Creation of the People, Not the States

A sharp difference had developed over whether the national judges (presumably of the Supreme Court only) should join the executive in putting a negative on acts of the legislature unless two-thirds of the legislature reaffirmed such laws. Those for bringing the judges to the help of the executive contended that this would strengthen his position in the eyes of the people; permit the judges to oppose laws which, while not unconstitutional, were unwise or unjust; help defeat the tendency of the legislature "to absorb all power into its vortex." In England the judges sat in the legislature, and could give their opinion against measures before they were passed. Wilson, Ellsworth, Mason, Madison, and

Gouverneur Morris used such arguments. Here was impressive support for associating the judiciary with the executive in the negative on the legislature.

Opposed to them were Gerry, Gorham, Strong (all of Massachusetts), and Rutledge of South Carolina. Ordinarily these could not have carried their point, but in this instance their reasoning was superior. The great departments of government must be kept distinct, not blended in their functions. The judges would determine when a law came before them in their official capacity whether it violated the Constitution. Otherwise they should have no say, for they were not law-makers, only expositors. The judges were not statesmen, and were less able than legislators, who were representatives of the people, to declare what was public policy. These clear-headed views narrowly prevailed in the vote. This division of responsibility was confirmed in later American practice, for the judges have refused to pass on hypothetical questions or to advise Congress or the President on the wisdom or expediency of intended actions.

How should the judges be appointed? In the clash of opinions, hard things were said about the competence and sincerity of both the executive and the upper house of the legislature. Madison proposed that the executive's choice of judges was to stand unless two-thirds of the Senate disagreed. Several were convincing when they objected that the executive, being "stationary," would not have a sufficiently wide knowledge of fit persons; the unfit would caress and intrigue with him; a compliant Senate would be apt to accept his suggestions; he had too much power anyhow, and it was wrong to permit him, by the right of appointment, to influence the judiciary. So naming of the judges was given at this stage of debate to the Senate alone. (Of course, this decision was later reversed, and the principle of Madison's motion—choice of judges by the President with consent of the Senate—was adopted. From an early period it has been accepted that Presidents nominate judges, especially of the Supreme Court, of whose political allegiance or at any rate views they approve.)

John Langdon and Nicholas Gilman, delegates from New Hampshire, arrived July 23. They had been delayed because the state had no money to send them, but rather than leave the state unrepresented Langdon supplied funds. A wealthy merchant, he was similarly public-spirited at other times.

This day saw some important actions. Debate was at first over whether the constitution should be referred for ratification to the state legislatures (as wished by Ellsworth and Gerry), or to conventions of the people of the states specially called for the purpose (as urged by Mason, Randolph, Gouverneur Morris, Gorman, King, and others). The bottom question was the old one—did the constitution being formed amend the Articles of Confederation (in which case the legislatures should pass on it), or supersede the existing government and thus require authority of the people themselves? Those for seeking sanction of the people had the better of the argument; the vote was 9 to 1 for this strategy; New York was not represented, as Hamilton had left June 29 and Lansing and Yates July 10. Chief opposition to the new system, declared Randolph, could be expected from "local demagogues who will be degraded by it from the importance they now hold. These will spare no efforts to impair that progress in the popular mind which will be necessary to the adoption of the plan, and which every member will find to have taken place in his own, if he will compare his present opinions with those brought by him into the Convention . . . therefore . . . the consideration of this subject should be transferred from the Legislatures where this class of men, have their full influence to a field in which their efforts can be less mischievous."

These were pertinent remarks. The members of the convention understood their state legislatures. Many of the best men, including the clergy, were not in them. Morris observed that recourse to the original power, of the people, was necessary since the Constitution was being framed by a body "unknown to the Confederation." That is, the articles provided for amendment by the state legislatures directly, and furthermore this constitution was a replacement, not a revision, of the old one. Often afterward the adoption of the new Constitution was referred to as a "second revolution." As Madison now said, "the difference between a system founded on the Legislatures only, and one founded on the people" was "the true difference between a *league* or *treaty* [which carried moral obligation], and a Constitution," which had political operation. Randolph's comment on the need for inducing "progress in the popular mind" in favor of the constitution foreshadowed the *Federalist* papers and others less influential. Much later, as we shall see, Chief Justice Marshall in Supreme Court decisions could not have vindicated the authority of the national over the state governments if the Constitution which the court interpreted had not sprung from the people themselves.

Also this day it was decided that each state should be represented by two (not more) in the Senate, and that these should "vote per capita," that is, as individuals. In the Old Congress—and in the Constitutional Convention itself—voting was by states, which put emphasis on states' rights rather than on national good. Further, if the delegation of a state was equally divided on an issue, the state and its delegates lost the vote.

A last action was to provide for a committee that would cast the decisions of the convention into the form of a Constitution. It was recognized that this "committee of detail" must elaborate at points, and fill in particulars where the convention had contented itself with general guidance. With this requirement in mind, Charles Cotesworth Pinckney "reminded the Convention that if the Committee should fail to insert some security to the Southern States agst. an emancipation of slaves, and taxes on exports, he shd. be bound by duty to his State to vote agst. their Report." Of course this ultimatum was an echo from the compromise, previously agreed to in principle, between popular rights and states' rights delegates. It was wisely determined to keep this committee small, of five members. Next day those elected to it were Rutlege (S.C.), Randolph (Va.), Gorham (Mass.), Ellsworth (Conn.), and Wilson (Pa.). These represented the different parts of the country. However, Ellsworth was the only one from what could be called a small state, and he himself spoke of Connecticut as of middle size and sentiments. The committee of the whole was discharged, and to the committee of detail were referred the plans of a constitution offered by Charles Pinckney and by Paterson.

However, the mode of choosing the chief executive was not referred to the committee of detail. This was not a matter of mere drafting, and the convention itself had a go at it for two full days of discussion. Much debate was given to designation of the electors, with no thought that these would later be shorn of all discretion, though retained, nominally, as a piece of constitutional machinery. It was moved to reconsider the earlier decision that electors be appointed by the state legislatures. Electors should be dropped, and the national legislature should appoint the executive. Several had no faith in electors. Capable men would not serve as electors, would not trouble to come to the capital from distant states. It was answered that election of the chief magistrate would "excite great earnestness" and command the attention of superior electors.

Then discussion was diverted to the character of the executive. A southern delegate thought executive power should be lodged not in one man but in three men taken from the three sections of the country. A single magistrate would be "an elective King, . . . spare no pains to keep himself in for life, and . . . then lay a train for the succession of his children." Fear of such a monarch rising in the new American democracy, and determination that the executive should not court the favor of the legislature produced demand that he should not be eligible for re-election. His term might be long—8, 10, 11, 15, even 20 years according to different suggestions—if only a definite end was put to it. The convention was confused by the variety of proposals. Gerry had a complicated method originating with the legislatures of the states. Wilson would avoid intrigue and dependence by choosing a small number of electors from the national legislature by lot. Let the fifteen who drew gold balls from a bowl "retire immediately and make the election without separating."

The purpose of this instant and on the spot choice of a President was to prevent appeals to constituents in different areas of the country and whipping up of popular clamors. The idea all along was to entrust the selection to prudent men who would act on their individual judgments. They must not form combinations within the group of electors, or be swayed by combinations of citizens. Our Founding Fathers feared what they called "faction," or organized forces contending against each other and disturbing the harmony of the nation. They did not foresee, much less approve, the formation of political parties. Of course they recognized that the convention itself was divided into the friends of a vigorous central government and those who wanted to keep more power in the states. This split was declared as soon as the Constitution was put into effect. Those of the dominant, more coherent majority called themselves Federalists. The others, for want of another name, were known as Anti-Federalists. Within a decade these became, in fact, distinct opposed parties. But it was not until a generation later that party conventions were held. It seems odd to present-day Americans that the party system for operating our government was not anticipated by the framers of the Constitution.

When all had tired of inventiveness, the delegates agreed that the national legislature should select a single executive for a term of seven years, to be ineligible a second time, and to be removable on impeachment and conviction of malpractice or neglect of duty. The convention adjourned for ten days to allow the committee of detail to present the draft of a constitution.

Qualifications To Vote

When this was submitted, earnest debate concerned qualifications of those voting for members of the House of Representatives, as it was now called for the first time. The draft made the qualifications "the same . . . as those of the electors in the several States, of the most numerous branch of their own legislatures." Dickinson, Gouverneur

Morris, and Madison would have the vote confined to freeholders (owners of land, but not further defined). Several of the states did not have this restriction, and the time would come when propertyless industrial workers would multiply. These, it was warned, would sell their votes or be otherwise controlled by their employers, who would thus dominate the House. Ellsworth, Mason, and Franklin pleaded with feeling for manhood suffrage, at least so far as it was permitted by the states. Said Mason, "every man having evidence of attachment to & permanent common interest with the Society ought to share in all its rights & privileges." Suffrage was the foundation of patriotism. Franklin observed solemnly "that we shd. not depress the virtue & public spirit of our common people; of which they displayed a great deal during the war, and which contributed principally to the favorable issue of it." He used a telling illustration. Our seamen, when captured, had preferred prison to serving on British ships against their own countrymen, while the British sailors taken by us readily agreed to cruise with us and share in our prizes. In the end it was wisely and unanimously agreed that the Constitution should not restrict the vote for members of the popular house.

King, Gouverneur Morris, and others protested vigorously when they were confronted with the compromise including three-fifths of the slaves for purposes of representation and taxation. In printed form it doubtless took on greater finality than when first debated. The draft placed no limits on importation of slaves. The northern states, said the objectors, were giving up too much. Exports—mainly the products of the labor of slaves—were not to be taxed. Morris was particularly scathing as he contrasted the "superior improvement" of the free states with "the misery & poverty which overspread the barren wastes of . . . the . . . States having slaves." The "inhabitant of Georgia and S.C. who goes to the Coast of Africa, and in defiance of the most sacred laws of humanity tears away his fellow creatures from their dearest connections & damns them to the most cruel bondages" was in effect importing votes for himself. Roger Sherman was conciliatory. He preferred to think it was "the freemen of the South. States who were . . . to be represented according to the taxes paid by them, and the Negroes are only included in the Estimate of the taxes." Only one Southerner replied, faintly. Nothing further was said.

However, action was taken on another feature of the compromise. The exclusive right of the House to originate money bills had been regarded as a concession to the large states which had more representation in that body. Leaders from both sections, though with opposition from George Mason and others, were for allowing the Senate the same control over the purse, and this was voted, in effect, by striking out the section as it stood in the report of the committee of detail. On a later day Randolph and others earnestly renewed the effort to confine extraction of revenue at least to the House, which represented the people. It was improper to permit the Senate, which represented the states in their political character, to tax the population. The new plan of government would not be approved by the country at large unless the purse strings were held by the House. In spite of arguments which have since seemed to be conclusive, the peculiar right of the House was not then approved.

Jealousy of foreigners was conspicuous in a controversy over the length of time one must be a citizen in order to qualify for election to the House. The committee of detail had proposed three years. Mason succeeded in getting seven years substituted. Otherwise, "a rich foreign nation, for example Great Britain, might send over her tools who might bribe their way into the Legislature for insidious purposes." Gouverneur Morris demanded that senators must be citizens for not four years but for fourteen. Mason supported him, but Madison, Randolph, and Franklin thought this restriction bespoke exaggerated fears. Franklin, particularly, reminded that during the Revolution "many strangers served us faithfully," while "many natives [Loyalists] took part agst. their Country." James Wilson remarked that, not being a native (he was born in Scotland) the proposal would make him ineligible for an office under the very Constitution "which he had shared in the trust of making." Gouverneur Morris was jingoistic. "As to . . . philosophical gentlemen . . . Citizens of the World, as they called themselves, He . . . did not wish to see any of them in our public Councils. He would not trust them." When his amendment for fourteen years was rejected he retreated to thirteen and this was whittled to nine before being accepted.

A few days later the qualifications for members of the House were reconsidered. Wilson and Randolph contended that four years of citizenship, not seven, were sufficient. Gerry, in opposition, talked as Gouverneur Morris had done before, and "wished . . . eligibility might be confined to Natives." Williamson preferred nine years. By now Alexander Hamilton had returned to the convention. He conceded that some dangers existed, but "on the other side, the advantage of encouraging foreigners was obvious & admitted." Why not require simply citizenship and leave any further restriction to discretion of the legislature? The Constitution itself ought not to be encumbered with limitations. Wilson, from Pennsylvania which had been notable for receiving foreigners, agreed, and withdrew his motion requiring four years. Besides himself, two of his Pennsylvania colleagues, Robert Morris and Thomas FitzSimmons, were not natives. He might have added, though everybody knew it, that Hamilton had not been born here. Hamilton's liberal motion was voted down, but so were others less favorable to foreigners. Gouverneur Morris, evidently mindful now of the presence in his own delegation of three outsiders, plus his friend Hamilton from New York, was willing that a limitation of seven years should not affect the rights of any person now a citizen, and so moved. Others were against this and after a wrangle the clause stood as it had been, seven years' citizenship without exception.

Responsibilities of Representatives, and Checks upon Them

The provisional draft of the Constitution (from the committee of detail) said that members of the two houses of Congress must not hold other offices under the United States, and senators could not accept such appointments until one year after their terms had expired. What was involved was confidence (or lack of it) in national legislators. Would they use their places to create profitable employment for themselves and their friends? Charles Pinckney thought not. The Senate particularly ought to become "a School of Public Ministers, a nursery of Statesmen." But if election to the legislature meant that one was ineligible for another post, men of talents would not go there. George Mason took the reverse position. His sarcastic remarks were not in line with the later notion that rich men in the convention created the Constitution for their own benefit. He was not for encouraging "exotic corruption" by "inviting into the Legislative service, those generous & benevolent characters who will do justice to each other's merit, by carving out offices & rewards for it." He went on to say that he had a low opinion of American morals; few would object to the Constitution because it gave "premiums to a mercenary & depraved ambition."

On the other hand the extreme democrat, Mercer of Maryland, agreed with Pinckney that the proposed disqualification "would . . . determine all the most influential men to stay at home, & prefer appointments within their respective States." Gerry would be agreeable to this. The senators would appoint themselves ambassadors, and the House must provide salaries for them. Many considered that we should send no ambassadors and receive none. Gouverneur Morris made an impression by reminding that the country would be endangered in case of war if the citizen most capable of leading the troops were a member of the legislature. Perhaps with a glance at Washington, he asked, "What might have been the consequence of such a regulation at the commencement . . . of the late contest for our liberties?" Several consented that members could quit Congress to serve in army or navy. Views of influential members were so contrary that debate on this question was postponed.

A crucial feature of the new plan of government was determined with little debate. It was that members of both houses of the national legislature should be paid from the federal treasury instead of by the states, as the committee of detail had specified. Carroll of Maryland rightly emphasized that the states, if they compensated their members, could say "if you do not comply with our wishes, we will starve you: if you do we will reward you. The new Govt. in this form was nothing more than a second edition of [the Old] Congress in two volumes, instead of one, and . . . with very few amendments." His colleague Luther Martin, ever the partisan of local sovereignty, differed; as senators represented the states, they should be paid by the states. Carroll answered, "The Senate was to represent & manage the affairs of the whole, and not to be the advocate of State interests. They ought then not to be dependent on nor paid by the States." Dickinson similarly believed "all were convinced of the necessity of making the Genl. Govt. independent of the prejudices, passions, and improper views of the State legislatures." It was agreed that members of the national legislature could be trusted to fix the amount of their own salaries.

Those against allowing the Senate to originate revenue bills reverted to their objections. They were willing to permit the Senate to propose or concur in amendments of money measures, but not to lay taxes or appropriate funds in the first instance. The Senate already had too much power. It could "sell the whole Country by means of Treaties." If Spain should seize Georgia "the Senate might by treaty dismember the Union." Those for restricting the Senate in direct command over funds doubtless remembered the point they had made earlier, that the upper house might conclude a treaty which would commit the lower house to provide moneys. Against the strong wishes of delegates who wanted to limit the Senate's command of funds, further discussion of this matter was deferred.

In the convention the desire for a national council of revision was recurrently manifested. This was not so much a willingness to repose authority in a small group as it was evidence of lack of faith in the wisdom of the legislature. As the provisional draft had it, all bills passed by the two houses should be submitted to the President, and a two-thirds vote in each house was necessary to pass the measure over the President's objection. Madison moved to amend by requiring that bills be submitted to the Supreme Court as well as to the President; if either objected, a two-thirds vote, and if both, a three-fourths vote of both houses was necessary for enactment. Wilson seconded; he was "most apprehensive of a dissolution of the Govt. from the legislature swallowing up all the other powers." Strangely, Mercer of Maryland was their ally, because he wanted "legislative usurpation and oppression . . . obviated." At the same time Mercer set limits to the power of the judges. They should not "as expositors of the Constitution . . . have authority to declare a law void. He thought laws ought to be . . . cautiously made, and then to be uncontroulable."

Madison's motion for an emphatic check on the legislature was rejected. But Gouverneur Morris got the question reopened. The lower house, prone to issue paper money, ought to be effectually corrected. Unless it was made difficult, the representatives would insist on ruinous measures, have their way, and become absolute over the executive. Morris proposed a complicated variant of Madison's motion; this led to the old suggestion that the matter be postponed. Numerous delegates were losing patience with constant deferments. Rutledge complained strenuously of the tediousness of proceedings. Gorham bemoaned stagnation because some would not agree to the form of government before powers were defined, while others would not consent to powers until the form was fixed. Ellsworth lamented, "We grow more & more skeptical . . . If we do not decide soon, we shall be unable to come to any decision." The members were fatigued, and the heat of mid-August did not help. Williamson of North Carolina cut the business short by moving to leave the negative with the President alone, but require a three-fourths vote in Congress to overrule his dissent, and this was accepted.

Central versus State Authority

The southern or "staple States" held tenaciously to the bargain they had made respecting representation, taxes, and the slave trade. When the section of the draft constitution giving Congress power to lay and collect taxes was reached, Mason wanted it stated in this place that no tax on exports was permitted. "He was unwilling to trust to its being done in a future article. He hoped the Northn. States did not mean to deny the Southern this security." Madison was from a staple state (Virginia, tobacco), but for half a dozen reasons he urged that taxes by Congress on exports were proper. Gouverneur Morris and Wilson of Pennsylvania were as emphatic in the same contention. Evidently Sherman was surprised that this question had flared again, for he thought "the matter had been adjusted . . . A power to tax exports would shipwreck the whole." The dispute was quieted only by agreement to resume the discussion when the clause regarding exports was reached in regular order. Delegates differed on how the "Treasurer" (secretary of the treasury) should be chosen. The draft gave this power to the legislature, where Mason contended it should remain; since the money belonged to the people, "the legislature representing the people ought to appoint the keepers of it." Others wanted this officer named by the President, likely to show more discretion than legislators. So far as appears from the meager record, the head of the Treasury was here regarded as the custodian of funds, not as one who would propose fiscal policies. At this time his designation was left to the two houses by joint ballot. (Later the secretary of the treasury was appointed by the President with the advice and consent of the Senate, but his peculiar responsibility to Congress—not true of other heads of departments—was defined by statute.)

Tenderness of numbers of the states for their local authority was constantly appearing. The draft constitution gave Congress power "to subdue a rebellion in any State, on the application of its legislature." Charles Pinckney, generally the friend of central authority, wished the limitation struck out. Luther Martin, of contrary views, insisted that "consent of the State ought to precede the introduction of any extraneous force whatever." Gerry similarly "was agst. letting loose the myrmidons of the U. States without its own consent." Coming from Massachusetts, which had so recently been torn by Shays's rebellion, he was in an embarrassing position in repelling federal correction. He went so far as to claim that "More blood would have been spilt in Massts in the late insurrection, if the Genl. authority had intermeddled." Gouverneur Morris, when champions of both sides were vocal, observed, "We are acting a very strange part. We first form a strong man to protect us, and at the same time wish to tie his hands behind him. The legislature may surely be trusted with . . . a power to preserve the public tranquillity." The difference was adjusted by approving Ellsworth's wording, that Congress might intervene on its own motion to subdue rebellion if the state legislature could not meet.

Inevitably, numerous powers that should or might belong to the national government had not been brought forward in the earlier weeks of the convention and remained now to be added to the items referred to the committee of detail. The authors were Madison, Charles Pinckney, Gerry, Rutledge, and Mason. Principal topics were exclusive authority over the federal capital district, the granting of charters of incorporation, funds for paying public creditors not to be diverted to any other purpose, expediency of the central government assuming war debts of the states, and regulation of the militia. The last two provisions provoked most debate.

Rutledge was decidedly for assumption of state debts, which had been contracted in the common defense. The states had surrendered import duties, their only sure means of payment, and the state creditors would demand that the central government, commanding the funds, must meet the obligation. The people of the states would be glad to be disburdened. King and Charles Pinckney agreed, but Mason, Sherman, and Ellsworth had doubts, and recommended that Congress should consider the matter, but without positive mandate. (It turned out that these last better understood the public temper, or a least the position that would be taken by many state leaders when the proposition of assumption came before Congress a few years later.) The question was referred to a grand committee of a member from each state.

Gerry and Martin were for severely limiting any standing army of the national government in time of peace, perhaps to 2000 men. But when General Pinckney, Langdon, and Dayton asked how the country was to be protected in case of attack, Mason urged that the state militia come under national regulation. When objection arose he much modified his proposal by confining federal discipline to one-tenth of the militia in any one year. General Pinckney and Langdon branded the division of responsibility for regulating the militia as thoroughly impracticable. The debate quickly revealed, from different quarters, trust or distrust toward the central authority, and this "most important matter . . . of the sword" was referred to the grand committee.

The convention, wishing to complete its business, had resolved to sit longer hours. This was fortunate, for immediately thereafter Charles Pinckney and Gouverneur Morris submitted a budget of further business for the committee of detail. Their recommendations, taken together, embraced important features of a bill of rights, and defined duties of heads of executive departments who should form a council (later the cabinet) advisory to the President. Both sets of proposals anticipated much that was accomplished later, including the first ten amendments and, long afterward, creation of the office of secretary of the interior.

Governor William Livingston of New Jersey, from the committee of eleven to which unresolved questions were referred, reported that the new national legislature "shall have power to fulfil the engagements which have been entered into by [the Old] Congress, and to discharge as well the debts of the United States, as the debts incurred by the several States during the late war, for the common defence and general welfare." One would think it would have been taken for granted that the new government stood in the shoes of the former one where financial obligations were concerned. Gerry wanted this stated specifically, and objected to making the authority or the duty permissive only. Otherwise the creditors of the United States lost their security, and would oppose the Constitution. Nor did Gerry like the last portion of the report, which compelled the national government to assume the war debts of the states. States which had exerted themselves to sink their debts would "be alarmed, if they were now to be saddled with a share of the debts of States which had done least." This was to become a bitterly controverted matter. Ellsworth, who never believed in looking for trouble, moved to postpone further discussion. This included deferring also a sensible recommendation of Livingston's committee that Congress should organize, arm, and discipline the militia, reserving to the states appointment of the officers.

Luther Martin, always shy of federal authority, wanted the states to decide the manner of laying direct taxes, if these were ever resorted to under the Constitution. Congress should first requisition the states for their shares, and only if the states failed to respond should the national government compel compliance. With no debate, his proposition was voted down unanimously. The general policy of preliminary requisitions had been discredited earlier.

South Carolina Determined To Import Slaves

The power of Congress to tax exports, now bruited again, brought a confusion of voices, both Northerners and Southerners differing among themselves. Langdon of New Hampshire, Wilson of Pennsylvania, and

Madison of Virginia gave reasons for it, while Sherman, Butler of South Carolina, Williamson of North Carolina, and Gerry of Massachusetts were as strenuously opposed. It was clear, as before, that the southern states, in most cases, were for prohibiting national taxes on their exported staples, for such would oblige them to bear a disproportionate burden. Maybe northern states would one day have large exports of provisions and lumber, but this was not yet true. Congress was forbidden to tax exports.

Southern states were successful not only in banning restriction on their exports, they had thus far ruled out any limitation on one of their principal imports, that of slaves. But they did not enjoy this immunity without brusque objection from Luther Martin of Maryland. Congress, he declared, should be able to stop this traffic or impede it by a tax. He offered three arguments: (1) unless checked, southern states would import more slaves in order to increase their representation in the House; (2) more Negroes increased the danger of slave revolts, against which the remainder of the country was bound to give expensive protection; (3) last (and most important) enslaving Africans "was inconsistent with the principles of the revolution and [it was] dishonorable to the American character to have such a feature in the Constitution."

South Carolinians were adamant against Martin's reasoning. Said John Rutledge, despising logic, free import of slaves did not encourage the trade. He was not afraid of insurrections, and he exempted the other states from any duty to protect the South against them. His reply on the moral issue was unworthy of him, of his state, and of the dignity of the convention. "Religion & humanity," he proclaimed, "had nothing to do with this question. Interest alone is the governing principle with nations." He issued his familiar ultimatum: "The true question at present is whether the Southn. States shall or shall not be parties to the Union." Lastly, if the northern states consulted their own interest "they will not oppose the increase of Slaves which will increase the commodities of which they will become the carriers."

Ellsworth's desire for peace did not permit him to take higher ground: "Let every State import what it pleases. The morality or wisdom of slavery are considerations belonging to the States themselves." (Here he was running contrary to what was to be the course of American constitutional development. To be sure, states should determine policy in questions genuinely local to them, but where their behavior damaged national welfare, their local authority must be superseded).

Ellsworth, like the South Carolinians, was content with material advantage. "What enriches a part enriches the whole, and the States are the best judges of their particular interest."

Charles Pinckney begged the question by declaring, "South Carolina can never receive the plan if it prohibits the slave trade." He softened his defiance a little by the pious hope that "If the States be all left at liberty on this subject, S. Carolina may perhaps by degrees do of herself what is wished, as Virginia & Maryland have already done."

The subject of the slave trade was resumed next day, August 22, and occupied much of the session. When Sherman of Connecticut was for keeping Congress out of it, believing that the states were on the way to abolishing slavery, and that anyhow the convention should get on with other business, George Mason could no longer contain himself. The issue of the increase of slavery by fresh imports must be faced and settled. His denunciation of "this infernal traffic" has become celebrated. Though Virginia and Maryland had forbidden it entirely and North Carolina had done so substantially, all was "in vain if S. Carolina & Georgia be at liberty to import. The Western people are already calling out for slaves for their new lands; and will fill that Country with slaves if they can be got thro' S. Carolina & Georgia." He plunged on in famous words. "Slavery discourages arts & manufactures. The poor despise labor when performed by slaves. They prevent the immigration of Whites, who really enrich & strengthen a Country. They produce the most pernicious effect on manners. Every master of slaves is born a petty tyrant. They bring the judgment of heaven on a Country. . . . By an inevitable chain of causes & effects providence punishes national sins, by national calamities . . . He held it essential in every point of view, that the Genl. Govt. should have power to prevent the increase of slavery."

This prophetic charge brought from Ellsworth only pleas in extenuation. With abolition in successive states, "Slavery in time will not be a speck in our country." Poor white laborers would increase and render slaves useless. "Let us not intermeddle." Charles Pinckney, himself opposed to slavery, yet reminded that "it is justified by the example of all the world . . . In all ages one half of mankind have been slaves." His cousin, Charles Cotesworth Pinckney, repeated his defiance: to exclude slaves was to exclude South Carolina from the Union. Baldwin spoke similarly for Georgia. Wilson made capital of optimistic assurances that the far southern states before long would themselves forbid importations. If that was true, they would not refuse to come into the Union because Congress did their work for them.

THE CONSTITUTION IS CONSTRUCTED

Dickinson went to the point: "The true question was whether the national happiness would be promoted or impeded by the importation, and this . . . ought to be left to the National Govt. not to the States particularly interested . . . He could not believe that the Southn. States would refuse to confederate on the account apprehended . . ." Rufus King met the proprietors of rice swamps squarely. "If two States will not agree to the Constitution . . . on one side, . . . great & equal opposition would be experienced from the other States." Rutledge was unmoved. "If the Convention thinks that N.C., S.C. & Georgia will ever agree to the plan [the Constitution], unless their right to import slaves be untouched, the expectation is vain." However, he would agree with General Pinckney that a tax on slaves imported might be pondered by a committee.

Compromise on Navigation Acts and Negroes

Amidst these antagonisms Gouverneur Morris saw the chance for "a bargain among the Northern & Southern States." Send to a committee the whole business of control by Congress over exports of goods and imports of slaves. Randolph supported him and, as tempers cooled, this was agreed to.

As we shall see later in these pages, a motive that induced New York to ratify the Constitution, after all the other states except Rhode Island and North Carolina had come in, was the fear of being isolated. If New York stood out she could not defend herself against military attack, and her southern counties, possessing the great harbor and access to the Hudson, might secede and join the Union. Is it possible that if the remainder of the country had refused to give in to the demand of South Carolina for continuance of the slave trade, that state similarly would have abandoned her objection rather than be left out? If importation of slaves had been stopped shortly after the Constitution went into effect, plantation states might have been less confirmed in the use of slaves and subsequent American history might have been different. George Mason in the Virginia convention lamented that under the Constitution, Congress could not forbid import of slaves for twenty years, and declared, "As much as I value a union of all the States, I would not admit the Southern States into the union, unless they agreed to the discontinuance of this disgraceful trade . . ." If Mason was prepared to take this stand, perhaps it was practicable.

As noted before, the framing of the Constitution involved a series of compromises. One that punctuated the running contest between the northern and southern states was reached at the end of August. Uniquely, this was accomplished with mutual cordiality. Earlier it was agreed, on demand of the planters, that no tax should be laid on exports (of tobacco, rice, or indigo), no tax on import of slaves, and of course no prohibition of the slave trade, internal or external. But exemption of slavery from any restriction struck the Northerners as yielding too much to the South. The special committee to which this was referred reported a modification: Congress should not forbid migration or importation of slaves prior to 1800, but a duty might be imposed not exceeding the average of duties laid on imports. The convention deferred the year to 1808. It was at first suggested that there be no prohibition on importation "until" the year 1808, but this was rejected because it looked like a commitment to end the trade then. The words "prior to the year 1808" were substituted and the duty was defined as a permissive tax "not exceeding ten dollars for each person."

The same committee which recommended a limitation on the slave trade offered further concession to the northern states by making it easier for them to pass "navigation acts"—that is, laws favoring American ships and seamen. The purpose would be to encourage our own merchant marine and furnish the basis of a navy, or to retaliate against foreign discriminations against our carriers. The proposal was to permit such acts to be passed by a mere majority of each house, instead of by two-thirds. Charles Pinckney wanted the two-thirds rule restored, as the power of regulating commerce was a "pure concession on the part of the S. States." At present the South did not need to encourage northern shipping to transport southern products. Martin of Maryland seconded, but other South Carolinians were more generous. General Pinckney considered the losses suffered by the eastern states in the Revolution, "their liberal conduct [in the convention] towards the views of South Carolina" (freedom to import slaves), and the wish of the weak South to be united to the strong North. His constituents would be reconciled to not putting fetters on power of the eastern men to make commercial regulations. He was cheerfully co-operative. "He had himself," he said, "prejudices agst the Eastern States before he came here, but would acknowledge that he had found them as liberal and candid as any men whatever." Clymer of Pennsylvania, and Gouverneur Morris, and Sherman of Connecticut, supported this stand. The northern and middle states would be ruined "if not enabled to defend themselves against foreign regulations." To require more than a majority would be embarrassing, as experience under the Confederation had proved. It was to the interest of the southern states to facilitate navigation acts, as "Preferences to american ships will multiply them, till they can carry the Southern produce cheaper than it is now carried." Williamson of North Carolina wanted the two-thirds requirement only as a precaution, "because if a majority of Northern States should push their regulations too far, the S. States would build ships for themselves . . ."

George Mason was more apprehensive on the part of the Southerners, who would be in the minority in both houses. Should they, by allowing a simple majority vote, "deliver themselves bound hand & foot to the Eastern States. . . ?" Madison, on the contrary, argued that "the disadvantage to the S. States from a navigation act, lay chiefly in a temporary rise of freight" that would be compensated by benefits which he listed. Now—as later in Congress—he was for discriminations in favor of our shipping if restrictions by foreigners made these necessary; we should be able to pass such acts by a majority only. Rutledge was against the motion of his South Carolina colleague demanding a two-thirds vote. The great object was to secure the West India trade to this country, "and a navigation act was necessary for obtaining it." Gorham of Massachusetts agreed.

Edmund Randolph, who had been active in presenting the basic plan of the constitution, now for the first time gave ominous notice that it already had been deformed by such "obnoxious ingredients" that he might feel compelled to refuse his assent to it. If the North was encouraged to limit shipping for southern staples, this might decide him. His challenge did not impress the delegates, who voted unanimously to allow navigation acts to be passed by a simple majority of each house.

Charles Pinckney and Butler of South Carolina wanted a compensation for this defeat of the planting states. This was a provision for the return of fugitive slaves. "If any person bound to service . . . shall escape into another State, he or she shall not be discharged from such . . . labor . . . but shall be delivered up to the person justly claiming their service . . ." The motion had first been put in a form more offensive, "to require fugitive slaves and servants to be delivered up like criminals." (How easily, from long habit, we invert morals! One who thrust his fellow into slavery was approved by the law, while the captive who asserted his right to freedom by running away was a criminal.) Sherman observed, dryly, that he "saw no more propriety in the public seizing and surrendering a slave . . . than a horse." In its more euphemistic form the demand was agreed to unanimously.

III FINISHING TOUCHES

The convention afforded a little preview of the confusion that would beset Congress three years later. The question was how to treat different classes of holders of the domestic debt. The debate arose on reconsideration of the recommendation of a committee that "The Legislature of the United-States shall have power to fulfil the engagements which have been entered into by [the Old] Congress" and discharge the national and war-incurred state debts. Mason "objected to the term, 'shall' fulfil the engagements & discharge the debts . . . as too strong. It may be impossible to comply with it." If the power to honor the debt was made definite that would "beget speculation and increase the pestilent practice of stock-jobbing." He went on to declare "a great distinction between original creditors & those who purchased fraudulently of the ignorant and distressed." He contradicted himself, for he first exculpated "those who have bought Stock in open market," but then found that "even fair purchasers" at low prices "did not stand on the same footing with the first Holders." He did not know how to draw the line between the meritorious who had loaned full value to the government and those who acquired their securities at much depreciated prices, but he did not wish to rule out the attempt.

Notice two features of Mason's statement. He was by no means sure the debt could be paid in full. He would leave the door open for a discrimination between original and later holders.

Gerry before offering his views explained that he "had no interest in the question" because he possessed so little of the debt. (Actually, his holdings were considerable.) "If the public faith would admit, of which he was not clear," he would not object to an adjustment of the debt to make restitution "to the ignorant & distressed, who have been defrauded." But he saw no reason to censure stockjobbers, for they maintained a market and kept up the value of the paper (Gerry was more in line with the policy that afterward prevailed.)

Gouverneur Morris was glad he was not a public creditor. He was free to urge what he believed complied with national faith: this was to promise repayment. If provision was first made for meeting the interest, the government could cancel the debt by purchasing it. (This is the position which Hamilton was to take as first secretary of the treasury.)

Randolph closed the discussion by offering a general declaration: "All debts contracted & engagements entered into, by . . . the authority of Congs. shall be as valid agst the U. States under this constitution as under the Confederation." This was accepted with the one negative vote of Pennsylvania.

A large committee considered a number of protections and guarantees. The delegates accepted the recommendation that "The trial of all crimes (except in cases of impeachment) shall be by jury . . ." Nothing was said about the right to jury trial in civil cases; this omission was a chief subject of complaint when the Constitution came before the people. There was strong objection to any suspension of the writ of habeas corpus, but it was afterward agreed to except "cases of rebellion or invasion [where] the public safety may require it."

The ghost of Daniel Shays had visited the convention chamber several times. The bloody outbreak in Massachusetts was a red signal run up before the eyes of the delegates. It warned that a single state was unable to cope with insurrection, especially if the rebellion sprang from widespread, deep-seated social grievances. So the national authority must be empowered to suppress such revolts in a state and to guarantee to each state a republican form of government—that is, not violent or dictatorial. But something more specific had come home to the members of the convention. The Massachusetts legislature, intimidated by threats of the debt-ridden farmers, had issued paper money and passed laws compelling creditors to accept livestock and land in settlement of their claims. These concessions damaged property rights. As the men of the eighteenth century saw it, liberty was a foundation stone of good government, but protection of property was another. Massachusetts had impaired the obligation of contracts, barged in between creditor and debtor, and said that the agreement they had reached in good faith, and by which both were bound, no longer held. What was to become of orderly dealings in the community if solemn engagements about what is mine and thine could be revised or overturned?

Therefore Wilson and Sherman moved that no state should "emit bills of credit, nor make any thing but gold & silver coin a tender in payment of debts." This being accepted, King wanted to add, on the same behalf, "a prohibition on the States to interfere in private contracts." Gouverneur Morris, Mason and others cited objections; within a state the majority must rule, "whatever may be the mischief done among themselves." Rutledge satisfied most by forbidding the states to "pass . . . retrospective laws."

No Bill of Rights in Original Constitution

This may be a fit place, in connection with discussion of certain civil rights and limitations on the powers of the states, to ask why the makers of the Constitution did not include protections to the individual citizen, for which there was clamor later, resulting in the first ten amendments. Many constitutional liberties, later spelled out so emphatically, were not mentioned in the convention, so far as the records show. Much of the protest in the convention against powers planned for the central government was on behalf of small states, else the privileges to be reserved to citizens in general, as against the central authority, might have come forward. Most of the members of the convention, promptly on assembling, agreed that their task was to construct a forceful national government, able to control the confusion of tongues that had plagued the Confederation. Consequently their minds ran on collective duties rather than on individual freedoms. In fact it was oftenest taken for granted that the people as a whole would approve the Constitution. Hostility to an effective Congress and executive would come from the state legislatures. These had their functions, but on the whole they were to be curbed and disciplined. Thus the convention was in the mood to defend the government against the citizens (as the latter were represented in the state legislatures), rather than citizens against government. Several delegates, opposed to a strong central power, who might have urged private rights rather than public authority, left the convention—Yates and Lansing early, Martin of Maryland ten days before the close. Madison, Hamilton, and others, while the Constitution was being framed, though it sufficiently guarded civil liberties, but they recorded this later and they may have recalled more concern on this score than they felt at the time. We shall return to this topic (freedom of speech, press, religion, and other essential guarantees) when we describe how the Bill of Rights was added to the fundamental law.

How many states must ratify the constitution before it would go into effect among themselves? All of the states, naming themselves individually, had formed the Confederation. But the precedent of unanimity for approval of the new Constitution had little appeal. Rhode Island had refused to send delegates to the convention. New York for much of the time was not formally represented (had no vote) because two of its three delegates had left, rejecting the shape the plan was taking. New Hampshire (her treasury empty) did not send delegates until they were urgently summoned, and the issue in that state was doubtful. What North Carolina would do was questionable. On days when conflicting forces in the convention seemed to be dead-locked, many wondered whether the reform would be accepted by enough states to make it feasible.

Therefore, consent of different numbers of states was put forward as sufficient—seven, ten, thirteen were suggested before the convention agreed on nine, the number stipulated in the Articles for passage of important measures in the Confederation Congress. Also if four states at first held off they were sure to be geographically scattered, for other reasons could not combine in a separate government, and would prob-ably soon come in for their own protection.

Then the convention reverted to the related query: after the docu-ment is submitted to Congress, how shall its fate in the states be deter-mined? By the state legislatures, said Gerry and Martin. Not so, ac-cording to others. The state governments would be inclined to thwart adoption; better depend on the people, who would favor the Constitu-tion. Therefore conventions were preferred, and these should be called speedily, before state officials could undermine the popular good will. This view prevailed.

In this discussion Gerry, Randolph, and Mason plainly showed their impending dissent from the plan as it was being framed. Gerry "repre-sented the system as full of vices." The prospect of approval got Mason in a lather; "he would sooner chop off his right hand than put it to the Constitution as it now stands." Both he and Randolph might be compelled to favor the calling of another general convention to reconsider the whole business or at least pass on amendments that might be proposed. From time to time they gave other evidence of their mounting disagreement with what was being done.

These three participated actively in the debates. The question arises, why did a third of the members of the convention, so far as our records disclose, take little or no part in discussions on the floor? These ab-stainers included men of unusual prominence, even in that company, particularly Robert Morris and Thomas Mifflin of Pennsylvania. No-body in the convention had more intimate official and personal knowledge of the shortcomings of the old government which was to be reformed than did Robert Morris, but he kept his seat throughout the sessions. Among some sixteen others whose views were not offered in the general discussions, several were tolerably known to the country, though most were prominent only in their own states. Some were absent during much of the convention, William Few of Georgia for a month, while attending Congress in New York. Numbers of the less conspicuous members served on committees, but whether they were vocal in these assignments is not recorded. Delegates who considered themselves poor speakers perhaps refrained from taking the floor for that reason. They doubtless communicated their opinions in private conversations. It is to be remembered that in any deliberative assembly —for example, the House of Representatives—a large proportion of the members are rarely or never heard except at times of voting, and often not then! The reserve of some who spoke, but chose to do so infrequently and briefly, is more remarkable. In this group fall men of talents like Thomas FitzSimons, William Samuel Johnson, Jared Ingersoll, and William Livingston.

Mechanics of Election of Executive

When less than two weeks of the convention's sessions remained, the mode of electing the President and Vice President was reconsidered. Wilson observed, "This subject has greatly divided the House, and will also divide people out of doors. It is in truth the most difficult of all on which we have had to decide." Earlier the plan had been for the national legislature to elect the President for a term of seven years, he not to be re-eligible. No Vice President was then contemplated, but the president of the Senate (how chosen, not said) was to succeed if the chief executive died or was disabled from serving.

On September 4 an all-state committee presented a revised scheme, intended, its sponsors said, to eliminate dependence of the President on the legislature and thus allow him to be re-eligible. Each state legislature would designate as many electors as the state had senators and representatives. The electors would meet in their states, each elector balloting for two candidates, one at least not to be an inhabitant of the same state. The lists should be sent to and be opened by the president of the Senate in presence of that body. The person having the greatest number of votes, if a majority, should be President. If more than one had a majority, and equal numbers of votes, the Senate should ballot for one for President. If none had a majority, the Senate should choose by ballot among the five highest on the list. After the President was elected, the person having the highest number of votes was Vice President; if two or more had equal votes, the Senate should select the Vice President from among them.

This change of method—election of the President by electors—may have been suggested by proposals previously made by Hamilton, who, incidentally, returned to the convention about this time, and said he preferred the new to old plan of naming the chief executive. In Hamilton's scheme the people (not the state legislatures) chose the electors, for both President and members of the Senate, but the significant feature was that holders of the highest offices were named at one remove from the citizens (in Hamilton's suggestion), or at two removes (in the plan under discussion).

Quickly several objected. Electors' votes would be scattered because poor communications would not permit a few characters to make superior impression in all the states, with the result that selection would be thrown into the Senate after all. What was the use of the cumbersome machinery? Indeed, the present plan was worse than the old one, because now the President—elected by the Senate in fact—was eligible for re-election, and would be subservient to that body. Moreover, the Senate would both appoint the President and try him on impeachment, which interfered with the impartiality of senators sitting as judges. Others replied that the working of this scheme would improve with "increasing intercourse among the people of the States," for that would make "Continental Characters" more known in all parts of the Union. The choice of the electors would be final, without reference to the Senate. However, if national legislators were to play a part, would it not be preferable to trust this duty to the House of Representatives rather than to the Senate? The representatives were more numerous, were constantly changing, and less favoritism would develop among them.

But on the other hand it was observed that if the House could choose in the end, the electors from the large states would concern themselves with promoting candidates, rather than with electing the officer. The reason was that in the House the large states would predominate and have the final choice among the candidates. The reverse would be true if the Senate was the arbiter, for there the small states were in the majority, and "the concerted effort of the large States would be to make the appointment in the first instance conclusive."

The danger of "cabal" (intrigue) would be reduced by requiring that a choice be made from fewer than five candidates. Immediate decision of the House would cut down on electioneering. (It was not considered that balloting for two candidates with an equal number of electoral votes might stretch over a long period, as actually happened in the first case to come into the House.)

The discussions running through several days must have been heated, or perhaps some of the members were testy from cumulative dissatisfaction. Mason thought it "utterly inadmissible" that the Senate should decide. "He would prefer the Government of Prussia to one which will put all power into the hands of seven or eight men, and fix an Aristocracy worse than absolute monarchy." Randolph talked similarly. This strong language may have had its effect, for agreement was reached (only Delaware voting no) that the House of Representatives—not the Senate—should choose if two or more candidates had a majority and an equal number of electoral votes. If no person had a majority, the House should select from among the five highest on the list. The members from each state would have one vote. A quorum of the House, in naming the President, should consist of members from two-thirds of the states, "and the concurrence of a majority of all the States, shall be necessary to such choice." That is, the President should not be named by representatives of a few of the largest states.

After the President was chosen, the person with the highest number of (remaining) electoral votes should be Vice President, but if two or more had equal electoral votes, determination between them should fall to the Senate.

The President should serve for four years and be re-eligible (not serve for a term of seven years, as previously proposed). As the plan worked out, unaffected by later amendment, the Presidents elected to that office (not Vice Presidents who succeeded) have in almost all instances come from the more populous states. Jackson was from the semi-frontier, Tennessee, but he was a military hero. Pierce was from New Hampshire. Wilson from New Jersey may be considered another exception.

The complaint of John Adams, when Vice President, that he had been elected to an office the most insignificant, was foreshadowed in the opinions of several in the Constitutional Convention that a Vice President was unnecessary. This was the view of Gerry and of Williamson. When several objected that the Vice President should not preside over the Senate (because that would confuse executive and legislative functions), Sherman answered that without this duty the officer "would be without employment."

From time to time different ones had argued that the Senate, by accumulation of functions, was being rendered too powerful. To check this tendency Mason revived an earlier proposal for creation of an advisory or privy council to the President. The Senate should appoint six members, two from each large section of the country, to serve for six years, to go out in rotation, two every second year. The President should look to this council for advice on most appointments. Wilson, Dickinson, Franklin, and apparently Madison agreed. Gouverneur Morris gave reasons of the small committee for rejecting the idea of a privy council, and the proposal was easily voted down.

When participation of the Senate with the President in making treaties was discussed, two members (Wilson and FitzSimons) were for permitting the House of Representatives to join in this act. As treaties were to have the operation of laws, both branches should give their sanction. This suggestion received the vote of the movers' state of Pennsylvania alone. The propriety of including the lower house came forward a few years later when Jay's Treaty with Britain was to be put in force. Then the representatives almost refused to make the appropriation for which the treaty called because they had not been consulted on the terms of the pact.

Expert Draftsmanship of Gouverneur Morris

Previous to this time (September 8), two committees had been appointed to review the work of the delegates and reduce it to tolerable form. The first restated, where necessary, propositions which had been settled upon. The second dealt with resolves which had been deferred or left incomplete. Now a small committee of five was chosen by ballot "to revise the style of and arrange the articles agreed to." The five selected were William Samuel Johnson, Hamilton, Gouverneur Morris, Madison, and King. All were known to their fellows as men of talents for the written word and eager to put the document in accurate, precise language before the people. It is doubtful whether the members of this drafting committee had a sufficient appreciation of the historic role they were being called upon to play. While, during debates, several had spoken of the convention as drawing up a plan for posterity, the delegates that gave it final form probably did not foresee how long their written constitution would endure. Nor could

they realize that, as the country grew in size and questions coming
before the federal courts increased in complexity, momentous consequences, affecting policies and property, would hinge upon their
chosen words, phrases, punctuation even. It is significant that four of
these practiced draftsmen agreed in turning the task over to Gouverneur Morris without interference on their part. They had complete
confidence in his skill and integrity. It is fortunate that the definitive
dress of the document was the work of one hand, for this favored
simplicity and a certain unity of character.

If the committee on style, said Williamson of North Carolina, was
to submit the constitution completed down to the last crossing of t's
and dotting of i's, a weighty matter should first be reconsidered. The
number of members in the House of Representatives should be increased. Madison seconded the motion. Sherman thought the size of
the House "amply sufficient," but Hamilton gave the proposal impressive support. Impressive not only for his reasoning, but because it
came from him. He was regarded by some (mistakenly) as wishing
government exclusively by the few—the enlightened, the secure, the
responsible—unhampered by the fumbling of the many. Attention to
his earlier statements would have saved this error. In any event,

Col. Hamilton expressed himself with great earnestness and anxiety in
favor of the motion. He avowed himself a friend to a vigorous Government, but would declare at the same time, that he held it essential
that the popular branch of it should be on a broad foundation. He
was seriously of opinion that the House of Representatives was on so
narrow a scale [65 members to begin with, later one for every 40,000
of population, counting three-fifths of slaves] as to be really dangerous,
and to warrant a jealousy in the people for their liberties. He remarked
that the connection between the President & Senate [acting together
on appointments, treaties, etc.] would tend to perpetuate him, by corrupt influence. It was the more necessary on this account that a
numerous representation in the other branch of the Legislature should
be established.

At the moment this revision was narrowly rejected, but it was soon
revived, as we shall see.

Alexander Hamilton now adopted the conciliatory role which aided
completion of the Constitution by the convention and its ratification
by the states. His friendly efforts were well received because he had
declared earlier "his dislike of the Scheme of Govt. in general" but

also his resolve "to support the plan to be recommended, as better than nothing." He now showed a respect for the Old Congress which some others would omit. The earlier mode of amendment of the Constitution was on application of the legislatures of two-thirds of the states, after which the national legislature should call a convention for that purpose. Hamilton reinforced the proposal of Gerry that the initiative in making amendments should lie with the central legislature. This body would be "the first to perceive and . . . most sensible to the necessity of amendments." Madison, Wilson, and Rutledge inserted particulars. As agreed to, the article provided that amendments might be proposed by the national legislature (two-thirds of each branch) or by two-thirds of the legislatures of the states. These amendments would be valid when ratified by three-fourths of the legislatures of the states, or by conventions in three-fourths of the states, depending on the method proposed by the national legislature. However (in deference to the demand of Rutledge of South Carolina), no amendment prior to the year 1808 should impose a tax on exports or interfere with the slave trade.

The next discussion was on the mode of ratifying the Constitution and putting the new government into effect. Earlier, the preliminary approval by Congress had been struck out. Hamilton supported Gerry in urging that politeness and due formality in eclipsing the old government required that the new Constitution be first submitted to the will of Congress. He framed a resolve that gave maximum volition to Congress, to the state legislatures, and to the state conventions. So far did he go that Randolph, who was turning against the Constitution, approved of Hamilton's permissiveness. But Randolph went further. The scheme of government as it was taking form violated the republican principles which he had intended it should contain. The state conventions should be free to offer amendments to a second general convention which should be final.

Wilson sharply opposed risking the Constitution for approval by Congress. He gave his reasons for fearing Congress would reject it; why should the convention, after months of work, throw an insuperable obstacle in the way of the plan's success? Others—King, Clymer, Rutledge—joined Wilson in his protest, and Hamilton's courteous and bold course was almost unanimously disapproved.

Randolph took advantage of the lull that followed to list at length his objections to the document. All added up to his repugnance to allowing the national government so much latitude. He implied that if he were chosen for a seat in the Virginia convention he would there fight the Constitution as an instrument of tyranny. (It was hard for Randolph, if he discerned true north, to keep his needle pointing to it. As it turned out, in the Virginia convention he swung round again and gave the plan his firm support.) He ended by moving for a second general convention to consider amendments. Strangely for a man of such experience and wisdom, Dr. Franklin seconded Randolph's wish. But Mason got the motion postponed for a few days until it could be seen whether some of Randolph's stumbling blocks were not removed.

All agreed in a useful suggestion of Charles Pinckney that the committee on style prepare an address to the people which should accompany the Constitution when it was laid before Congress to be transmitted to the States.

The committee on style did its work promptly, submitting its revision, together with the introductory letter addressed to Congress, on September 12. The letter frankly declared that the convention had "kept steadily in . . . View that which appears . . . the greatest Interest of every true American [,] The Consolidation of our Union in which is involved our Prosperity Felicity Safety perhaps our national Existence." It was hoped that the states themselves, like their delegates in the convention, would receive the Constitution in "a Spirit of Amity and . . . mutual . . . Concession." This was necessary where certain rights of the states must be surrendered in order to preserve the rest.

Now began the process of amending here and there the seven articles, most of them with numerous subsections, which the committee on style had presented. Some feared, on second thought, that the requirement of three-fourths majorities in each branch to override the veto of the President gave too much power to the President and a small minority in the legislature. After debate, two-thirds majority was substituted for three-fourths to carry a law even though the President had sent it back with his veto.

Power of Congress To Charter Corporations

Absence of a guarantee of jury trial in civil cases was regretted by several. It was explained now and later that this was omitted only because law and practice differed in different sorts of civil suits and in the separate states. It was thought best to leave this for regulation by Congress, which would no doubt accommodate rules to varying customs. The purpose was not to sacrifice a valuable right by an inaccurate definition of it.

Mason and Gerry wanted the Constitution to be prefaced by a bill of rights, which could be prepared in a few hours by a committee which they moved should be appointed. This was rejected unanimously. After the Constitution went to the people, failure of the delegates to incorporate a bill of rights produced loud protest. However, several with perfect sincerity exculpated the convention. Among these were Washington, Wilson, Madison, Hamilton, Ellsworth, and C. C. Pinckney. It was recalled that the inclusion of a bill of rights was not so much as mentioned until nearly the end of the meetings. (Madison and others were mistaken in saying no motion was made in this behalf.) The bills of rights in the state constitutions were deemed full protection, as the states retained all powers which they did not surrender to the central government. Also it was feared that if an enumeration of rights was attempted, it might later be argued that others were omitted intentionally. Pinckney told his fellow South Carolinians, with grim humor, why delegates of the state wished no bill of rights inserted in the Constitution. "Such bills generally begin with declaring that all men are by nature born free. Now, we should make that declaration with a very bad grace, when a large part of our property consists in men who are actually born slaves."

Most of the alterations made in the revised draft of the constitution were minor, often merely verbal. But major proposals were offered. Williamson of North Carolina renewed the motion to increase the size of the House of Representatives, this time by one half, allowing two members from the smallest states. It barely failed of passage. An important change was made when appointment of the secretary of the treasury was taken away from the two houses of the legislature and put under the same rule with other heads of departments, that is, nomination by the President and approval by the Senate. This was put through by the delegates from South Carolina, in which state naming of the treasury chief by the legislature had resulted in poor choices and the mischief could not be corrected because the legislators felt partial to their officer.

Giving the selection to the President with approval of the upper chamber proved to be wise. The first secretary of the treasury, Alexander Hamilton, was obliged to urge fiscal solutions which met prolonged and violent hostility in the House as it was, and without the moral support of the President his principal plans might not have carried. Further, being the President's choice, he had undisputed place in executive councils. He helped to give unity and decision to principal policies at the outset when Congress, split into factions, required firm guidance. The statute establishing the Treasury department made it the secretary's duty to report directly to the House, and he was empowered to recommend expedients on his own initiative. Thus he had immediate access to the lawmakers but was sufficiently independent of them. He could be summarily removed only by the President, though of course he could be dislodged by the legislature by the process of impeachment and conviction.

An effort was made to require the secretary to publish Treasury operations annually, but when it was shown that this was impracticable, the words "from time to time" were preferred.

More than three weeks earlier Madison and Charles Pinckney had recommended giving Congress authority to create corporations. When this section of the report of the committee of style was reached Franklin made a motion which had no result at the time except to provoke a discussion which soon became and for years remained a subject of dispute. He proposed that, in addition to establishing post roads, Congress be given "a power to provide for cutting canals where deemed necessary." Wilson was the seconder. These words are from Madison's notes. The only mention in the official journal is in the detail of votes, where the description is (No. 534) "To grant letters of incorporation for Canals & ca [et cetera]." Madison's record shows that those who took part in the debate considered that Franklin's motion implied the power in Congress to incorporate banks and confer mercantile monopolies as well as charter canal companies. Madison himself used words of this import, for he "suggested an enlargement of the motion into a power 'to grant charters of incorporation where the interest of the U.S. might require & the legislative provisions of individual States may be incompetent.' " However, his explanation indicates that he had in mind, chiefly or exclusively, the utility of interstate canals.

This was the idea of Sherman and of Mason, but Wilson approved and Rufus King opposed the broader objects, especially banks, on which Congress could enter if Franklin's motion was adopted. King was sure that to confer on Congress a general power of incorporation would divide the states and militate against adoption of the constitution. Wilson disagreed; banks would not be objected to and "As to mercantile monopolies they are already included in the power to regu-

late trade." It is not possible from the contemporary record to determine what was the final form of the motion, whether it permitted the
incorporation by Congress of canals alone, or of other enterprises as
well. In any event it was voted down, 8 to 3.

The reader may wonder why the foregoing is here spelled out. It is
because a few years later when Hamilton urged incorporation of the
Bank of the United States, Madison and others opposing it cited this
debate as proving that the convention had refused such an authority
to Congress.

The fact is that Hamilton was correct in dismissing this argument
when he gave to President Washington his opinion that the bank was
constitutional. He declared that "the precise nature or extent" of the
proposition for the power of incorporation as raised in the convention,
"or what the reasons for refusing it, is not ascertained by any authentic
document, or even by accurate recollection." The record that we have,
though better than anything of documentary sort which Hamilton
possessed, is equivocal. The memories of those who had part in the
discussion, let alone hearsay reports of others, were contradictory.
Hamilton justified incorporation of the bank on another ground, that
of the "implied powers" given by the Constitution to Congress.

The committee on style, among prohibitions laid on the states, forbade any law impairing the obligation of contracts. As we noted
earlier, the recent behavior of Massachusetts in passing stay laws and
permitting debts to be paid in commodities rather than in money was
in the committee's mind. In any case, Gerry of Massachusetts immediately commended the provision. He urged that Congress also should
be forbidden to impair the obligation of contracts, but his motion was
not seconded. Had he succeeded, presumably the United States government would have been prevented from abandoning the gold standard during the Civil War and from abrogating the gold clause in
private contracts in the Great Depression (1933).

Charles Pinckney and Gerry reverted to the former's proposal of
three weeks earlier that the constitution should pledge "The liberty
of the Press shall be inviolably preserved." Sherman objected that the
power of Congress did not extend to the press, and the motion was
lost. This was another reason why a distinct bill of rights was later
insisted upon.

Saturday, September 15, when the convention was almost at the
close of its work, Daniel Carroll of Maryland noted that no address to
the people, to introduce the Constitution to them, had been pre-

pared. The people would expect it, it would be serviceable, and he moved that a committee be appointed for this purpose. Others objected that the convention should not go to the people "before it was known whether Congress would approve . . . the plan." If an address be thought proper, Congress could prepare a good one. (Actually, while Congress placed no obstacle in the way of the Constitution, that body could hardly be expected to plead eloquently for its adoption, since it meant the exit of the old government). Had the convention framed persuasive reasons for approval, this might have smoothed the path of the Constitution in several states. Sessions of the convention had been secret; suspicions out of doors would have been dispelled, partly at least, by a friendly communication to the people accompanying the completed document.

The addition of one representative each for North Carolina and Rhode Island was pressed but failed of approval. Delegates, eager to button up the business, were not in the mood for delays.

Amendment of the Constitution was made easier by permitting two-thirds of the states to call a convention without the intermediation of Congress.

Three Refused To Sign

The delegates sat late Saturday, September 15, in order to take the final vote on the Constitution in finished form. Then nothing would remain but to have the document engrossed for signatures. It was nearly six o'clock when Edmund Randolph arose to explain, with sorrow more than resentment, that he could not approve the plan as it stood. He moved—evidently with no hope of agreement—that the state conventions be allowed to offer amendments "which should be submitted to and finally decided on by another general Convention." If this proposal for revision was rejected, he could not lend his name to the Constitution.

George Mason seconded Randolph's despairing motion. He gave his own bitter testimony against "the dangerous power . . . of the Government, concluding that it would end either in monarchy, or a tyrannical aristocracy." The people had not been consulted in the work of the convention. It was improper to say to them, "take this or nothing." He would not support the document here or afterward in Virginia.

These last-minute dissents had been expected. Charles Pinckney, whose hopes had not been fulfilled, solemnly deplored the defection of respected members. It would be worse than futile to throw the whole subject back into debate of a second convention. "Nothing but confusion & contrariety could spring from the experiment." He mentioned his own objections. But rather than risk "a general confusion, and an ultimate decision by the Sword, he should give the plan his support."

So far from fetching Randolph and Mason to sign with the rest, his plea was followed by another protest. Elbridge Gerry of Massachusetts enumerated the fatal shortcomings of the instrument. Probably the delegates attended little to his list. Their afflicting thought was the damage to the prospects of the Constitution if it could not go before the country with the unanimous endorsement of all who had remained in convention to the closing scene. Here were leading men from principal states not only refusing their assent, but, what was more ominous, practically giving notice that they would fight ratification. In this crisis of America, with the old government in ruins and rescue through a reorganization hanging in the balance, the members' fears were all alive. Suppose the new plan, so earnestly projected to save the situation, was to meet with refusal. We know that many, with Charles Pinckney, foresaw further distraction, fragmenting of the nation, or actual civil war. Rhode Island had flatly declined any part in the reform. Two delegates from New York had long since departed in disgust, leaving their minority colleague with no vote for his state. Other members, like Martin of Maryland, had quit the convention with fierce mutterings. Now valued companions who had remained till the last were issuing an ultimatum: Invite a new convention or battle for this Constitution without us. The reply of all the states, on the motion for a later reconsideration, was a determined No

Then "On the question to agree to the Constitution . . . All the States ay," and the document was ordered to be engrossed.

Monday, September 17, 1787, after four months of deliberations, came the final episode. Over Sunday the body of delegates favoring the scheme must have racked their wits to discover how to put the best face on the refusal of a few to sign. Now Dr. Franklin rose and gave to his friend Wilson a speech to read. It was a mellow appeal for tolerance that would produce unanimity. "I confess that there are several parts of this constitution," he began, "which I do not at present approve, but I am not sure I shall never approve them: For having lived long, I have experienced many instances of being obliged by better information or fuller consideration, to change opinions . . . which I once thought right, but found to be otherwise." He hoped that all would respect the judgment of the majority. "Thus I consent, Sir, to this Constitution because I expect no better, and because I am not sure, that it is not the best. The opinion I have had of its errors, I sacrifice to the public good." Franklin trusted that "we shall act heartily and unanimously in recommending this Constitution . . . wherever our influence may extend, and turn our future . . . endeavors to the means of having it well administered." He entreated that every man yet harboring objections would "with me, on this occasion doubt a little of his own infallibility, and to make manifest our unanimity, put his name to this instrument." He read a form of signing which, though he did not say so, had been devised by Gouverneur Morris "in order to gain the dissenting members." The adroit wording was, "Done in Convention, by the unanimous consent of *the States* present . . . In Witness whereof we have hereunto subscribed our names."

At this point, when it seemed that all might be concluded the next moment, Gorham put in an eleventh hour request, "for the purpose of lessening objections to the Constitution," that the number of representatives should be increased from one to every 40,000 to one to every 30,000. This was promptly seconded by King and Carroll. Before taking the vote Washington departed from his rule of abstaining from debate to give the proposal his earnest sanction. The change would contribute security to "the rights & interests of the people." The proposition was agreed to unanimously.

Closing Scene

As the members were about to come to the secretary's table to sign, Randolph offered another apology for his refusal. He was the one of the trio of abstainers who wavered. Now he must have been strongly tempted to go along with those prepared to sign. Perhaps he was stung by Franklin's strictures. At least Franklin got that impression, and took the earliest occasion to disclaim scolding any individual. His little homily on the merits of endorsement by the full convention was written before he knew there would be dissenters. "He professed a high sense of obligation to Mr. Randolph for having brought forward the plan in the first instance, and for the assistance he had given in its progress," and hoped that Randolph would yet determine not to withhold his name. But Randolph had a new reason for remaining adamant. Since the states must accept or reject the Constitution in toto, without the liberty of first demanding amendments, he believed there would not be nine to ratify. This would "produce the anarchy and civil convulsions" which the majority in the convention—the signers—were desperately anxious to prevent.

Others, evidently making a last effort to bring Randolph over, told of their own misgivings which, nevertheless, they put aside in loyalty to the common welfare. Gouverneur Morris was one who prophesied, "The moment this plan goes forth all other considerations will be laid aside—and the great question will be, shall there be a national government or not?" If not, "general anarchy" would be the country's sorry fate. Williamson spoke similarly and persuasively. Hamilton "expressed his anxiety that every member should sign." He used famous words, often recalled with admiration in the years of his labors for the success of the Constitution: "No man's ideas were more remote from the plan than his own were known to be; but is it possible to deliberate between . . . Convulsion on one side, and the chance of good to be expected from the plan on the other?"

These exhortations evidently converted William Blount of North Carolina, at least sufficiently to secure his signature. He had previously declared that he would not give it, but now "he . . . would without committing himself attest the fact that the plan was the unanimous act of the States in Convention." Randolph, though "he took a step which might be the most awful of his life," could not violate his conscience by a mere shift of words in the signing. Gerry repeated Randolph's resolve. "The proposed form made no difference with him." Before he sat down he loosed a shaft against the venerable Franklin, whose "remarks . . . he could not . . . but view . . . as levelled at himself and the other gentlemen who meant not to sign." Franklin's only answer, in which he was joined by his colleague Jared Ingersoll, was to hope once again that objectors would be able to give the document the benefit of their names. George Mason had said earlier why he could not support the Constitution, and now sat silent. We know, from Madison, that "Col. Mason left Philadelphia in an exceeding ill humor indeed." Fatigue at the end of the convention and his impatience to get away "conspired to whet his acrimony. He returned to Virginia with a fixed disposition to prevent the adoption of the plan if possible."

General Pinckney, ever forthright, spurned ambiguity. "He should sign the Constitution with a view to support it with all his influence, and wished to pledge himself accordingly."

The handsome, huge mural painting, by Howard Chandler Christy, in the national Capitol vividly re-creates the signing scene. The dominating figure is that of Washington, who surveys the room as the secretary, William Jackson, in crimson coat, calls the delegates to affix their names. They are talking animatedly, in groups, testifying to the emotion with which they acted. In the center of the floor, in cordial conversation, are Franklin and Hamilton, the oldest and one of the youngest members of the convention. The prominence given them is appropriate, for they had been among the most zealous to secure common consent to the Constitution. The benign philosopher and his spirited junior had alike been peacemakers, who are blessed.

The motion of Franklin and Gouverneur Morris that the Constitution be signed so as to show unanimous consent of the states present was approved. On the question of what to do with the journals and other papers of the convention it was decided that they should be deposited with the presiding officer, Washington, "subject to the order of Congress, if ever formed under the Constitution." Perhaps it was during this discussion that Hamilton, eager to see the document signed and sealed, went to the table and entered the names of the states with space left opposite each for the signatures of her delegates. He included New York, with pardonable disregard of his inability, as the lone delegate, to commit his state.

George Washington as "Presidt. and deputy from Virginia" and thirty-eight other delegates signed; the order was that of the states, from New Hampshire in the north to Georgia in the south. Thereafter the members dined together at the City Tavern "and took a cordial leave of each other." Major Jackson, the secretary, sped to New York to lay the Constitution before Congress.

Chapter Four

CHAMPIONS AND CRITICS

As the Constitutional Convention was held behind closed doors and members were pledged not to reveal proceedings, then or afterward, it was necessary for the new plan of government to be explained to the representatives of the people before they could pass on it. Election speeches, public letters, and newspaper essays described, attacked, and defended. We may be sure that most people had only the vaguest notion of the provisions of the document, or of how it differed from the Articles of Confederation. With our superior education and remarkable communications today, what proportion of the millions intimately affected by social security legislation know its particulars? Probably most citizens in 1787-88 felt burdened by debt and low land values and were ready to accept a remedy sanctioned by Washington and Dr. Franklin. Faith in the former, especially, was the greatest single force making for approval of the Constitution. Objectors like Luther Martin and others, competent to scrutinize the scheme in all its parts, refused to be swayed by men instead of by measures. But surely most said, "If George Washington thinks this reform is good for the country, I think so too." They knew that if the Constitution was put into effect the government would be headed by General Washington, and that was enough argument for its success. Anyone who reads the record of those times is impressed by the trust placed in Washington.

Those who offered themselves as delegates to the state conventions, however, were influenced by local political leaders. Governor George Clinton in New York and Patrick Henry in Virginia brought behind them a majority of delegates who were prepared to reject the Constitution. In Massachusetts suspicion of the Shaysites of anything to be done in Boston, and the failure of Sam Adams and John Hancock to come out firmly for the Constitution endangered ratification. The appeals in print, for and against the Constitution, were directed chiefly to the members of the conventions. Even so, large numbers took their seats uninformed, and learned features of the Constitution only from debates on the floor. As always, loyalty to leaders rather than independent reasoning and conviction was apt to determine votes. In critical states friends of the Constitution must win over some of those committed against it as well as persuade the wavering.

The printed polemics preceding ratification were of three sorts— the personal, the political, and the expository or analytical. Distinctions between them were not sharp, except that addresses of the last type—examinations of the Constitution in detail—were freer of emotional appeal and attacks on antagonists. Of course those who were members of the Philadelphia convention had superior knowledge of arguments, pro and con, on all features of the Constitution. Without betraying confidence, they could be illuminating and accurate beyond what was possible for those confronted with the document only after it was completed. However, some who had been in the Philadelphia convention busied themselves afterward with charges against colleagues and vindications of their own position and conduct. These personal controversies made spirited newspaper reading, but shed little light on the subject under review. Thus Oliver Ellsworth assailed Luther Martin for his inconsistencies: "One hour you sported the opinion that Congress, afraid of the militia resisting their measures, would neither arm nor organize them, and the next, as if men required no time to breathe between such contradictions, that they would harass them by long and unnecessary marches, till they wore down their spirit and rendered them fit subjects for despotism. . . You cannot have forgotten, that by such ignorance in politics . . . you exhausted the politeness of the Convention, which at length prepared to slumber when you rose to speak." And Martin answered: ". . . if the framing and approving the Constitution . . . is a proof of knowledge in the science of government . . . I glory in my ignorance; and if my rising to speak had such a somnific influence on the Convention as the Landholder [Ellsworth] represents . . . the time will come, should this system be adopted, when my countrymen will ardently wish I had never left the Convention, but remained there to the last, daily administering to my associates the salutary opiate. Happy . . . would it have been for my country, if the whole of that time had been devoted to sleep, or been a blank in our lives, rather than employed in forging its chains."

Ellsworth had flung at Martin: "You espoused the tyrannic principle, that where a State refused to comply with a requisition of Congress for money, that an army should be marched into its bowels, to fall indiscriminately upon the property of the innocent and the guilty, instead of having it collected as the Constitution proposed, by the mild and equal operation of laws." And Martin came back: "That I ever suggested the idea of letting loose an army indiscriminately . . . is a falsehood so groundless, so base and malignant, that it could only have . . . been devised by a heart which would dishonour the midnight assassin." Gerry, also, was a butt of Ellsworth's attack. Martin came to his rescue, and so the acrimonious exchanges were remote from the merits of approving or rejecting the Constitution.

Worthier of serious consideration were essays by men not in the framing convention but who discussed the principles and purposes of the plan. Such were the contributions of James Sullivan and James Winthrop of Massachusetts, and George Clinton of New York. These were well adapted to influence opinion—the first for the Constitution, the others opposed—precisely because they were couched in general terms and did not go into minutiae. These were plain, brief, and dealt with principal aspects. They were not free from personal bias, but none of the writings when the Constitution was in prospect was completely objective. Some readers doubtless were glad to have the tedium of over-seriousness relieved by the clowning of Hugh Henry Brackenridge of Pittsburgh in his "Cursory Remarks on the Constitution." His comments were not so sportive as to conceal his distaste for the whole performance. The pieces we have mentioned were intended to be tracts for the times and would not have survived longer had not painstaking scholarship rescued and reprinted them.*

Also meant to serve in the emergency were the essays signed "Publius" (better known since as *The Federalist*) prepared by Alexander Hamilton, James Madison and John Jay. They aimed to persuade the New York convention to ratify. But due to their thoroughness, learning, patriotism, and wisdom they have continued to be famous as authoritative commentary on the American system of government. They formed by far the longest series examining the Constitution. The essays, eighty-five in number, appeared about three times a week in various newspapers—for they were widely copied—during the eight

---

* See P. L. Ford, editor, *Pamphlets on the Constitution of the United States* (1888), and *Essays on the Constitution* . . . (1892).

months from October 1787 until the following June. Before serial publication was completed the essays appeared in two bound volumes. Hamilton seems to have proposed the project, and enlisted the others. He wrote two-thirds of the papers, Jay five, and Madison, or Madison and Hamilton jointly, the remainder. Though the work was done in haste and under pressure, the tone was just right to capture attention and win approval. The drastic disappointments of the Confederation and benefits to be expected from the new plan were fully set forth, while men's minds were disabused of false fears industriously being circulated by enemies of the Constitution. Not ideal possibilities, good or bad, but calculable probabilities formed the subject matter of discussion. A series had commenced earlier, counter-thrusts at letters of Governor Clinton, who was violently opposed to the Constitution. It is possible, though not probable, that Hamilton was the author; in any event he saw that this dueling should be dropped in favor of calm exposition of the reform offered to the people. The chances of failure were too imminent, and the prospect of success was too alluring for supporters of a firm national government to indulge themselves in a mere swapping of epithets. The contest for agreement of voters and delegates called for cool appraisal and diligent exploration, not to carry a debater's point, but to win solid conviction.

The authors of *The Federalist*, from their early advocacy, practical participation, and moral commitment, moved with perfect familiarity in the materials they were handling. They knew all of the arguments, and were as aware of the defects of the Constitution as of its benefits. With high diplomacy they chose the method of candor rather than select the favorable and conceal the adverse. Hamilton, more than his collaborators, doubted whether the Constitution furnished sufficient strength to the central powers. In arguing for it, he was sustained by his belief that once in effect, declamation about mere words in the Constitution would disappear, and men would seize the opportunity to set in motion a workable government. He and his friends had confidence in their capacity to help in this task.

The writers of *The Federalist*, alive though they were to popular hopes and fears, failed to appreciate the vigor of the demand for a bill of rights, protecting the people against oppressive acts by their own chosen rulers, to be incorporated in the fundamental law. Happily, this omission did not discredit their recommendations. They could not be expected to anticipate certain developments in American political practice which were to loom large—formalized parties, nomination of candidates by conventions, and the evils of local boss rule. But they dispelled apprehensions which history proved to be unfounded—for example, that the President would become a despot and that the small states would be obliterated by the large ones. On the whole, their description of how the Constitution would operate was remarkably accurate in the light of more than a century and a half of experience. Constantly quoted by the Supreme Court as evidence of what the makers of the Constitution intended, *The Federalist* is also read with profit by those who want to know the principles of our government today.

Debates in conventions in the states had many of the qualities of a theatrical performance. There was tension, a problem, a cast of characters to work out the plot. There was a sort of script, for both sides caucused, laid out the lines of argument, appointed speakers for first presentation and for rebuttal of opponents. Many speeches were eloquent, for this was the day of oratory. Flourishes did not so much greet the few in the Philadelphia meeting that framed the Constitution as in the state gatherings with more delegates to form an audience. As one said in the Richmond assembly, "Is not the influence of popular declaimers less in small than in great bodies?" Being used to these arts, critics were always ready to deflate windy opponents. And yet the outpourings continued. The formula was for the member to rise with apologies for his ignorance, crudity, age (too young or too old), feebleness of body, as compared with the masters so much more worthy of being heard. With this diffidence and disability at the outset he soon gathered strength, skill, fire, and pathos, with frequently the added embellishments of interjected apostrophes to liberty or to patriotism. He was apt to range through history ancient and modern for precedents to illustrate his thesis. As such a speaker had long premeditated his remarks, he often repeated in substance what others had offered. He was not to be done out of his turn, even if he trod familiar ground.

The chair seemed never to stop a haranguer; no time limit was set for those taking the floor. In the end, perhaps after hours, the delegate would sink to his seat, explaining reluctantly that he was too much exhausted to continue now, but doggedly promising to resume on a future occasion. But what of the patience of his audience? Was that not spent? Doubtless yes, as would be vented in sarcastic reproofs from those who followed next. But the stern etiquette was to grin and bear it, those that were to deliver themselves later remembering that they too would demand to be indulged.

This is not to say that all of the proceedings were smoothly undulating, or marked by flowing periods. Extemporaneous staccato exchanges there were; sharp personal accusations were met by instant resentment and demand for retraction. Once in a while the stately decorum of discussion was broken by downright disorder, so that the reporter could not record the rapid charges and retorts.

As was to be expected, in the state conventions more than in that at Philadelphia the main participants were few, either self-selected or put forward by their respective contingents. For instance, in Virginia a dozen debaters accounted for most of what was thrown back and forth. For every member that took the floor, ten sat silent in the sessions, content to listen in the hall, doubtless to pass animated remarks in lobby or lodgings, and of course to give their votes. It was the same in the other state conventions, Massachusetts and New York, which give us our fullest accounts. Many of the quiet members were genuinely bashful, or felt that they came to listen and learn, not to instruct. If those who were to decide on the Constitution understood its chief features when they took their seats, they could not appreciate the interaction of its parts until the ingenuity of its construction had been explored in the debates. While a minority of delegates came instructed one way or the other, and more refused to give up existing prejudices, on the whole the delegates were open-minded, willing to be convinced. The heaviest majority against the Constitution when the delegates assembled was in New York, and even there determined proponents, by dint of logic, skill, and zeal, were able in the end to win enough votes to ratify the new government.

Varying Reception in States

The Federalists in Pennsylvania were in the heavy majority, especially in and around Philadelphia. They were eager to make their state the first to ratify the Constitution, for this prompt pledge of loyalty would aid the selection of Philadelphia as the national capital. Federalists literally dragged dissenting members of the Assembly to the floor to make a quorum so that the convention to consider the Constitution might be called. In convention the Federalists sped the discussion to a favorable issue. In vain did Smilie and Findley, leaders of what Gouverneur Morris called the "cold and sour temper of the back counties," inveigh against the Constitution. They charged that it set up a consolidated government which obliterated the sovereignty of the states. Nor did it contain a bill of rights to protect the liberties of the people who were said to be the contracting parties. Tyranny of the aristocrats must be the result. Said the overmountain men, "The militia of Pennsylvania may be marched to New England or Virginia to quell an insurrection occasioned by the most galling oppression." (Actually, these westerners within a few years were to give aid and comfort to a rebellion in their own locality against the national authority, put down by militia from their own and neighboring states.)

James Wilson and other Federalists gave impressive answers to these accusations. The Constitution was ratified by a two-to-one vote, a few days after Delaware unanimously became the first state to give approval. The Anti-Federalists in the Pennsylvania convention published their "Reasons for Dissent," a mixture of objections to the Constitution and to the high-handed methods of the majority in hastening ratification.

Thereafter the order of the states in approving the Constitution was New Jersey and Georgia, both unanimously; Connecticut by more than three to one; Massachusetts by a narrow majority (see below); Maryland by almost six to one. Next came South Carolina, the stronghold of slavery, angry that Virginia had been willing to abolish forthwith importation of Negroes, and fearful of northern domination. The sharpest conflict between upcountry Anti's and low-country Federalists came beforehand, in the legislature on the question whether to call a state convention to pass on the Constitution. Rawlins Lowndes was the mouthpiece of opponents. He went full length in praising the old "most excellent constitution" (Articles of Confederation), and damned experiment with a new one which threatened "loss of political existence." He defended the slave trade "on the principles of religion, humanity, and justice," and wanted his tombstone inscribed, "Here lies the man that opposed the constitution, because it was ruinous to the liberty of America." The Charleston Federalists who had helped make the Constitution, especially Rutledge and the Pinckneys, removed misapprehension on one score after another.

The South Carolina convention, held after a few months, traversed much the same ground, rejected a proposal to adjourn (evidently to see what Virginia would do), and ratified the Constitution, 149 to 73. A month later the adjourned convention of New Hampshire approved by a similar majority, but this made the ninth state and the new Union was assured. Virginia and New York ratified in time to participate in organization of the national government, but North Carolina did not come in until November 1789 (eight months after Washington was inaugurated), and Rhode Island not until six months after that (May 1790).

We shall review in some detail the discussions in three ratifying conventions, those of Massachusetts, Virginia, and New York. We choose these for several reasons. In each the momentous issue was long in doubt, though the willingness of this trio of states to accept the Constitution was in fact necessary to the success of the new nation. They were among the foremost in population and wealth. These assets, and the part they had played in the movement for independence, gave them major influence. Their geographic placement was a further crucial factor. Massachusetts (embracing then what later became the state of Maine) comprised the larger part of New England, and was a bulwark against possible southward extension of Canada. In the middle section, New York had the finest ocean port and hence prospect for commercial development. If Virginia, at the head of the South in more ways than one, refused to come in, the other planting states would be separated from the remainder of the country.

Because the eyes of America were on these problematical states, we have full reports of the debates in their conventions. By the same token, in reviewing what was said for and against the Constitution in these meetings, we shall know most of what was brought forward elsewhere, and learn how the Constitution was received by the public, or by public leaders. In the Philadelphia convention that framed the instrument most of the argument had been serious and sincere, as became men planning for the whole people. Now that discussion had fanned out, local preferences and prejudices came more to the fore. Declamation often took the place of deliberation, and mere politics intruded. But these battles in the states, however conducted, furnished the perilous test of the project of a reform of government.

I STRATEGY IN MASSACHUSETTS

The Massachusetts convention that opened in Boston January 8, 1788, was populous, had almost as many delegates as there are days in the year—355—and would have had far more except that 46 towns registered their hostility to the proposed Constitution by refusing to send representatives. The large assembly shifted its place of meeting twice before finding a hall that suited. This state had the maximum of local sentiment, nurtured in town government. While it was thus fragmented, a sharp division ran between those fearing power and those willing to confer authority, between poor and rich, debtors and creditors, between the unlearned and those of the professions, particularly lawyers. The immediate reason was Shays's insurrection of recent and evil memory. Massachusetts was in an ironical position. Shays's rebellion had shown that a state could not keep promises, or keep the peace even, within its own borders, and yet a large contingent in the convention was hostile to erecting a national monitor.

The intimacy of the town meeting engendered profound distrust of any outside or superior control. The state government at Boston at last had mustered troops to suppress the Shays insurgents. Boston was far enough from Northampton and Great Barrington. A national capital, much more distant, was viewed with horror. As in other conventions, President and Congress tended to be equated with King and Parliament as tyrants threatening liberties of the people. Some of this fear was conjured up for effect, but with many it was genuine.

Those wanting the Constitution put John Hancock in the chair, which inclined that handsome, popular, but uncommitted leader to their side. Debate by clauses as they appeared in the Constitution, and then discussion of the whole before any vote was taken was agreed to without difficulty. Opponents forthwith assailed the two-year term for members of the House of Representatives. This was too long. One year was enough. The people should be able to hold a tight rein on their spokesmen in Congress. If these were not subject to being unseated annually they would ensconce themselves. Here was the town meeting talking, the political awareness of nothing beyond the neighborhood. Give the representative a longer tether and he would cease to be the servant and become the master of the people.

The wise counsel of Fisher Ames should have routed this prejudice. Popular apprehension, he explained, was misplaced. "We need not talk to the power of an aristocracy. The people when they loose [lose] their liberties are cheated out of them. They nourish factions in their bosoms, which will subsist so long as abusing their honest credulity shall be the means of acquiring power. A democracy is a volcano, which conceals the fiery materials of its own destruction. These will produce an eruption [read Shays], and carry desolation in their way." Then he soothed while he corrected. "The people always mean right, and if time is allowed for reflection and information, they will do right. I would not have . . . the momentary impulse of the public mind become law. I consider biennial elections as a security that the sober, second thought of the people shall be law."

All now looked to Samuel Adams, *par excellence* "the man of the town meeting," to pronounce on this. He had the wit to declare himself satisfied by Ames's reasoning that the convention should accept the two-year term for congressmen.

But the jealous and timorous were not silenced. General Samuel Thompson, a loud declaimer from Topsham (District of Maine), cited the recent benefit of annual election in Massachusetts. This had given a new legislature that pardoned Shays's followers and restored peace. This pointed allusion to the insurrection produced a sudden adjournment "to put out every spark of the fire that appeared to be kindling." When the convention had cooled a few hours Rufus King repeated the remonstrance of Fisher Ames. King (Newburyport) like Ames (Dedham) was a resident of the seaboard, and had been in the Philadelphia assembly that made the Constitution. He was an offset to Elbridge Gerry, who, although he had refused to sign for Massachusetts, was invited to a seat in the state meeting to answer questions. If objects of the legislator's decision were local, said King, and within his constant observation, a one-year term was sufficient. But "where the complicated interests of united America, are mingled with those of foreign nations, and where the great duties of national sovereignty will require his . . . attention," the two-year span of office was not too long.

Opposition then shifted to the power of Congress to regulate elections. This seemed an alien, menacing force, subversive of freedom. Ingenious oppressions that Congress might practise were devised on the spot and elaborated. The Rev. Mr. Samuel West expostulated against such extravagant alarms. "Gentlemen," he said, "have only started *possible* objections. I wish the gentlemen would shew us, that what they so much deprecate is *probable*. Is it probable that we shall choose men to ruin us?" This comment fitted much that was urged against the Constitution. It was proper, since the document was up for acceptance or rejection, to explore the likelihood of abuses, but there was no point in raising mere phantoms of excited imagination. In the terror of deputing power men brought specters to the convention floor. Thompson answered West's faith in good intentions of representatives by declaring that humankind grew worse day by day. "Sir, I suspect my own heart, and I shall suspect our rulers." Both Ames and King had to argue against making the term of senators one year instead of six. Of course they showed, what critics were constantly forgetting, that the framers of the Constitution had confronted these problems and that the instrument itself, in its several parts, guarded against dangers. The upper branch required longer tenure of members. Reasons were that senators preserved the integrity of the states, must advise on enduring treaties, should moderate precipitate action of the

House. Though they could not be quickly replaced, one-third of their number were subject to change every two years.

Twin bugaboos were possession by the central government of "the sword and the purse." The changes were rung on the irresistible combination of standing army and power to tax. What was left to the citizen if he must hand over to Congress the strings to his money-bag and bare his breast to the national bayonet? Exaggerated alarms were sounded. The peacetime army, as all knew, would be tiny—a few battalions to give token protection to the coast and man posts on the Indian frontiers. Revenue would be furnished by import duties and excises (the last mainly on distilled liquor). Both of these levies were indirect, would be paid in the price of goods. Direct taxes (principally on land, which was the commonest form of property) would not be resorted to unless other sources proved insufficient. Much of the outcry was because under the Constitution, Congress could draw income from individuals instead, as under the Articles, of asking the states to fill requisitions. The state, for revenue purposes, was to be disregarded by the federal government. The authority of the state was thus diminished.

Rufus King and others had the perfect answer to objectors. Pleas to the states to furnish funds to Congress had operated unevenly, unjustly. Massachusetts had supplied more than its share, with corresponding burden on its people, while many states had been delinquent. Two states had paid in not a farthing from the adoption of the Confederation to the present. ". . . if we mean to support an efficient national government, which under the old confederation can never be the case, the proposed constitution is . . . the only one that can be substituted." Foes replied with nothing better than empty accusation. Thus Major Kingsley: ". . . after we have given [Congress] all our money, established them in a federal town, given them the power of coining money and raising a standing *army* . . . what resources have the people left?" Christopher Gore countered with the reminder that Congress under the new plan was not to be a usurping despot, similar to the British Parliament taxing Americans. We were not represented in Parliament, but Congress belonged to us. The British by taxing us relieved themselves. Congressmen by contrast, must help pay the taxes they imposed.

Authority of the national government to protect commerce was especially coveted by New England shipping interests. "In the states southward of the Delaware . . . three-fourths of the produce are exported, and three-fourths of the returns are made in British bottoms.

This is money which belongs to the New England states, because we can furnish the ships . . . much better than the British." Nor should America be confined to sending out raw materials and taking back finished goods made elsewhere. With national encouragement we could manufacture much that we raised, and skilled immigrants were available to promote this object.

Agriculture and Democracy Equated

Reading the records of the Massachusetts and other conventions, we remember that our ancestors, of classical education, relied principally on examples from ancient history. As confederations in classical times had gone to smash, these sorrowful examples were cited by men who viewed the experiment in America with alarm and pessimism. From supposed precedents in Sparta, Athens, and Rome, delegates "deduced . . . arguments to prove that where power had been trusted to men, whether in great or small bodies, they had always abused it, and . . . thus republics had soon degenerated into aristocracies." Others with more faith in the Constitution, and with more discrimination, rebutted these gloomy predictions. They pointed out that ancient leagues had fallen apart precisely because they lacked "an efficient federal government." Over-all authority must be conferred. True, this central capacity must be properly checked and rendered responsible, but to argue that power might be abused was to condemn all social control and invite return to a state of nature. This was the sufficient answer to all who proclaimed the depravity of man and thus dismissed wise plans for ensuring protection, peace, and prosperity. Further, usurpation in America was impossible "as, from the great preponderance of the agricultural interest in the United States, that interest would always . . . elect men [who] would . . . prevent the introduction of any other than a perfectly democratical form of government."

Notice that our forefathers, living mostly from the land, were prone to assume that liberty exuded from the soil. Farmers tilled their own acres, prized their independence. Close to nature, they exemplified natural law, which had the highest validity. By contrast, cities bred social inequality. In these human hives the grasping oppressed the poor. Hirelings in workshops, though industrious, could not assert their rights, being at best second-class citizens. This was an idea as old as the Greek philosophers. It was Jefferson's insistence that America would remain democratic so long as it was agrarian. Those who made this bland assumption overlooked the fact that slavery was an agricultural institution, and that slavery, by definition, was the denial of freedom, let alone democracy.

One opponent of the Constitution had the candor to admit that "the quoting of ancient history was no more to the purpose than to tell how our forefathers dug clams at Plymouth."

The eighth section of Article I, reciting the powers of Congress, brought delegates for and against to the clinch. Authority of the central government to tax and collect from citizens was the chief bone of contention. Though the melancholy history of mere requisitions was convincingly rehearsed, the familiar proposal was revived: let Congress assess the states and step in to possess itself of funds only when a state defaulted in its duty. "For, sir, . . . the power to collect, which is here vested in Congress . . . is a power, sir, to burden us with a standing army of ravenous . . . harpies, perhaps, from another state . . . who . . . were never known to have bowels for any purpose, but to fatten on the life-blood of the people . . . and when the Congress shall become tyrannical, these vultures, their servants, will be the tyrants of the village, by whose presence all freedom of speech and action will be taken away." Those upholding it were begged to "enlarge upon this formidable clause." Thompson of Topsham, in his pride in Massachusetts, disregarded all confronting dangers to the country. Massachusetts could always protect herself; meantime (taking Jefferson's advice?) "she may be one of the four dissenting states; then we shall be on our old ground . . . Let us amend the old Confederation. Why not give Congress power only to regulate trade?"

To this language of escape, shutting eyes to national perils, or reckless procrastination, Bowdoin gave thorough and patient reply. Remedy unpaid public debts, trammeled trade, and languishing agriculture "By giving Congress . . . proper power . . . such power, so far from being an objection, is a most cogent reason for accepting the Constitution. The power of Congress . . . is the power of the people, collected . . . to a focal point, at all times ready to be exerted for the general benefit."

Parsons, the colleague of King from Newburyport, developed further the theme of positive government. Members of the legislature were servants of the nation, popularly elected. ". . . the people divest themselves of nothing; the government and powers which the Congress can administer, are the . . . result of a compact made by the people with each other, for the common defence and general welfare. To talk, therefore, of keeping the Congress poor . . . must mean . . . depriving the people themselves of their own resources."

Several delegates urged that the convention quit discussing the Constitution by paragraphs; they should be at liberty to descant on the whole, for they wanted to be done and go home. These were people who would have rejected the new government out of hand. Of several who replied that the document should be examined in all its parts in orderly fashion, Samuel Adams spoke with special emphasis. His doubts about some provisions had induced him "rather to be an auditor than an objector." "We ought not . . . to be stingy of our time, or the public money," and the public expected of the convention a thorough investigation. The motion to hurry forward to an airing of general views was voted down without a roll-call. Nevertheless, opponents fired broadsides at the right of Congress to raise an army or to have exclusive jurisdiction over a federal town. The expression "We, the people" in the preamble proclaimed "a dissolution of the state governments."

King, Ames, and more refuted these fears, but their arguments and pleas had only the effect of loosing fresh charges from Amos Singletary of Sutton, an old-timer in the General Court since 1775. He regarded himself as a sort of legislative minute-man, more simple and more patriotic than latter-day sophisticates who had contrived this Constitution and for ignoble reasons plotted to foist it on the people. His tongue ran on: "These lawyers and men of learning, and moneyed men, that talk so finely, and gloss over matters so smoothly, to make us poor illiterate people swallow down the pill, expect to get into Congress themselves; they expect to be the managers of this Constitution, and get all the power and all the money into their own hands, and then they will swallow up all us little folks, like the great *Leviathan*, Mr. President; yes, just as the whale swallowed up *Jonah*."

Testimony from the Heart

This demagogic speech brought to his feet a man who was a better representative of the common people, appropriately identified in the proceedings simply as "Mr. Smith." He was Jonathan Smith of Lansboro, and his reply to Singletary's censures was the aptest utterance during the convention. The admired eloquence of His Excellency John Hancock could not carry the conviction of Smith's indisputable simple story.

"Mr. President," he began, "I am a plain man, and get my living by the plough. I am not used to speak in public, but I beg your leave to say a few words to my brother ploughjoggers in this house. I have lived in a part of the country [the Berkshires, western Massachusetts] where I have known the worth of good government by the want of it. There was a black cloud that rose in the east last winter, and spread over the west [Shays's Rebellion] . . . the cloud . . . burst upon us, and produced a dreadful effect. It brought on a state of anarchy, and that led to tyranny . . . People that used to live peaceably, and were before good neighbors, got distracted, and took up arms against government." (A member from Worcester County, which was a center of the disturbance, "called to order, and asked, what had the history of last winter to do with the Constitution. Several gentlemen, and among the rest Hon. Mr. Adams, said the gentleman was in order—let him go on in his own way.")

Probably Jonathan did not need this encouragement, for he was in full career. "I am going to show you, my brother farmers, what were the effects of anarchy, that you may see the reasons why I wish for good government. People I say took up arms; and . . . if you went to speak to them, you had the musket of death presented to your breast. They would rob you of your property; threaten to burn your houses; oblige you to be on your guard night and day; alarms spread from town to town; families were broken up; the tender mother would cry, 'Oh, my son is among them! What shall I do for my child!' . . . Then we should hear of an action, and the poor prisoners were set in the front, to be killed by their own friends . . . Our distress was so great that we should have been glad to snatch at any thing that looked like a government," even though our savior was a monarch.

"Now, Mr. President, when I saw this Constitution, I found it was a cure for these disorders. It was just such a thing as we wanted. I got a copy of it, and read it over and over . . . I did not go to any lawyer, to ask his opinion . . . I formed my own opinion, and was pleased with this Constitution. My honorable old daddy there [pointing to Mr. Singletary] won't think that I expect to be a Congress-man, and swallow up the liberties of the people. I never had any post, nor do I want one. But I don't think the worse of the Constitution because lawyers, and men of learning, and moneyed men, are fond of it. I don't suspect that they want to get into Congress and abuse their power. I am not of such a jealous make." He went on with homely illustrations, taken from the rural setting, to show that little people would do well to welcome alliance with the powerful in a firm Union. And he ended, "Some . . . say, Don't be in a hurry; take time to consider . . . I say, Take things in time; gather fruit when it is ripe. There is a time to sow and a time to reap; we sowed our seed when we sent men to the federal Convention; now is the harvest, now is the time to reap the fruit of our labor; and if we won't do it now, I am afraid we never shall have another opportunity."

Massachusetts men who cried up state sufficiency and fought competent authority for the federal government were in an especially vulnerable position. Shays's Rebellion demonstrated the inability of Massachusetts to prevent prolonged violence and bloodshed within her own borders. Smith did right to bring home this lesson which others had preferred to forget. The fact was that the disgrace of Massachusetts had spurred delegates in the Philadelphia convention to restrict state powers and give larger responsibility to the central government.

William Widgery of New Gloucester (now Maine), though he blustered, and threw out sarcasms against the optimism of Smith and others who praised the Constitution, was glad enough to escape further discussion of the duties of Congress. The convention should move on to the next topic. But Ames, Gorham, and more would not let their critics off so easily. They reinforced the need of Massachusetts, for selfish reasons if no other, to welcome the protections offered in the new structure of government.

All in this Massachusetts meeting condemned the slave trade, and of course slavery itself. The only difference between them was that some demanded earlier abolition than the Constitution permitted, while others "rejoined that a door was now to be opened for the annihilation of this odious . . . practice, in a certain time." The debate produced one of the few attacks, to be found in public discussion of this period, on Washington, who "has immortalized himself" but "he holds those in salvery who have as good a right to be free as he has."

Enemies of the Constitution weakened their case by objecting to almost every feature of the plan. If the powers to be exercised must be approved, then the manner of administration was sure to be despotic and dishonest. If detail was included, then it would have been safer to omit it; if principles were expressed in the large, as became the fundamental law, then particulars should be specified as in a statute. The provisions for the judiciary and court procedure were favorite targets. Those accused in criminal actions and defendants in civil suits lacked protections which should have been incorporated and defined. Supporters explained that the restrained wording of the document was in deference to the variety of judicial practices of the different states. Presumably the national courts would adopt what was customary in the states where they sat.

Still, critics drove home the need to declare certain basic immunities and privileges, as that a man must not be compelled to testify against himself, and Congress must be "restrained from inventing the most cruel and unheard-of punishments, and annexing them to crimes." These useful limitations were afterward included in the "Bill of Rights" or first amendments to the Constitution, and for such improvements opponents were to be heartily thanked. Friends of the Constitution made this easier by pointing constantly to the machinery for supplementing and correcting the plan, once adopted, as experience suggested. What other scheme of government carried within itself such a means of peaceable change? Further, beneficial amendments were more likely from concurrence of nine states, according to the process provided in the Constitution, than from a new convention which would require unanimous call of the states. If the present plan was rejected, another, if formed and offered, would not be more perfect.

Cavillers in Massachusetts found the Constitution in one respect too liberal. This was the stipulation that "no religious test shall ever be required as a qualification to any office." The Plymouth forefathers "who came here for the preservation of their religion" were dishonored by a Constitution that "would admit deists, atheists, &c., into the general government," for this invited "a corruption of morals." Rebuke came from two clergymen, Daniel Shute and Phillips Payson. In speeches worthy of remembrance they placed dependance in integrity, not in profession of creed. "Upon the plan of a religious test," said Shute, "the question . . . must be, Who shall be excluded from national trusts? Whatever answer bigotry may suggest, the dictates of candor and equity . . . will be, *None.*"

At this point we must look behind the scenes.

Hancock and Adams Managed

The two most influential members of the convention were Sam Adams and John Hancock. They were historical Revolutionary figures, Patriots with a capital P. Both were inclined against the Constitution, especially Hancock. Adams was less popular in the western part of the state, for he had bitterly opposed the Shaysites and had urged harsh punishment of convicted insurgents. Hancock had won favor in that quarter because as governor he pardoned the prisoners. It became a prime object of friends of the Constitution to commit both of these leaders to acceptance of the new and stronger Union. A preliminary step with Hancock had been to place him in the chair of the convention. But he felt uncomfortable in this position and absented himself, pleading illness (the gout). The first progress with Adams was when Fisher Ames, by luminous argument on the floor, got him to consent to the two-year term—not annual election—for members of the House of Representatives, as provided in the Constitution.

But Adams and Hancock must be brought along further, must be persuaded to declare positively for the Constitution. Unless this was accomplished, Massachusetts would probably turn the plan down, other important states would follow suit, and the project of an invigorated national government would be sacrificed. Skillful pressures must be applied. The device with Hancock was to flatter him out of the flannels in which he had wrapped his tortured frame. He must be made to believe that he alone could save the convention and the country. The Federalists seized on the demand for a bill of rights. They drew up a list of restrictions on the central government, and guarantees to the citizens. This list they took to Hancock, together with a speech (written by Theophilus Parsons) which Hancock should deliver to the convention in offering the amendments. The speech urged that Massachusetts ratify the Constitution, but recommend to Congress that the fundamental law be improved by the specified additions. That is, prior amendment—which would entail a second national convention—should not be a condition of acceptance of the Constitution. The Constitution would go into effect, and then the representatives of Massachusetts would work to have the amendments adopted in the way provided in the Constitution itself.

The Federalists, appealing to Hancock's well-known ego, secured his consent to this strategy. They gave complete service. To get him before the convention with his all-important proposal, they would furnish several strong young men to lift him from his sickbed into his carriage, convey him to the hall, and assist him to mount to the president's chair.

So much for Hancock. How ensure that Adams would approve the proposition that Hancock would put before the delegates? Adams had written of the Constitution to Richard Henry Lee of Virginia a few weeks before the Massachusetts convention assembled, ". . . I stumble at the Threshold. I meet with a National Government, instead of a Federal Union of Sovereign States." But Adams would follow the demands of the mechanics of Boston who had regularly been his trusted supporters. Therefore the Federalists called the mechanics to their favorite Green Dragon Inn where they were supplied with a set of resolves for ratifying the Constitution as it stood, amendments to be considered later. One narrator has said that the redoubtable Paul Revere delivered these mechanics' resolves to Sam Adams. As we shall see, these blandishments worked. Hancock, for his part, suddenly discovered that his gout had improved to the point where he could risk his health for the honor of the commonwealth.

This was the crisis of the convention, which had been in session three weeks (January 30, 1788). General William Heath, of Roxbury, opened the last phase of the debates. The delegates had discussed the Constitution by paragraphs, now approached the momentous decision on the whole. Heath devoutly hoped that Massachusetts would not fancy that she could stand alone, but would join with her sister states to preserve and strengthen the Union. He and other friends of the Constitution obviously feared their opponents were in the majority.

Theophilus Parsons moved that "this Convention do assent to, and ratify, this Constitution."

This was the moment for Hancock to play his hand. He made Parsons's speech so impressively that delegates believed it came from Hancock's own deepest conviction. Others praised his masterful stroke of conciliation.

Adams did not at once assent. He had not heard from his mechanics at the Green Dragon. He was for accepting the Constitution if and when protections to the people and the states were written into it. If Massachusetts took this stand now, conventions of six other states, yet to deliberate, were likely to adopt the same course. Dr. John Taylor, of Douglas, finding the convention so evenly divided, thought it would be a pity to endorse or reject the Constitution by a slim majority. Better to adjourn while the people pondered further. Bowdoin answered these doubts with a stout plea to embrace the Constitution "and thereby confirm the liberty, the safety, and the welfare of our country." Another supporter at this critical moment was the Rev. Mr. Thatcher (Ames's colleague from Dedham), who vividly sketched the perilous position of the Confederation. Opponents were violent. They paid their devotions to the spirit of liberty which was compromised by this Constitution. The Constitution annihilated the states, substituted a hateful consolidation.

Federalists exulted when the committee named to consider Hancock's amendments reported more than two to one (15 to 7) in favor of recommending them, but meantime the Constitution was to be ratified.

Diehard enemies were ready with retorts. Major Thomas Lusk, from Shays country (West Stockbridge), declared the amendments would never be adopted by nine states. Anyhow the Constitution was wicked because it countenanced slavery and imposed no religious test for holding office. Papists might set up the Inquisition on these shores. And Thompson of Topsham, fearing to lose his following, called amendments only bait to bring wary delegates to the trap; "the amendments—might be voted for by some men—he did not say Judases."

Massachusetts Line-up For and Against

Somewhere along here Sam Adams got word from the Green Dragon. He was ready to be swayed if the meeting of mechanics was large, if friends he inquired for approved the resolves. He was eagerly reassured on these points, withdrew some additional amendments he himself had proposed, and went over to the supporters of the Constitution. Several waverers joined him. Ames argued persuasively. Evidently he, Sedgwick, Bowdoin, King, and other Federalists felt the tide had turned in their favor. Their opinion was confirmed when a motion to adjourn to a future day to allow Constitution and amendments to be submitted to the people was negatived, only 115 out of 329 present voting for this delaying action. The Rev. Mr. Stillman heaped praise on Hancock. Parsons's motion "that this Convention do assent to, and ratify, this Constitution" was called up. Hancock pronounced his blessing: "That a general system of government is indispensably necessary, to save our country from ruin, is agreed upon all sides." The plan before them had defects, but "I give my assent to the Constitution, in full confidence that the amendments proposed will soon become a part of the system."

Of a total of 355 votes, 187 were for ratification and 168 opposed. The affirmative majority of only 19 in that large convention testified to "a great division" of sentiment in Massachusetts which Hancock had estimated, but the decision was as binding as if it had been resounding. When the Constitution had been ratified, several delegates who had voted against it rose to say they would support the majority decision. Thus "Dr. Taylor . . . had uniformly opposed the Constitution; . . . he found himself fairly beaten, and [was determined] to go home and endeavor to infuse a spirit of harmony and love among the people."

What prompted the delegates to divide as they did? Charles A. Beard's famous contention that the Constitution reflected the economic interests of the framers at Philadelphia is borne out to a degree in the Massachusetts ratifying convention. Forrest McDonald (*We, the People, The Economic Origins of the Constitution*), after painstaking inquiry into occupations and property holdings of delegates, has concluded that the Constitution was favored by merchants on a large scale and shippers, artisans and mechanics, professional men, and farmers. Ratification was opposed by the majority of retail shopkeepers, manufacturers as distinct from mechanics, and those who may be described as capitalists.

It is significant that of the delegates whose occupations could not be discovered (that is, relatively obscure men), almost two-thirds were opposed.

However, the line of economic interests is blurred, for "a large number of delegates who could expect to derive economic gain from the adoption of the Constitution voted against ratification. A large number favored ratification on philosophical or political grounds, and an even larger number opposed it on similar grounds."

The geographic division (partly occupational, partly to be described as political) may be as significant as the economic alone. Massachusetts was torn internally as the result of hard times following the Revolution —loss of shipping income to Britain, and a large debt that bore heaviest upon the poor. In this state, and in New England generally in contrast to the middle and southern states, the town was more important, in identifying the sentiments of the citizen, than was the county. Delegates for the Constitution were, broadly speaking, from towns on the coast, those against were from towns inland. The main concentration in favor was in the counties of Suffolk (including Boston), Essex (north shore), and Plymouth; heaviest concentration against was in the counties of Worcester and Berkshire (Shays country). Middlesex (where Revere had galloped to "every village and farm") was against by a smaller majority. On the other hand, Hampshire (including Springfield and Shays's native place) was almost two to one for ratification.

The best inference is that when the delegates assembled, a majority opposed ratification. On the floor, and off it in publications and personal persuasion, the Federalists did better in winning farmers and mechanics than would be supposed if we think of the Federalists as the moneybags. The capture of Hancock and Sam Adams may well have determined the result for the Constitution.

II DEBATERS' DUEL IN VIRGINIA

The Virginia convention was in session in Richmond between June 2 and 25, 1788. Before it concluded, the ninth state (New Hampshire) had ratified, but the consent of Virginia was practically necessary to success of the Constitution, for she was the state foremost in area, population, and wealth. Her neighbor, North Carolina, disinclined to come into the closer union, would follow Virginia's example. Besides Virginia's geographic, economic, and political importance, her moral support was needful. Among her citizens were leaders in the independence movement, Washington the chief, and the Constitution had been based on her plan.

It has frequently been said that the Virginia convention furnished the only full-dress debate on the Constitution, as well as being critical in the result. We shall find reason to question this when we come to describe the New York convention, which followed. In the Richmond assemblage there was never the overwhelming majority of delegates against the Constitution which appeared at Poughkeepsie. The presiding officer in Richmond, Edmund Pendleton, was a chief advocate of ratification, as was George Wythe who took the chair in committee of the whole. Of even greater force, while Washington was not a delegate, his eagerness for the Constitution was universally known, and his influence in the proceedings was acknowledged equally by friends and foes of the reform of government. Governor Edmund Randolph, who had refused to sign the Constitution at Philadelphia, was now converted to it and was an active protagonist on the floor.

In New York, by contrast, Governor George Clinton, president of the convention, was the unyielding enemy of adoption. Furthermore, the Virginia champion of opposition, Patrick Henry, who exercised his persuasions almost every day, practiced demagogic appeals. His armor of oratory could be penetrated by reason because it was fashioned of emotion and excited prejudice. Henry, in spite of his unexampled gift for attracting popular response, was vulnerable to counterattacks by those employing calm inspection instead of passion. He was too often the actor, substituting the mask for the man. The determined men who fought him—Madison, Pendleton, George Nicholas, John Marshall, Randolph—knew how to tear off the false face. Henry was assisted by the more solid, less brilliant George Mason and by others not so experienced and prominent, but Henry himself was chief duelist and determined the strategy of his supporters. The burden of criticism of the Constitution in New York was carried by Melancton Smith, whose method was persevering, cold analysis, and therefore harder to discredit.

On the other hand, the issue in Virginia perhaps remained more problematical because the decision in New York was still in doubt. The friends of ratification at Poughkeepsie, by the same token, before they were through had the advantage of the news that Virginia chose to come into the new Union.

The Richmond debates packed the floor and gallery of the Academy building on East Broad Street opposite what is now Capitol Square.* We have from a Virginia historian of the convention, Hugh Blair Grigsby, sketches of the appearance and manner of principal figures, for he knew some of the delegates and witnesses of the scene. Patrick Henry, as became a democrat, arrived from his home in distant Charlotte County in a "stick gig" (two-wheeled, open cart). He was somewhat stooped by his fifty-two years, but his eyes flashed as always. Pendleton, the chief justice of Virginia, drew up to the Swan tavern in his phaeton. His finer conveyance did not in itself betoken his aristocracy, for he was lame, obliged to walk on crutches. Thirteen of the delegates had been long on the road from "Kentucke," the vast western district then a part of Virginia. These, with special problems and prejudices, made a bloc in the convention, courted by speakers on both sides.

Among the 168 delegates were anatomical curiosities. James Innes, the attorney general, was said to be the largest man in Virginia. "He could not ride an ordinary horse, or sit in a common chair, and usually read or meditated in his bed or on the floor." George Nicholas, like Innes an advocate of ratification, was so broad as to obstruct the members' view of the presiding officer. The thin little frame of George Wythe suited his name. While most wore everyday clothes, some of station and fashion were handsomely garbed in blue and buff; William Grayson had elegant ruffles at throat and wrists. John Marshall, one of the best liked in the hall, did not depend on dress; his unkempt hair and loose wash coat were without benefit of barber or tailor.

The speakers ran the gamut from Patrick Henry of consummate art, in his agitated flights pushing his brown wig out of position on his bald pate, to the diffident Madison referring to notes held in his hat.

* Erected with subscriptions collected by Chevalier Quesnay, a grandson of the French philosopher of the same name. It was intended for the home of a literary and scientific society on the European model, but this ambition was disappointed. The hall was later used as a theater until it burned. Another theater on the same site also burned, with fearful loss of life. This disaster happened while the mother of Edgar Allan Poe was an actress in the company, and her death in Richmond soon after (1811) led to the adoption of Edgar by a wealthy family of the place.

Sometimes the shorthand reporter could not put down fast enough Henry's soaring sentences, but frequently Madison's voice was so faint that he could not be heard.

Besides delegates and spectators were lobbyists in both camps. Robert and Gouverneur Morris from Philadelphia advised with pro-Constitution men on tactics such as the order in which debaters should take up the argument, who should answer whom. For the foes of ratification Colonel Eleazer Oswald, the ebullient Philadelphia newspaper editor, was visiting wiseacre. As in other conventions, as many minds were changed by buttonholing as by formal debates in the sessions.

Virginia Did Not Need the Nation?

In Virginia the over-all obstacle to approval of the new government was what was discovered in other states in less emphatic form. It was fear that national power—in Congress, executive, and judiciary—created by the Constitution would be tyrannous like that of British king and Parliament which had been overthrown. The central authority was viewed as alien and hostile. The only safety was in local self-determination by means of pure democracy, the direct, immediate voice of the people. This was the ideal. The collection of states covered an area too large to be managed under this simple plan. Representative government, a republic, seemed distant and dangerous. Of course even the state or the county used this device, but that was on a smaller scale and those charged with control were or were felt to be closer to the individual voters. Remember that the states were then more diverse in character and interest than they have since become. They were vastly farther from each other, especially at the extremities of the country, in travel-time and in dissemination of news. Nowadays one is a citizen first of the United States, and secondarily of a particular commonwealth or community. Then it was the other way around; primary loyalty went to Pennsylvania, or Massachusetts, or South Carolina.

Virginia's distaste for, or rejection of, national sovereignty was emphasized by conditions more or less peculiar to her. These were four in number. First, she was largely self-sufficient: she had her own commerce and shipping, domestic and foreign, which produced in customs enough revenue to carry on her government and pay off already much of her state debt; she had one-fifth of the population of the entire country. Second, the people of Virginia wanted to avoid creditors—

private creditors (British merchants to whom they were heavily indebted), and the public creditors of other states which had been less successful in discharging their obligations incurred for the Revolution. Third, thousands of land titles were shaky. What if huge estates of loyalists which had been confiscated during or after the war were restored to their hated original owners, or payments for them were compelled? Also, enormous reaches of western lands, held by individual settlers or by speculative land companies, rested on disputed Indian titles which might be disallowed. Fourth and last, free navigation of the Mississippi river, vital to the overmountain people (of what are now Ohio and Kentucky, then Virginia), might be bartered away to the Spaniards by the national government. Willingness to do this was already attributed to the Continental Congress, and worse might be expected from a new Congress and executive of supreme powers.

These fears of their constituents, partly genuine, partly pretended, were the cards in the hands of Patrick Henry, George Mason, and the others in the convention who repelled the proposals for a tighter union. Those who framed the Constitution in Philadelphia had met behind closed doors. This bred suspicion and resentment. The people knew next to nothing of what went forward until the completed Constitution was published and submitted to the states. Most, especially in remote parts, learned nothing even then. Some delegates came to Richmond without ever having seen the document. If they read newspapers, those sheets carried little of what was proposed. Discussions of the new provisions hardly penetrated except to the towns. The patient explanations, clause by clause, of "Publius" (Hamilton, Madison, and Jay in the *Federalist* essays) were taxing for the attentive, and made little or no impression on those less disposed or less able to inform themselves. In spite of valiant efforts of friends of the Constitution, large sections of the population and many of their delegates were unprepared in advance for the problems posed in the state conventions. Though the case is different, let us ask how many persons in the United States today can name even the main features of the charter of the United Nations, though it has been in operation for years?

Ignorance of the Constitution being so general, and fears of its effects being all alive, its enemies in the Virginia convention, as an opening gambit, claimed that the framers of the document had exceeded their authority and therefore the paper should be disregarded. This effort to discredit the Constitution at the threshold was frustrated. Its friends showed that the extent of reform of the old Articles of Confederation was within the discretion of the delegates at Philadelphia. Further, the document was properly before the Richmond meeting by order of Congress and the Virginia legislature, and must be considered on its merits. The next best move of foes, if the Constitution could not be tossed out as *ultra vires*, was to assail it in the large, as providing a consolidated—no longer a confederated—government, perilous to the state. George Mason, who had refused to sign at Philadelphia, immediately gave advocates an advantage which, as we shall see, they were obliged to maneuver to secure in the subsequent New York convention. He successfully urged that the document be taken up clause by clause in order. He wanted discussion to be systematic and thorough. The effect was to give time for supporters to supply justifications piecemeal and in detail, and prevent opponents from taking the fort by storm. Patrick Henry and others freely violated the agreement by assailing several or all provisions at once, but after some days of this they were called to task and the agreed procedure was restored.

Throughout, Henry's method was that of persuasion, while Madison and his friends, determined to recommend the Constitution, plied argumentation. Rarely has the difference between the two stratagems been better illustrated. Henry, past master at swaying opinion, alarmed fears with vivid portrayals of insults, cruelties, usurpations by the national Congress, President, and courts which the Constitution authorized. The very preamble betrayed the wretched mischief which the document would work, for it professed to spring from "We the *people*; instead of the *states*." The Virginia orator proclaimed that the most precious rights of the individual were to be sacrificed—liberty of conscience, jury trial, freedom of the press. Besides overleaping state boundaries to abuse the citizen, what iniquities would be practiced in the ten miles square of the capital where Congress and President would rule without check!

The shorthand report of debates does not reveal the eloquence of Patrick Henry to which hearers eagerly testified. No man, it was said, could take eyes from him to commit his words to paper. The result was imperfect report, paraphrase, or, in the rush of his passion, helpless omission. Where verbatim, the written record cannot convey the manner which was inseparable from his meaning—his insinuating or commanding gestures, his flashing eyes, "his startling exclamations, or horror-breathing tones." The story has been told how, in one of his transports, he pictured ethereal beings anxiously hovering over the proceedings. At that moment an electric storm broke, and the orator, said a beholder, seemed "rising on the wings of the tempest, to seize upon the artillery of Heaven, and direct its fierce thunders against the heads of his adversaries." The scene became "insupportable." Doubtless Henry wove spells, but also hearers in that day were susceptible.

Defects of Confederation

The friends of the Constitution pressed for a prompt start of the convention's work, reminding that it would be portentously interrupted when the legislature met three weeks later. George Wythe being in the chair of the committee of the whole, George Nicholas led off for ratification. He defended features of the plan which he anticipated would be attacked. He said the Constitution conferred necessary powers while preserving full control by the people. Patrick Henry in reply plucked strings on which he was to harp in the days following. The country was blissfully tranquil until the promulgation of "this fatal system . . . a proposal to change our government—a proposal that goes to the utter annihilation of the states . . . of those solemn treaties we have formed with foreign nations. Who authorized [the framers at Philadelphia] to speak the language of We, the *people*, instead of, We, the *states*? States are the . . . soul of a confederation. If the states be not the agents of this compact, it must be one great, consolidated, national government, of the people of all the states . . . The people gave them no power to use their name. That they exceeded their power is perfectly clear . . . The federal Convention ought to have amended the old system; for this purpose they were solely delegated . . ."

The makers of the Constitution being thus stigmatized, Edmund Randolph answered. Embarrassed because he had notoriously changed his tune from objector to advocate, he at once explained his motives. He had refused to sign because he insisted on previous amendments of the document. But then the Virginia convention was postponed to so late a day that hope of prior amendment was impossible "without . . . ruin to the Union, and the Union is the anchor of our political salvation." He pleaded for immediate ratification with recommendation of amendments afterward. He was compromised as a supporter, and was not allowed to forget it, but he did well to declare at the outset the grounds of his change of heart. He refuted Henry's criticisms. The country had not been content under the inefficient Confederation, but suffered every misfortune and disability at home and abroad. The delegates at Philadelphia spoke in the name of the people because the new government was for them, and "are not the people the proper persons to examine its merits or defects?"

George Mason, the other Virginia member of the Philadelphia convention who had refused to sign the Constitution, was more specific than Randolph in his misgivings. He said truly "the assumption of this power of laying direct taxes does, of itself, entirely change the confederation of the states into one consolidated government." Congress, levying on the people of Virginia, would have "neither knowledge of our situation, nor a common interest in us, nor a fellow-feeling for us." Far better to use the old method of requisitions, "with an alternative of laying direct taxes in case of non-compliance." Most power should reside locally, for, Mason asked, "Does any man suppose that one general national government can exist in so extensive a country as this?" His approach was negative. "I always fear," he declared, "for the rights of the people." It did not occur to him—indeed he rejected the intimation—that the rights of the people could best be defended by a competent central government. The record in American history of the protection of civil liberties, as between national and state authorities, is mixed, but in notable instances, since the Civil War, Congress and the federal courts and executive have been obliged to override repugnant laws and practices of certain of the states.

Madison promptly undertook to disabuse Mason of the conviction that the representatives of Virginia in the national House would be too few to know and reflect the peculiar needs of their constituents. They would be informed by the state laws, the state legislature, "from their own experience, and from a great number of individuals." The incredulity of Mason and of many on his side nevertheless persisted, and the point came up again and again in subsequent debate.

Edmund Pendleton, president of the convention and speaking from the eminence of his chief judgeship, did his excellent best in the same behalf. With patience he argued away what Mason and Henry conceived to be dire dangers in the proposed reform. Like Randolph earlier, he showed that if under the Confederation "the public mind was . . . at ease" it must have been due to "unaccountable stupor." For "Our general government was totally inadequate to the purpose of its institution; our commerce decayed; our finances deranged; public and private credit destroyed . . ." The Confederation was "no government at all. It has been said that it has carried us, through a dangerous war, to a happy issue. Not that Confederation, but common danger, and the spirit of America, were bonds of our union" and "The moment of peace showed the imbecility of the federal government." To cure this the Constitution did not go over to a consolidated system. "It only extends to the general purposes of the Union. It does not intermeddle with the local, particular affairs of the states." Actually the central authority was in many respects dependent upon the states, could not "annihilate" them without destroying itself. Pendleton like other friends of the Constitution showed beyond dispute that if Congress was to tax only after a state had refused to comply with a requisition, "resistence [must] terminate in confusion, and a dissolution of the Union."

This old man did not spare Patrick Henry's behavior. After acknowledging the famous orator's "éclat and brilliancy" on former occasions, Pendleton rightly charged that this time Henry, instead of investigating the merits of the new plan, "informed us of horrors which he felt, of apprehensions in his mind, which made him tremblingly fearful of the fate of the commonwealth. The question before us belongs to the judgment of this house. I trust he is come to judge, and not to alarm." Henry in rejoinder continued to abuse the Constitution. It was a project to produce prosperity merely. "Liberty," exclaimed Henry, "the greatest of all earthly blessings—give us that precious jewel, and you may take every thing else!" He reverted, not obliquely, to his record. "Twenty-three years ago was I supposed a traitor to my country? I was then said to be the bane of sedition, because I supported the rights of my country." His mission now was the same. In his "invincible attachment to the dearest rights of man" perhaps he had "become an old-fashioned fellow." In reading Henry's self-defense and his violent protests later in the convention one feels that he had waked from a Rip Van Winkle sleep, that unbeknown to him others, no less patriots, had found it necessary to preserve rights by devising security. These agreed with him on the desired end—which was freedom; the problem was the means.

Patrick Henry was too persistent and too fertile in raising objections to the Constitution to be accused of insincerity. The representatives in the lower House of Congress might be whittled down to one from each state, he suggested, and this clique of tyrants, with troops at their command, could work their will against the defenseless people. Once the proposed plan was adopted, it was futile to expect amendments. The boasted checks and balances existed in theory only. The "mighty President" was to have "the powers of a king." "Among other deformities [the Constitution] squints towards monarchy; and does not this raise indignation in the breast of every true American?" Then the orator went on quixotically to declare he "would rather infinitely . . . have a king, lords, and commons, than a government so replete with . . . insupportable evils."

Governor Randolph was sure that Virginia would be excluded from the Union by a ratification merely conditional. In case of military attack, as an isolated state, she would be vulnerable. Indians would be excited to horrid ravages on the frontiers, the Negro slaves (two-fifths of the population) might rise against the whites; of manufactures and military stores Virginia had none. States in the Union would dispute Virginia's boundaries. These were speculative perils, but Madison, who followed Randolph, was factual and practical. Henry had charged that adopting states were hurried into a decision of which they were repenting. Madison gave his reasons for believing that "the satisfaction of those states is increasing every day." Doubtless thinking of the *Federalist* papers of which he was an author, he was persuaded that "the grounds of proselytism extend every where . . . and the inflammatory violence wherewith [the new plan of government] was opposed by designing, illiberal, and unthinking minds, begins to subside."

Motives of Constitution-Makers

The bottom difference between friends and foes of the Constitution was the belief of the former that government is a good and of the latter that it is an evil. Nicholas taxed Henry with contending "that the powers given to any government ought to be small." Rather, coercive authority "given for some certain purpose, ought to be proportionate to that purpose, or else the end . . . will not be answered." It was as dangerous to delegate too little as to entrust too much. Throughout these debates, in Virginia especially, opponents were apt to take dogmatic positions which they clothed with the merit of principles. On the other hand those favoring the reform must be discriminating, choosing between extremes, exercise judgment. Antagonists tried to make them appear opportunist, devoid of praiseworthy conviction. It was harder to be selective and reasonable than to be merely adamant. Any device for contributing to order, security, and solvency must be put in broad terms or be specifically defined. If stated generally, objectors charged that too much discretion was allowed; if limited, then the particular restrictions should have been different. The technical advantage in debate seemed to belong to those determined to say "No." The situation of the country, they answered, was not as bad as was represented; perhaps something should be done, but less than was proposed; or let us delay, see what actions other states will take; if these ratify the Constitution, they may still be persuaded to let us in on our own terms; if not, it will then be time to consider our own course.

Nor could advocates of the plan expect hostile or inert delegates, much less the mass of the people, to appreciate nicely contrived balances which had been worked into the written document. The delicate poise of governmental powers, sufficient yet safe, and combining central and local needs, have been the admiration of later generations, but could not then be perfectly conveyed. The real strength of advocates lay in their appeal for rescue of the country from imminent discord and dissolution. Political and economic breakdown under the Confederation supplied the exciting force for reform, and particulars of the plan were of secondary, though never negligible, importance. The embarrassment of opponents was that they must acknowledge defects in the existing system, while they had little of a corrective character to advance.

The decision on the Constitution was made not in the state conventions, but was in effect taken when delegates were sent to Philadelphia at the call of Congress. The next step was when the heavy majority of these delegates, once assembled, agreed, as Randolph put it, that "this shipwrecked vessel" of the Confederation could not be repaired to be "safe for us to embark in." Or as another said, "Our state vessel has sprung a leak; we must embark in a new bottom or sink into perdition." The design of hull, spars, rigging as the new craft was ready to leave the ways surely mattered, but the impressive feature was that she promised to float and be navigable with her burden.

In the construction and adoption of the Constitution, events dictated theories. The Constitution illustrated the economic force in history. It is worth noting that in all of the scrutiny which the document received in the state conventions the makers of it were rarely accused of being disingenuous. They were charged with framing a new instrument instead of patching up the old one as many in the country had thought them commissioned to do. But if they exceeded their authority it was agreed that they did so in good conscience, and discussion promptly shifted to the merits of the plan they offered as a substitute for the Articles of Confederation. It remained for others (Charles Beard pre-eminently) a century and a quarter later to seek to demonstrate that the constitutional fathers executed a selfish plot to retrieve the property interests of themselves and the class to which they belonged. If this was the case, would not keen contemporary critics have detected and exposed the fraud? Antagonists were bursting with political and moral suspicions in favor of liberty and human rights. They would have damned a motive so unworthy of public servants. Though the plan of government was formed behind closed doors it was bared to public view and debated for a year before it was confirmed by representatives of the people. If it was shot through with ulterior purpose would not this disgrace have been set in the forefront of hostile attack?

Other contemporary evidence is even more persuasive against the contention that the Constitution was a piece of pocketbook patriotism. Leave aside its enemies, call them fumbling and obtuse in their refusal to crush the proposal because it was self-serving on the part of its authors. What of its friends? Surely among them were honest men who would have been disgusted by attempted cunning deception. Could they have supported the plan for its merits without denouncing hidden purposes that gave it birth? If they distrusted the integrity of colleagues among the framers, could they have been whole-souled espousers of their work? No, their advocacy is stamped with earnest sincerity.

Of course the historian may say that mean incentives were so subconscious as not to be recognized at the time. Calm inspection long afterward, with all the helps of scholarly review, may identify forces at work which were not suspected by actors in the scene. This is doubtless true, but is different from blaming architects of the Constitution as bold impostors. It is one thing to see members of the Philadelphia convention as instruments of history; it is another to call them perpetrators of a private salvage operation which they pretended was a public benefit. Statesmen are human, and readily confuse personal advantage with the common good. We may search the records for property possessions and claims of individuals and communities. We may contrast characteristic occupations—commercial, agricultural, professional—in different sections, states, even counties, and to these attribute attitudes on the burning question of the Constitution. However significant the conclusions, this is the wisdom of hindsight. A careful examination of what men said and wrote when the Constitution was formed and adopted convinces one that the document was an act of honesty in a sinning world.

But back to our muttons of the Virginia convention considering ratification or rejection of the Constitution. It had frequently been a plea in avoidance that the geographic area of the United States was too large to be embraced in any republican government unless a loose confederation. Francis Corbin, in reply, asked, "How small must a country be to suit the genius of republicanism?" He went on to explain that "The extent of the United States cannot render this government oppressive. The powers of the general government are only of a general nature" (to defend and strengthen the nation), "but the internal administration of government is left to the state legislatures, who exclusively retain such powers as will give the states the advantages of small republics, without the . . . weakness of such governments." (When one reflects on the expansion of this country from ocean to ocean, and beyond, it is plain how completely Corbin's confidence has been justified.)

Speakers rightly tenacious of popular self-government often failed to see that pure democracy (where the voters could assemble, as in a Swiss canton) had a reasonable substitute in representative democracy, where the people, widely scattered, sent delegates to express their wishes. This alternative is now a commonplace, indeed pure democracy is a curiosity. In examining views in the constitutional period we are many times reminded that Americans then were exploring a new proposition, whether citizen control was feasible over a wide territory. The ancient and contemporary democracies were by comparison petty. Further, these other governments which reflected, more or less, the people's will were growths. Ours was to be—with some earlier experimentation—an invention out of hand. The crucial question arose, over and over, "Can direct taxes be laid on the people by a central authority without imperilling liberty?" It was necessary for Corbin to stress that "Government cannot exist without the means of securing money . . . this power can never be dangerous if the principles of equal and free representation be fully attended to. While the right of suffrage is secured, we have little to fear." In fact, he reminded his fellow Virginians, the Constitution went to the illogical length of counting, for purposes of representation, "three fifths of those who are not free." Southern whites as persons were over-represented.

Corbin closed with sound advice. "The loss of the union, sir, must be the result of a pertinacious demand [for] precedent conditions. My idea is, that we should go hand in hand with Massachusetts [which had acted four months earlier]: adopt it first, and then propose amendments of a general nature; for local ones cannot be expected." Massachusetts in the north and Virginia in the south "are the two most populous, wealthy, and powerful states in the Union . . . their influence would have very great weight in carrying any amendments."

A common charge of those who attacked the new plan (George

Mason, for example) was that the dozen representatives of Virginia (ten in the House, two in the Senate) "will have no fellow feeling for their constituents." Once ensconced in the sacrosanct federal district, they would oppress the people who sent them there. Randolph exclaimed against this absurdity. "Will their honor and virtue be contaminated and disgraced in one instant?" Would they "be suddenly changed from upright men to monsters"?

The anemia of the Confederation was often described by advocates of an effective government. Madison at the end of the first week of the Virginia convention devoted a speech to this topic. "A government which relies on thirteen independent sovereignties for the means of its existence, is a solecism in theory and a mere nullity in practice." He discredited supposed contradiction elsewhere. "I . . . say that no instance can be produced . . . of any confederate government that will justify a continuation of the present system, or that will not demonstrate the necessity of . . . substituting, for the present pernicious and fatal plan, the system now under consideration, or one equally energetic." Madison's known competence in constitutional history, ancient and modern, must have given him an attentive audience. Those who foretold hardships on citizens from the new plan should rather remember the record of the late war. "We are now, by our suffering, expiating the crimes of the otherwise glorious revolution. Is it not known to every member . . . that the great principles of free government were reversed through the whole progress of that scene? Was not every state harassed? Was not every individual oppressed, and subjected to repeated distresses? Was this right?"

Dependable revenue for Congress, such as the Constitution provided, would have done most to obviate these abuses. "The Confederation is so notoriously feeble, that foreign nations are unwilling to form any treaties with us," for any engagement of the general government "may be violated at pleasure by any of the states." We had no prospect of paying what we owed to foreign nations. "We have been obliged to borrow money even to pay the interest of our debts. This is a ruinous . . . expedient . . . How are we to extricate ourselves" except by a reorganized government capable of commanding the resources of the country?

Jefferson's Misgivings Flaunted by Patrick Henry

Patrick Henry had worshipped the Virginia bill of rights. Similar guaranties of civil liberties must be added to the national Constitution before he could consent to that plan. But he was reminded that the purity of Virginia had not prevented her legislature from executing one Josiah Philips without indictment or trial. Henry brazened it out, not helping his standing in the convention as a logical debater. "That man," he protested, "was not executed by a tyrannical stroke of power . . . He was a fugitive murderer and an outlaw . . . He committed the most cruel and shocking barbarities. He was a enemy to the human name . . . He was not executed according to those beautiful legal ceremonies which are pointed out by the laws in criminal cases . . . I am truly a friend to legal forms and methods; but, sir, the occasion warranted the measure."

Henry was sure the Constitution would burden the people taxwise, for besides supporting the states, the "splendid maintenance" of the enlarged central government "will cost this continent immense sums . . . A change of government will not pay money." Friends of the Constitution might have answered, as they did not answer in so many words, that for increased taxes the people would get improved security and other services. Further, if "a change of government" induced prosperity, it might then be easier to pay a larger revenue, especially from import duties, than a smaller one if stagnation continued. It was to be proved that adoption of the Constitution did in fact relieve the burdens of citizens.

Henry damned "your constructive, argumentative rights" of Congress " 'to make all laws which shall be necessary and proper to carry their power into execution.' " Here he misquoted, and went on: "Implication is dangerous, because it is unbounded . . . every implication should be done away." Perhaps Henry recalled this sally two years later when the secretary of the treasury invoked the implied power of Congress to charter the first Bank of the United States. Henry would have said, "I told you so!"

Essaying to speak for the settlers in the western parts of Virginia (now Kentucky and Ohio), Henry feared that the federal government, given more power, would sacrifice the right of navigation of the Mississippi. "If a bare majority of Congress can make laws, the situation of our western citizens is dreadful." The northeastern states even under the Confederation had temporized with the Spaniards on the Mississippi. This was a sore point with the frontier people whose lifeline was that river. Henry on the floor could be parried, but how capture the votes of overmountain men who took Henry's bias as gospel?

Henry believed he played a high card when he quoted Jefferson against adoption of the Constitution by Virginia. Jefferson was then

United States minister in Paris. "I . . . say . . . from . . . good information, that his opinion is, that you reject this government . . . This illustrious citizen advises you to reject this government till it be amended. His sentiments coincide entirely with ours . . . At a great distance from us, he remembers and studies our happiness. Living in splendor and dissipation, he yet thinks of bills of rights . . ." This report was accurate. Jefferson had written his qualified approval of the new plan; his hope was that nine states would form the government, but that four would refuse to enter the Union until those joining consented to additional safeguards to civil liberties.

Of course Jefferson had every right to communicate his views on the proposed Constitution. Those who had worked ardently to bring it into being, and who were now clinched in the struggle that would mean success or failure, were nettled when Jefferson's authority was used to strengthen their foes. Jefferson, long absent, could not know the urgency of the situation in America. Friends of the reform felt that for four states—Virginia, New York, North Carolina, and Rhode Island—to refuse the project unless and until prior demands were met, invited many dangers. It would be hard enough to cope with confronting problems—domestic conflict, debt payment, foreign relations—if all thirteen states united in resolve and good will. The consent of Virginia and New York was considered to be essential. North Carolina and Rhode Island might hold off temporarily, but they would soon be obliged to come in. If strategically placed large states imposed conditions the result might be fatal. It is easy to see that Federalists on the ground and straining every effort resented the attempt of Jefferson, overseas, to thwart them at the critical moment. Perhaps if Jefferson in Paris had better understood the case at home he would have held his hand. Maybe Jefferson could not foresee that the orator, Patrick Henry, would trumpet his misgivings about the Constitution. Though this mischief was overcome, Federalists did not forget the attempt. Jefferson's equivocal position on the Constitution was repeatedly urged against him in after years.

Patrick Henry was not always tilting at windmills. Sometimes he was usefully realistic, as when he discredited opponents' alarms that if the states did not unite to pay the public debts this country would be forcibly attacked by foreign creditors, France and Holland. Both, Henry thought, would continue to be friendly and forbearing. Nor, if Virginia declined to enter the new union on the instant, would she be invaded and her contiguous territory snatched by Maryland. These were dangers which Federalists had raised unreasonably. On the other hand Henry presumed in declaring that New Hampshire had rejected the Constitution and that New York and North Carolina would do so.

Here he let himself in for sharp correction by Henry Lee of Westmoreland ("Light Horse Harry"), who followed on the floor. Lee damaged Henry, too, by contrasting his "rage for democracy" and his adoration of liberty with his often-expressed "admiration of that king and Parliament over the Atlantic." Also, multiplying his inconsistencies, Henry condemned a standing army, on which the British monarchy relied, and placed his faith in a militia. Lee, from a soldier's knowledge, which Henry did not possess, praised the bravery of militiamen at times during the Revolution, but illustrated their cowardice on critical occasions. Lee's candor on this touchy topic showed his earnestness. "Let the gentleman recollect the action of Guildford. The American regular troops behaved there with the most gallant intrepidity. What did the militia do? The greatest number of them fled . . . Had the line been supported that day, Cornwallis, instead of surrendering at Yorktown, would have laid down his arms at Guildford."

Patrick Henry's charge, said Lee, that "public liberty . . . is designed to be destroyed" by the Constitution was empty of reason. "What does he mean? Does he mean that we, who are friends to that government, are not friends to liberty? No man dares to say so . . . when it will be necessary to struggle in the cause of freedom, he will find himself equalled by thousands of those who support this Constitution." It was time that an opponent met Henry's declamation head-on. Lee countered Henry's demand for a bill of rights by declaring that while suffrage was widespread and "the privilege of representation is well secured, our liberties cannot be easily endangered." He believed the Constitution of enumerated powers "is infinitely more attentive to the liberties of the people than [is] any state government." This was because, in the states, "the people reserved to themselves certain enumerated rights, and . . . the rest were vested in their rulers," who were allowed much latitude as compared with national officers who were held to defined objects. Lee contended this demonstrated "the inutility and *folly* (were he permitted to use the expression) of bills of rights."

Randolph had been chafing under the personal aspersions of Patrick Henry, who pointed to his change of front on the Constitution. Randolph explained again that he opposed it until "after the ratification . . . by so many states, the preservation of the Union depended on its adoption by us." If Henry by his "illiberal . . . insinuations" wanted an end to their friendship, so be it. Henry did not want that, said so, and Randolph's temper subsided. Like others who helped form the Constitution, Randolph saw no occasion for including in it a bill of rights. America was not menaced by a king. "What have we to do with bills of rights? Six or seven states have none." Bills of rights in Massachusetts and Virginia were no part of their constitutions. "A bill of rights . . . is quite useless, if not dangerous to a republic." However, he proposed no rights for Negro slaves; instead, only union under the Constitution would permit military strength "formidable" enough to put down possible slave revolts.

John Marshall Argues for Constitution

Now was presented a contrast in long speeches by James Monroe and John Marshall. The first confessed that the Confederation was "void of energy, and badly organized." He considered the substitute system "safe and proper" if shorn of "one power only—I mean that of direct taxation." But his assaults on this vital faculty led him to rule out other features, so that in the end he called it "a dangerous government" unfit to secure interests or rights of the country. Monroe throughout the debates was heavy without being weighty. Nor did his deliberation save him from confusions and contradictions. He was sincere but had not the clarity to be consistent.

Marshall, supporting the Constitution, was another matter. He had thought the problem through. His principle—now as later—was that freedom required system and strength in a national government. He did not expect democracy from the monarchy which Patrick Henry admired. But a safe society required the sure public revenue which Monroe would deny to Congress. The impost, back lands, supplicating requisitions, and borrowing would not serve. Direct taxation reaching the citizens was a necessary resource. This much was right, though Marshall stumbled at the mode of laying direct taxes. He conceded to opponents that to "regulate the taxes so as to be equal on all parts of the community" Congress might have to "make thirteen distinct laws" in order to embrace "the general objects of taxation in each state." This admission afterward rose to plague his side. This was a problem, how to get uniformity of levies amidst diversity of bases. Hamilton, in the Treasury, wisely avoided it, and solution was not found until federal income taxes were used.

Justifying direct taxation, Madison did a neat bit of divining. He foresaw renewal of war between Britain and France. America would be the neutral carrier until the British, still denying the principle that free ships make free goods, would pounce on our vessels and draw us into the conflict. Then we should need money promptly and in plenty for defense.

Opponents of the Constitution constantly complained that the states were to be eclipsed. Madison turned this about, declared the danger was that the states, with predominance of officers and claiming the local attachments of the people, would enfeeble the central authority. He believed amendments might be needed, not to weaken but to invigorate Congress. Madison, like others, had discussed the new plan in the large, but begged that the convention now return to its resolve to proceed clause by clause. Patrick Henry, as before, preferred a general canvass, refused to be limited, and for days afterward debate ranged over the whole subject as speakers chose. This was to the advantage of the anti's, for the less specific the examination the better their opportunity to raise alarms.

George Mason improved this chance, picturing fanciful oppressions of the people by poll taxes ("light on the rich, and heavy on the poor") and by burdensome levies on land. He quoted Robert Morris as having projected such iniquities. The new government was to be aristocratic, violative of common interests. For a solid, sober man Mason worked himself into surprising extremes. Others on his side were extravagant, but often with the unspoken admission that they were talking for effect. Mason, without the saving grace of oratory, offered unlikely contingencies as probable fact and thus mocked his own earnestness. In his sullen anger at the reform, he took no pains to guard his reasoning. Further, he hurt his cause by objecting to everything that was proposed.

The frequent interjections of William Grayson formed a puzzle. He was against the Constitution, but more selectively than Mason or Henry. Often he seemed to be arguing for it. He credited the members of the Philadelphia convention with honest intent. "Although I do not approve," he declared, "of the result of their deliberations, I do not criminate or suspect the principles on which they acted." In the determination to protect their states, it was a misfortune that "they did not do more for the general good of America." Grayson's belief in the sincerity of the makers of the Constitution is worth noting in the light of much later accusation that the men at Philadelphia schemed selfishly to set up an overweening central power.

Edmund Pendleton was always a help in bringing the discussion back to actualities. He absolved the friends of the Constitution from

Henry's charge that they thirsted for a government of the "well-born." The distinction of economic classes in American politics was an unworthy invention of the enemies of a firm system. "I consider every man well-born," said Pendleton, "who comes into the world with an intelligent mind, and with all his parts perfect." Government was to serve not the fortunate, but the industrious and honest. He voiced the famous expectation, not then a shibboleth, that the poorest, by economy and effort, might rise to opulence. Was the law to be condemned if it encouraged and protected their success? The broad suffrage was the true defender of liberty, "far superior to paper bills of rights."

Pendleton ended by rejecting what became the final stand of opponents—that Virginia should not approve the Constitution until her demand for amendments was acceded to. This proposition was afterward examined in all its bearings, but Pendleton, at this point in the discussion, was sufficiently specific. Eight states had accepted the plan, were prepared to try the experiment, reserving modifications for the future as experience dictated. "Do gentlemen believe," Pendleton asked, "that, should we propose amendments as the *sine qua non* of our adoption, they would listen . . . ? I conceive . . . that they would not retract. They would tell us—*No, gentlemen, we cannot accept of your conditions . . . Your amendments are dictated by local considerations. We, in our adoption, have been influenced by considerations of general utility to the Union. We cannot abandon principles . . . to gratify you.*" Far better to drop hostility and embark with the rest, trusting to future changes which seemed useful. By quoting the exact words of Jefferson's letter, vaguely cited as supporting previous amendments, he showed that this distinguished Virginian cherished and would by no means imperil the prize of union of the states.

"Old Man River" in the Picture

Patrick Henry was not to be mollified. He wanted powers reserved to the people to be enumerated, not taken for granted because not delegated to Congress. He exemplified the old observation: when you want to discredit a reform you declare that it is against religion. Lacking a bill of rights, "Holy religion, sir, will be prostituted to the lowest purposes of human policy." From this impiety Henry went on to threaten a different trespass by Congress. Seven northern states were minded to shut the western settlers from transporting their products on the Mississippi river. Advocates of the Constitution were quick to say that

Henry, by this charge, was "scuffling for Kentucky votes." The complaint, once it was brought, got a thorough airing.

Monroe and Grayson, from their own knowledge in the Old Congress, reviewed the history of negotiations with Spain. Southern and northern states had both shifted ground on the issue. During the war the former, overrun by the enemy, sought and secured from Congress authority to relinquish navigation of the Mississippi for a term of years. They hoped that Spain, in return, would lend us money and acknowledge our independence. At this time the northern states opposed the concession. They believed that if the Mississippi was given up the southern states would not support northern rights in the Newfoundland fisheries, "on which their very existence depends." But once the war was won the situation was reversed. The shipping states, eager for a commercial treaty with Spain, were willing, even anxious, to thwart expansion of population and formation of new states in the West. Seven northern states, in disregard of the Articles of Confederation which said that no fewer than nine states could make a treaty, empowered the secretary for foreign affairs to relinquish the river as the price of commercial benefits for the upper seaboard. The southern states as stoutly objected.

Nothing came of all this. But opponents of the new government in the Virginia convention made capital of the accusation that the Constitution revived the danger to the western people. Why? Because two-thirds of senators present (representing at most seven states) could approve a treaty excluding those settlers, for twenty-five or thirty years, from the Mississippi. Thus the North would ensure its continued dominance of national councils.

Patrick Henry, introducing the Mississippi issue, had "sprung a mine" under the friends of the Constitution. Instantly debate took this turn, visitors packed the gallery. The Kentuckians were petitioning Congress to be admitted as a state, but if the new government might rob them of the river they might fling off from the Union. Their ties with the East were tenuous. We must remember that their huge district was more distant, in travel time, from Richmond, Philadelphia, or New York than is today the remotest spot in the world by airplane. More than once the convention had heard of the ability, and maybe the inclination, of the overmountain men to vindicate their rights against Spain. A dozen years before, at the start of the Revolution, in petitioning the Virginia legislature for a favor, they had impressed "how impolitical it would be to suffer such a respectable body of prime riflemen to remain in a state of neutrality." The original Scotch-Irish settlers, while always self-assertive, were disposed to be loyal. But now mixing in with them, loud and irresponsible, were many adventurers ready to exploit an explosive situation for their own ends. Some at the convention believed that if Patrick Henry and others succeeded in arousing Kentucky fears they would at once press for a vote on the Constitution and accomplish its rejection then and there.

Madison, Nicholas, and others repelled this sortie of the anti's. It was their admired Confederation which had threatened to surrender the Mississippi. The right to the river would be better secured by the strong government in prospect from the Constitution. Further, the "carrying [northern] states" were developing their own solicitude for western settlement. They would transport the agricultural products of the interior, and northerners as well as southerners were emigrating to that region. Madison was sure the House, with increasing numbers of representatives from the West, would oppose yielding navigation of the Mississippi. His argument was legitimate, but Patrick Henry attacked it. The House would have no part in treaty-making. This was true in strict interpretation of the Constitution. (In fact, the question whether the House could negative the Senate on a treaty remained in doubt for some years.) This discussion in the Virginia convention was another incident in the momentous rise of the West as a third great section of the nation, political as well as geographic.

Opponents of the Constitution objected to every feature of it. One would have supposed that provision for the militia would have been approved. Militia did not hold the menace of a standing army. The states were to appoint militia officers and train the militia according to rules of Congress. Only when called into national service, to suppress insurrection or repel invasion, was the militia under national orders. But Henry and Mason found peril in every part of this arrangement. Congress would neglect the militia to furnish an excuse for raising a regular army. Or, on the other hand, Congress would use the militia irresponsibly, hale them to distant quarters and deprive the states of self-protection. Congress clutched the purse and now was to be handed the sword. Friends of the Constitution (John Marshall in particular) emphasized that in a government springing from the consent of the people, power over the militia was one least likely to be abused. Much time was needlessly consumed in debating this item.

More extravagant were forecasts of tyrannies of President and Congress in the ten miles square which was to be the seat of the central government. This small spot, under unlimited national sway, was to become the refuge of scoundrels who would here embattle themselves.

Implied powers would be invoked to pervert the press, for hostile editors would be dragged to the national district to be tried without juries. Here "any man who shall act contrary to their commands . . . shall be hanged without benefit of clergy." Villains in the national government might in the ten miles square "keep a powerful army continually on foot . . . to aid the execution of their laws." The vivid recollection that Congress had been driven from Philadelphia by a mob five years before had prompted the sensible provision that national authority should police the capital. Nothing more was intended than safety for the functioning of government. But foes took fright at every gift of power. If power was absolute—over the national district, forts, and arsenals—all manner of evils would issue. These planters little knew that sixty years would pass before their slave-pens would be abolished in the capital city.

Mason was indignant because the slave trade had a twenty-year guarantee against interference by the national government. Then, contradicting this moral outburst, he protested because the Constitution gave "no security for the property of that kind [slaves] which we have already." The other side seized the invitation to discredit Mason's reasoning, and explained that limited permission for slave imports was the price of keeping far southern states in the Union under the new scheme. Which did Virginians choose, a temporary evil, or sure disruption of the nation?

Limits of Power of Congress

Shadow-boxing was put aside when debate focused on the scope of the authority of Congress. The right to pass laws "necessary and proper" to carry delegated powers into effect (what Henry called the "sweeping clause"), and the "general welfare" provision came under attack and were as vigorously defended. These seeds in the Constitution, as was apprehended by its enemies, have grown and flourished beyond others planted in the fundamental law. Patrick Henry and his friends contended that restrictions on the ability of Congress (to suspend *habeas corpus*, pass *ex post facto* laws, etc.) implied that other powers (which should have been explicitly reserved to the people of the states) were given without limit. The proper defense against this portentous latitude in the national government was to incorporate in the Constitution a bill of rights.

Supporters explained with precision the wording of the document. Here they were vindicating the draftsmanship of Gouverneur Morris, who had come to Richmond to advise friends of ratification. They protested that the "sweeping clause" bore no such interpretation. It granted no extra authority, but only the capacity to carry stipulated powers into effect by legislation "necessary and proper." In a constitution, as distinguished from a statute, not all could be defined in advance. Discretion must be allowed, so long as action was appropriate to the constitutional object. Randolph was wiser than colleagues in refusing to attribute to the word "necessary" the meaning of indispensable.

Equal dispute, then and since, attached to the welfare clause. Those for the Constitution showed that it did not vest "complete legislation" in Congress. Congress had not "an independent, separate, substantive power, to provide for the general welfare of the United States." Rather, Congress could "lay and collect taxes, duties, imposts, and excises, to pay the debts and provide for the common defence and general welfare. . . ." Congress could not adventure upon any project designed for the general welfare, but such a purpose must be subordinate to the authority to tax.

Time and changing circumstances have blurred the strict textual denotation. As the American people have come to look more and more to the national government for correction and promotion in the public interest, the welfare clause has been stretched. This is true in the common understanding, in decisions of the courts, and in the freedom exercised by Congress itself. Commitments of Congress have proved superior to commas in the Constitution. History has taken command of syntax. Through the years the Constitution has been warped to fit manifest new utilities, while the words as they were set down by Gouverneur Morris's pen have remained the same. The alternative was constant formal amendment which would have altered the document from its broad purpose. Amendments, in the absence of circumspect informal reinterpretation, would themselves have required amendment, as in many of the state constitutions, until the fundamental law was deformed.

Dissatisfaction over the mode of choosing the President led to ingenious conjectures and the calculation (by Grayson) that in a particular contingency a candidate might win by the votes of 2 state electors and 15 members of the House, a minority of 17 against a majority of 139. Friends of the system scouted the notion that this could ever happen, but, in the view of everyone, the business remained complicated, as indeed in practice it proved to be.

For visitors, and doubtless most members of the convention, the

dullest and longest discussion was on the federal judiciary, its impinge-
ment upon the state courts, and whether it violated accepted principles
of justice in the appellate jurisdiction. National courts formed a new
proposal, for the Confederation furnished no judiciary, except for admiralty courts. Further, the convention was replete with lawyers, technically equipped and eager to dispute. Madison, Randolph, Pendleton,
and Marshall were leading supporters, while the fight against was led
by Mason (though law, he said, "lies out of my line"), Grayson, and
Henry. After this full-dress encounter the remainder of the Constitution was gone through. Particular attention was given to the mode of
amendment prescribed in the document.

This brought the beginning of the end of the debates, for next
morning George Wythe, after a masterly little speech, introduced a
decisive resolution. He was one of the most esteemed members of the
convention, for he was professor of law in the College of William and
Mary, had taught many of the delegates, and had been elected chairman of the committee of the whole. The friends of the Constitution
could not have done better than choose him for their spokesman. If
one wants evidence, in brief compass, of how a superior mind operates,
reducing thought to language, let him read the single page of Wythe's
remarks. They are reported in substance, but the version is doubtless
correct. The glorious issue of the Revolution, he reminded, was poorly
served by defective Articles of Confederation "and the consequent misfortunes suffered by the people." The plan of a new government had
imperfections, but undenied excellence too. Try as the convention
might to amend beforehand, more amendments would be found necessary. "The extreme danger of dissolving the Union" recommended that
the Constitution be accepted in confidence that serviceable changes or
additions would be agreed upon later as experience dictated. The document itself provided the means of amendment, and other states were
favorable to corrections. "He then *proposed* that the committee *should
ratify the Constitution*, and that whatsoever amendments might be
deemed necessary should be recommended to the consideration of . . .
Congress." In all sincerity, and to sweeten his motion to opponents,
Wythe in his preamble recited the principles of a bill of rights, but
his proposal was definitely for trial first, and alteration afterward.

Patrick Henry's Last Stand

Immediately Patrick Henry was on his feet. He complained that
Wythe's motion was premature, as much remained to be mulled over.

The mention of only a couple of reserved rights implied that Virginia was prepared to forgo others. He heard of so much opposition to approval before changes were made that if Virginia adopted in mere anticipation of satisfactory amendments afterward she would actually promote discord. He offered his motion that the other states be asked to incorporate a bill of rights and other amendments (forty items in all) before Virginia would ratify the Constitution. Grayson repeated this demand, more moderately. He counted on New York and North Carolina to take the same stand, and the three, essential to the Union, would be received "with open arms" on their own terms. Virginia's importance alone was enough, for "Tobacco will always make our peace with them."

The final challenge had been sounded. The issue was touch and go. Grayson had written, "Our affairs in the Convention are suspended by a hair." And Madison reported to Washington, "The majority will certainly be very small, on whatever side it may finally lie; and I dare not encourage much expectation that it will be on the favorable side." As few of the delegates had expressed themselves on the floor, and no significant votes had been taken, the sentiment of the body was only to be guessed. Members from the frontier doubtless remained against the Constitution; others had been instructed by their districts to veto it. Most had come little informed, so the query was whether the few who would determine the outcome had been converted, one way or the other, by what they had heard in the convention.

Now was the moment for friends of the Constitution to persuade votes or, as they believed, forfeit salvation for the country. Randolph, Madison, and Nicholas stepped forward as champions. They had long readied themselves for the encounter. They showed, one by one through the list, that Henry's amendments were unnecessary, mischievous, or worse. Madison made a particular impression in demonstrating the futility of the project of bringing eight states, which had approved the Constitution, to reverse themselves. At best, they must call new conventions to deliberate on Virginia's demands. Many and diverse as these were, other states, pressing *their* local objections, would produce hopeless confusion.

At this time New Hampshire had not approved. If Virginia ratified, she would make the ninth state and usher the Constitution into effect. Nicholas, after a solemn appeal to ratify and rely upon amendments in the prescribed mode afterward, moved that George Wythe's resolution for this purpose should be put to a vote. John Tyler at once moved similarly for Henry's proposition of previous amendments. Supporting

Tyler, Benjamin Harrison declared that if Virginia ratified she need not expect later amendments. The little states had fashioned the plan to their liking and would refuse changes. Madison was quick to deny this charge. Harrison himself had shown that several ratifying states had recommended improvements. If Virginia followed their course, all that was desirable would be accomplished in an orderly way. Friends of the system would go along in this process. Randolph in a last word warned that, since eight states had approved, the question before Virginia was "*Union or no Union.*"

Wythe's motion (ratify and recommend desirable amendments) was twice read. This was temporarily set aside for Henry's substitute resolve (reject until alterations were made). Conditional adoption was voted down by a narrow margin, 88 to 80. In the fateful majority were only 3 of 14 Kentucky delegates. Then the main motion, to ratify, was carried, 89 to 79 (one David Patteson shifting his vote to aye). The victory was won. Henry's proposal for a bill of rights and other amendments—now recommended only—was accepted. Select committees reported a form for engrossing. Only one of Henry's wished-for amendments was thrown out. This would have refused Congress the power of direct taxation unless the states failed to fill requisitions.

III DRAMA IN NEW YORK

The New York convention that met in the court house at Poughkeepsie June 17, 1788, was critical for the success of the Constitution and the new Union. Eight states had ratified, and it was supposed that New Hampshire, whose convention reopened the same day, after an adjournment in which the Federalists had been industrious, would make the ninth necessary to inaugurate the national government. However, both Virginia and New York were essential to the Union. Delegates had been in session a fortnight at Richmond when the Poughkeepsie assembly commenced, but the outcome to the southward was doubtful. The prospect of approval in New York was drearier. There two-thirds of the members, almost the whole representation from upstate, under the command of Governor George Clinton, were against the Constitution, and confident of its swift rejection. In the Philadelphia convention, New York was the only state that opposed the document when it was being framed. Yates and Lansing, so long as they remained, cast the vote against essential provisions, leaving Hamilton powerless in his approval. When Yates and Lansing left the convention, New York had no vote, and Hamilton signed the Constitution, legally speaking, simply as an individual. Moreover, Yates and Lansing, in a letter to Governor Clinton, had advertised their antagonism to the reform. The "consolidation" worked out at Philadelphia invaded "the individual states in their uncontrolled constitutional rights," was not feasible for a country so extensive, and, they implied, the New York convention ought not to ratify it.

Even if Virginia came in, the Union could not prosper without New York. Her central position would divide New England from the middle and southern states. Her superior harbor, admitting to the great waterway of the Hudson, would be missed. If New England was cut off the British, already suspected of intriguing with insurgents in Vermont, might try to join the northeastern states to Canada.

The foes of the Constitution in New York were more formidable than those in the Virginia convention. Governor Clinton, chief enemy, brought both soldierly and political prestige to his chair as presiding officer. "A set of ignorant Dutchmen," as a critic called them, were entirely under his control. Melancton Smith, who was Clinton's majority leader on the floor, was a close reasoner in his arguments. We have mentioned the contrast in Virginia, where Edmund Pendleton, president of the convention, was a friend of the Constitution, as was also Governor Edmund Randolph. Principal attacker was Patrick Henry, but his impassioned charges were not so dangerous as the cold thrusts of Smith. George Mason in Virginia carried weight, but the opposition was less compact than in New York. The estimated majority against ratification was far smaller in Virginia than in New York. Virginia had a peculiar reason for approving the Constitution; her foremost citizen would surely be President when the new government was launched. On the other hand, George Clinton took prodigious pride in being governor of New York, and hated to lose any of his power by assenting to a superior national authority.

In spite of valiant men like Robert R. Livingston, John Jay, and James Duane, New York could not have been won to the Constitution except for the determined, resourceful leadership of Alexander Hamilton. He had exerted himself beforehand for the election of delegates who were favorable. More importantly, with Madison and Jay, he had published the *Federalist* essays—first in newspapers and then in book form—intended to persuade public opinion in New York and elsewhere to accept the Constitution. These papers were masterpieces, combining exposition and advocacy. If we wonder at the influence they exerted, we must remember that at that time those who read formed a far smaller proportion of the population than since, and they were content with frugal philosophical and political fare while we are distracted to subjects more sensational. Besides, discussions of impending momentous reorganization of their society commanded the attention of thinking men with property and liberty at stake.

Hamilton hoped that favorable news from the conventions in New Hampshire and Virginia would help to win over the New York delegates to the Constitution. He therefore arranged with President John Sullivan at Portsmouth and James Madison at Richmond to send him expresses (messages by relays of horsemen) if their states ratified, and he would pay the considerable cost of this service from his own pocket.

At the very start of the meeting in Poughkeepsie, Hamilton and Robert R. Livingston pressed through a motion without which New York would not have adopted the Constitution. The agreement was that the document should be discussed article by article and no vote would be taken until all had been debated. This prevented opponents from taking a swift summary view and rejecting the plan. The Clinton forces (against the Constitution, and in a vast majority in the convention) accepted this procedure because they did not want to be accused of precipitate action without real examination of the new government. They were sure they were strong enough to dismiss the scheme in the end no matter how long it was under consideration. After the motion was passed they were sorry they had consented to allow every part of the document to be explored, for this gave time to its friends to argue away fears. Also, while debate was protracted, other states might ratify, which would have an effect on the delegates at Poughkeepsie.

Each side formed strategy for presentation of its case. Chancellor Robert R. Livingston opened for the advocates of the new government. At the end of his speech he offered the resolve that the Constitution should be fully examined before any vote was taken, particular or general. In collaboration with Hamilton, he had prepared himself with care. His address—the manuscript of it is held by the New-York Historical Society—was a model of exposition and persuasion. He laid bare the shortcomings of the Confederation, showed why the central authority must be strengthened, and argued that New York could not preserve herself except by entering the closer union. Delegates should not demand perfection which, anyway, differed in the minds of different persons. Rather, embrace gratefully what was the practicable best. His object was to counter the specious plea that the Constitution should be rejected because it did not suit the views of everyone.

Since this convention was to decide the action of New York, he would show "from our particular situation . . . that our existence, as a state, depends on a strong and efficient federal government." This was shrewd, for state pride, he knew, pitted the heavy majority against the proposal for national consolidation. The assets of New York had "excited an improper confidence in ourselves; . . . produced an inflexibility, which has rendered us regardless of the . . . expectations of the other states . . ." Actually, Livingston showed, the very wealth of the state invited invasion; New York, in the absence of union, was helpless to defend herself. Vermonters, independent and ambitious, were ready to pounce from the northeast, and the British and Indians from the forts in the northwest.

The existing league (Confederation) had not been able to repel invaders, maintain domestic peace, support public credit, nor extend commerce. The "old Confederation was defective in its principle, and impeachable in its execution, as it operated upon states in their political capacity, and not upon individuals." The "common consent of America" must give to Congress not only the power of forming laws, but of "carrying them into effect" instead of entrusting execution to the individual states.

Livingston himself held one of the highest posts in the state government. Addressing himself to fellow delegates in magisterial positions —he had Governor Clinton chiefly in mind—he begged: "Let us, on this solemn occasion, forget the pride of office; let us consider ourselves as simple citizens, assembled to consult on measures that are to promote the happiness of our fellow-citizens."

First reply came from John Lansing, Jr., who had left the Philadelphia convention because it proposed a union too compact. He sought to counter the points made by Livingston. Throughout he cherished the authority of the individual state. There the interests of the people were better represented than in the general government. He did not expect perfection, but was sure the existing Confederation could be sufficiently amended without being superseded. For example, it would be enough to requisition the states, and extract money directly from individuals only after the requisition had not been complied with. If there was delay in the interval, Congress might borrow.

Misfortunes experienced were not due to the demerits of government, but to exhaustion from the war, followed by extravagant importations from Europe, which "contributed to embarrass and distress us." If the union, unless tightened, was destined to dissolve, New York would not stand alone and surrounded by enemies. Instead, New York would combine with friendly New England neighbors for an effective defense. He resented the Chancellor's charge that officeholders opposed the new government rather than lose their present importance.

Livingston was quick to explain, not convincingly, that he had not meant to attribute unworthy motives to state officers in the convention. He was better in answering the old proposal that Congress should tax citizens only after the state had refused to fill its requisition. This acknowledged that the Confederation was "totally incompetent to federal purposes." Further, how would the scheme operate? Revenue officers must be appointed. If the state complied punctually, the federal collectors were a useless expense. If the state proved delinquent, national officers must enter to coerce citizens in direct opposition to the local legislature. This must provoke internal disorder and finally self-destruction of the government.

Hamilton in Answer to Melancton Smith

Then came Melancton Smith in a speech that called for careful rejoinder. The question, he began, "was not whether the present Confederation was a bad one, but whether the proposed Constitution was a good one." Livingston himself had shown that "the intent of the Constitution was not a confederacy, but a reduction of all the states into a consolidated government." This was a radical change likely to destroy freedom. Smith held, in effect, that what was needed in America was not a new constitution, but a new conscience, an improvement in public behavior. Of course this retreat into the moral sphere begged the question, which was whether the structure of government now offered should be adopted in place of the old one.

The power of Congress threatened the liberties of the people because, instead of being confined to great national objects, "it extended to every thing dear to human nature." The plan of representation in Congress was a cause of quarrel. Slaves, with no will of their own, should not be included; he would consent to this only as a matter of necessary compromise. He ended by moving that the states should now have twice the number of representatives offered in the Constitution, and later one for every 20,000 of population until the House had 300 members.

Hamilton's turn was next. He was serious throughout. He regretted that opponents had accused Livingston of "having wandered in the flowery fields of fancy . . . I will not agree with gentlemen who trifle with the weaknesses of our country, and suppose that they are enumerated to answer a party purpose, and to terrify with ideal dangers. No. I believe these weaknesses to be real, and pregnant with destruction." He would never sacrifice our liberties, but would have the Constitution canvassed soberly to judge of the corrections it promised. He could not accept the "lurking favorite imagination" that the existing system could be amended to be safe and permanent. "We contend that the radical vice in the old Confederation is, that the laws of the Union apply only to states in their corporate capacity . . . Hence there have ever been thirteen different bodies to judge of the measures of Congress, and the operations of government [especially in seeking revenue] have been distracted by their taking different courses."

New York had complied fully with the requisitions, but most others had responded only partially or not at all. If this was to continue, New York was vulnerable. "This is a weak state . . . Your capital is accessible by land, and by sea is exposed to every daring invader; on the north-west you are open to the inroads of a powerful foreign nation." The salvation of New York was in a cemented union. "Sir, if we have national objects to pursue, we must have national revenues." A federal standing army to enforce requisitions would produce civil war, but without that the federal treasury would be without supplies and the government without support. "What . . . is the cure for this great evil? Nothing, but to enable the national laws to operate on individuals, in the same manner as those of the states do."

He was sustained by the belief that the more the new Constitution was explained, the more the reasons for it would appear. "The fundamental principle of the old Confederation is defective; we must totally eradicate . . . this principle before we can expect an efficient government." The compromise concerning the slaves was inescapable; as it was the price of union it was prudent. He put it in the best light possible. As to the number in the House, soon it would be as large as desirable.

Melancton Smith replied to Hamilton. He still complained that membership of the House was too few, for the clause of the Constitution did not compel Congress to prescribe one representative for every 30,000 of population of a state; it might set 40,000 or 50,000 or more, so long as each state had at least one member in the House. The smaller the number, the greater the tendency to compose the House of privileged persons, belonging to the "natural aristocracy" of "birth, education, talents, and wealth." This would exclude the solid yeomanry, who had not the vices of "the great," but were prudent, moderate, felt for the "common people" from constant contact and experience. The yeomanry should make the majority in the House. A small legislature was liable to corruption. Smith did the favorite arithmetic of those who feared conspiracies against the public. "The whole number, in both houses," he observed, "amounts to ninety-one; of these forty-six make a quorum; and twenty-four of those, being secured, may carry any point. Can the liberties of three millions of people be . . . trusted in the hands of twenty-four men? . . . Reason revolts at the idea."

However, Smith did not discredit all features of the new plan. The compromise including three-fifths of slaves in the representation he admitted must be accepted. The old Confederation "too much restricted the powers of the general goverment. "But now," he objected, "it is proposed to go into the contrary, and a more dangerous extreme —to remove all barriers, to give the new government free access to our pockets, and ample command of our persons . . ." Men wanting concentration of authority "are increasing; they have influence, talents, and industry. It is time to form a barrier against them." The barrier must be that of a broad democracy.

Hamilton resumed his argument. All features of a government, he reminded, could not be fixed in a paper constitution. If good principles were embodied, and actual administration was serviceable, the people would approve. He was trying to prevent imaginary defects from balking adoption. Thus the number of representatives was of small consequence beside "a train of prosperous events" which would win the confidence of the citizens. In the Massachusetts legislature were 300 representatives, in New York's, 65. Avoid a number manifestly too small, like 10, or unwieldy, like 1000, and approximate what promised to be useful. In the national legislature 91 men were sufficiently conversant with the general matters coming before them. It was unnecessary, as it was impossible, for them to know peculiarities of productions and habits in every state.

Those whom Melancton Smith had stigmatized as aristocrats were in fact men who were likely to be regarded by the voters as possessing merit. A rich man had no special claims under the Constitution. The people would place in office whom they chose. So long as "unbounded liberty" in popular election was preserved, tyranny was a fiction. The old Confederation, hastily framed while we were fighting off hated British domination, was so zealous for freedom in the abstract that government was left feeble. The people were now convinced of this, and would gladly embrace the proposed Constitution which afforded "genuine . . . representative and republican government, and . . .

will answer, in an eminent degree, all the beneficial purposes of society."

The exchanges between Hamilton and his friends on the one hand, and Smith, Clinton, and Lansing on the other illustrate what may be called the ordeal of the Constitution. It sprang from the fact of a written document specifying powers to be exercised and the mode of choosing those who were to govern. In proportion as the Constitution departed from the familiar Articles of Confederation it invited attack simply because it was new, aside from any question of its merits in correcting old errors and omissions. Once a fundamental law is in effect, a court interpretation of it, though significant, will be acceded to without major objection. A formal amendment to an operating scheme of government will be debated without risk to the validity of the whole. But when a comprehensive plan is presented, *de novo*, it provokes fears of how it may function. Often these misgivings are genuine, but other men, who for different reasons do not want a change, will put forward spurious objections. Thus Hamilton observed, "Events merely possible have been magnified, by distempered imagination, into inevitable realities; and the most distant and doubtful conjectures have been formed into a serious and infallible prediction." Hamilton and those of his persuasion were confident that once the Constitution was accepted, it would prove workable. The problem was to bring it to the point where its actual benefits would be manifest. The plan had been devised, after long effort, by able men of good will. Those who ardently wished its success, when they met the most violent antagonism in certain of the state conventions, were sustained by the trust that the body of the people would receive it gratefully and live under it happily.

Lansing at length announced that the opposition did not wish to dwell longer on the need for a larger House. It was time for this concession, as the committee of the whole had worn out the subject. But other members, for and against, worried it, like a dog with a bone. The Chancellor would have done better to keep his seat, for he had nothing to add to his satisfaction with the size of the House as it stood except a few barbs flung at his adversaries. He was inclined to be scornful and indulged his facility in language in this direction. It was unfortunate, for the favorite accusation of the upstate men, that the Constitution was made by and for aristocrats, seemed to be supported by Livingston's behavior. Undoubtedly Hamilton, who was trying mightily to confine the discussion to reason, squirmed when his colleague gave any cause for resentment and demagogic retort. John Jay smoothed Smith's ruffled feathers. Perhaps Hamilton, managing the support of the Constitution, prompted the cool Jay to interpose when he did.

Functions of the Senate

Finally, Gilbert Livingston, the Poughkeepsie lawyer who was to play a surprising part in the convention later, shifted attack to the Senate, which he believed was fatally vulnerable to corruption unless protections were introduced. He proposed an amendment, that no one could serve as senator more than six years in twelve, and that senators should be subject to recall by their states. Gilbert Livingston made a florid little speech and must have been embarrassed when the company guffawed at a comical mixed metaphor into which he led himself. A bright red vest of his (preserved at Newburgh, and which he may have worn this day) reminds of his colorful character. The objects of the amendment, as Lansing went on to point out, were to place senators at all times under control of their state legislatures, and to compel senators, after one term, to return to the body of their fellow citizens. Otherwise the Senate would be subject to corruption. Lansing, closing his defense of the amendment, illustrated the suspicion that was prominent in the minds of many. The community must be protected against its governors. In line with this, government must be purely negative. Thus, "Scruples would be impertinent, arguments would be in vain, checks would be useless, if we were certain our rulers would be good men; but for the virtuous government is not instituted; its object is to restrain and punish vice; and all free constitutions are formed with two views—to deter the governed from crime, and the governors from tyranny."

Richard Morris, Richard Harison (the admirable New York attorney), and Chancellor Livingston combated the proposal with arguments that received new force as elaborated by Hamilton. He and his colleagues had taken pains to claim, in favor of the Constitution, whatever their opponents conceded. These became bench-marks from which friends of ratification proceeded. Thus Richard Morris: "I am happy . . . to perceive that it is a principle on all sides . . . that an energetic federal government is essential to the preservation of our Union; and that a constitution for these states ought to unite firmness and vigor in the national operations, with the full security of our rights and liberties." This much established, Hamilton urged sanction of each provision, as it arose, without change. His remonstrance against

weakening the national loyalty of the Senate by making it amenable
to local state demands was among the most impressive of the convention. His earnest plea this day, after a week of sessions, helped win
the hostile majority to adopt essential reform. Weighty as was his
logic favoring each particular part of the new structure, his enforcement of the whole was yet more commanding. He conveyed to his
hearers his vision of the future stature of America if only the capacities
of the nation were released. He was the mastermind of the meeting,
confirming friends of the Constitution, sympathetically removing the
fears of those who doubted. No summary of what went forward can
picture his unremitting vigilance as an advocate. After years of effort
to procure a good frame of government he had assisted to work the
project along until now it was to be rejected or embraced by his own
state. Here at Poughkeepsie was an important crisis of his career and
of the career of his country. Happily, with valiant aid from others—
Livingston, Jay, Duane—his powers were equal to the demand.

He did not stigmatize; rather, the strength and sincerity of his own
appeal made shallow and disingenuous complaints appear unworthy.
"We all," he began, "profess to be anxious for the establishment of a
republican government on a safe and solid basis. It is the object of
the wishes of every honest man in the United States; and I . . . shall
not be disbelieved, when I declare that it is an object, of all others, the
nearest and most dear to my own heart. The means of accomplishing
this great purpose become the most important study which can interest
mankind." The Revolution was a death struggle against tyranny. "In
forming our Confederation ... . we . . . had no other view than
to secure ourselves from despotism. The object . . . deserved our utmost attention; but, sir, there is another object, equally important, and
which our enthusiasm rendered us little capable of regarding: I mean a
principle of *strength* and *stability* in the organization of our government, and *vigor* in its operations." Then he came to the defense of
the Senate. Firmness in our government required "some select body
. . . to correct the prejudices, check the intemperate passions, and
regulate the fluctuations, of a popular assembly." Such a body "should
be small . . . hold its authority during a considerable period, and
. . . have such an independence in the exercise of its powers, as will
divest it . . . of local prejudices." He went on to observe, with brave
candor, that "the body of the people, in every country, desire sincerely
its prosperity; but . . . they do not possess the discernment and stability necessary for systematic government. To deny that they are frequently led into the grossest errors by misinformation and passion,

would be a flattery which their own good sense must despise." He appealed to the example of the constitution of New York, in which a more prudent Senate was expected to countervail the "misguided . . . ignorance" and "sudden impulses" of the popular Assembly.

Our foreign affairs as a nation could not be conducted without the consistency which the Senate would supply. To make senators recallable was to make them dance to the tune of the state, which might act capriciously without knowledge of national policy. Men were too much afraid of danger to the states. "The state governments are essentially necessary to . . . the general system." If anything, they were apt to have too much influence on the national government.

Those who urged recall cited the existence of this power under the Confederation; they noted that while it was a salutary deterrent, it had not in fact been exercised. Hamilton was quick to show that the experience of a few years did not prove that senators would not be bidden home in future if the amendment was approved. If this had not happened under the existing government it was because it had been "difficult to find men who were willing to suffer the mortifications" of serving in a feeble central body. Republican government was apt to be too fluctuating. The Senate was designed to provide an element semipermanent and responsible. If the upper house was rendered anemic and tentative, "prejudices would govern the public deliberations, and passions rage in the counsels of the Union."

Lansing and Smith answered. Hamilton had made an impression. Lansing agreed that a purpose of two branches of the national legislature was to make one a check upon the other. Smith went farther and accepted in principle Hamilton's arguments for "the propriety of giving stability to the Senate." Having admitted so much, however, Smith went on to picture a perpetual Senate, engulfing the functions of the states, erasing local government. We must remember that Smith's anxiety to keep senators responsive to state desires had more plausibility then than since. It was supposed that the Senate would be sitting continuously. Senators would entrench themselves at the national capital, politically and physically, for life.

Plea for Requisitions Is Discredited

June 24 news was brought in an express dispatch from President John Sullivan to Hamilton: New Hampshire had ratified the Constitution. This made the ninth state to approve, and therefore the old Confederation was dissolved. Chancellor Livingston next day brought this prominently forward; "the circumstances of the country were greatly altered, and the ground of the present debate changed." Did New York dare to remain outside the new Union which was now a fact? Chief opponents declared they were not influenced by determination of the requisite number of states to establish the new national government. As New Yorkers they would persistently examine the Constitution and weigh the choice before their state. Smith brushed off the momentous event by saying he had long expected it, but his feelings were not affected. Lansing similarly would continue to fasten his attention on the rights of New York. "We acknowledge that our dissent cannot prevent the operation of the government: since nine states have acceded to it, let them make the experiment . . . We ought not . . . to suffer our fears to force us to adopt a system which is dangerous to liberty." Nor would Clinton be moved by "gloomy reflections upon the situation of the state."

Not only did skeptics continue to probe features of the Constitution as they were reached, but they brought forward amendments and amendments of amendments. Numbers of these changes, quite apart from the subjects they dealt with, were unsuitable because too detailed for a fundamental instrument of government. Also as proposed amendments multiplied it was obvious that foes of ratification planned only a conditional adoption by New York, perhaps pending a second constitutional convention in which alterations should be considered.

John Williams, from the far up-state counties of Washington and Clinton, introduced a restriction on the taxing power of Congress which had been a staple of debate in the Confederation. He grew eloquent on the certainty that Congress, providing for the general welfare, would claim every sort of revenue for the national government, starving the state treasuries. Congress if it chose could destroy the states. He therefore resolved that no excise should be imposed on any article of the growth or manufacture of the United States; that Congress should not lay direct taxes unless proceeds of import duties and excises proved insufficient, and not then unless a state had refused to fill the requisition upon it. Melancton Smith took a fresh breath to defend this proposal. He tried to exculpate the states in their record of faulty response to requisitions under the old system. Two-thirds of the amounts required by Congress had been paid.

Chancellor Livingston rebutted this demand. Requisitions—"these pompous petitions for public charity"—had brought little cash into the treasury. New York would be the theater of any future war on America. "If we form this Constitution so as to take away from the Union the means of protecting us, we must, in a future war, either be ruined by the enemy, or ruined by our exertions to protect ourselves." The fact was that the Constitution gave Congress no exclusive power of laying taxes except in a few cases. The national and state taxing powers were concurrent.

In the face of such charges that the Constitution plotted a despotism over the states, Hamilton almost lost patience. He explained the protections which were carefully built into the plan, and then solemnly admonished: ". . . what do gentlemen mean by . . . declaiming against this government? Why do they say we ought to limit its power, to disable it, and to destroy its power of blessing the people? Has philosophy suggested, has experience taught, that such a government ought not to be trusted with every thing necessary for the good of society? Sir, when you have divided and nicely balanced the departments of government; when you have strongly connected the virtue of your rulers with their interest; when, in short, you have rendered your system as perfect as human forms can be,—you must place confidence; you must give power." He hoped to hear no more of idle accusations that Congress must be corrupt and menace the very existence of the states. The duties that must be performed by the central government were vaster than those within the purview of the states. It was not prudent or possible to draw a line beyond which Congress must not go in commanding the resources of the country. The national government could not borrow unless it could exact revenue with which to pay its debts. To compel the government to ask for means instead of empowering it to possess them in case of need was "to destroy all confidence and credit."

The states were in his view "absolutely necessary to the system." They should tax for their objects concurrently with Congress for its objects. The states formed to the national legislature "an indispensable support, a necessary aid in executing the laws, and conveying the influence of government to the doors of the people." Those devoted to the integrity of the state (New York) must not conjure up fanciful fears. "When we leave common sense," Hamilton warned, "and give ourselves up to conjecture, there can be no . . . security in our reasonings."

Next day Hamilton, in co-operation with James Duane, introduced telling reminders of the dismal defects of the system of requisitions which their opponents would retain in recruiting revenue for the national government. This was in the form of New York official documents of the Revolution complaining of the failure of sister states to respond to the requests of Congress for funds. One was a message of Governor Clinton, others were resolves -of the legislature. They condemned the present apologists of requisitions out of their own mouths. Naturally, Clinton and his friends objected to having them read without certain explanations that would temper the effect, but they did not have their way and the embarrassing evidence was presented. These cries of distress of New York showed "that requisitions have been unable to draw forth the resources of the country; that requisitions have been the cause of a principal part of our calamities; that the system is defective and rotten, and ought forever to be banished from our government." Hamilton taxed Governor Clinton with having refused to grant the Old Congress an independent income (through import duties) because he would not consent to the only method of collection which Congress declared was feasible. These proofs cut the ground from under Clinton and his cohort. They stood convicted of urging now a method of support of the national government which they themselves earlier had condemned.

Federalists Afraid To Risk Vote on Ratification

Of course Hamilton and his friends in the Poughkeepsie convention were constantly appealing to the interest of New York state. They pointed out that the proposal to forbid Congress to lay excises on American manufactures would actually increase the federal burdens of New York. This was because New York had less industry than several of its neighbors, and consequently, in a selfish view, would wish to see manufactures an object of taxation by the central government.

In closing this speech, Hamilton begged to be forgiven if, in the warmth of debate, he had uttered criticisms that offended opponents. He went on to discredit the charge that the Constitution was being urged by men who meant "to derive peculiar advantages" from it. He knew no such set of men. Were there any, he would not be among them. "If, to-day, I am among the favored few, my children, to-morrow, may be among the oppressed . . . suffering the . . . distresses to which my ambition has reduced them." His statement is to be remembered, first because he rejected the accusation that the Constitution was contrived by men who wished to protect their wealth and privileges, and second because his own devotion to public service did, in fact, impoverish his family.

Lansing, who was always in the forefront of the battle against the Constitution, replied that Hamilton was too sanguine when he declared that the states would fill an important role in the new system. Lansing believed that "if you do not give the state governments a power to protect themselves [against federal taxation], if you leave them no other check upon Congress than the power of appointing senators, they will certainly be overcome . . ." The states and Congress must be hostile to each other. He charged that Hamilton, in the Philadelphia convention, was convinced of this "and argued, with much decision and . . . plausibility, that the state governments ought to be subverted . . ." Hamilton immediately interrupted to deny that he was guilty of this contradiction, and the "personal dispute" between them consumed the remainder of this day and most of the next. Melancton Smith came in at the end of this altercation to explain that his conduct (in distinction to Hamilton's) "had been uniform and consistent." Throughout he had "objected to this Constitution, because it gave too much power to the general government, however it might be organized."

Duane took the floor to reinforce the proofs that "requisitions had ever had . . . fatal operation . . . would never answer the purposes of government, and . . . the principle ought to be forever discarded from our system." Requisitions could not serve in the emergency of war, nor maintain the large armies and navies which this country would one day require. John Jay as usual was thoughtful and tried to conciliate with realism. This was welcome, but Smith still accused friends of the Constitution of using extreme arguments. The states, he assured, though opposed to forms of federal taxation, would never combine against the Union. (He could not guess that within fifty years South Carolina nullifiers were to attempt this in protest against import duties.)

Chancellor Livingston, with "a luxuriancy of fancy which [he] is famous for," poured sarcasm on debaters of the other side. They contradicted themselves and each other. Instead of examining serious problems, they were like "children making bubbles with a pipe." His "torrent of illiberality" riled his kinsman, Gilbert Livingston, and equally so Williams, who had moved the amendment to check the taxing powers of Congress. He concluded that the Chancellor's ridicule might excite laughter, "but, trust me, sir . . . will . . . instead of frightening, be considered with contempt." Melancton Smith, also, was stung because the Chancellor made sport of him "to the no small entertainment of the ladies and gentlemen without the bar." (The galleries were daily crowded, we know from other sources, by onlookers attracted by the spirited exchanges of debaters on the floor.) Smith in his fencing made a touch, a palpable touch. The Chancellor had been sure that Hamilton's "reasoning was so conclusive that it seems to have carried conviction to every mind." Smith replied that whether the members "have received conviction can easily be settled by a vote." At this stage of the debates Smith knew, and friends of adoption knew, that if the temper of the convention was now tested the Constitution would be rejected by New York.

News Received That Virginia Had Ratified

Governor Clinton was speaking a little after noon on July 2, when he was interrupted by "a buz through the House." A dispatch rider had dismounted before the door—he had covered the eighty-two miles from New York in less than ten hours, changing horses only twice—and handed in to Hamilton momentous news. A letter from Madison and a certificate from the president of the convention at Richmond showed that Virginia had ratified the Constitution. This meant that New York, if she refused, would be isolated, for North Carolina was expected to follow Virginia's example, and even the obstinate Rhode Islanders would be bound to come in. One would think that Virginia's acceptance of the Constitution decided the issue in New York. Perhaps so, but four more weeks of arduous argument at Poughkeepsie were necessary before a slender majority could be won for ratification. In the end the fear of Clinton's upstate delegates that the southern counties would break away and join the Union may have been decisive.

For a time the convention went along much as before. Jay summarized the reasons for adoption, while Tredwell with flourishes proclaimed at length that "a union upon the proposed plan is certain destruction of liberty." Thereafter, as successive articles were read, opponents offered more than two dozen amendments that could have cluttered up the Constitution, if indeed they did not cripple it fatally. Evidently to digest this mass of material the convention adjourned business for two days. Lansing had presented a bill of rights, and soon rearranged the amendments in three groups. Some of these explained New York's understanding of certain parts of the Constitution, others set conditions on which the state would ratify, and final ones recommended changes which it was hoped would be made.

John Jay moved that the Constitution be ratified. His only concession to opponents was that the convention should state its construction of doubtful clauses and should recommend any useful amendments for later adoption. Debates on this for several days were brisk. Then Melancton Smith offered an amendment to Jay's resolution, making ratification conditional. Until a second general convention should be called to consider alterations in the Constitution, New York militia should not be continued in service outside the state for more than six weeks, Congress should not interfere with the state election procedure, and no direct tax should be laid in New York unless a requisition of Congress had been refused.

Hamilton laid before the convention Madison's opinion that New York could not be received into the Union with the right to withdraw if stipulated conditions were not met. A committee appointed to "fix on some accommodating scheme for an adoption" got nowhere. Hamilton made an impassioned plea for outright ratification. If New York was to join the Union the convention could do no more than recommend changes in the Constitution. Hamilton's earnestness sent a "murmur of admiration" through the hall. Some were coming over to his view. However, Clinton was implacable as ever, but tried to throw the blame on "the advocates of the Constitution [who] are determined to force us to a rejection." For himself, he would risk civil war rather than vote for unqualified ratification. Moreover, foes of adoption downed, two to one, a proposal that the convention adjourn for an interval to allow delegates to consult their constituents. Friends of the Constitution urged that this would be proper, since it was now certain that the new government would be launched, and the people might demand that New York adhere. Refusal to adjourn to test public opinion was taken as a confession of weakness on the part of Clinton's forces.

Actually, principal enemies of adoption were prepared to change sides. Melancton Smith moved that the Constitution be ratified "in confidence" that amendments "will . . . receive an early consideration." Samuel Jones bettered this by proposing that Lansing's "words *upon condition* should be obliterated, and the words *in full confidence* should be substituted in their stead." Smith, who had been the stoutest champion of the opposition, recanted. Until Virginia ratified he had hoped New York could force amendments before the Constitution went into effect. Now he was satisfied that this was impossible. New York must make sure of being received into the Union, otherwise he foresaw convulsions in the state. He still believed the Constitution was defective, but would work for amendment in the way prescribed in the document itself. His party, if it demanded alterations beforehand, would "be dispersed like sheep on a mountain." He begged those who had stood with him "to vote against any proposition which would not be received as a ratification of the Constitution."

Immediately some of his vocal followers echoed his decision. Gilbert Livingston had decided to abandon his prejudice for his duty. Only the conviction that he must serve his country by voting New York into the Union persuaded him to "differ from so many of my friends on this floor." Judge Zephaniah Platt, also of Poughkeepsie, was of similar mind. These defections were a blow to Governor Clinton, but he declared that he would never shift his ground. His constituents of Ulster County would not approve unless the rights of the state were first protected. He would vote against unconditional adoption.

However, the tide had turned. The motion to ratify "in full confidence" that the Constitution would be corrected passed by the narrow margin of 31 to 29. This was July 23, 1788. Lansing, faithful to Clinton's leadership, made yet another effort (still in committee of the whole) to escape irrevocable ratification. He moved that New York should reserve the right to withdraw from the Union if after blank years the amendments had not "been submitted to a convention in the mode prescribed in . . . the Constitution." Hamilton, Jay, the Chancellor, and Duane fought this, begged for harmonious approval, and Lansing's expedient was rejected, 31 to 28. This was decisive. All that remained was for the convention as such to adopt the report of the committee of the whole, which it did by a slightly larger majority, 30 to 25. The friends of the Constitution, determined that New York must be brought into the new Union, had won what long seemed a hopeless contest. After five weeks of struggle, an overwhelming opposition had been converted to a bare margin for ratification. American public life has witnessed few superior achievements of reasoning and patriotism.

The victors could afford to be magnanimous; they moved that Governor Clinton send a circular letter to the legislatures pressing for a general convention to consider amendments that had been proposed. Jay, Lansing, and Smith drafted this appeal. (No second constitutional convention was held, but amendments, comprising a bill of rights, were adopted in the manner laid down in the Constitution.)

Chapter Five

AFTERTHOUGHTS

The "Bill of Rights," comprised in the first ten amendments, is perhaps the best known, most cherished feature or portion of the Constitution.* The reasons for this are several and plain. These guarantees of civil liberties have the most ancient lineage in Anglo-Saxon polity, commencing before Magna Carta of 1215. These protections and immunities of citizens are thought of as absolute and moral, and not —like the remainder of the Constitution—expressions of governmental policy. They most closely concern the individual person; they proclaim his dignity, his equality with all others in the society. Thus, at bottom, they define democracy, the origin of government in the consent of the governed. They are rights, retained by the citizen though power over him in other respects is assigned to his political representatives or rulers. This part of the Constitution is readily visualized as separable from the rest; it has acquired its own name.

The question at once arises, why was not this vital section embodied in the document as framed at Philadelphia and presented to the people for adoption? Why did these essentials have to be added after the Constitution went into effect? Why did wise and informed men, during months of anxious discussion in constructing the fundamental law, fail to embrace provisions for which there was general popular demand immediately the plan was unveiled? Why did chosen representatives of the people so miscalculate the people's wishes?

Numerous answers became evident in the fierce debates in the state conventions and in the essays on the Constitution, pro and con, when

* The text of the Constitution appears on pages 373-93.

it was submitted for approval. Men like Madison, Hamilton, Wilson, and Gouverneur Morris, confronted by objectors, explained that the omission of a bill of rights as such was not due to a blind spot in the majority at Philadelphia. First, the federal Constitution was one of stipulated powers, proceeding from the people in the states. The assumption was that authority not delegated was reserved. Consequently, if basic rights, not given to the central government, were to be defined, they should be looked for in the constitutions of the states. Here in fact, in all states except one, New Jersey, such solemn declarations existed, though not in all cases as a formal part of the constitution of government. Thus citizens had already protected their most precious freedoms of religion, speech, press, assemblage, proper trial on alleged offenses, immunity from cruel and unusual punishments, unwarranted searches and seizures, and the like. A state constitution, "which has the regulation of every species of personal and private concerns" was the correct place for "a minute detail of particular rights." This was not suitable in the federal Constitution, "which is merely intended to regulate the general political interests of the nation."

Second, and nevertheless, the Constitution did contain, explicitly, appropriate ones of the protections contended for, including *habeas corpus*, trial by jury in criminal cases, strict definition of treason, prohibition of *ex post facto* laws and of titles of nobility. It would not have been fitting to forbid, in the federal instrument, other abuses, "For why declare that things shall not be done which there is no power to do? Why, for instance, should it be said that the liberty of the press shall not be restrained, when no power is given by which restrictions may be imposed?" Artful legislators might claim that the very prohibition implied authority to regulate the press (or religion), and thus what was to be protected might be invaded. From another motive the national Constitution did not require jury trial in civil cases; no single procedure could be set up, for practices differed in the states, and juries were commonly not used in equity and admiralty causes.

These, and other reasons, were not afterthoughts, put forward as excuses for the Constitutional Convention. As noted earlier, civil rights were discussed at Philadelphia, and certain delegates—George Mason and Luther Martin especially—had vainly made particular point of including them. Most members felt no compulsion to do so and perhaps for a reason which nobody put into words. The convention busied itself to replace the feckless Confederation with a competent government; concern was with giving powers, not denying them. The framers at Philadelphia conceived their mandate to be political, not ethical. In fashioning a system they guarded abundantly against internal abuses, as by building in checks and balances of one branch against another, and making sure that direct taxation should be geared to representation. These precautions were for functional excellence, and did not defend against possible invasion of deepest human rights. It must be remembered that they felt less obligation to incorporate civil liberties since the Articles of Confederation contained no such category of protections. Also, the framers recalled that the great English monuments in this department—Magna Carta, and the Bill of Rights accepted by William and Mary in 1689—limiting the power of sovereigns, were extracted from monarchs. The men at Philadelphia were expressing the authority of the people themselves. Should these fear self-tyranny?

Popular Demand for Bill of Rights

But many of the citizens, perhaps a majority, when the Constitution was at length presented to them, made no such historical distinctions. They had been kept in ignorance of what was going forward in the convention hall, and now could have their say. Confronted for the first time with the prospect of a central government of positive powers, their impulse was to be cautious if not suspicious. Obliged to decide on a complicated structure of government, novel too, it was easier to say no than to agree. "Rather bear those ills we have than fly to others that we know not of." Many came to the state conventions ignorant of what the Constitution contained. Of those who sent them, a larger proportion depended on vague report. Furthermore, numbers who opposed the Constitution on other grounds chose to plead the omission of a bill of rights. The states would surrender sovereignty, lands would be heavily taxed, northern shipowners would secure the monopoly of southern agricultural exports, property in slaves was threatened. Complaint of absence of a bill of rights served as stalking-horse for these misgivings.

But more were entirely sincere in deploring the failure of the Constitution to defend basic freedoms in so many words. At worst these prohibitions could do no harm, and might be expected to work much safety. America had recently, in the Revolution, freed itself from certain concrete oppressions by a distant government, and these should not be allowed to creep in again by any eventuality. The Declaration of Independence, while not a bill of rights, carried the approved aura in its phrases—"life, liberty, and the pursuit of happiness," "free and equal." "Unalienable rights" had the highest sanction. In a professing age these proceeded from what the Continental Congress of 1774 called "the immutable laws of nature." God's law was before man's laws. Massachusetts townsmen rejected a state constitution because it did not "describe the Natural Rights of Man as he inherits them from the Great Parents of Nature, distinguishing those, the Controul of which he may part with to Society for Social Benefits from those he cannot." What else is revolution but the collective upsetting of secular law in vindication of inborn personal rights?

Most of the state constitutions, formed during the war, were prefaced or accompanied by a bill of rights. Running back to English examples, and borrowing from the philosophy of John Locke, the most influential of these documents was the Virginia Declaration of Rights framed by George Mason. This became almost the copybook for other states, though several made additions to Mason's enumeration. Also Jefferson's Bill for Establishing Religious Freedom, adopted by the Virginia legislature in 1787, and the bill of rights in the Northwest Ordinance of the next year, were fresh in men's minds.

When the Constitution was formed and published, James Madison considered that it contained sufficient protections to personal liberties. Nevertheless, the first ten amendments, embracing the "Bill of Rights," are directly owing to his persistent efforts in the opening session of the new national Congress. Madison was beaten in Virginia for a Senate seat by notable objectors to the Constitution as adopted, William Grayson and Richard Henry Lee. This was through the enmity of Patrick Henry, who continued his hostility by supporting Monroe against Madison for a place in the House of Representatives on the Anti-Federalist ticket. Madison, detained in New York, returned to Virginia for the campaign barely in time to overcome the charge that he was opposed to any amendments and would do nothing in Congress to obtain them. These damaging insinuations were directed to the Baptists and other independent sects (Madison's friends), who were insistent on a guarantee of religious freedom. Madison quieted these fears, and in the process of his promises was himself convinced that popular demand for additional defenses of the citizen against the powers of government was deep and must be satisfied.

He early brought the subject forward in Congress, but suffered postponement. In June 1789 he would wait no longer, but moved that the House go into committee of the whole on amendments to the Constitution. This he felt himself "bound in honor and in duty to do." It was necessary to show constituents who had amendments "much at heart" that the House was making a beginning to this end. ". . . it would have been of advantage to the Government if it had been practicable to have made some propositions for amendments the first business we entered upon; it would have stifled the voice of complaint, and made friends of many who doubted the merits of the Constitution."

He met a barrage of objections, some from those who craved no amendments, more from members who agreed they were desirable, but ought to be deferred to later discussion. Should the Constitution be overhauled before it was fairly in operation? It could not be known what changes were expedient until the new plan had been tested. Congress must not be interrupted in the initial task of setting up the government, providing immediate revenue, and organizing departments. Already duties on the spring importations had been forfeited because a collection system was not in readiness. The plea that Congress should not be distracted from pressing practical problems was sincere and legitimate. However, the inconvenience of halting to consider amendments at that juncture would not have appeared so evident if objectors had paid stricter attention to the small budget of alterations and additions to the Constitution which Madison proposed. The "farrago," as one called it, of amendments called for by Virginia, and by New York, had been introduced earlier and provoked fear that debate on them would occupy weeks, months, or, according to Jackson of Georgia, a year!

Bill of Rights Introduced by Madison

Madison, ever systematic, had collated the recommendations of the several state conventions, and chose to present a few of them. But the body of his resolutions came from the Virginia Declaration of Rights composed by George Mason. What Madison offered was substantially the first ten amendments as we have them, plus a few proposals which did not survive the legislative process and eventual action by the states. They concerned almost exclusively civil liberties; they were precautionary, and made few changes in provisions of the Constitution as it stood. Madison declared, in support of his resolutions, that rights could be protected "without endangering any part of the Constitution, which is considered as essential to the existence of the Government by those who promoted its adoption."

But many of his hearers were alarmed by the prospect of protracted debate on what Madison did not include—the multiplicity of amendments proffered by the states and that might be hatched in Congress. Gerry had refused to sign the Constitution without amendments, but was now positive "that the salvation of America depends upon the establishment of the Government, whether amended or not." However, if amendment was to be broached, it would not be enough "to consider of a few propositions brought forward by an individual gentleman" (Madison). The whole matter must be entertained at large. Jackson of Georgia lamented that the system of essential operative laws was incomplete, "And how long it will remain in such a situation, if we enter upon amendments, God only knows . . . We are not content with two revolutions in less than fourteen years; we must enter upon a third, without necessity or propriety."

Thus urged, Madison consented that his rights resolutions be referred to a select committee (Vining of Delaware, Sherman of Connecticut, and himself). Then more delay in which the select committee was enlarged to embrace a member from each state, with Vining still chairman. With some maneuvering, Madison's proposals, not improved, plus some urged by state conventions, were got before committee of the whole. Here the question was whether the amendments, if sanctioned by the House, should be interwoven in the Constitution, thus altering the form, and to a degree the substance, of that document, or simply added in a block. Both procedures found supporters. The first would be an intricate task, would sacrifice the wording of the Constitution as originally ratified, and as more changes were introduced later, confusion would be worse confounded. Yet Madison himself, strangely, was for this expedient.

Others argued forcibly that any amendments should be merely supplementary, and the Constitution, left intact, could be interpreted in the light of amendments grouped to themselves. Vining, begging that amendments be kept separate, pictured the exasperation that would result from unending internal alterations. "He had seen an act entitled an act to amend a supplement to an act entitled an act for altering part of an act entitled an act for certain purposes therein mentioned. If gentlemen were disposed to run into such jargon in amending and altering the Constitution, he could not help it; but he trusted they would adopt a plainness and simplicity of style . . . which should be easily understood." Another of the same mind advised "the original Constitution ought to remain inviolate, and not be patched up, from time to time, with various stuffs resembling Joseph's coat of many colors."

It was pointed out that the English constitution is a succession of documents, not an integrated whole. This discussion involved more than form. It took its energy from the difference of purpose in members of Congress as they expressed their own preferences or reflected the pleas of their constituents. Should the Constitution be changed in essentials—basis of representation, power of direct taxation, procedure of the judiciary, and much more—or should amendments be confined to certain prohibitions? Among those favoring the first method lurked numbers who were essentially hostile to the Constitution; those content with a supplemental protection of rights were prepared to support the new system once their distrust on fundamental points was removed.

Debate in Congress

Vining, chairman of the special committee reporting desirable amendments; Madison, the original proposer; Gerry and others urged that changes be written into the body of the Constitution; this method was at first accepted. Debate commenced in committee of the whole on the merits of the several propositions.

The first was that in the preamble, after the words "We, the people," be inserted "Government being intended for the benefit of the people, and the rightful establishment thereof being derived from their authority alone." Promptly Smith of South Carolina and Gerry of Massachusetts wanted the wording altered. Gerry objected that most governments are not instituted for the benefit of the people; he would qualify the statement by inserting "of right." Others thought the amendment unnecessary. Tucker observed that the preamble was not a part of the Constitution; if the principle contended for was important, put it into a bill of rights. Madison admitted that it might be tautological or self-evident, though "it appears important in the estimation of three states, that this solemn truth be inserted in the constitution." Sherman considered the statement gratuitous. "The people," he observed wryly, "have given their reasons for doing a certain act. Here we propose to come in and give them a right to do what they did on motives which appeared to them sufficient to warrant their determination." Evidently for the sake of playing safe the amendment was accepted.

The second proposal was to insure a larger representation in the House (a change in Art. I, sec. 2, par. 3). Instead of "The number of representatives shall not exceed one for every thirty thousand, but each state shall have at least one representative," the provision should read, "after the first enumeration, there shall be one representative for every thirty thousand, until the number shall amount to one hundred. After which the proportion shall be so regulated . . . that the number of representatives shall never be less than one hundred, nor more than one hundred and seventy-five; but each State shall always have at least one representative." This proposal produced a sharp clash between members from Massachusetts. Ames argued that one representative for 40,000 was preferable because "in proportion as you increase the number of representatives, the body degenerates . . ." If choice is in larger districts "nothing but real dignity of character can secure an election." If the House is larger there "will be an excitement and fermentation in the representative body." Gerry in reply made a demagogic speech. Ames, he charged, was bent on keeping his official importance "at the risk of the liberties of America."

Madison did not mollify Ames by reminding that several states demanded more representatives. Also if passions were more rife in a larger body, it would be less a prey to venality and corruption. Ames was swift in answer. It was not the function of Congress to recommend changes because states wanted them; otherwise why not propose the entire undigested list of what the various conventions had put forward? All local information necessary "was to be found as fully among the ten members from Massachusetts, as if there had been one from every town in the State." Stone of Maryland countered Ames with arithmetic. If the House had only 100, a quorum would be 51, a majority of the quorum 26. Add 7 senators and 33 men could give law to the United States. Ames's restriction of the size of the House was easily voted down. Sedgwick wanted the maximum pushed up to 200, and with this alteration the amendment was carried. (Actually, as we shall see, the discussion was abortive because the proposal was not ratified by the states.)

The third proposition was to prevent members of the House from raising or reducing their own pay, since "no law varying the compensation shall take effect, until an election of representatives shall have intervened." (The change was to be in Art. I, sec. 6). The likelihood of a cut in legislative wages has not often excited alarm, but our ancestors could be suspicious. Sedgwick feared two dangers in the practice. The representatives might lower their salaries to prevent poorer men from serving. Or they might do it to court popularity. His subtle apprehensions were not shared; the proposal was approved, though, like that enlarging the House, finally it was not ratified.

The committee of the whole then moved into what became, with minor modifications, the Bill of Rights. Farther down in Article I, section 9, among the prohibitions on Congress should be inserted, "no religion shall be established by law, nor shall the equal rights of conscience be infringed." This was greeted with divergent reactions. A New York member feared it might have a tendency to abolish religion altogether, and Huntington of Connecticut hoped the amendment would not "patronize those who professed no religion at all." Sherman of the same state, always for keeping the Constitution terse, declared the precaution was superfluous. Congress had no delegated power to make religious establishments. Strike the amendment. But others cried down the objectors. Carroll—Maryland being tolerant of different faiths—supported the many sects who contended the rights of conscience were not well secured by the Constitution as it stood. This protection "would tend more towards conciliating the minds of the people to the Government than almost any other amendment he had heard proposed." Madison, who had befriended Baptists and other dissenters, reverted to the argument of some state conventions. Might not Congress, under the power to make all laws necessary and proper to carry the Constitution into execution, infringe rights of conscience? Why not at least forbid establishing any "national" religion?

This last precipitated the committee into the familiar contest between the concept of a federal as opposed to a consolidated or national government. Gerry was for preserving a larger measure of state authority. He observed that all along the Federalists had been for ratifying the Constitution as it was, the Anti-Federalists for amendments first. Their party names were ambiguous. They should have been called the rats and the anti-rats. After this quip the committee approved a slightly altered wording: "Congress shall make no laws touching religion, or infringing the rights of conscience."

Freedom of Speech and Assembly

The next clause of the fourth proposal, since treasured for itself, led the committee into a bypath. The provision was "The freedom of speech and of the press, and the right of the people peaceably to assemble and consult for their common good, and to apply to the government for a redress of grievances, shall not be infringed." Sedgwick would edit by striking out "assemble and." To speak freely implied the right to assemble. Benson thought that speaking and assembling were separable. Both were inherent rights, to be defended against invasion by government. Sedgwick came back with a *reductio ad absurdum*.

Inherent rights made a long list. Why did not the committee declare a man should have a right to wear his hat, get up, go to bed when he pleases? Government did not intend to violate the right of free speech and press.

Gerry and Page reproved Sedgwick for trifling with a serious matter. They showed foresight in predicting that government might deny the liberty of assemblage on specious pretexts. Vining considered the precaution was harmless; if it would gratify the states that urged it, he would not object. Hartley quoted conventions of Pennsylvania and other states that recommended a sweeping prohibition. He would include words that later were accepted: "all the rights and powers that were not given to the Government were retained by the States and the people thereof." Sedgwick's motion to prune the amendment by omitting freedom of assemblage was lost by a large majority.

Then the committee explored the bypath. Tucker moved to insert, as an adjunct of free assemblage, freedom of the people to instruct their representatives in the House. Both Virginia and North Carolina had wished this. Page asked, why should people consult if they may not instruct? Instruction and representation go together. Gerry called instruction an expression of popular sovereignty. Hartley of Pennsylvania was opposed. Congress would be the best judge of measures. If all representatives came with varying instructions and followed them, "what possibility would . . . exist of accommodating each to the other . . . to produce any act whatever?" Instructions, said Jackson, would often put the representative in a quandary, for he must obey his constituents and break his oath to uphold the Constitution, or follow his conscience and disregard his clientele.

Madison saw the error of cluttering the amendments; let us "confine ourselves to an enumeration of simple, acknowledged principles," for then "ratification will meet with but little difficulty." Lugging in the doubtful device of instructing members of Congress would "prejudice the whole system." The representative may know what his constituents do not know. Gerry had asked whether sovereignty did not lie with the people at large. Madison turned this against him. "Does he infer that the people can, in detached bodies, contravene an act established by the whole people? My idea of the sovereignty of the people is, that the people can change the constitution if they please; but while the constitution exists, they must conform themselves to its dictates. But I do not believe that the inhabitants of any district can speak the voice of the people; so far from it their ideas may contradict the sense of the whole people," and if delivered as instructions to their delegates would be "of a dangerous nature." This was correct doctrine, but ironically Madison was one of the first to contradict it, for within a few years he was penning the Virginia resolution (provoked by the Alien and Sedition Acts) defying the national authority.

Smith from South Carolina pointed out that if members of the House were to be instructed, one from a state would be enough, yet yesterday men contended for a numerous representation. Stone considered that a system of instructions would change the representative government "to a democracy, wherein all laws are made immediately by the voice of the people," as in a Swiss canton. This would subvert the Constitution. The question was called for, but Gerry wanted more time for deliberation. In fact, he would have "all the amendments proposed by the respective States" brought on the boards. Vining answered that the special committee, canvassing the whole mélange, found some superfluous or dangerous and "many . . . so contradictory that it was impossible to make anything of them . . ." Gerry defended himself by charging that opponents were not for a democracy, but an aristocracy. The committee was bored, inattentive, impolite to several more speakers who called for a full parade of changes sought by the state conventions. Burke, of North Carolina, displaying demands of his own state and others, was exasperated. The amendments reported and likely to be adopted by the House "are not those solid and substantial amendment which the people expect; they are little better," he cried, "than whip syllabub, frothy and full of wind, formed only to please the palate . . ." The committee had only wasted time.

When they finally got to the motion for authorizing instruction of representatives it was overwhelmingly rejected, and the proposal for free speech, press, and assemblage was approved without change.

Other Guarantees

When the committee of the whole rose, and the speaker resumed the chair of the House, Ames moved to discharge the committee from any further consideration of amendments. Time had been consumed uselessly. Moreover, if amendments adopted in committee failed of a two-thirds majority in the House itself the effect would be injurious. But so many objected to this summary action that Ames withdrew his motion.

But his impatience propelled the committee two days later through a succession of amendments familiar to us. "A well regulated militia composed of the body of the people, being the best security of a free state, the right of the people to keep and bear arms shall not be infringed; but no person religiously scrupulous shall be compelled to bear arms." This reflected the fear of a standing army at command of the central government. The only objection offered was the strange one that those in power might use the amendment to destroy the Constitution. "They can declare," said Gerry, "who are those religiously scrupulous, and prevent them from bearing arms." But the clause as reported was accepted.

An historic grievance against the British had been the forcible quartering of troops on citizen householders. So the next proposition read, "No soldier shall, in time of peace, be quartered in any house, without the consent of the owner, nor in time of war, but in a manner to be prescribed by law." Sumter, albeit a general in the Revolution, was for no quartering without consent of the owner, but most conceded that in wartime the practice was allowable under proper restrictions, and the provision was approved.

The next clause contained more fundamental guarantees: "No person shall be subject, in case of impeachment, to more than one trial or one punishment for the same offence, nor shall be compelled to be a witness against himself, nor be deprived of life, liberty, or property, without due process of law; nor shall private property be taken for public use without just compensation." Benson and Sherman wanted to strike out the limitation to "one trial," since the accused, if found guilty, was entitled to a new trial if he could show good cause, but the motion was lost. To this point the immunity from testifying against oneself had not been confined to criminal prosecutions. Lawrence of New York objected that this protection should be restricted to criminal charges, and with this change the clause was adopted.

The next prohibitions had further to do with judicial procedure: "Excessive bail shall not be required, nor excessive fines imposed, nor cruel and unusual punishments inflicted." Livermore wondered whether the terms might not prevent inflicting punishments sometimes necessary though undoubtedly cruel—hanging, whipping, or cropping of ears. But others thought the meaning sufficiently clear, and agreed to the wording.

Next came a protection to privacy. "The right of the people to be secure in their persons, houses, papers, and effects, shall not be violated by warrants issued without probable cause, supported by oath or affirmation, and not particularly describing the place to be searched, and the persons or things to be seized." Gerry moved to strengthen the language by banning "unreasonable seizures and searches," and with this addition the clause was approved.

Among those who thought it inadvisable to amend the Constitution were some who believed rights not specifically claimed would be violated. The excuse would be that the people did not reserve this or that freedom, so Congress or the executive or the courts could trespass upon it. This possibility was sought to be prevented by a precautionary sentence: "The enumeration in this constitution of certain rights shall not be construed to deny or disparage others retained by the people." This was endorsed without question.

Now came the proposal to deny to the states certain actions already forbidden to the national government or its agents. In Article I, section 10, after the first paragraph should be inserted "no state shall infringe the equal rights of conscience, nor the freedom of speech or of the press, nor of the right of trial by jury in criminal cases." Tenderness of the people for the states, or perhaps we should say superior trust reposed in local governments as compared with the national authority, was expressed by Tucker of South Carolina, who had been insistent on restricting the central power. He moved to strike out the whole proposition as an unwarranted interference with the capacities of the states. Madison was emphatic in reply. He thought this "the most valuable amendment in the whole list." If the United States government was to be prevented from invading these rights it was equally necessary to restrain the state governments. Livermore supported him, and the stipulation was agreed to by the committee.

The judicial power as it stood in the Constitution gave special dissatisfaction in the states, where many believed the federal courts would intrude, or, in appealed cases, would override determinations of local juries. As we have seen, part of the difficulty was that the Philadelphia convention had been unable to define the federal system more precisely because of the variety in state judicial practices. Since so many of the leaders were lawyers, they put forth their objections with particular knowledge and vehemence. Therefore, when amendments were being discussed, it was natural to find a proposal for a modification in Article III, section 2, paragraph 2, where conditions of appeal formed the subject. These, under the Constitution as ratified, were to be regulated by Congress. The following limitations were now urged and adopted: "But no appeal to such [Supreme] court shall be allowed, where the value in controversy shall not amount to one thousand dollars; nor shall any fact, triable by a jury according to the course of the common law, be otherwise reexaminable than according to the rules of common law."

Next, the whole of the third paragraph of this section, covering criminal trials, should be canceled in favor of new wording to spell out procedure. Thus "In all criminal prosecutions the accused shall enjoy the right to a speedy and public trial, to be informed of the nature and cause of the accusation, to be confronted with the witnesses against him, to have compulsory process for obtaining witnesses in his favor, and to have the assistance of counsel for his defence." Livermore (himself Chief Justice of New Hampshire) urged that the right of the accused to be tried in the state where the crime was committed be restored. With this improvement the provision was adopted.

The States: Amendments Proposed and Powers Reserved

The following day, in the House itself, Gerry renewed his effort to get all of the amendments proposed by the states into the picture. If not already in substance considered by committee of the whole they should be referred there and all amendments agreed to by that committee should be included in one report. Tucker was fervid for this attention to the wishes of five important states which "have pretty plainly expressed their apprehensions of the danger to which the rights of their citizens are exposed." If their plans were not entertained they would seek a second general constitutional convention, and imperil harmony of the country. If their recommendations were at least received by the House they would be gratified even if they must be disappointed in the end. Madison was not against referring the whole collection of state amendments, but he opposed including them in one report of committee of the whole. The House considered that enough was better than too much, and voted down Gerry's motion by more than two to one. All those of Federalist views were opposed to loosing this heterogeneous mass of proposals, which had already been culled for eligible amendments.

Again in committee of the whole, the members accepted without change a precaution that trial of all crimes, except in the military forces, should be by an impartial jury of the vicinage, and no person should be tried for a capital or otherwise infamous crime unless on presentment by a grand jury. Similar unanimity greeted the stipulation that "In suits at common law, the right of trial by jury shall be preserved." Then an amendment declaring the separation of powers in the national government, though not strictly necessary, was approved on Madison's plea that it would reassure the people.

Another effort to leave nothing to chance produced debate that had a prophetic ring. Wording was "The powers not delegated by the constitution, nor prohibited by it to the States, are reserved to the states respectively." Tucker, strict constructionist, wanted it to read "all powers not expressly delegated." This provoked Madison to beg that the central government be allowed scope within the Constitution. ". . . it was impossible to confine the Government to the exercise of express powers; there must necessarily be admitted powers by implication, unless the constitution descended to recount every minutia. He remembered the word 'expressly' had been moved in the convention of Virginia, by the opponents of the ratification, and, after full and fair discussion, was given up by them, and the system allowed to retain its present form." Sherman agreed, citing the fact that "corporate bodies are supposed to possess all powers incident to a corporate capacity, without being absolutely expressed." Tucker's motion to straitjacket the national authority was lost. It was out of harmony with the Constitution as originally adopted. If Tucker's strict limitation had been approved by Congress and by the states, it might have destroyed the elastic quality of the Constitution that has proved so necessary to America's progress.

Carroll of Maryland proposed to add four words at the end of the statement which echoed the all-important principle of the preamble, namely, that the Constitution sprang not from the states, but from the body of citizens. The last words should be that powers not delegated "are reserved to the States respectively, *or to the people.*" The phrase here italicized was incorporated.

The committee of the whole—what we may call the House in shirt-sleeves—then rose, and reported its suggested amendments to the House in formal dress prepared for legislative enactment. Tucker persisted in his attempt to get other amendments considered. He named seventeen which should be referred to committee of the whole. All were inspired by the desire to restrict central power. Thus he would limit the number of terms a representative might serve in a stated time period. Senators should be elected annually. Eliminate authority of Congress to regulate elections of senators and representatives. Tucker revived a favorite proposal often before rejected: "No direct tax shall be laid, unless any State shall have neglected to furnish, in due time, its proportion of a previous requisition . . ." Then only could Congress impose a direct tax, together with interest and charges. There should be no inferior federal tribunals except "courts of admiralty." The states should be allowed to lay import, export, and tonnage duties, if uniform in operation on foreign nations and on citizens of all the states. No one should hold the office of President more than eight years in any period of twelve years.

Tucker's effort to bring these restraints under discussion was turned down.

Action by House of Representatives

The next day (August 19) the House had before it amendments adopted by committee of the whole. Sherman renewed his motion that amendments should be added to the Constitution in a block, not insinuated in the document at different points. Debate repeated pros and cons urged before. Sherman's motion was carried by a two-thirds vote of the House. Then the proposed amendments were considered on their merits. The first—declaring that all power originates in the people —did not receive the required support, but was adopted next day. On the second proposition (enlarge membership in the House), Ames moved to limit the increase, but his and some similar motions were tabled. The third proposal (representatives may not alter their own pay) was approved. On the fourth amendment Ames moved a slight change of wording to read "Congress shall make no law establishing religion . . . or to infringe the rights of conscience," which was accepted.

Numbers of the suggested amendments were approved without difficulty. When the House reached the ninth proposition Gerry revived the desire to hold the national government to the exercise of powers "expressly" delegated. The vote was almost two to one against him.

This completed amendments sanctioned by committee of the whole. Promptly members who had all along wanted additional changes advanced them. Burke moved that Congress's liberty to regulate elections of senators and representatives should not apply unless a state refused, neglected, or was unable because of invasion or rebellion to conduct them. Gerry chimed in that Congress, by control of elections, intended to establish arbitrary government. This wide authority given Congress was "obnoxious to almost every State." Stone, of Maryland, Smith and Tucker of South Carolina were vehement in the same behalf. Not so Ames, who declared the right of Congress to supervise election of its members was essential in the interest of all the people. Improper state restrictions must be prevented. Goodhue was equally emphatic; the states might thwart the federal government, which should "possess every power necessary to its existence." (Though these men could not name "white primaries," "grandfather clauses," poll tax obstacles, and registration frauds, they foresaw that states would practice such abuses.) Burke's motion was narrowly rejected, 28 to 23.

The House returned to and accepted Ames's proposal of a formula to prevent the number of representatives from increasing in the same proportion as population grew.

Madison had begged that no more amendments be introduced. The House, that had first been unwilling to enter on this business, was now in danger of unreasonably postponing other duties. But he could not stop Tucker, Livermore, and Gerry, who fought to the last against direct taxes, subordinate federal courts, and mercantile monopolies, but were voted down on every count. Those determined to preserve in the central government adequate powers were in the large majority and disallowed crippling amendments.

The epilogue of the Philadelphia Constitutional Convention was almost concluded. Changes in the recently ratified fundamental law which the states had demanded with more or less sincerity had been reviewed and reduced to a feasible number. The House could feel that these would satisfy requirements and remove the threat of a second convention, sure to be disorganizing. Though North Carolina and Rhode Island still stood aloof, these states could be expected to accept what others, firmly in the Union, found sufficient.

Benson of New York brought the matter to a head with the resolve, anticipating Senate action, that amendments to the Constitution having been agreed to by two-thirds of both houses of Congress be submitted to the legislatures of the several states; those ratified by three-fourths of the legislatures should be valid as parts of the Constitution. This resolution was referred to a committee of Benson, Sherman, and Sedgwick, who should arrange the amendments and report them in final form. This was Saturday, August 22, 1789. Benson reported, the following Monday, seventeen amendments which the House adopted and sent to the Senate for concurrence. Here there was delay while efforts of Grayson and Richard Henry Lee to induce consideration of the whole list of changes urged by the Virginia legislature were frustrated.

Bill of Rights in the Senate

The Senate whittled the amendments down to fourteen. The chief loss, in Madison's view, was the restraint on violation of civil liberties by the states as well as by the central government. Ellsworth, Charles Carroll, and Paterson from the Senate met Madison, Vining, and Sherman from the House to reconcile differences. September 25 both chambers sent twelve amendments, as they came from conference committee, to President Washington for transmission to the states, including the executives of Rhode Island and North Carolina.

While ratifications were pending, North Carolina, Rhode Island, and Vermont entered the Union. This made it necessary for eleven states to ratify the amendments. Two of the amendments submitted to the states were not ratified—those concerning number of representatives and the pay of members of Congress. By December 1791 the remaining ten amendments had become part of the Constitution. Virginia, which had been so clamorous for alterations and had demanded a second convention for the purpose, was the last of the required eleven to ratify. Massachusetts, where the cry for amendments had threatened to block endorsement of the Constitution, omitted to ratify those the other states accepted until she finally gave her voice in 1941 on the hundred and fiftieth anniversary of the Bill of Rights.

The first ten amendments, protecting personal liberties, were an increasingly valuable supplement to the Constitution. Though regarded by many leaders at the time as superfluous or even mischievous, their adoption was due to the superior instincts of the body of citizens. The most vital of them—freedom of speech, press, religion, assemblage— have been overridden in certain periods of stress, but with later admission of error. Efficient government, if it is to remain democratic, demands these guarantees to the self-respect of the individual. Many have felt, down through the years, that the Tenth Amendment, in a total constitutional view, is of chief importance: "The powers not delegated to the United States by the Constitution, nor prohibited by it to the States, are reserved to the States respectively, or to the people."

Later Amendments

In keeping with the fact that the Constitution is a relatively short instrument of government, it has been amended surprisingly few times. A total of twenty-six amendments only has been added in the 183 years

between 1791 and 1974. This total includes, of course, the first ten—
the Bill of Rights, already discussed.

The later amendments fall into obvious time groups. The Eleventh
and Twelfth were adopted in the early Federal period, to remedy flaws
which became apparent in the actual operation of the Constitution.
The next three are known as the Civil War amendments, and were
ratified between 1865 and 1870. Their interpretation will be found in
later pages discussing civil rights cases before the federal courts. The
Sixteenth and Seventeenth did not come until more than forty years
later. Ratified in the same year (1913), the income tax and direct
election of senators amendments may both be regarded as the fruit of
the initial twentieth-century movement for political reform. Amendments Eighteen and Nineteen (prohibition and women suffrage) were
adopted in the immediate post-World War I period. The "lame duck"
amendment and repeal of prohibition were ratified in the midst of the
Great Depression, 1933. The next two were separated by ten years;
the Twenty-second, limiting the number of presidential terms, was
ratified in 1951, the Twenty-third, giving residents of the District of
Columbia the right to vote in presidential elections, in 1961. The next
three—concerning poll tax, presidential succession, and lowering the
voting age—were spread over the years 1964-71.

The length of time necessary for ratification of different amendments is of interest. The amendments setting a limit to the number
of presidential terms required the longest period of ratification, almost
four full years; the Twenty-first and Twenty-third each took only nine
and one-half months. However, the Twenty-sixth, lowering the voting
age, required the shortest period for ratification, slightly over three
months. Average time for the last sixteen has been under a year.

When the amendments are looked at from the point of view of content, it is apparent that seven are concerned with altering or amplifying
the operation of the constitutional structure itself. These include prohibiting federal jurisdiction over suits against individual states, the
machinery for election of the President and Vice President, the right
of the federal government to levy income taxes, direct election of
United States senators, the "lame duck" amendment, limitation of the
number of presidential terms, and succession to the presidency and vice
presidency. Three are concerned with the civil status and rights of
Negroes. Five deal with extension of the suffrage—to Negroes, to
women, to residents of the District of Columbia, to those who may
not have paid poll taxes, and to 18-year-olds. Two cancel each other,
and represent, of course, the one unhappy effort to deal constitutionally

with sumptuary legislation—a notoriously difficult matter for governments throughout history.

Eleventh and Twelfth Amendments

The background for the Eleventh Amendment is in Article III, section
2, paragraph 1 of the Constitution, which provides that the judicial
power of the United States extends to controversies "between a State
and Citizens of another State." There was some objection to this
clause while ratification was in progress, since on the face of it a private
individual might take a state before a federal court. The rebuttal offered
was that, because of the doctrine of "sovereign immunity," a state
could never be sued without its own consent.

In the post-constitutional period, while all Revolutionary War debts
were assumed by the federal government, there was dispute over other
state debts of a more private nature. The Jay Treaty recognized validity
of debts to British subjects and increased the difficulty. A suit brought
against the state of Georgia in the United States Supreme Court by
the executors of a British creditor (*Chisholm v. Georgia*, 2 Dallas 419,
1793) was decided by the Court on the basis of the literal provision
in the Constitution. This decision paved the way for a flood of other
such suits, and provoked an outburst of indignation throughout the
country. Reaction in Georgia was naturally more extreme than elsewhere. The Georgia legislature passed a bill providing that any federal
official who tried to enforce this decision should be hanged "without
benefit of clergy." But there was also a general demand for a constitutional amendment to prevent this sort of action. Congress proposed,
and the states ratified, the Eleventh Amendment: "The Judicial power
of the United States shall not be construed to extend to any suit in
law or equity, commenced or prosecuted against one of the United
States by Citizens of another State, or by Citizens or Subjects of any
Foreign State."

This amendment was declared effective in January 1798, and attempts by subterfuge to gain access to federal courts in such cases have
been generally unsuccessful. Swisher concludes that "On the whole,
the losses resulting from inability of individuals to sue states have not
been great. Whether on grounds of improved ethical standards or of
business expediency, the states have usually fulfilled their obligations.
The elimination of friction may well have justified enactment of the
constitutional amendment."*

* Carl B. Swisher, *American Constitutional Development* (Houghton Mifflin,
1943), p. 88.

The Twelfth Amendment proceeded from a much more basic flaw in the Constitution, the failure to provide for separate balloting for President and Vice President by the presidential electors. If division into political parties, and consequent disappointment of the expectation that the electors would be distinguished citizens who would in fact choose the President and Vice President, had been foreseen by the Constitutional Convention, this defect might have been avoided.

By 1800 the electors had become party representatives, pledged to vote for the candidates nominated by their respective parties. Although a constitutional amendment had been proposed after the presidential election of 1796 (when a Federalist had been elected President and a Republican Vice President), no action had been taken. In 1800 the Republican-Democratic electors were a majority, but they cast the same number of undifferentiated votes for Jefferson and Burr. The tie threw the election into the House of Representatives, controlled by Federalists.

After the battle in the House which resulted in the election of Jefferson through Hamilton's intervention, an amendment requiring separate balloting for the two offices was again introduced. It could not secure the necessary two-thirds majorities until the second Congress under Jefferson, and even then the Senate vote—a two-thirds majority of those present and voting, but not of the total membership—was challenged. (This question was not finally settled by the Supreme Court until 1920, in a case testing the validity of the Senate vote on the Eighteenth Amendment.)

Opposition to this amendment, in and out of Congress, was supported by several arguments. There was the cogent advice of Washington that it was unwise to make changes unless absolutely necessary, until the Constitution was well established. Another objection was the belief that it would downgrade the office of Vice President; that, while hitherto the Vice President had been the nation's second choice for President, he would now be only a shadowy stand-in for the President. In the course of Congressional debate, it was even proposed that the vice presidential office be eliminated entirely. Further opposition came from small states. It appeared unlikely (and has proved so in fact) that many elections would wind up in the House of Representatives if the amendment were adopted. Since the small states had a disproportionate influence in the House if it *did* have to decide a presidential election, they took a stand in advance against curtailment of this power.

When the amendment was finally accepted by both houses, it was ratified quickly (in less than ten months), so as to take effect in time for the election of 1804. It has successfully adapted the original presidential machinery to the two-party system. In only one election since its adoption, that of 1824, has the House of Representatives been called upon to choose the President. That election was marked by the temporary breakdown of the two-party system, with several small factions and no electoral majority at the regular election.

At least one modern constitutional historian takes seriously the argument that the Twelfth Amendment did, in fact, tend to downgrade the Vice Presidency. The rebuttal to that view could not be better put than in the words of the man who first filled that office. Whatever the intention of the Constitutional Convention, the vice presidency seems always to have been frustrating to any man having political ambitions. John Adams, in a letter to his wife Abigail, dated December 19, 1793, said: "My country has in its wisdom contrived for me the most insignificant office that ever the invention of man contrived or his imagination conceived."

The essential difference between Article II, section 1, paragraph 3 of the Constitution and the Twelfth Amendment is the requirement in the latter that the electors vote separately for President and Vice President, making "distinct lists of all persons voted for as President, and of all persons voted for as Vice-President." If the House of Representatives must choose the President because a majority of electoral votes is lacking, their choice must be among those three persons having the highest number of electoral votes, instead of the five highest. The Vice President is chosen by the Senate from the two candidates having the highest number of electoral votes, if there is no electoral majority for one. The same requirements for eligibility to be President apply to the Vice President.

Amendments Provoked by Civil War

The Thirteenth Amendment, made inevitable by Civil War and Emancipation Proclamation, was the only one of the "Civil War" amendments to be proposed before Lincoln's death. Prior to its adoption, whether slavery was permitted or not was a matter for each state to determine individually, and in the loyal border states and the District of Columbia slavery remained legal until the adoption of this amendment deprived both states and national government of the right to decide this question.

Proposed February 1, 1865, and declared in force December 18 of the same year, the amendment was of course aimed at Negro slavery. However, whether other forms of coercion come within the prohibitions of the amendment has sometimes had to be decided by the federal courts. It has been held that compelling persons to help build public roads, to pay alimony, to serve on a jury or in the armed forces are all permissible without violating the Thirteenth Amendment.

Only two of the amendments—the Thirteenth and the Twenty-first—can be directly violated by individuals.* The Thirteenth is termed "self-executing;" that is, no action by Congress was required to put it into effect, although Congress had in fact passed legislation setting penalties for its violation.

Nearly twenty years after the ratification of the amendment, the Supreme Court ruled that discrimination against Negroes by private individuals cannot be regarded as imposing slavery or involuntary servitude upon them (109 US 3, 1883). Congress did, however, in Reconstruction times use its power to prohibit "peonage"—involuntary servitude to work off a debt. Certain loopholes in these laws make the protection incomplete.

The Fourteenth Amendment, more controversial and more complicated than the Thirteenth, sought to counter the immediate post-Civil War legislation of states of the former Confederacy. Because of unexpected interpretation of the "due process" clause, and the enormous importance today of the clause about "equal protection of the laws," this amendment will be treated more fully in the later section on civil rights cases; here we content ourselves with a brief statement of what is included in its text.

Proposed in June 1866, the first section serves to shore up constitutionally the congressional reversal of the Dred Scott decision holding that Negroes were not citizens within the meaning of the Constitution. Also it overrides discriminatory legislation by southern states, in the following words:

All persons born or naturalized in the United States, and subject to the jurisdiction thereof, are citizens of the United States and of the State wherein they reside. No State shall make or enforce any law which shall abridge the privileges or immunities of citizens of the United States;

The same section includes the prohibitions against deprivation of "life, liberty or property, without due process of law" by any state, and the denial to "any person within its jurisdiction the equal protection of the laws."

* If the equal rights amendment is ratified, it too could be directly violated by individuals.

Section 2 provides a sanction against states unlawfully denying any males the right to vote which has never been used—the threat to reduce representation from any such state proportionately to the number denied the right to vote. Section 3, denying the right to vote to any persons who had as officials taken an oath to support the Constitution of the United States and then "engaged in insurrection or rebellion against the same" was, of course, intended to disfranchise leaders of the Confederacy. The section further provided, however, that Congress might by a two-thirds vote of each house remove such disability, and Congress did so on June 6, 1898. The amendment also invalidated the Confederate debt.

The Fifteenth Amendment (proposed February 27, 1869, and declared in force March 30, 1870) forbade suffrage discrimination on racial grounds. It was made necessary, Reconstruction Congresses felt, because the southern states resisted threats of curtailed representation in the Fourteenth Amendment. Framers of the earlier one had believed these threats would be sufficient to coerce southern states into giving voting rights to Negroes, but it was quickly apparent that this would not happen. Discrimination on the basis of race, color, or "previous condition of servitude" was therefore specifically prohibited in the Fifteenth Amendment, and Congress was given power of enforcement.

The Fifteenth Amendment is a pre-eminent instance of the fact that the Supreme Court alone cannot always protect the rights guaranteed by the Constitution. All sorts of devices, legal or informal, have been used to evade the plain meaning of this amendment. Some of these, although intended to disfranchise Negroes, are not on their face discriminatory on the basis of race, and do actually disfranchise also many poor or uneducated whites. Poll taxes came within this category until ratification of the Twenty-fourth Amendment, outlawing them in federal elections. Restrictive residence requirements and technical requirements covering registration, such as the provision that one must register in the year preceding the election, are other examples.

Other more clearly discriminatory tactics are in process of being whittled away by the Supreme Court. The "grandfather clause," requiring a literacy test for all persons whose ancestors did not have the vote before January 1, 1866, was held to be a violation of the amendment, since no Negroes could vote at that time, but whites could. The "white primary" was more difficult to attack; not until 1944 did the Court begin a series of decisions which affected it. In most of the South winning the Democratic primary has in the past been equivalent to election, and Negroes were kept from voting in the primary on the ground that the Democratic party was a private organization and might make its own rules about membership. In *Smith v. Allwright* (321 US 649, 1944) the Court held the white primary in South Carolina to be a direct violation of the Fifteenth Amendment, on two grounds. It was a part of the machinery for choosing officials, and was therefore subject to the same criteria as to discrimination as the general elections. Also, the discrimination practiced by a party entrusted by law with determining the qualification of participants in the primary was enforced by the state. This constituted state action within the meaning of the amendment.

Other subterfuges directed to the same end, such as the repeal by South Carolina of all laws related to the primaries, and requirement of an oath to support segregation as a prerequisite for voting, have also been struck down by the Court. Since 1944 the Court's decisions and the civil rights legislation of the 1960's have been responsible for bringing practice in the South into much closer conformity with the Fifteenth Amendment than at any time since its adoption, but we are still some distance from securing to Negro citizens the right to register and vote on an equality with white citizens in the South.

The Court itself, early in the history of the amendment, rendered a decision that hampered its operation. In the *Civil-Rights Cases* (109 US 3, 1883) it was held that, while the amendment forbade discrimination on the basis of race, etc., it did not *confer* suffrage upon anyone. A judicial splitting of hairs, perhaps, but it points up the fact that in the requirements for registration lay the power for nearly a hundred years to defeat the intention of the amendment.

Income Tax and Direct Election of Senators

The Sixteenth Amendment (1913) gives the federal government power to lay and collect taxes on income, from whatever source derived, without apportionment among the states according to population. The amendment was proposed and ratified because without it Congress could not draw on a source that promised to furnish large and needed revenue, by a tax that illustrated the country's idea of social justice. Income taxes, personal and corporate, have come to yield the largest proportion of Treasury funds.

During the Civil War and for a few years thereafter a national income tax supplied substantial returns and was sanctioned by the Supreme Court. This law lapsed and the expedient was not resorted to again for more than twenty years, in 1893, a period of depression when the government required more revenue. Promptly (1894) the lawfulness of this income tax was tested in the Supreme Court. The justices now reversed their previous stand. They held the levy unconstitutional because it was a direct tax and yet was not apportioned according to population, or representation in Congress, as the Constitution demanded. Two decades more were consumed in discussion before the Sixteenth Amendment cut the Gordian knot and made the Treasury master of a rich resource. The developments leading to the Sixteenth Amendment are here given only in brief because in later pages we shall treat the history of the federal income tax in some detail.

The Seventeenth Amendment, providing for the direct election of United States senators, belongs to the same period as the Sixteenth. Provision in the Constitution for election of senators by the state legislators reflected, as did the electoral system for choosing the President, the distrust in the Philadelphia convention of popular voting. The adoption of universal manhood suffrage by mid-century and the growing strength of the democratic spirit generally made it inevitable that sooner or later direct election by the people would be substituted for the constitutional method.

By the time the constitutional amendment was introduced the question had already come up repeatedly. As early as 1826 a resolution for an amendment had been introduced, because of dissatisfaction with the election by state legislatures. By the end of the century the movement for popular election was so strong that, between 1893 and 1902, the House five times passed resolutions calling for an amendment. Each time the Senate failed to take action (not unnaturally, since its members had all been elected by the method under fire). After that, however, resolutions were introduced into both houses regularly, year after year.

Many objections, apart from the greater desirability of popular vote, were made against election by state legislatures. Deadlocks over election of senators were not infrequent, always resulting in a waste of time and money, and sometimes leaving a state lacking full representation in the Senate for a considerable period. Bribery and corruption were alleged, sometimes with cause and always to the damage of legislative reputations. It was natural to find that members of legislatures were frequently chosen on the basis of their attitudes toward senatorial candidates, rather than for their ability to deal with state legislative matters.

As early as 1866 Congress had by legislation attempted to prevent deadlocks between the two houses of a legislature in choosing a senator. This act was based on the authority of Congress to legislate about the times and manner of choosing senators and representatives, and provided that if no person obtained a majority in the two houses sitting separately, they should meet in joint session and vote as a body (14 Stat. 243). Even so, delays continued.

Although opposed by party bosses and other entrenched interests, the tide of democracy finally proved irresistible. Several states had, in fact, instituted what amounted to popular election earlier, by binding state legislators to vote for senatorial candidates approved by the voters of the parties, in primary or general elections.

Opposition came, also, from conservative forces for a variety of reasons. Elihu Root, for example, believed that the proposed amendment would change the basic character of the Senate, on the ground that it was intended to be both more deliberative and more conservative than the House of Representatives. The amendment would result in the election, he argued, of candidates more responsive to the immediate wishes of the people, and would discourage the type of senator who accepted membership as a patriotic duty, but who would not subject himself to the political campaign necessary for popular election. He said in Congress, "It is not wise that the people of the United States should contract the habit of amending the Constitution . . . Reverence for that great instrument, the belief of mankind in its perpetuity, the unwillingness of our people to tamper with it or to change it, the sentiments that are gathered around it—these, constituting the basis of stability in our government, are the most valuable of all the possessions of the nation that inhabits this rich and fertile land."

This attitude, apparently, was less influential than the fear of Southerners that white supremacy might be endangered by federal prescription of regulations for elections which they would not want to obey. In the debate, it was even proposed that the amendment strip Congress of the power to make regulations about the time and manner of election of senators. An amendment to that effect was killed in the Senate, but was retained by the House long enough to halt progress for several months. The joint resolution was finally adopted May 16, 1912; ratification was completed by May 31, 1913.

Contrary to the hopes of some and the fears of others, direct election of senators has not brought about any sweeping changes. White supremacy in southern elections did not disappear. State legislatures, while they enjoy no great prestige usually and may fairly be said to be of generally mediocre caliber, did not get that way because they lost the right to elect United States senators. Nor has the fact that they no longer have this obligation resulted in increased efficiency in attending to the states' business.

As to the senators elected by popular vote, although both the average age when elected and the amount of formal education possessed increased, probably the most significant change has been economic. There is objective evidence that the average wealth of senators elected since the amendment became effective has decreased, and it could probably be demonstrated that their obligations to important economic interests have also decreased. While business interests can still bring pressure to bear on members of the Senate, we do not hear nowadays of "railroad" senators, "steel" senators, "oil" senators, as used to be commonplace, often connecting individual senators with specific companies.

Prohibition and Repeal

The episode of Prohibition and its repeal, constitutionally contained in Amendments Eighteen and Twenty-one, is more intelligible when considered as a whole. It is a sad, even tragic, story, but with many other elements as well if all the details could be examined. Those who would have liked to destroy the "demon Rum" were active for seventy-five years before national prohibition became a possibility. A Prohibition party candidate has run in every presidential campaign since 1880, and as early as 1842 the state of Maine went dry. But only World War I and its accompanying curtailment of personal liberties created a political climate in which the experiment of forbidding alcohol to an entire nation could be made. Patriotism and the propaganda arm of the Anti-Saloon League were shrewdly joined to bring off the passage of the Eighteenth Amendment.

The first steps were taken in forbidding the sale of intoxicating or spirituous liquors at any military post, or to military personnel in uniform, as a part of the Selective Service Act. A Food Control Act of August 1917 forbade the use of food materials in the manufacture of distilled spirits for beverage purposes, and the importation of spirits. Fuel and foodstuffs used for the manufacture of beer were reduced by

30 to 50 per cent, and later there were other restrictive wartime measures.

But the major effort lay in launching a constitutional amendment. Expressions of opinion by our allies helped to provide ammunition for the cause. Lloyd George, the British Prime Minister, was quoted in May 1917 as saying, "We are fighting Germany, Austria, and Drink; and . . . the greatest of these deadly foes is Drink." Action on the proposed amendment was speeded in Congress, in an access of patriotic zeal, partly because opposition to it was poorly organized. Objection in the general public had always come largely from the big cities and heavily industrial states, where there were many foreign born, Roman Catholics, or both. The Prohibition proposal therefore had a strong flavor of rural, white Anglo-Saxon Protestantism, and of an unattractive Native Americanism as well.

Proposed by Congress on December 3, 1917, ratification was similarly hurried. It became a part of the Constitution on January 29, 1919, to take effect a year later. The time lapse was supposed to give brewers, distillers, and others involved opportunity to liquidate their businesses in orderly fashion. The amendment was ultimately ratified by all the states except Rhode Island and Connecticut.

Several court cases were instituted to test the Wartime Prohibition Act (November 1918), which prohibited the sale of spirits, wine, and beer from June 1919 until demobilization was completed. The Supreme Court decided that ample proof existed that the war was not yet at a formal end, and that the act was constitutional as a war measure (*Hamilton v. Kentucky Distilleries and Warehouse Co.*, 251 US 146, 1919, and *United States v. Standard Brewery*, 251 US 210, 1920).

Scarcely had the amendment been officially declared a part of the Constitution than it was attacked in the courts on many different grounds, presaging judicial, constitutional, political, and social conflict which was to endure throughout the life of this ill-conceived experiment.

One of the earliest cases to reach the Supreme Court upheld the constitutionality of the amendment, but was also productive of much confusion. It is impossible to avoid the impression that the Court itself was confused. Constitutionality was upheld unanimously, but only five justices concurred in a statement on a number of points, without giving their reasons. Chief Justice White gave his own reasons on certain points. Another justice said that, although he did not dissent from the disposition of the cases made by the Court, "Because of the disposition of the cases made by the Court, "Because of the bewilderment which it [the amendment] creates, a multitude of questions will inevitably arise and demand solution here. In the circumstances I prefer to remain free to consider these questions when they arrive." Another remarked that declaring conclusions without reasons "will undoubtedly decrease the literature of the Court if it does not increase its lucidity" (*Rhode Island v. Palmer*, 253 US 350, 1920). One is reminded of Alice in Wonderland, "sentence first, verdict afterward." amendment not be operative unless ratified within seven years. In a case involving violation of the enforcement legislation (Volstead Act), the defense charged that Congress had no power to base ratification of an amendment on the fulfillment of a time-provision (*Dillon v. Gloss*, 256 US 276, 1921). The Court decision analyzed the periods of time required for the ratification of previous amendments. All of those which had been adopted were ratified within four years, and the Court found that a stipulated period of seven years was not unreasonable. It held also that the Constitution did not suggest that, once proposed, an amendment was to be indefinitely open to ratification.

Problems of Enforcement

The really insoluble questions, from any long-range point of view, arose concerning enforcement. The Volstead Act was passed by Congress in 1920, providing more stringent measures than those in the Wartime Prohibition Act. Difficulties in enforcement fell into two main categories, even before they were hopelessly entangled in the rise of new and outrageous criminal methods and organizations. These were first, the constant violation of civil liberties involved, or at least alleged, and second, how Congress and the states should use their "concurrent power" to enforce the amendment by legislation.

Since the law could not be enforced at all without constant search of different sorts of buildings, it was often charged that these visits violated the Fourth Amendment forbidding unreasonable searches and seizures. It was in connection with Prohibition enforcement that the vexing question of wiretap evidence arose. The Supreme Court upheld the use of such evidence as constitutional; Chief Justice Taft said that "no searching and no seizure" were involved in tapping telephone wires, since the evidence was secured "by the use of the sense of hearing" only (*Olmstead v. United States* 277 US 438, 1928).

The Court's decision, however, left open the possibility that Congress might legislate against the use of wiretap evidence, which Justice Holmes had called a "dirty business." After a number of earlier attempts, Congress finally prohibited, in the Federal Communications Act of 1934, the giving of information received by wire or radio to persons not entitled thereto. Federal courts have interpreted this to prohibit the use in federal courts of such information.

Specifying the power to enforce the Prohibition amendment as concurrent between federal and state governments was an innovation, productive of much confusion. A basic question at issue was whether the amendment conferred the power on the states, or protected the exercise of powers already existing. The Supreme Court in 1922 clarified this, saying "each state possessed that power in full measure prior to the amendment," and that the probable purpose of including it specifically in the amendment was to confirm this authority (*United States v. Lanza*, 260 US 377, 1922). This decision meant that the states had, however, no *obligation* to enforce prohibition, unless they chose, which frequently left the federal officers in a woefully weak position. Without the aid of the states there was virtually no enforcement machinery. To do a really effective job would have meant creating a federal structure of courts, prisons, and investigators to parallel those in the states. This was opposed, the amendment itself was unpopular, federal funds for enforcement were always inadequate.

Although nearly all the states passed Prohibition laws either before or after ratification of the amendment, antagonism made itself felt in a number of states before many years had passed. New York repealed its law in 1923, followed by several other states despite the denunciations of the Anti-Saloon League and its supporters. Lax enforcement became the rule rather than the exception, partly because the states would have liked the federal government to foot the bill, partly because of mounting public opposition.

No real effort was made by the Republican Presidents of the period to provide the money that would have been necessary to make the amendment effective. Harding referred to this lack as a "nation-wide scandal" and Coolidge's contribution was an abortive attempt to solve the problem by authorizing the appointment of state officials as prohibition officers of the Treasury. Not until Hoover was elected (and added to common parlance the phrase characterizing Prohibition as a "noble experiment") was anything further done. Under an act of Congress appropriating $250,000 for a "thorough inquiry into the problem of the enforcement of prohibition," the President appointed the

Wickersham Commission. Its final report in 1931 reflected faithfully the nation's divided view. It was proved factually that enforcement was impossible for a variety of reasons ranging from geography to the magnetic attraction of high profits, and that the federal courts had suffered grievously in loss of dignity and respect. However, the commission nevertheless recommended that federal appropriations for enforcement be increased. Some members of the commission said openly that the amendment had proved unworkable and should be modified; the only change suggested was to authorize Congress *either* to regulate or to prohibit the sale and use of liquor.

President Hoover supported the Wickersham report, so far as proposed statutory changes went, but not the modification of the amendment. No action was taken, however. The election of 1932 was imminent, and the nation was in deep economic trouble which preoccupied the public mind. Indeed, one of the objections to Prohibition was beginning to be the loss of important revenue to the federal government.

Movement for Repeal

Both party platforms in 1932 contained proposals for change in the Eighteenth Amendment. The Democratic platform advocated outright repeal, while the Republicans were more subtle and less clear. Essentially the position was that the states should be given the right to deal with the problem as they saw fit. Whether the more forthright stand taken by the Democrats contributed to the Roosevelt landslide is impossible to say; at any rate, the vote was interpreted as a mandate for repeal.

Congress proposed an amendment to repeal the Eighteenth Amendment, in February 1933, specifying ratification by convention. Since no earlier amendment had this provision, the fact that the Twenty-first did so gave rise to a certain amount of discussion and uncertainty. It was not clear whether the federal government or the individual states might set up the requirements for the conventions. In the end it was left to the states (thus setting a precedent for the future), although several unsuccessful procedural bills were introduced into Congress. In some states, delegates were elected at large, in others, in essentially the same way as the state legislatures. Most of the conventions were expected simply to meet and vote, not to deliberate on the matter. In a number of states, voters had a chance to express an opinion; either there was a "wet" slate of delegates and a "dry" slate, or a referendum was held when delegates were chosen, the outcome of which bound the delegates. Ratification was promptly completed by December 1933.

The President's proclamation of repeal urged the public to help in restoring law and order by buying legal liquor only, from legally licensed dealers. In some states, selling was restricted to state liquor stores. The President also urged against restoration of the saloon and its evils, although the evils of bootlegging and gangsterism attendant on the era of Prohibition had been much worse. One of the pressing problems of the new federal administration was control of the underworld organizations which had flourished on bootlegging, and which after repeal moved into other fields such as kidnapping and extortion. Efforts at control had some success, although the genie was not so easy to get back into the bottle. Probably organized crime is more prevalent in American cities than it ever was before the Eighteenth Amendment was passed.

The second section of the amendment, designed to protect "dry" states against the violation of their laws, has become by interpretation something not intended at all. The Supreme Court has held that the amendment permits states to levy taxes on the importation of liquor from other states—a kind of tax until that time clearly unconstitutional. Article I, section 8 gives Congress the power to regulate interstate commerce, and provides that customs duties must be uniform throughout the United States. But since the language of the Twenty-first Amendment did not distinguish between "wet" states and "dry" states, state laws prescribing what are really customs duties on the importation of liquor from other states were upheld. The result has been retaliatory legislation between states, discriminating against their various alcoholic products. Such "tariffs" have been extended to other products; for example, California levies a "use tax" on automobiles brought into the state but bought elsewhere.

It is impossible to avoid the conclusion that the Eighteenth Amendment proved a colossal and costly mistake. Had the leaders of the Anti-Saloon League been more widely read in the history of sumptuary legislation, or the effects of unpopular legislation on the attitude toward law in general, they might have been less eager to see the nation embark on the "noble experiment." In terms of the Constitution itself, it was a mistake. The strength of the American system is that the Constitution provides a broad structure for the functioning of government, with enough flexibility to reflect changes in institutions, customs, and popular opinion. The attempt to legislate permanently within the Constitution about a matter on which the public has always been sharply divided was a blunder soon requiring correction in another amendment. The Prohibition episode illustrates the difference in character between a constitution and a statute. The first is designed to be basic and enduring, the second may be experimental, short-lived, or readily modified.

Amendment for Woman Suffrage

The first agitation to include women in the right to vote was directed toward state action, since federal suffrage, under the Constitution, was determined by the states. As provided for the House of Representatives in Article I, section 2, and for the Senate in the Seventeenth Amendment, electors for members of both houses were to have "the qualifications requisite for the most numerous branch of the state legislature." The movement for woman suffrage in the individual states goes back to the 1840's, by which time manhood suffrage had generally been achieved.

The Civil War amendments and their discussion, however, partly changed the focus of action. When the extension of voting rights to Negroes was under discussion, women began to suggest that they also be included. Most of the effort at that time was to secure the elimination of the word "male" from section 3 of the Fourteenth Amendment: "But when the right to vote . . . is denied to any of the *male* inhabitants of such State . . . the basis of representation therein shall be reduced in the proportion which the number of such *male* citizens shall bear to the whole number of *male* citizens . . . in such State." If this move had succeeded, there would have been an entering wedge for woman suffrage.

When the Fifteenth Amendment was being proposed, woman suffrage advocates took the opportunity to suggest including sex as one of the prohibited grounds of discrimination as to voting, along with race, color, and previous condition of servitude. This attempt also failed, but the national woman suffrage movement was on its way. Beginning in 1878, a constitutional amendment permitting women to vote was introduced session after session, until it became a commonplace of the Washington political scene.

Action in the states was not stopped, however. Beginning with Wyoming in 1890 (when it was admitted as a state), by the time the constitutional amendment was finally adopted a total of twenty-nine states had given women either complete or presidential suffrage, and two more allowed women to vote in primaries.

Woman suffrage achieved a major victory when New York was added in 1917 to the ranks of those states which permitted voting by women citizens. New York had been regarded as a principal center of opposition.

A parallel movement was elimination of some of the legal disabilities of women which had helped to produce the suffrage campaign. Chiefly at issue were property rights and rights affecting control of minor children. In several states, conditions were improved in the hope of avoiding the necessity of giving the right to vote.

The campaign for woman suffrage picked up momentum in the period before World War I, with the move for "popular government" reforms, such as the referendum, recall, and direct primary. As the number of states where women had the vote increased, so did the number of representatives and senators who, like it or not, had to take the opinions of women into account.

As had been true of the debate over the Prohibition amendment, part of the argument about woman suffrage turned on the question of whether state rights were being curtailed by proposed federal action. Amending state constitutions was in a number of cases so difficult, however, that this pragmatic fact was made the excuse for advocating federal interference, as many termed it. By 1916 the platforms of both major parties advocated woman suffrage by state action, so strong had the suffrage movement become. Governor Charles Evans Hughes, the Republican candidate, went further and supported also a constitutional amendment. President Wilson's failure to do so was probably a factor in his narrow margin of votes for re-election, since the militant suffragists were active in a vote-for-Hughes-in-protest movement.

By this time it was clear, however, that the suffragists' demands would have to be seriously considered. On January 8, 1918, a House committee took a stand in favor of a suffrage amendment. This was after an extensive review of the question, which covered charges that woman suffrage would overturn the social order, that women would become masculine or at least "unfeminine," and that political parties would be overthrown. The report also included a plea for an amendment as a "war" measure.

At this point President Wilson changed his position publicly, and, while this was attacked in the *New York Times* and elsewhere as political, his influence was important. The House passed the resolution by the necessary margin on January 10, 1918, in the presence of many suffragists.

It was a surprise to suffragists that the resolution was delayed in the Senate. Many southern Democrats opposed it, because they feared that passage of the amendment would upset white control of the South. A Mississippi senator proposed an amendment to the text which would have limited its operation to white citizens of the United States. He explained that he wished to leave to the states the question of whether or not to give the vote to non-white women: "If California wants to enfranchise the Chinese and Japanese women, let her do it; if Mississippi wants to enfranchise the Negro women, let her do it; but do not force upon California and Mississippi the enfranchisement of those women who are not of our race, who are not of our aspirations, who are not of our ideals, who are not of anything that makes an essential part of us." In spite of a personal appearance of the President in the Senate to urge passage of the resolution, it was defeated in October 1918. Another attempt failed in December. Not until June 1919, at a special session of Congress, was a joint resolution passed in both Houses by the necessary majorities.

Ratification was completed by August 1920 in time to permit women in all states to vote for President in November. No southern states ratified. Operation of the Nineteenth Amendment indicates that neither the hopes of its supporters nor the fears of its enemies have been wholly justified. The white population retained control of the South, and women were not "coarsened" by the right to vote. The structure of politics has not been notably purified by the fact that women can vote, nor is it yet true that women are given political preferment in anything like the same proportion as men. It is difficult to prove that there is a "women's vote," though after the presidential election of 1952 it was asserted that women had voted for General Eisenhower in larger proportions than had men. Women have played an important educational role since being given the vote, notably in organizations such as the League of Women Voters (national) and the Women's City Club of New York. Removal of legal discriminations and enactment of protective legislation for women were both due in considerable measure to the enfranchisement of women.

"Lame Duck" Amendment

The Twentieth Amendment differed sharply from the Eighteenth and the Nineteenth, for it was directed toward improving the machinery of federal government, and aroused no deep-seated emotional discussion.

When the Constitution was adopted, the Continental Congress provided for beginning the functioning of government, including the appointment of presidential electors, the casting of their ballots, and the actual initiation of the constitutional system. The date chosen for this last was March 4, 1789—a date based on nothing more sacred than an estimate that it would take that long for the necessary preliminaries to be completed. Terms of senators and representatives, therefore, began on that date, and expired in later (odd) years on that date also. The Constitution itself, however, provided that the regular sessions of Congress should begin on the first Monday in December, "unless they [Congress] shall by law appoint a different Day." This combination of facts meant that members of Congress elected in November could not take office until after the expiration of the terms of their predecessors the following March, and the first regular session of Congress in which they would sit would not begin until the following December, thirteen months after they were elected to office.

In presidential years, therefore, the Congress which convened in early December invariably included some persons who had been defeated for re-election—and yet these "lame ducks" remained the de facto legislators for the country for four months. And, should that session of Congress need more time to complete its business, there was no way to provide it, since the terms of its members expired at noon on March 4. Worse still, under some circumstances, a President repudiated by the voters continued to hold office for an additional four months.

Proposals for change commenced as early as 1795, and by 1840 the first suggestion of reform by amendment was made. No action was taken, but between 1875 and 1900 many measures were introduced to change terms of office and dates of congressional sessions, some to make the process effective later in the year, some to make it earlier. Not until 1921, however, did the move for a constitutional amendment gather sufficient force to be taken seriously.

Use by the Harding administration of legislators defeated in November 1922 to try to pass a ship-subsidy bill which had wide public opposition, appears to have precipitated the introduction of the Twentieth Amendment as a joint resolution from the judiciary committee of the Senate. The measure provided that the terms of federal legislators should begin on the first Monday in January following their election. Hearings revealed widespread public support, although it was opposed by the President. It passed the Senate by a large majority, but was prevented from coming to a vote on the floor of the House. Senator

George W. Norris was the sponsor and perennial reviver of the proposal. Between 1922 and 1930 he had four experiences similar to the first.

By January 1932, however, the Hoover mid-term elections had returned a Democratic majority to the House, and the Republican Speaker, Nicholas Longworth, who had been the resolution's chief tactical opponent, had died. Introduced for the final time, it passed both houses by the required majorities by March 3. Ratified in short order, the amendment became part of the Constitution on February 6, 1933.

The amendment as adopted provided for an earlier beginning of the term for members of Congress, which not only allows time for organization, but also to elect a President or Vice President if there should be no electoral majorities. The third and fourth sections provide against eventualities for which no procedure had previously been specified—what to do if a President-elect died, failed to qualify, or if one of those from whom the House of Representatives may by law choose a President should die. The provision that the amendment must be ratified within seven years was again included.

Presidential Tenure and Votes for District of Columbia

Soon after Franklin Roosevelt died, at the beginning of his fourth consecutive term in the presidency, Republicans brought forward resolutions in the Eightieth Congress that would ensure more frequent change of tenants in the White House. The proposal of a maximum of two elections for any one candidate passed the House, 285 to 121, with no votes of Republicans against it and 47 Democrats for it. A rival resolution stipulating a single term of six years drew mixed support but was dropped. Republicans protested that their motive was not political; the purpose was to protect the health of our Presidents, and prevent spread of the world trend toward dictatorship. The amendment would merely write into the Constitution the tradition, coming down from Washington, of limiting a President to two four-year terms —a tradition preserved until the fateful year 1940 when Roosevelt was elected to his third term. In the heated debates Democrats insisted that no limitation was necessary or desirable. The attempt by their opponents implied that "the people of this great Nation cannot think for themselves, and . . . we must . . . place them in a strait-jacket."

The House agreed to a change by the Senate, providing that one (i.e. a Vice President) who served more than two years of a term for which another man was elected might be elected in his own right for only a single term. This meant that the maximum service is for ten years. A Mississippi Democrat demanded that the measure be submitted to special conventions in the states, not to the legislatures, but this despairing device failed.

The proposal went to the states March 24, 1947, and was proclaimed as part of the Constitution almost exactly four years later, March 1, 1951. States generally Republican were earliest to ratify, but later eight southern states joined them and three more in that section gave their approval after the necessary three-fourths had agreed.

Residents of the parts of Virginia and Maryland which became the District of Columbia lost their voting rights in 1802. Many in the Constitutional Convention expressed fears that the federal preserve would become a refuge of scoundrels. They were not thinking of the members of Congress, but of criminals fleeing prosecution by the states, who would perhaps find national officers more tolerant of their sins. After long agitation, Congress recommended to the states (June 16, 1960) an amendment permitting District residents to choose three members of the electoral college (the number assigned to the least populous state). Attempts to give them also a nonvoting delegate in the House of Representatives and home rule (instead of being governed in local affairs by three commissioners appointed by the President) were dropped.

Practically all of the opposition came from southern states, apparently unwilling to enfranchise Negroes who then constituted almost 54 per cent of the District population. Not one state of the deep South ratified; Arkansas rejected the proposal outright. In spite of sectional objection, the amendment was ratified in 286 days. The amendment was proclaimed part of the Constitution April 3, 1961. President Kennedy favored eighteen as the voting age, but the statute executing the amendment stipulated twenty-one. It also placed careful restrictions on political campaign expenditures.

Anti Poll Tax Amendment

Poll taxes which must be paid as a qualification for voting were levied in southern states chiefly for the purpose of barring Negroes from use of the ballot. Poll taxes were regressive, bearing more heavily on persons of low income. They disenfranchised large numbers of poor white persons as well as poor Negroes. Partly by this means members of the Senate and the House from southern states, controlling small bodies of electors, were able to maintain themselves in office for long periods. By virtue of seniority they rose to the chairmanship of important committees where they powerfully influenced legislative policies.

Between 1942 and 1949 bills to bar the poll tax as a requirement for voting in federal elections were five times passed by the House, but always died in the Senate. They were killed by filibusters in 1942, 1944, and 1946. Senator Holland, Democrat of Florida, abandoned attempts by statute, and introduced an anti poll tax constitutional amendment in every Congress beginning in 1949, but it was never reported out by the Senate Judiciary Committees. In 1962 Senator Holland sponsored a Senate joint resolution proposing a constitutional amendment. He argued that an amendment was necessary because no language in the Constitution barred poll taxes; by Article I, Section 2 and by the Seventeenth Amendment the qualifications of voters in federal elections were the same as those "requisite" for electors of the most numerous branch of the state legislature. If Congress undertook to eliminate poll taxes in state voting requirements there was no telling how far the national government might go in invasions of state electoral machinery. The advocates of a statute urged that to prefer the method of a constitutional amendment was to admit that Congress could not eliminate abuses in voting laws, and would weaken other proposals for civil rights legislation.

President Kennedy supported Senator Holland's proposal for an amendment. Attorney General Robert Kennedy endorsed the amendment approach, but also gave the opinion that Congress could outlaw poll taxes by statute without violating the Constitution. Both Senate and House passed the proposed amendment with votes to spare above the needed two-thirds. By the time the amendment was ratified in 1964 it affected only five states that retained the poll tax requirement for voting—Alabama, Arkansas, Mississippi, Texas, and Virginia. The Civil Rights Act, passed the same year, greatly enlarged the liberties of citizens of minority groups.

Presidential Succession

The Constitution as adopted lacked detail on what should happen if the office of President or Vice President became vacant, or either of these officers was unable to discharge his duties (Article II, Section 1, Clause 6). Laws of 1792, 1886, and 1947 prescribed the succession to the presidency, after the Vice President. The first act designated the president pro tempore of the Senate, the second named instead the secretary of state, and the third substituted the speaker of the House; in each law the further succession, of officers of Congress and the cabinet, was stipulated. But what determined disability of principal officers—when it commenced or how long it continued—was not covered. Nor was there any rule for filling the office of Vice President if that became vacant.

President Garfield lived eighty days after he was shot in 1881, but in that period performed only a single official act. President Wilson suffered a paralytic stroke in September 1919, did not meet his cabinet until the following April, and assumed few duties before his term ended in March 1921. In neither instance did the Vice President take over the President's powers.

President Eisenhower had a heart attack in June 1955, a surgical operation in 1956, and a mild stroke in 1957. Each time, until the President recovered, Vice President Nixon presided over cabinet meetings. Thereafter Eisenhower and Nixon had an agreement that should Eisenhower become incapacitated again Nixon would become Acting President following "such consultation as it seemed to him appropriate under the circumstances." President Kennedy and Vice President Johnson made the same agreement in 1961, adding that consultation should include the cabinet. After the assassination of Kennedy in 1963 President Johnson repeated this arrangement with House Speaker John W. McCormack, then next in line, and practically the same understanding held between President Johnson and Vice President Humphrey. These informal agreements were never tested in the courts.

The United States had been without a Vice President 16 times for a total of 37 years, because the Vice President succeeded to the presidency, or died, or (in the case of John C. Calhoun) resigned.

Lyndon B. Johnson, when majority leader of the Senate in 1955, had a heart attack which kept him from his duties six months. Then as President he had surgical operations in 1965 and 1966 from which his recovery was more rapid.

The temporary disabilities of Presidents Eisenhower and Johnson prompted the adoption of the Twenty-fifth Amendment in 1967. Its provisions were first invoked in 1973 when Vice President Spiro Agnew resigned and was succeeded by Gerald R. Ford. The text of the amendment is long, its chief features are as follows:

(1.) If the presidency becomes vacant the Vice President becomes President. (2.) If the Vice Presidency becomes vacant, the President nominates and both houses of Congress by majority vote confirm his successor. (3.) If the President declares in writing to the president pro tem of the Senate and speaker of the House that he is unable to discharge his duties, the Vice President becomes Acting President and so remains until the President declares his fitness to resume his responsibilities. (4.) If the President cannot or does not admit that he is disabled, other officers may establish the fact. The Vice President, together with cabinet officers or other authorized body notifies the president pro tem of the Senate and speaker of the House, and the Vice President becomes Acting President. However, if the President declares that he is not disabled, he resumes his duties. But there is another catch. Suppose the Vice President, cabinet officers, etc., within four days repeat their written assertion that the President is incapacitated. Then Congress within twenty-one days decides the issue by a two-thirds vote.

On August 9, 1974, Vice President Ford became President on the resignation of Richard Nixon. Thus within eight months the operation of the Twenty-fifth Amendment had put in office a President who had not faced national election. Confirmation by Congress of Vice-President-designate Nelson Rockefeller will accomplish the same for the next in succession. Particularly when President Ford's elevation was followed within thirty days, by an unconditional pardon for his predecessor, many wondered whether the amendment on presidential succession might not be improved.

Lowering Voting Age

At hearings on extension of the 1965 Voting Rights Act to permit 18-year-olds to vote Gov. Lester G. Maddox of Georgia charged that the act constituted "discrimination in its vilest form. When are you going to stop warring on the South? If the Government must make war, let it be upon Communism, crime, pornography, and the drug traffic, not upon the God-fearing, country-loving, industrious people of the South." Gov. Maddox then retired to the House restaurant where he handed out autographed pickaxe handles reminiscent of the weapon he used to bar Negroes from a restaurant in Atlanta.

The Voting Rights Act, which was to expire in 1970, almost doubled the proportion of Negroes registered to vote in seven southern states, an increase of 897,000. It forbade literacy tests and lowered to thirty days the residency requirement for voting in federal elections, and provided against other discriminatory practices.

The Senate added an amendment reducing to age 18 the right of citizens to vote in national, state, and local elections. Only four states then permitted voting under the age of 21: Georgia and Kentucky (18 years), Alaska (19 years), and Hawaii (20 years). Three states had rejected proposals to lower the voting age, and 14 states had scheduled referenda on the question.

President Nixon believed that Congress had no power to direct the voting age by statute. However, he signed the bill because of its other manifestly popular features, but he urged Congress to reach its object by proposing a constitutional amendment.

Most of the states were in consternation at the prospect of dual age voting. Many believed that they could not prepare registration books, ballots, and furnish voting machines in time for the 1972 federal elections. It would not be possible to alter state constitutions by that date. A Senate subcommittee reported that lowering the voting age to 18 in federal but not in state and local elections would entail additional election costs of $10 million to $20 million.

The President requested prompt decision by the Supreme Court on the constitutionality of the age 18 feature of the Voting Rights Extension Act. On December 21, 1970, only ten days before the act was to go into effect, the Court by a 5 to 4 ruling declared that Congress could open federal elections to 18-year-olds, but not state and local elections.

The result was that Congress proposed the Twenty-sixth Amendment, March 23, 1971, lowering to 18 the voting age in all elections. Witnesses who carried weight had testified that young people were far better educated than half a century earlier, that they could be expected not to demonstrate violently in the streets if they were given the right to help shape society by their ballots. The proposed reform would extend the suffrage to 14 million Americans. A frequent argument was that if young men were required by the military draft to fight for the country they were old enough to vote.

The amendment was ratified in little more than three months, reducing by more than half the fastest time achieved earlier. This was the fifth amendment to enlarge the electorate: the Fifteenth gave the vote to Negro citizens, the Nineteenth extended the suffrage to women, the Twenty-third permitted voting for President in the District of Columbia, and the Twenty-first added those previously unable to pay poll taxes.

Proposed Equal Rights Amendment

Alice Paul, of Quaker descent and highly educated, had witnessed the militant suffrage campaign in England. In the nineteen-twenties she and her indomitable cohort of the Woman's Party demanded an equal rights amendment to the Constitution. The suffrage amendment for which they had pressed seemed not to have freed women from complained-of discriminations. Piecemeal reform measures were not speeded. A fundamental corrective, applying to women as a class in American society, appeared to be required.

From the first the absolutist feminists were opposed by spokesmen of the majority of women who feared to lose legal protections which they considered outweighed many injustices suffered by their sex. The New Deal of Franklin Roosevelt in the Great Depression of the 'thirties gave new impetus to selective reform. Rescue from desperate poverty appealed as the most insistent right. This social legislation preserved sex distinctions to the disadvantage of women, but it accustomed the public to massive federal intervention in the conditions of life of the people.

The efforts of the Woman's Party dwindled, but other developments promoted the cause of the equal rights amendment. World War II multiplied the number of women wage-earners. At the same time technological advances were freeing women from housework and inviting them into manufactures, trade, and the service industries. By the mid-1970's 44 per cent of women worked outside of the home, and 8.5 million of these took employment to support themselves and their families. Collective action to solve social problems had made the United States a Welfare State. The Civil Rights Act of 1964 removed many discriminations against women, but a more inclusive guarantee was needed in the fields of education, employment, and control of property. One after another objection to equal rights economic, social, and legal was weakened or refuted. Protective labor laws were less necessary where mechanical power was substituted for muscular exertion. Many "protective" limitations in fact excluded women workers from better-paying employment; men equally with women should be defended against economic exploitation.

The capacities of the individual, not of the sex-class of 53 per cent of the American people, should govern restrictions. Those who boggled at the prospect of the military draft being extended to women were reminded that General Eisenhower expected that in another world conflict women would be taken into the armed services equally with men. Most assignments in the military are non-combatant, and army service offers training, promotion, and security. Legally established rights of privacy preclude mixing of the sexes in sleeping quarters and restrooms.

Proposed by Congress in 1972, the equal rights amendment had been ratified in January 1974 by 32 states of 38 required to make it a part of the Constitution. The provision of a delay of two years before becoming operative is to allow the states to make necessary changes in their laws to bring them into conformity with the national mandate.

Proposed Reform of Electoral College

The feature of the Constitution longest and most often complained of as obsolete or positively injurious is the machinery for choosing President and Vice President—the "electoral college." This was settled upon by the Philadelphia framers only after much discussion, and misgivings as to how it would operate. All agreed that the President should represent the whole people of the nation. Some, like James Wilson, contended for direct popular election. Others (Madison and Randolph, sponsors of the Virginia draft) preferred selection by Congress. Hamilton urged choice by the people of electors, "men most capable of analyzing the qualities adapted to the station" of President; these, possessing "the information and discernment requisite to so complicated an investigation," should be entrusted with the "immediate election." Luther Martin in an adaptation of Maryland practice recommended that the executive be chosen by electors "appointed by the several legislatures."

From these various expedients came the combination plan adopted almost at the end of the convention, as Article II, section 1. Each state should designate, "in such manner as the legislature thereof shall direct, a number of electors, equal to the whole number of Senators and Representatives to which the State shall be entitled in the Congress . . ." That is, Hamilton's plan of election of electors by the people could be followed, or the legislature of the state might appoint them. The electors, meeting in their states, should each vote for two persons. The list of those voted for, with the number of votes for each, should be directed to the president of the Senate for counting in the presence of both houses of Congress. The person with the greatest number of votes, if a majority of the whole number of electors, should be President. If more than one had a majority, and an equal number of votes, the House should immediately ballot for one. If nobody had a majority as the lists came up from the states, the House should choose from the five highest. The votes should "be taken by States, the representation from each State having one vote." After election of the President, the person with the next highest vote should be Vice President, and if two or more had the same number of votes, then the Senate should choose. This scheme was modified by the Twelfth Amendment in 1804, which made the votes of electors for President and Vice President distinct. This change was prompted by the experience in 1800-1801 when Jefferson and Burr had an equal number of electoral votes. Many ballots in the House were necessary before Jefferson won, though it was generally recognized that he had been the preference of the electors. Other changes in the amendment were of less importance.

Actually this complicated system never worked as intended. Initially it was a foregone conclusion that the electors must register the overwhelming choice of Washington for President, and for further terms if he would consent to serve. By 1796 there were two acknowledged political parties. The leaders of each put forward a ticket—the Federalists, John Adams and Thomas Pinckney, and the Republicans, Jefferson and Burr. Thus the party conference or "caucus" made nominations and largely supplanted the electors. This practice was repeated in 1800 and continued until the first party conventions made nominations in 1832.

But the machinery outlined in the Constitution remained. Its central vice, in practice, was that frequently the President, supposed to represent the majority of the people, had a majority of the electoral vote but a minority of the popular vote. This was because in each state, increasingly, the electors voted in a bloc for the candidates (for President and for Vice President) having the majority of popular votes in that state. The successful electors considered themselves instructed to report the will of those who chose them. They exercised no discretion of their own. Thus the rule became, in each state, "winner takes all." A candidate with a bare majority in populous states—those with a large electoral vote—could win the presidency though he had few popular votes in other states and a minority of popular votes in the country as a whole. Minority Presidents were John Quincy Adams (1824), Polk (1844), Taylor (1848), Pierce (1852), Buchanan (1856), Lincoln (1860), Hayes (1876), Garfield (1880), Harrison (1888), Cleveland (1892), Wilson (1912, 1916), Truman (1948), Kennedy (1960), Nixon (1968). Two of these, Hayes and Harrison, actually polled fewer votes than their respective major opponents.

Party campaign efforts are concentrated in the doubtful states and candidates are often chosen from these states in the hope of winning their electoral votes. Little attention is paid to citizen voters in "sure" states, those considered certain to go for one or other of the major parties. Political apathy may be the result where there is no contest between candidates.

At the time the Twelfth Amendment was under debate there was practically no discussion of changing the electoral machinery, but more recently proposals have come mainly under two heads: (1) divide electoral votes proportionately within the various states, on the basis of division in popular vote; (2) sweep away the whole system, and rely entirely on the popular vote. There has been little popular demand for reform, and repeated proposals for change have always met with defeat. Even the extremely close popular vote in 1960 seemingly did not bring about a more serious consideration of possible change. The basic criticism has been that expressed by Representative Ross of Pennsylvania as far back as 1816: "Might not the election be better trusted at once to the people? Why the intervention of electors? . . . It did appear . . . that to the people and to them only could the election be safely confided; and that all the present machinery for electing a President, which sometimes is wielded by mere legerdemain, corruption, and unfair influence, be put out of the way."

Chapter Six

CONSTITUTION IS WHAT
SUPREME COURT SAYS IT IS

I THE MIGHTY MARSHALL

It is frequently said that the Supreme Court is "a continuing constitutional convention." Its interpretations of the Constitution may be revisions of the document. The Court, bit by bit, and here and there is adding to the instrument or taking from it, is in fact creating fundamental law. This is plainest where an earlier decision has been contradicted by a later one, or where a development appears through a succession of decisions. An example of the latter would be the treatment of due process, which was at first limited to property rights, but has come to be concerned with civil liberties, or the status of citizens.

When the Court says what the law is, does it in effect make law? If so, do the justices usurp the legislative function? Should the Court confine itself as closely as is discoverable to the intent of the framers of the Constitution, and, if the result is unacceptable to Congress or the country, rely on alteration of statute or on constitutional amendment to serve the contemporary need? How permissive is the duty conferred on the Court?

The Constitution itself gives the Supreme Court no authority to negative acts of Congress or of the state legislatures. The latter power was conferred in the federal Judiciary Act of 1789, but only where the highest state court had declined to hold the disputed statute invalid. This right of the Supreme Court was first exercised in 1797 when a state law was nullified as violative of the treaty of peace with Great Britain. Thereafter hundreds of state statutes, mostly after the Civil War, were struck down by the Supreme Court. In 1914 the appellate jurisdiction of the Supreme Court was enlarged to permit it to pass on state acts which state courts had condemned as against the federal Constitution. This was because state courts sometimes held invalid state legislation—for example, regulating hours of women workers— which the Supreme Court had ruled constitutional!

Though the Constitution was silent on the function of "judicial review" of federal statutes by the Supreme Court, this duty was approved in the Philadelphia convention by such influential members as Madison, Mason, Wilson, Gouverneur Morris, Luther Martin, and impliedly by Ellsworth, Strong, and Rutledge. This discretion was flatly opposed by Mercer and Dickinson, who declared "no such power [to set aside laws of Congress] ought to exist."

Many in the convention, echoing American hostility to Parliament, were sure the public liberty was in greater danger from legislative usurpation than from any other source. The President, holding office for a brief term of years, would be a feeble check upon the lawmakers; "there is the greatest ground to fear his want of firmness in resisting encroachments." Several urged that the judges of the Supreme Court be associated with the executive in approving acts of Congress before these could take effect. This would be serviceable to Congress in forestalling departures from constitutional mandate, support the President in his vetoes, and protect the public against "those unwise and unjust measures" which were blameable for "so great a portion of our calamities." Notwithstanding the double defense, of court and executive, danger was that the legislature would "absorb all power into its vortex." Judges in England were consulted in advance on disputed intended laws; as members of the Privy Council, they might advise the executive. It was as stoutly objected that judicial and legislative duties should not be mixed. The constitutionality of statutes would "come before the Judges . . . in their proper official character," when "they have a negative on the laws." To consult them beforehand "was making Statesmen of the Judges," though, as judges, "they are not to be presumed to possess any peculiar knowledge of the mere policy of public measures." These and other arguments killed the proposal.

It is clear that the framers of the Constitution believed the President's veto was sufficient check on the expediency of legislative acts, and the Supreme Court should be confined to passing on their legality. The justices were to apply the Constitution rather than interpret it with any degree of discretion. Said Hamilton in *The Federalist*: "The courts must declare the sense of the law; and if they should be disposed to exercise *will* instead of *judgment*, the consequence would be . . . the substitution of their pleasure to that of the legislative body." Wilson and Mason, in the debates, lamented that unless the judges were consulted in advance on the propriety of statutes, they would be compelled, on the bench, to give effect to laws not plainly repugnant to the Constitution though in their view "dangerous" or "destructive."

One must be bold to suppose the constitutional fathers were naïve enough to envision the Supreme Court as charged with rendering open and shut decisions on the validity of statutes. Did they not foresee that in the actual experiment, over time, with the progress of the country, the Constitution must be plastic? However this may be, the Constitution, as formulated, was necessarily general in character, an outline of broad principles. But social behavior constantly evolves. Somewhere in the political system must be the authority to countenance changes in practice as in conformity with the basic plan, or disallow them because out of harmony with the scheme. This power may not be exercised mechanically, as in putting square pegs into square holes, round pegs into round holes. Judgment is the essence of the process. What is wise for the convenience, efficiency, integrity of the on-going society?

Doubtless most Americans agree that this discretion is sensibly lodged in the Supreme Court. It is desirable that changes of policy in the national community should be deliberate, not eccentric, and gradual rather than sudden. For this purpose of giving the final word—or final for the time being—a few judges are superior to a more numerous legislature. The judges are chosen for their learning, awareness, and responsibility. They sit for life, do not have to respond to political influence or popular whim. Since they are mouthpieces of a Constitution designed to endure, they have always at hand a frame of reference, are apt to be conservative. Better so than be capricious or volatile. Society is tough, makes a myriad of informal internal adjustments all the time, and will not be seriously injured by some delays.

Judicial Review Makes for Flexibility

Evidence is that the framers of the Judiciary Act of 1789 saw the Supreme Court as arbiter of the constitutionality of statutes of Congress. In the first ten years in only one case (*Hylton v. U.S.*) was the power of the Supreme Court to declare a law void considered. The federal carriage tax was upheld, but the implication surely was that the Court possessed authority to refuse agreement. *Marbury v. Madison* (1803) furnished the first decision in which the Supreme Court unequivocally asserted its liberty to strike down an act of Congress as violative of the Constitution. The particulars of this history-making opinion are given elsewhere in these pages. In the following half-century the Court passed on the validity of acts of Congress but sustained them all. Then the unhappy policy of perpetuating slavery in the Dred Scott decision, 1857, blasted the Missouri Compromise. In the next decade two more acts were pronounced void before the Court proved cagey in the Reconstruction period. The century closed with a score of statutes thrown out, among others those covering civil rights and the income tax. Redoubled negatives in the early 1920's provoked Senator LaFollette to propose an amendment giving Congress power to re-enact a law held unconstitutional. A barrage of decisions condemned measures devised by Franklin Roosevelt's New Deal to rescue the country from depression—national recovery, railroad retirement, coal conservation, bankruptcy, and agricultural adjustment acts.

Roosevelt's answer was the plan to enlarge the numbers on the highest bench from nine to fifteen, ostensibly to clear the clogged docket and unburden aged justices. But Congress and country, which had been responsive to emergency measures, rejected the real motive of "court packing," which was to ensure favorable opinions from the new justices to be appointed. The attempt pressed the President's popularity to his discredit. The verdict of the public was that judges had their personal economic and social predispositions, to be sure, but trust in the integrity of the Supreme Court was crucial to our constitutional system. It would be fatal to make the Court an instrument in the hands of any administration. On this occasion tension was eased when the court approved labor relations and labor standards acts which went far to regulate manufacturing and commerce within the states.

Thus our Constitution, quite aside from amendments, has proved to be flexible, answerable to emerging needs. The process of Court interpretation is not as simple as in Britain where the constitution, instead of being a single document, is a series of historic charters supplemented by decisions, statutes, and in fact by tradition. In the United States the letter of the law sometimes gets in the way of the spirit. Application of given words to new situations is frequently awkward. The Supreme Court may be driven to the dodge of sanctioning a doubtful law because of the purpose which Congress assigns to it. A tax which furnishes no revenue because it is intended to prohibit a commodity or practice may be held by the Court to be a tax because Congress says it is that. But the Constitution in important instances is not verbally specific, much less constricting. Collecting revenue for the "general welfare" admits of a variety of objects. Implied powers take in vast territories. "Due process" is a reminder of caution but allows latitude. The Court invents for itself escape clauses, such as the "rule of reason" applied to the lawfulness of business combinations. Use of such an expedient permits the bench discretion in passing on the meaning of statutes, apart from their constitutionality. This comes close to placing the judges in the seats of the legislators.

One often finds citation of precedents cluttering Court decisions. The effort is to keep the record straight, or tolerably straight. Previous decisions are apt to be imperfect guides to later judgments. The issues and facts may not be precisely alike, the cases not "on all fours" with each other. The devil may quote scripture; justices of contrary views do not lack earlier pronouncements to bolster their arguments. They will ascribe different meanings to the same precedent. Usually this habit of appeal to past wisdom is beneficial—to legislators, litigants, lawyers, to the Court itself. But when former determination may not be reconciled with present requirement, precedent becomes embarrassing. Perhaps it is consciously twisted to make the chain of reasoning at least plausible. Where there is flat contradiction the Court is in the situation of the Australian bushman who was given a new boomerang but could not throw away his old one.

Then there are several choices before the Court. It may reverse itself, repudiate the old position, make a fresh start on a more promising course. It may find the law unconstitutional—if that is inescapable—expecting that the legislature may re-enact it with changes to make it acceptable. Or the Court may say, perhaps with regret, that the Constitution by no stretch will permit a power to Congress, and point to the alternative of an amendment. This means reverting to the will of the people which is the supreme authority. This method entails delay, though perhaps justified to allow of deliberation. Far more amendments have been proposed than have been ratified. Were this not true the federal Constitution would lose its merit as a fundamental charter, couched in broad language, permissive as well as limiting. It would come to resemble many state constitutions, which amount to an accumulation of statutes and grow so unwieldy as to require recurrent conventions to revise them.

Suppose Congress recommends an amendment but it drags in approval by the people (actually by the state legislatures). A minority of states, maybe in a geographical bloc, may thwart it. If there is sufficient demand the object may yet be accomplished. It may be embodied in statutes by most of the states. Or it may be ensured for the whole country in an act of Congress which the Supreme Court may find valid. This happened in the satisfactory restriction of child labor.

First, laws of Congress were held unconstitutional. Next, the child labor amendment did not receive approval of three-fourths of the states. But, at long last, the evil was successfully attacked in the Fair Labor Standards Act. There is more than one way to skin a cat.

A chief reason for admiring the Constitution is its durability with slight formal change. The first ten amendments (Bill of Rights) were added almost immediately; they might be considered as inadvertently omitted from the original plan. Since then only a baker's dozen of amendments have been found desirable. But think of the changes in the nation in the span of more than 200 years! We have grown from five million people in thirteen states along the Atlantic coast to 210 million in fifty states reaching to the Pacific and beyond. Immigration has brought a variety of cultures into a population once homogeneous. Subsistence agriculture and trade, local for the most part, have developed, with the addition of industry, transport, and communication, to continental and international proportions. Corporate organization and finance dominate a scene once marked by small-scale personal enterprises. The states have shrunk in self-sufficiency, while the central government fills a role—political, economic, social—never foreseen. When the Constitution was adopted the country was only emerging from colonial status, our erstwhile enemy still had troops on our soil, and we were fearful of Spanish rivalry on this continent. Long since we have become the leading world power with military, diplomatic, and moral commitments around the globe.

Through all this expansion and transformation the Constitution has continued to serve. We must not forget, amidst this praise, that the Civil War was, on the surface at least, a calamitous quarrel over the meaning of our fundamental law, which threatened a disastrous end to the experiment. Fortunately, the economic differences which underlay the political and military conflict were reconciled, so that unity and progress were resumed.

The wisdom of the framers has been matched by the discipline and responsibility of after-comers from many lands who have lived under the plan outlined long ago. The secret is in tolerant interpretation of the master document. If the fathers could return would they recognize their handiwork as now applied? Many would be astonished. Their puzzlement would be the measure of the constitutional achievement of the generations which have succeeded them.

Marbury versus Madison

Crusty John Adams has been pictured as driving his quill at the presidential desk until the moment of midnight, March 3, 1801. He was signing the commissions of a flock of national judges. This was to place Federalists in long-tenure posts before Jefferson's administration took over. According to the story, Adams had little rest that night, being obliged to pack his baggage for Braintree. He made an ungracious exit from Washington, refusing to remain a few hours longer to help usher his successor into office. The part about Adams quitting the capital before Jefferson's inauguration is true. That about dashing down his name with one eye on the commissions and the other on the clock is not literally the fact. However, he did, at the very end of his term, press through appointment of party men to openings created by the (Federalist) Judiciary Act of 1801. The last were forty-two justices of the peace for the District of Columbia. The Senate had confirmed them, their commissions were signed and sealed, and passed on to John Marshall, secretary of state, to be delivered. Marshall did not get around to this final act and absent-mindedly left the commissions lying on his desk when he relinquished office to President Jefferson's secretary of state, James Madison.

President Jefferson ordered that most of the commissions be sent to those for whom they were intended. Among the certificates of appointment withheld were those of William Marbury and three others, who applied to the Supreme Court for a mandamus to Madison. Accordingly Chief Justice Marshall in December 1801 directed Madison to show cause why the mandamus should not be issued. Before the case could proceed further a tumultuous debate in Congress, taking some of its violence from Marshall's preliminary move, radically changed the posture of national affairs. The Judiciary Act of 1789, which organized the national courts, deserved correction. It wearied and misapplied the energies of Supreme Court justices by requiring them to travel through the country to sit in circuit courts. They must review, on appeal, cases which they had heard below. After a dozen years this awkward system was reformed by the Judiciary Act of 1801, which freed the Supreme Court justices for their proper duties in the highest tribunal (two terms a year), and provided judges for an increased number of circuit courts. To these permanent posts President Adams appointed dependable Federalists.

When the Republicans came in, President Jefferson asked for a review of the judiciary system. He was persuaded to delete from his message a challenge which his spokesmen in Congress boldly expressed: the federal courts had no power to hold acts of legislature and executive invalid. The other branches of government had the right to interpret the Constitution for themselves. Jefferson believed that every state possessed this autonomy. The mess that would have resulted from departments within the administration pulling against each other, and states working at cross purposes, with no one authority entrusted to say what was the law, impugns the common sense of these political theorists. The definition of liberty is self-will amenable to agreed rules, and of course this involves reposing somewhere the duty to interpret and apply the fundamental charter.

The Republicans set themselves to repeal the Judiciary Act of 1801. The hated Federalists had plotted to make the courts their last refuge. Driven from control of Congress and the national executive, they would still reign through judges' writs. Had not Marshall dared to reach into the very cabinet by demanding that the secretary of state answer to the Court? Judicial robes must not be allowed to cover tyranny. Wicked doings of the federal judges under the Alien and Sedition acts were recalled. Every instance where a court had held a law unconstitutional was remembered for revilement. So far from being multiplied, the number of national judges should be reduced. And those who remained had best be careful if they hoped to escape impeachment.

Federalists in Senate and House Couverneur Morris, Uriah Tracy, James A. Bayard, John Rutledge, Jr.—remonstrated against the charges of leading Republican debaters such as Giles and John Randolph. The last mentioned was severe against the arrogated power of the Supreme Court to negative laws passed by national and state legislatures, and to direct certain actions on the part of the President and his secretaries. Legislators were chosen by the people, and better than appointed judges, could determine what the Constitution intended. The Federalists answered, as always, that the people, and their direct representatives, were fluctuating, not to say turbulent in their demands. Guarantee of liberty and the security of property required the wisdom of learned justices, on indefinite tenure, as far as possible immune to buffetings of party storms.

These sensible counsels of the Federalists—which were to be approved by subsequent experience—were for the time in vain. The existing judiciary law was repealed on a strict party vote, 59 Republicans against 32 Federalists. By this action the old judiciary system of 1789, which crippled the operation of this branch of the government, was restored. The *Washington Federalist* (newspaper) was typical of others of that party in announcing, "The fatal bill has passed; our Constitution is no more . . . the President . . . has gratified his malice towards the judges, but he has drawn a tear into the eye of every thoughtful patriot . . . and laid the foundation of infinite mischief." But it was predicted that the judges would sit as usual and declare the repeal law invalid.

To prevent this last the Republicans promptly pushed through a law suspending sessions of the Supreme Court for fourteen months. They hoped that in this hiatus the clamors of the displaced Federalist judges would be stilled, any intention of the Supreme Court to declare the repeal law unconstitutional would be relinquished, and further action in the case of *Marbury v. Madison* would be postponed. Postponed it was, but it took on unexpected meaning when the Court reconvened in February 1803. Chief Justice John Marshall used this stale case to rebuke the dominant Republicans who denied the right of the Supreme Court to pass finally upon the lawfulness of an act of Congress.

The suit was mostly shadow boxing, but in the course of his decision Marshall delivered a blow which fight fans call a "sleeper"—lightly felt at the moment, but revealing its powerful effect later. The circumstances were well adapted to Marshall's purpose, (and we must assume that he had a purpose, since he was human, and not a mere abstraction of Justice). He could say that the appointees of President Adams had a right to their commissions, and that the secretary of state, on mandamus if necessary, was bound to deliver them. At the same time he could pronounce that the Supreme Court had no authority to issue the mandamus, thus excusing the secretary of state from doing, in fact, what the Court declared was his duty. But—and this is what in time since has given celebrity to the opinion—the Supreme Court could not issue the mandamus because the Judiciary Act of 1789, which conferred this power, was unconstitutional in this respect.

Court Will Declare a Statute Invalid

The opening of the case was comic, much like the libretto of a Gilbert and Sullivan operetta. Marshall himself, before he quit as secretary of state, had custody of the commissions, but he was obliged to preside gravely on the bench while counsel for Marbury strove to prove that the papers had been made out in form. Madison had refused to answer Marbury's questions and if the commission was demanded he referred Marbury to his chief clerk, Wagner. Wagner said the commissions had gone to Attorney General Lincoln, but in court he objected to giving any information, since that would be to disclose what he knew as a subordinate of the secretary of state. Similarly Lincoln objected to testifying, but later, in answer to written questions approved by the Court, said he had seen some completed commissions but did not know whether commissions for Marbury and the other petitioners were among them. After further disputes about the laws of evidence it was proved, on testimony of a clerk, that some of the commissions in question were signed and sealed.

Marshall decided that Marbury and the others were justices of the peace. Their commissions were merely formal evidence of the offices they held. Delivery of the commissions by the secretary of state was a ministerial act incumbent on the secretary, Madison. He had no discretion in the matter, nor did the President. Why, then, not compel Madison by mandamus to give Marbury his right?

Here, judging from the large number of words Marshall used in his opinion, he recognized his quandary. If he did not issue the mandamus, and dismissed the case, this would admit what the Republicans contended, that the Court could not give directions to executive officers, nor override a law of Congress because unconstitutional. If the Court issued the writ, Madison would refuse to comply with it, the President would support him, the Court would be powerless to enforce its demand and thus be made ridiculous.

But Marshall knew how to have his cake and eat it. The Constitution, he propounded, gave the Supreme Court original jurisdiction in specified cases, and thus excluded all others. The authority to issue the writ of mandamus was not specified. Therefore Section 13 of the Judiciary Act of 1789, on which Marbury's counsel confidently relied as conferring the power of mandamus, was contrary to the Constitution and void.

Marshall needed to be impressive in declaring this conclusion. The Constitution did not say that the Supreme Court could annul a statute if held to be violative of that document; however, the possibility of such action had long been the subject of heated discussion and judges, state and federal, had claimed the authority. Further, the statute containing the section which Marshall now voided had been acquiesced in for years, and this very Court had accepted the mandamus power without question. The Constitution itself might have been interpreted more broadly to make the statute perfectly legal. In fact, except for the emergency in national affairs, as Marshall viewed it, which called for a declaration of the power of judicial review, Marshall would hardly have chosen this case for his momentous announcement. But if he had not then illustrated the right of the Court to strike down an act of Congress this supreme power, ever after accepted, might not have been established. No such authority was exercised in the earlier history of the Court, and it was not employed again for forty-two years. So, as Beveridge observes, if Marshall had not intervened when he did, "nearly seventy years would have passed without any question arising as to the omnipotence of Congress. After so long a period of judicial acquiescence in Congressional supremacy it seems likely that opposition to it would have been futile." The foremost position ever taken by the Supreme Court—that this body is the final arbiter in what is law—might never have been claimed. By the same token, the chief contribution made by America to jurisprudence might have gone by default.

We have spoken of Marshall more than of his brothers on the bench. Able and conscientious men though they were, we must assume from their previous behavior that the Chief Justice persuaded them to embrace his bold resolve. If we forget the appropriateness of the features of this particular case as that on which to hang the epochal decision, which is disputable, the logic of Marshall's reasoning is not to be questioned. Like all enduring statements of principle, his was simple, understandable by anybody. The purpose of the people, in ordaining a written constitution, is to limit the powers conferred on government in its several departments. The justices are sworn to uphold the Constitution. If they find that a law passed by Congress is repugnant to it, they must declare that law invalid. Marshall illustrated by striking examples how the efficacy of the written Constitution would be broken down, and the authority of the fundamental law would become a mockery, if the Court enforced statutes which flouted the solemn will of the people.

However, we must remember that a society may not live on dogma. Growth means change. Nobody knew this better than Marshall. He was saying that departures from old practice must not be made at the sole will of the legislature or of the executive. In disputed cases such laws and actions must be referred to national judges who will pass on their validity. Decisions of the courts are not mechanically foreordained. They are interpretations. The Supreme Court itself must be flexible, must discard old meanings, discover new ones. All is relative, there are no absolutes. The final word rests with the Court because it is best fitted, by training of its members and by its procedure, to act as conservator. If it is cautious, in instances, about approving what afterward appears to be progress, it is also alert to discountenance what later will be recognized as precipitate and dangerous. Americans have decided from experience that wise government consists in the ready expression of popular demand which is then filtered to remove unwanted ingredients. Public discussion must be free. The House of Representatives presumably refuses what is most prejudicial. The Senate uses further prudence. The President may disapprove what both houses of the legislature have proposed. Lastly the Supreme Court, in cases brought before it, may affirm or reject. It all comes down to the axiom "better safe than sorry." In this "make haste slowly" process, much of speed and spontaneity are lost. Nor is the Supreme Court infallible. On occasion it frankly reverses its former decisions, and oftener it does so with face-saving words which nonetheless have their own value. Paradoxically, the variability of the Court is testimony to its integrity.

Marbury v. Madison (1 Cranch 137, 1803) provoked criticism from Republicans because the Court took to itself the power to cancel an act of Congress. From the fuss made about this beforehand, we would expect it to form the chief basis of complaint. Not so, for resentment was directed against the lecture read to the President and secretary of state for withholding the commissions. The justices as much as said that lower federal courts could issue mandamuses. This was repulsed by Republicans as interference with the executive department. Could the judiciary direct action of the President and his ministers? Further, Marshall's observations on this head were *obiter dicta*, thrown in, not necessary to the decision, since the Court went on to say that it had in fact no power to issue the mandamus.

Jeffersonians Attack Supreme Bench

In this book we are not concerned with the history of the Supreme Court as such, but rather with principal decisions interpreting the Constitution. However, the complexion of the Court, the political and social outlook of the justices, is pertinent, as is also the attitude at different times of the President, Congress, and the public toward the Court. In this last connection we must mention the efforts of Republicans at the beginning of the 1800's, about the time of *Marbury v. Madison*, to discredit federal courts by impeachment of judges. It may be that President Jefferson and his most eager party lieutenants wanted by this means to remove a substantial number or all of the Federalist justices of the Supreme Court, including John Marshall. If this was the design, only a beginning was made before the attempt was dropped.

First, an able but arrogant state judge, Alexander Addison, who had regularly preached his Federalist doctrine in charging grand juries, was impeached by the Pennsylvania House of Representatives and was convicted by the Senate in January 1803. A few days later the national House of Representatives was urged by President Jefferson to take appropriate action against Judge John Pickering of the district court of New Hampshire. Joseph Nicholson and John Randolph of Virginia pressed through a resolution for impeachment and presented it to the Senate at just the time when Marshall was delivering his opinion in *Marbury v. Madison.*

Judge Pickering had twice been relieved of his judicial duties during periods of insanity, and afterward he went too promptly from the bottle to the bench. It was cited against him that when a ship and cargo were libeled for violation of customs regulations he ordered both restored to the owner. However, the case was again brought to trial because the collector complained that the judge had behaved in an incompetent manner. This time Pickering was drunker than before. Amidst much confusion in the court he was prevailed upon to grant a postponement until the next morning for, he observed, he would "then be sober." On the morrow the government hoped for better treatment, but found His Honor as wild as ever. He refused to hear any but the owner's side, and accordingly ordered vessel and goods freed.

The "trial" of the judge was held a year later, in March 1804. Pickering did not answer when his name was called. His condition of insanity was explained by his son and by Robert Goodloe Harper. What to do? Was a judge admittedly out of his wits responsible for "high crimes and misdemeanors" on the bench? If the Senate could not pronounce an insane man guilty, how could a judge so afflicted be deposed from the bench? The Republican-controlled Senate was in a box. The (Federalist) Judiciary Act of 1801 had provided another method of removal in such a case, but the Republicans had repealed that law and were now on the horns of a dilemma. They must call a crazy judge sane, in order to hold him guilty, or leave a demented man on the bench. The Republicans in the Senate, though with broken ranks, still mustered a party majority to find Pickering guilty.

The Republicans next levelled on Associate Justice Samuel Chase of the Supreme Court. He was bigger game than poor demented Pickering who had been unseated from the district bench in New Hampshire.

For a couple of years Chase had been pictured in pamphlets as a political judge, venting his spleen against Republicans, especially where these were defendants before him. Under the Alien Act he had helped convict Callender and Cooper—English visitors who loudly proclaimed popular rights—and, under the Sedition Act, John Fries, the Pennsylvania auctioneer who had rallied disobedience to the federal direct tax. Only another of Chase's outbursts was needed to precipitate the attempt at his impeachment.

Soon after the Supreme Court unanimously decided in *Marbury v. Madison* that an act of Congress was unconstitutional and that a high executive officer was answerable to a command of the bench, Chase instructed the grand jury in Baltimore. Being a Marylander, Chase felt a special liberty—an excuse which he did not need—to inveigh against "the recent change in our state constitution, by the establishing of universal suffrage." This would "take away all security for property and personal liberty . . . and our republican constitution will sink into a mobocracy . . ." He had some choice words for the recent Republican Judiciary Act (beloved of Jefferson); how could "justice be impartially administered by judges dependent on the legislature for their . . . support?"

When these sentiments met President Jefferson's eye he dispatched them to a lieutenant in Congress with the query: "Ought this seditious and official attack on the principles of our Constitution, and on the proceedings of a State, go unpunished?" Jefferson did not need to spell out "the necessary measures." His House leaders promptly (in the same hour that Judge Pickering was convicted) secured the impeachment of Judge Chase. Management of the case was placed in the hands of John Randolph of Roanoke. Of his six companions Caesar Rodney was a man of force, Joseph Nicholson of Maryland was possessed of parts and partisanship, but the others were distinctly third-rate. Randolph was the worst choice of all. Vain, violent, and ignorant of law, the charge which he drew against Chase was vulnerable in all its eight counts. His nerves, which needed no exhaustion, were frazzled because he had just been beaten in his assault on Jefferson's compromise of the Yazoo land fraud. This not only made him more than ever temperish, but he was at odds with his own party when unity was essential if Chase was to be pulled from the bench. The Republicans in the Senate numbered 25, the Federalists 9. Two-thirds of the total, or 23, were required for conviction. Thus if three Republican senators disagreed with their party fellows, Chase was safe, and more than that small contingent were known, on various grounds, to be doubtful. Still, Federalists were ready to despair because the conduct of Chase was to be weighed in political scales. Fisher Ames lamented that "party reasons are the only ones . . . regarded . . . You may broil Judge Chase and eat him, or eat him raw; it shall stir up less anger or pity than the Six Nations would show if Cornplanter or Red Jacket was refused a belt of wampum."

The springboard of the managers for the House was that an officer could be impeached for other than acts deliberately illegal. Behavior held by the House to be intemperate, extra-legal, and abusive was enough.

Giles had often before been the spokesman of a Virginia junto hostile to central—especially if Federalist—power. Beginning with Chase he wanted to "sweep the supreme judicial bench clean" except for the judge last appointed (by Jefferson). For conviction upon impeachment it was not necessary, according to Giles, to show criminality or corrupt conduct. Congress could monitor courts, and say to the judges, "You hold dangerous opinions, and if you are suffered to carry them into effect you will work the destruction of the nation. We want your offices for the purpose of giving them to men who will fill them better." This was the opposite of what had just been done in Judge Pickering's case. There a crazy man, incapable of knowing right from wrong, had been convicted of high crimes and misdemeanors. However, inconsistency did not trouble the Republican party managers.

Trial of Judge Chase a Popular Show

After a delay of one month, granted to Chase to prepare his defense, the trial opened in the little Senate chamber on February 9, 1805, and neither branch of Congress gave ear to much else during the remainder of that session. A temporary gallery, below the regular one—a sort of mezzanine—had been erected to accommodate the Washington ladies, and members of Senate and House and the diplomatic corps filled every available seat on the floor. The upper public gallery was crowded with visitors who came to see the show. The capital's boarding houses had no rooms left. It has been said that the hall was decorated in bright colors which heightened the spectacle, but these garlands seem to have been nothing more than the red and green felt covers for the desks of legislators.

Doubtless most of those who craned their necks and drank in the oratory with approval or received it with snorts did not know the magnitude of the decision that was to be reached. It was no less than whether the federal judiciary was to be sustained as an independent branch in the triumvirate of governmental powers, or whether the judges were to be subordinated to executive and legislative policy of the moment. Was the Constitution our permanent fundamental law, to be sagely interpreted by men secure in their positions, or was the document to be applied according to temporary, and perhaps passionate, demand?

True, there were farcical features of the proceeding. Aaron Burr, Vice President of the United States and president of the Senate, who occupied the chair, had just returned from his flight to southern parts. His scamper was to escape action on indictments in two states, New York and New Jersey, for the murder of Alexander Hamilton (in a duel). It was an open question whether the Senate sat as the nation's highest court, to judge of alleged crimes of Chase, or was a mere civil inquiry to determine whether the accused should be removed from the bench for reasons which to the senators seemed good. John Randolph's colleagues differed among themselves in their speeches for the prosecution. Some pressed particular charges which others disregarded as invalid. John Randolph, ignorant of law, floundered and blustered. Finally, "with much distortion of face and contortion of body, tears, groans, and sobs," he broke down and could only congratulate the senators that this was "the last day of my sufferings and of yours."

The dignity of the doings was saved, if at all, by the businesslike competence of Chase's counsel. Allotted a box over against the accusers from the House, they were among the foremost advocates the country boasted. Luther Martin, Chase's fellow-Marylander, was prepared to make the greatest effort of his career, and he was supported by Robert Goodloe Harper, Charles Lee (former attorney general), Philip Barton Key, and, youngest but not least, Joseph Hopkinson. Their insistence, first to last, was that Chase, if guilty, must be convicted of offenses indictable at law. This was the meaning of the Constitution, and no amount of distaste for his views, or reproaches because he read a political lecture to the Baltimore grand jury, would serve to touch him. Actually, the political participation of other federal judges, from the Supreme Court down, had been accepted for years, without the blame now fastened on Chase. Whenever one of the prosecutors ventured to cross swords with Chase's practiced counsel on the score of the legality of the judge's actions he found his weapon hacked and himself thrust through.

Probably something between the principles of prosecution and defense would have been a truer ground of impeachment. The political or constitutional slant of Chase, though hateful to the Republicans, was not cause for censure. On the other hand, the interpretation of Luther Martin and the other lawyers for Chase was too narrow; other offenses besides those for which a man could be indicted might make him ineligible to hold his post. Savage sentences, irresponsible and extravagant action, while not crimes in definition of law, might call for impeachment. Chase had not flown in the face of the law, but he was impetuous in voicing his political convictions (or prejudices), and took no pains to preserve judicial detachment. Judge Richard Peters, of the district court, who had been on the bench with Chase in the Fries trial, and who at first was proposed to be impeached along with Chase, said of him at this time, "Of all others, I like least to be coupled with him. I never sat with him without pain, as he was forever getting into some intemperate and unnecessary squabble."

Three weeks were consumed in taking evidence and hearing arguments. On March 1 judgment was to be pronounced. Senator Bayard, a Federalist, successfully moved that the vote be on the question, "Is Samuel Chase guilty or not guilty of a high crime or misdemeanor as charged . . . ?" This was all in Chase's favor, for it ruled out mere disagreement with Chase's politics, and dislike of the man's methods, and confined his judges to deciding, on each count, whether the conduct of the accused was illegal in the strict sense. From that moment Chase's acquittal was foreseen. So it turned out, for on the first article (Chase's handling of the Fries trial), many Republican senators, along with the Federalists, voted "Not Guilty." Among those who refused to stand with their party were the "hot impeachers," Giles of Virginia and Jackson of Georgia. A majority of the Senate exculpated Chase on this count. On the fifth article, Randolph's doing, in which Chase was accused of some technical errors, but without bad intent, every senator found the judge innocent. The highest vote against him was 19, on his charge to the Baltimore grand jury, but this was four short of the 23 required for conviction.

John Randolph, thus frustrated, immediately entered the House, where he proposed an easier way of getting rid of judges held obnoxious by the majority party. This was to be by an amendment to the Constitution—"The judges of the Supreme and all other courts of the United States shall be removed by the President on the joint address of both houses of Congress." One of his supporters, angry at Republicans who had voted with the Federalists, moved another amendment empowering a state legislature to recall a senator. But these were outbursts of anger following defeat, and had no practical issue. President

Jefferson, in the failure of his design to purge the bench of Federalists, pronounced impeachment "a mere scarecrow." Jefferson could survive the blow of Chase's acquittal, but his agent, John Randolph of Roanoke, never recaptured his sway. He had his moments afterward, but his career was to close in excesses and insanity.

That Chase was saved was something, but that the integrity of the Supreme Court was rescued, and thereby the Constitution preserved, was more. This was the year 1805. John Marshall remained as chief justice for thirty years longer. During this period he and his fellows established the Constitution as the undoubted guide of our national course. Most of the men who made the Revolution, the Constitution, and launched the new nation were, one after another, removed from the scene, but Marshall remained as interpreter of their legacy. In other hands the document might have become a nullity, and the form of government been changed to something less steady and progressive. The merit of Marshall, as we shall see, was that he kept the Constitution tough, but elastic.

Sanctity of Private Contracts

Marshall respected the acts of the states unless they ran counter to federal authority, then they were disallowed. The case of *Fletcher v. Peck* (6 Cranch 87, 1810) was the first in which a state law was held void because it conflicted with a provision of the Constitution of the United States; previously nullifying grounds had been national statutes or treaties. *Fletcher v. Peck* originated in occurrences as early as 1795 when the Georgia legislature sold the better part of what later became the states of Alabama and Mississippi to companies of speculators for $500,000. Immediately popular outcry denounced the deal because obtained by bribing practically all members of the law-making body. The following year a new legislature was elected and repudiated the sale. The state offered to return the purchase price to the buyers, but this and other terms of settlement were rejected.

Parcels of the land were sold all over the country to innocent third parties. Robert Fletcher had bought 15,000 acres from John Peck for $3000. "Peck, in his deed to Fletcher, convenanted . . . that the title to the premises as conveyed by the state of Georgia, and finally vested in the said Peck, has been in no way constitutionally or legally impaired by virtue of any subsequent act of any subsequent legislature of the . . . state of Georgia." Fletcher sued Peck for breach of contract, contending that Georgia had rescinded the original sale. The circuit court of the district of Massachusetts found for the defendant Peck. The case came on appeal to the Supreme Court of the United States.

The question was whether a state could abrogate a contract in violation of the prohibition in the Constitution. Thus *Fletcher v. Peck* raised the ghost of Daniel Shays, as is explained more fully below. By the time the case reached the highest court, fifteen years of discussion of the Yazoo land sales, as they were called, had made familiar every argument for and against their validity.

Top counsel of the day were engaged. Luther Martin for the plaintiff, Fletcher, stressed the bribery of the legislators in 1795, "by reason whereof the said law was a nullity . . . and . . . the title which the . . . state of Georgia had in the aforesaid premises at any time whatsoever was never legally conveyed to the said Peck. . . ." On the other hand John Quincy Adams and Robert Goodloe Harper for the defendant, Peck, stressed that their client's title was good by reason of the original sale which could not be undone by act of a later legislature. Alexander Hamilton, consulted in the case, gave his opinion that the state could not revoke a contract. Peck's lawyers and Chief Justice Marshall in his decision took this line: a legislature could repeal or modify acts of a preceding one, but not where contract rights were conferred.

The legislature of 1796, said Marshall, may have had proof of fraud, which would have justified abrogation so far as concerned those to whom crime was imputed. "But the grant, when issued, conveyed an estate in fee simple, clothed with all the solemnities which law can bestow. The estate was transferable, and those who purchased part of it were not stained by that guilt which infected the original transaction." While Marshall deplored corruption in a legislature, he refused to take notice of the motives of that of Georgia in granting the lands. He would not allow the court to be involved in suspicious prying, which would have forfeited its legal function. He took the act of Georgia for what it purported to be, a valid sale. "When . . . a law is in its nature a contract, when absolute rights have been vested under the contract, a repeal of the law cannot divest those rights. . . ."

The nature of society, Marshall held, prescribes some limits to legislative power, and "where are they to be found, if the property of an individual, fairly and honestly acquired, may be seized without compensation?" Further, Georgia could not be viewed as a single sovereign power.

She is a part of a large empire; she is a member of the American union; and that union has a constitution, the supremacy of which all acknowledge, and which imposes limits to the legislatures of the several states, which none claim a right to pass. The constitution of the United States declares that no state shall pass any bill of attainder, *ex post facto* law, or law impairing the obligation of contracts.

The contract between Georgia and the purchasers was executed by the grant. . . . It is . . . the unanimous opinion of the court that, in this case, the estate having passed into the hands of a purchaser for a valuable consideration, without notice, the state of Georgia was restrained, either by general principles which are common to our free institutions, or by the particular provisions of the Constitution of the United States, from passing a law whereby the estate of the plaintiff in the premises so purchased could be constitutionally and legally impaired and rendered null and void. . . .

The judgment of the court below was affirmed.

The validity of a contract made by a state was amplified two years later in *New Jersey v. Wilson.* The Delaware Indians had surrendered certain lands to New Jersey in exchange for other lands on which the state granted exemption from taxation. When the Delawares later moved out of New Jersey and sold their lands to white men, these purchasers refused to pay taxes. They contended that freedom from taxation was a part of the original contract and had enhanced the price paid for the lands. Marshall's opinion in the Supreme Court was that New Jersey could not tax the lands because that would impair the obligation of the contract.

At first sight there is little connection between Daniel Shays and Daniel Webster. The former, a rebel against courts and legislature of Massachusetts, sped to the "New Hampshire Grants" to escape the wrath of the law. The latter, a native of New Hampshire, progressed to Massachusetts as an expounder of the law and was forever a bulwark of orderly government. The link that unites them is in the Constitution (Article I, section 10, paragraph 1). Daniel Shays's indebted farmers, in the hard times that followed the Revolution (1785-86) begged the state legislature for means of meeting the demands of their creditors. Additional paper money would help most, but they also urged stay laws permitting them to defer payment of what they owed. For a while the lawmakers, seated at Boston, allowed them to discharge their debts in country produce—corn, wheat, or cattle—instead of cash. Then this leniency ended, the judges were busy in foreclosing mortgages, and sheriffs packed the insolvents into the county jails. Thereat the debtors rose in protest, at first with petitions from middle and western county towns, soon with pitchforks, flails, and muskets. They collected at courthouses and compelled the judges to quit the bench. As we have seen, with Daniel Shays at their head—he had been a captain in the Revolutionary army—they attacked the continental arsenal at Springfield. This defiance brought against them local militia and soon a large force dispatched by the governor under General Benjamin Lincoln. A little internal war ensued. Fights in various parts divided loyalties and announced to all the states that the authorities of Massachusetts could not enforce the law or maintain the peace. Finally, in a surprise night march through the snow, General Lincoln routed the insurgents at Petersham. The survivors, including Shays, fled for their lives, and the outbreak was put down.

Shays's Rebellion was one of the warnings that produced the Constitutional Convention that year at Philadelphia. Among the conservative men who labored through the oppressive summer to establish government on a surer footing were many, including George Washington, who had been alarmed by the terrors in Massachusetts the previous winter. If a state, populous and proud of its competence, could not preserve its power over its own citizens, then surely the central authority must be strengthened in a new fundamental law. The independence which Sam Adams proclaimed for the continent could not endure if the likes of Daniel Shays could take arms against governor and legislature. Remembering that Massachusetts had encouraged the revolt by yielding in its early stages, the makers of the Constitution provided in their document that no state in future should "coin money; emit bills of credit; make anything but gold and silver coin a tender in payment of debts; pass any . . . law impairing the obligation of contracts . . ."

General Lincoln had dispersed the Shaysites and the Constitution had limited the freedom of a state to invade the claims of private property. Often these claims were in the form of contracts. A contract was sacred in the eyes of the law, and could not be altered or broken without the consent of all of the parties who had agreed to it. And Daniel Webster? He comes in a generation later by convincing the Supreme Court that a charter granted by government to a college was a private contract and could not be changed or undone by the legislature simply at its own will. In a way that nobody guessed at the time this was to give enormous scope to American corporate enterprise.

Now our scene shifts to an earlier period—before Webster, before the constitutional fathers, before Shays and his enraged farmers. Our locus is Lebanon, Connecticut, where young Eleazer Wheelock was a principal figure. This ambitious preacher, a graduate of Yale, belonged to the "new lights" Presbyterians. He was on the emotional side, energetic in converting unbelievers. He was viewed with distaste, even alarm by the majority of clergymen in Connecticut, who were content to deal with public morals and education in time-honored ways. Wheelock, besides exhorting his flock on Sundays, took youngsters into his own home to teach them the four R's—reading, 'riting, 'rithmetic, and religion. Among these was a Mohican Indian, not so famous as Cooper's Uncas, but a stout fellow nonetheless, Samson Occom by name. He proved such an apt scholar that he dropped the scalping knife for the scriptures and returned to the forests to round up more converts to Wheelock's teachings. Thus encouraged, the Reverend Eleazer took most of his pupils from the tribes of the Six Nations. The boys were given books (the Bible not least) and better ways of agriculture. The girls forsook grubbing in the fields to learn the arts of homemaking.

No sooner were these young savages civilized and "graduated" from Wheelock's instruction than he dispatched them back to the woods to preach and teach their unregenerate people. So well did they appear to succeed that Wheelock, ever reaching out for the bigger and better, sent a couple of solicitors (the Mohican Samson was the exhibit to clinch the plea) to England to collect funds to enlarge his school. Soon £12,000 (a tidy sum for a faraway project) were corralled in the hands of sponsors headed by Lord Dartmouth. Wheelock, who had transferred to a new flock and an ample farm in the wilderness of New Hampshire, to make sure of the future of his endeavors, made his will. He pitched into the endowment of the institution all that he possessed, chose a board of managers from New England clergymen, and appealed to Governor Wentworth of the colony of New Hampshire to grant His Majesty King George's charter for the perpetuation of Dartmouth College. This was issued in 1769.

Rarely has a grant of rights and powers been made in finer form. All was done in the name of the King, who could be perfectly liberal since he was contributing majesty but no money. All that Wheelock could ask for recognition of his private charity, now increased and extended by the benefactions which he had attracted, was vouchsafed. Ownership and direction of the property were vested in "twelve trustees and no more," and these were protected in their charter powers against any and all persons, including the King himself.

Dartmouth College Case

Eleazer Wheelock, by the letters patent, was authorized to name his own successor as president, professor, and trustee, and he chose his son John. The father would have designated John's older brother Ralph, had he not been an epileptic. John was far from having unaccountable mental or emotional seizures. Instead he continued the founder's liberal administration of the College in spite of growing dissatisfaction among his fellow trustees, who were all Congregationalists and Federalists—that is, conservative in religion and in politics. In one way and another over a span of years the anti-Wheelock minority in the board became the majority. John Wheelock was ousted as president, trustee, and professor, and the Rev. Francis Brown was chosen in his place. This was in August 1815. A year later Judge William H. Woodward, the secretary of the board, was also displaced because he was Wheelock's supporter.

Warfare in the College was bound up with bitter conflict in the larger community, both religious and political. New Hampshire had been steadily Federalist and Congregational, but now Democratic winds were blowing through the mountain ranges and valley farms. Jefferson and Madison had been in command of the national government for sixteen years, while the Federalists had dwindled to a New England faction. Citizens resented being taxed to support Congregational clergymen, who were themselves exempt from public levies. William Plumer, long prominent in state and national legislative office as a Federalist, ran for the governorship of New Hampshire on the Democratic ticket. Wheelock, to get back at his old enemies among the Dartmouth trustees, turned Democrat and helped elect Plumer.

Swift on this victory the Democratic legislature, instructed by Plumer and Wheelock, passed a law (June 1816) changing the College to Dartmouth University with a board increased to 21 members, and overseers, 25 in number, with veto powers. The purpose was declared to be to improve the services of the institution to the people of the state, but the real object was to transfer its control to the state administration. Wheelock was elected president, and Woodward secretary, by the new trustees.

The president and professors of the College were expelled from the buildings and menaced with heavy penalties if they tried to conduct the institution; but they persisted. In emergency quarters across the village street they taught most of the students, while the University attracted only a handful. The two institutions lived uneasily cheek by jowl for several years.

In November 1817 the suit of the College to recapture its records and seal from Woodward, its erstwhile secretary, was determined in the superior court of New Hampshire. In spite of six hours of argument for the College by Jeremiah Mason, Jeremiah Smith, and Daniel Webster (who was an alumnus), against half as many hours by counsel for the University, the judges were unanimous against the old board. However, the Jeremiahs and Webster at once appealed to the Supreme Court at Washington.

There Webster opened the argument for the College, as plaintiff in error, March 10, 1818, all the Supreme Court justices being present. He scarcely glanced at his brief, which owed much, as Webster later said, to "materials furnished by Judge Smith & Mr. Mason," who had been his colleagues in the New Hampshire trial. As he spoke for nearly five hours, it is not surprising that his argument was "in the calm tone of easy and dignified conversation." Webster contended that the charter granted to Dr. Eleazer Wheelock, the founder of the College, and the trustees he named, created a private corporation for charitable purposes. Though the institution was designed to benefit the community, it was not a public corporation such as a town, the charter of which, for sufficient cause, could be amended by the governmental power granting it. The trustees of the private corporation, Dartmouth College, were not bound to accept any alteration in their charter without their consent. The state of New Hampshire had no power to pass the law of 1816 which not only changed the character of the old corporation, but in fact abolished it and transferred its property to a new corporation with different name, different duties, different control. The charter of the College was a contract, as had indeed been declared by the Supreme Court in *Fletcher v. Peck* (6 Cranch 87, 1810). If violated, owners were deprived of their property without judgment of their peers. The legislature of New Hampshire was not a judicial tribunal. Its acts substituting Dartmouth University for Dartmouth College were forbidden by the state's Bill of Rights.

But further, and only this could be declared by the Supreme Court, the acts of New Hampshire were repugnant to the Constitution of the United States which forbade a state to "pass any . . . law impairing the obligation of contracts" (Art. I, sec. 10). Webster quoted Madison in *The Federalist*, justifying this prohibition in the Constitution as a protection to the citizen against the acts of local legislatures swayed by unprincipled speculators. Webster did not dwell long on this plea. This at first glance seems surprising, for it was the Court's assent to this argument that made the Dartmouth College case famous in our constitutional law. He was brief on this point because he had been compelled to consume time in laying his groundwork (that the charter was private, and inviolable). Also, as noted above, he demonstrated that the Court had already pronounced the judgment he sought, in the previous decision of *Fletcher v. Peck* (1810). We think of the Dartmouth case as buttressing powerful business corporations, but its significance in these respects did not appear until years later when the corporate form of commercial, financial, and industrial enterprises became important.

Immortal "Nonsense"

Webster thought of himself as protecting charitable corporations— schools, colleges, hospitals endowed by private benevolence. In fact it was his appeal at the end for Dartmouth in this character of an eleemosynary institution which is remembered and often referred to as a sample of Webster's eloquence. We owe the preservation of this short passage to Chauncey A. Goodrich, then professor of oratory at Yale, who attended the trial because his college at New Haven was vitally concerned in the outcome. Goodrich recorded his recollection thirty-six years after he heard Webster's utterance. We may believe that the sentiment lost nothing of its pathos in the hands of the admiring reporter. Webster had completed his argument. He stood in silence for a moment while his personal affection for the College and his gratitude for what it had given him filled his memory. Then, "addressing Chief Justice Marshall, he said,—

'This, sir, is my case. It is the case, not merely of that humble institution, it is the case of every college in our land . . . of all those great charities founded by the piety of our ancestors to alleviate human misery, and scatter blessings along the pathway of human life . . . Sir, you may destroy this little institution: it is weak, it is in your hands! I know it is one of the lesser lights . . . You may put it out: but if you do, you must carry through your work! You must extinguish, one after another all those great lights of science, which . . . have thrown their radiance over the land! It is, sir, as I have said, a small college, and yet there are those that love it . . .'

No shorthand report of Webster's speech was made. Soon afterward, in an abstract of his argument, he said he had "left out all the nonsense"—the emotional part at the end. Later still, when he wrote out his address for publication, he included nothing but the straightforward argument and citation of authorities, and it appears so in the Supreme Court report of *Dartmouth College v. Woodward* (4 Wheaton 518, 1819). However, as an advocate Webster did not need to be ashamed of his sentimental flight. William Wirt, attorney general of the United States, who opposed him in this case, attempted something similar, but without the same success. One of the trustees of Dartmouth University, listening in on the case, recorded, "Mr. Wirt closed a very able argument in our cause. His peroration was eloquent. The ghost of Wheelock was introduced exclaiming to Webster, 'Et tu Brute.' " Of course Wirt and the counsel with him urged their legal points but Webster had been convincing, and his colleague Joseph Hopkinson, closing for the College, sought to remove any stray doubts.

Next morning Chief Justice Marshall announced a continuance, as some on the bench had not reached opinions and others differed. In the interval the University officers, fearing their cause was lost, planned to have it reargued by William Pinkney of Maryland. When notified of this, Webster and Hopkinson objected that the justices should not allow such a proceeding. However, Pinkney prepared himself, and was present in court February 2, 1819, to make his motion. He was about to rise when Marshall announced that decision had been reached in the Dartmouth case and he read it. Only Mr. Justice Duvall dissented, but he offered no reasons.

The opinion agreed on all points, was on all fours, or, as Hopkinson said, went "all lengths" with the argument for the College. The charter was an undoubted contract, private in character, not amenable to alteration as was attempted by the New Hampshire legislature. What the state tried to do ran counter to the Constitution; consequently those laws were void and the decision of the highest New Hampshire court upholding them must be reversed. What impressed newspaper editors and public men at the time was the choice of the Court, predominantly Republican in its make-up, to defend national against state power, and private rights against popular interference. But few foresaw the application the decision was to have in after years. It was rendered at the time when America, taught by embargo, non-intercourse, and the isolation of the War of 1812-14, was turning attention to internal development. This country must be united and more than previously self-sufficient in manufactures and markets. Means of transportation must be developed to bind East to West—first turnpikes and canals, then railroads. Industrial enterprises must supply our own needs in war and peace.

These objects called for business corporations which permitted combination of many small capitals, limited liability of the individual investor, and provided permanence of the undertaking. But people would not venture their money in chartered companies if they feared the legislatures which granted the charters would alter their terms or raid property claims whenever lawmakers felt so disposed. The decision declaring the charter of Dartmouth College to be a contract gave the highest, most solemn assurance that vested rights, whatever other risks they encountered, were safe against legislative meddling. This furnished confidence to corporate initiative, without which economic growth would have been long retarded. Later, by interpretation of the courts, legislatures were allowed more authority over corporations than was at first contemplated, but these modifications were plainly in the public interest and were not a check to business progress.

The Supreme Court decision in the case of *Proprietors of the Charles River Bridge v. Proprietors of the Warren Bridge* (II Peters, 420, 1837) signalized a stricter interpretation of corporate privilege. The Massachusetts legislature chartered the Charles River bridge, between Charlestown and Boston, in 1785. Conjecture at the time that investors took a risk because the structure might not hold up against the tides so near the sea proved unfounded. The bridge, exceedingly profitable, paid for itself many times over in the tolls charged. In 1828 the legislature chartered the Warren bridge a few rods from the old one. The Warren was to revert to the state when paid for, in a maximum of six years, and thereafter was to be toll-free.

The Charles bridge proprietors sued in the Supreme Judicial Court of Massachusetts to prevent construction of the new bridge on the ground that it would destroy their monopoly which was conferred in their charter. Of course nobody would pay to cross the old bridge after the new one became free. The state court found against the Charles bridge. On appeal to the Supreme Court of the United States the case was first argued in 1831, but then there were postponements until 1837. In the meantime John Marshall had died. Justice Joseph Story, who shared Marshall's interpretation of the Constitution, had written an opinion which upheld the claim of the old bridge company.

Roger B. Taney succeeded Marshall as chief justice in 1836. His early Federalism had been long exchanged for Jacksonian democracy. He was fresh from his victorious battle, as President Jackson's henchman, against the second Bank of the United States. The Industrial

Revolution had come from Britain to the United States, and it was apparent that enterprisers were eager to avail themselves of the opportunities of incorporation without claiming monopoly privileges.

In 1837, when the bridge case was decided, the Warren bridge was in use toll-free and was "a nuisance" to the Charles bridge proprietors —an understatement of the total ruin they had suffered. Webster, the hero of the Dartmouth College defense, was counsel for the old bridge. His position was the same as earlier, on the sacredness of a contract contained in a legislative charter, but he now extended the principle. The charter of the Charles bridge implied guarantee of a monopoly in consideration of the risk the investors had assumed. The question before the court, Webster said, "was one of a private right, and was to be determined by a fair construction of a contract . . . property has been taken from [the plaintiffs] by proceedings which violate a contract; and is a case where this Court has a constitutional right to interpose for its protection and restoration."

Taney was mindful that the decision to be taken was important to thousands of corporate investors in the country. However, Marshall's permissive approach toward corporations found an exception. In *Beatty v. The Lessee of Knowles* (4 Pet. 168, 1830), the former chief justice had said, "The exercise of the corporate franchise being restrictive of individual rights"—that is, limiting competition—"cannot be extended beyond the letter and spirit of the act of incorporation."

Government, Taney declared, was for the public benefit and could not surrender its powers. The rights of the community had pretensions against those of private property. Technological progress had meant the obsolescence of more primitive means, and would continue to do so. Turnpikes had been superseded by railroads, ferries by bridges. The advances of society could not be held back by legal limitations. Unless the charter of the Charles River bridge specifically gave the right of monopoly that right did not exist.

Story dissented on the merits of the case, and Thompson similarly; McLean dissented because, he believed, the Supreme Court had no jurisdiction of the case. The others followed Taney in affirming the judgment of the state court. Undoubtedly in the narrower sense contemporary politics bore a part in the decision. Five of the seven justices were President Jackson's appointees. Democratic indignation against the autonomy of the Second Bank was in vivid memory. But, more largely, the decision was right in inviting the new to displace the old if it could do so. American enterprise no longer needed to be sheltered as once, but was entering on a period of free expansion.

May a State Destroy a Federal Agency?

The case of *McCulloch v. Maryland* (4 Wheaton 316, 1819) determined that the Constitution was made by the people, not by the states; that the central government was dominant over the states within its allotted sphere; and that the means which the federal authority could employ for its designated purposes must be liberally interpreted. The decision, read by Chief Justice John Marshall for a unanimous court March 6, 1819, has been held to be perhaps the foremost of his expositions of our fundamental law. The case was argued during ten days by leading lawyers, including Daniel Webster, Luther Martin, and William Pinkney. The gallery in the little courtroom in the basement of the capitol at Washington was crowded to hear them.

And yet in essential features the issue was concluded twenty-eight years before. The precedent which the Court followed was chiefly the opinion of Alexander Hamilton, submitted to President Washington February 23, 1791, defending the constitutionality of the first Bank of the United States. Of course presumptive evidence was not wanting, for Congress had established the first Bank, President Jefferson had approved the opening of branches, after an interval President Madison had acknowledged that a second Bank would be constitutional, and signed it into law.

But the reasoning, which counsel for the bank, and the Court adopted without change, was in Hamilton's statement. Of his many cabinet opinions, this was a master one, for it developed the doctrine of the implied powers of Congress. It fixed the principle that the national government in discharging its agreed responsibilities must be allowed scope, not be plucked back at every turn by a grudging interpretation of its capacities. The spirit of the Constitution, not the letter must be consulted and cherished. It is this which made room for growth in American society. As population expanded, as transport and communication knit all parts together, as large-scale production extended in widening circles, local differences tended to disappear. Foresight was required to recognize that this would happen. If those who insisted on keeping the Constitution rigid and inert had prevailed, they would have condemned the Union to weakness, dissension, and extinction. This was the issue belatedly tried, or retried, in the agony of civil war. Then the triumph of the national principle was beyond question, but how much bloodshed and lingering hatred and suspicion would have been prevented had we gone on in the enlightened course which Hamilton and Marshall pointed out long before!

It is convenient to attach ideas to the names of individuals who on conspicuous occasions expressed them with fullness and precision. Thus we say that the doctrine of implied powers of the central government was announced or invented by Hamilton. Actually that is not true, for the benefits and perils of flexible construction of the Constitution were heatedly debated in Congress and in the country when Hamilton's recommendation of a Bank of the United States was submitted in December 1790. Indeed the whole proceeding turned on the question whether Congress was at liberty to incorporate a bank when neither the power of incorporation nor a bank as the object of a charter was included in specific terms in the Constitution. What Hamilton did (and Webster and Marshall a generation afterward) was to examine the proposition in every light, discard the extravagances that had been urged pro and con, and enforce the affirmative with convincing reasoning.

Similarly we should note that the axiom "the power to tax is the power to destroy," which is attributed to Marshall in the Supreme Court opinion upholding the second Bank of the United States, was not original with him. If Marshall did not know of it from much earlier occurrence in English jurisprudence, he had heard it repeatedly used by counsel in the case before him. As with Hamilton and implied powers, he gave the principle definition and emphasis, and we rightly speak of it as his own.

The case of *McCulloch v. Maryland*, which is our topic, involved the second Bank of the United States, but as the second Bank was patterned after the first, we are accurate in examining Hamilton's argument for what he proposed. So far as the Constitution is concerned, the two banks were one, just as though the first had enjoyed continuous existence, without the gap of five years between them. The debate in Congress on the first Bank was focused on the true meaning of the Constitution. Hamilton's proposals nearly a year earlier for dealing with the public debt had produced bitter differences on matters of policy, but not of principle. Congress early declared that the debt should be discharged. Discussion concerned how this should be done, and whether the debts of the states should be assumed by the national government. The recommendation of a national bank gave peculiar alarm to the strict constructionists. How the central government should act directly in its own behalf was one thing. But could it extend itself, create a powerful instrument (a bank) able profoundly to affect the life of the nation and the interests of individuals, though the bank was largely private in ownership and operation? If Congress could charter a bank, with numerous branches, what other tentacles might it not sprout to bind and maybe strangle the citizens in the states? A procedure in public finance seemed relatively abstract, but the proposition of setting up a bank—with president, directors, physical places of doing business—was concrete, easily visualized, readily made into a bugaboo. At the same time that a bank had shape and size, its operation was to many a mystery and was therefore suspect. How could a bank create credit and purchasing power beyond the gold and silver deposited in it? Many people at that time, and some of them in high places, looked on a bank as a piece of sleight of hand and therefore dangerous.

Hamilton's Argument for Implied Powers

When the bank bill was passed, President Washington, mindful of the dispute whether it was in accordance with the Constitution, asked for the written opinion of the attorney general (Edmund Randolph), who gave lengthy reasons for holding it was invalid. The secretary of state (Thomas Jefferson) condemned it also, but more briefly. Since the bank was Hamilton's proposal, the President furnished the negative arguments to him for his answer. Hamilton worked on his reply (almost fifty pages of ordinary print) for a week. He toiled most of the last night (and his wife helping with the copying) to complete it in time for Washington to approve the bill before it would become law without his signature.

Hamilton had the affirmative of the argument, which invites to courage, warmth, and ingenuity. His personal reputation and the efficiency of the Treasury which he administered were at stake. But his anxiety was deeper, in no way selfish. The objections of his opponents —narrow and timid, though he did not call them that—if they prevailed would "be fatal to the . . . indispensable authority of the United States." He was pleading for the future, for the greatness of America. One had but to read his defense to discard the counterarguments as inferior. While his colleagues were inspired by fears, he was moved by faith that the young nation could use power wisely for the enlargement of the liberty and prosperity of the people. Not only did he have technical knowledge, which his antagonists lacked, and thus enjoyed an advantage; he had thought about the problem for a decade, had repeatedly framed plans, had satisfactorily answered for himself every refutation that could be urged. Hamilton put his heart into what he was about.

In his opinion for the President, Hamilton immediately took the offensive. The national government was sovereign within areas committed to its management, and sovereignty included the power to erect a corporation. This power did not need to be specifically delegated. It was implied as incident to authority in so many words conferred by the Constitution. A corporation was not, as some in Congress had pictured it, a separate menacing entity, but was no more than a convenient means to an end. The Constitution authorized Congress "to make all laws necessary and proper for carrying into execution" the powers expressly entrusted. "Necessary" did not mean indispensable, but, like "proper," referred to what was needful or useful. Granted that Congress was commanded to perform certain duties, the means chosen were matter of discretion. The principle was "every power vested in a government is . . . *sovereign*, and includes . . . a right to employ all the *means* . . . fairly applicable to the attainment of the *ends* of such power, and which are not precluded by . . . exceptions specified in the Constitution, or not immoral, or not contrary to the *essential ends* of political society."

Hamilton went on to show that a bank would be serviceable in assisting the central government to collect taxes, borrow money, regulate trade between the states, and maintain fleets and armies—all of these being functions unmistakably deputed by the Constitution. The fact was that strict constructionists wanted government but were afraid to permit it to operate. They were like maids who wish to marry but insist on remaining virgins. Another figure would be that they preferred a bicycle, like that in a gymnasium, propped off the ground, so that the pedals and wheels would revolve, but the machine could go nowhere. Hamilton's view was the sensible one; define certain powers, and then allow freedom to exercise those powers in appropriate ways.

He had plain words for those who objected that federal authority would conflict with laws of the states. Where the national government acted within its orbit, it was supreme and any law of a state running counter must give way.

Opponents of the bank, at the end of its career two decades later, claimed that President Washington consented to the charter reluctantly, and would not have done so except that the secretary of the

department immediately concerned insisted the bank would be serviceable in Treasury operations. This was hearsay. Since Washington required opinions on the constitutionality of the bank, we have no
reason to believe that consideration of administrative convenience
determined his judgment. On pondering Hamilton's argument the
President signed the bill.

Excellent First Bank Disestablished

The first Bank of the United States ran a good course, satisfying the
hopes of its projectors in benefits to stockholders, government, the
business community, and the economy generally. For several years
before the term of its charter ended, in 1811, renewal of the charter
was actively agitated. The bank's resources and its obligations to the
government were both to be increased. The secretary of the treasury,
Albert Gallatin, was decidedly favorable, as were associations of mechanics, manufacturers, and merchants. But by the time Congress had
to decide, in the beginning of 1811, vocal opponents mustered their
strength. For the previous decade the Republicans, traditional foes of
the bank, had been in power nationally, while the Federalists, who had
sponsored and supported the bank, were on the way to disappearance.
The Louisiana Purchase had enormously enlarged territory and potency
of the South and Southwest. State banks had multiplied. The prosperity of the country was rightly attributed to the war in Europe, and
the merit of the national bank and its branches in steadying this
progress was overlooked by many.

The debates in Congress on the bill to extend the bank's charter
were as lengthy and animated in the Senate as in the House. Friends
of the institution easily made an impressive case for its continuance
on the basis of its performance. They took its constitutionality for
granted, for that had been established in the beginning and Republican-controlled Congresses had frequently confirmed and augmented
its operation. However, these advocates of recharter were forced by
the bank's enemies to reargue the old question of legality. Experience
and expediency were largely neglected, while construction of the Constitution was reinvoked as of yore. Proponents reprinted and circulated
Hamilton's brief for the bank, and this buttress was assailed by the
time-honored weapons. The conflict was sustained not by new reasoning for or against, but by the energy of political differences. Those
against the bank said that its exit would cause no inconvenience, since

their favorite state banks would supply all financial and fiscal services. A few years later, seeing that the bank was sorely missed during the War of 1812-14, they were compelled to eat their words.

Recharter of the bank was lost by the narrowest margin. In the House, January 24, 1811, the bill was indefinitely postponed (that is, killed) by a vote of 65 to 64. In the Senate, February 20, the enacting clause was struck out by the deciding vote of the presiding officer, George Clinton; before casting his fateful ballot he made a little speech (the same one he had been making for a generation) explaining that his strict construction of the Constitution ruled out a national bank.

This plight of the country compelled the Republican administration, beginning in January 1814, to respond to appeals of New Yorkers and others to re-establish a national bank. During two years of worsening fortunes, including the burning of Washington, six attempts failed. The Republicans were themselves at odds on every plan proposed. The strict constructionists thought any bank unconstitutional; the new secretary of the treasury, Alexander J. Dallas, did not agree with the sensible demands of William Lowndes and John C. Calhoun of his own party; the Federalists were critical, not creative. In 1815 when a feasible bill was passed President Madison vetoed it, though his objections were not on constitutional grounds. Another year of distress persuaded all to consent to a similar measure, which was signed into law April 10, 1816.

The second Bank of the United States commenced business in January 1817 under handicaps. During the war the finances and currency rapidly became disordered. The government borrowed at heavy discount and was paid in depreciated paper—its own Treasury notes were at times worth less than the state bank notes. The latter circulated only in the areas where the different sorts were issued, with the result that the government could not transfer its deposits from one part of the country to another. In late summer of 1814 the banks, except those in New England, suspended specie payments, and a few months later the Treasury was unable to pay interest on the national debt held in Massachusetts or redeem Treasury notes at Boston, New York, and Philadelphia. Government departments were put to it to scrape together small sums of a few thousands of dollars. Successive heads of the Treasury—William Jones and George W. Campbell—were incompetent.

Second Bank Misbehaves

The second Bank, though more than three times as large in capital ($35,000,000), closely resembled the old one which Hamilton had devised and which the Republicans, unfortunately, had refused to recharter five years before. It had taken national confusion, dishonor, and peril to produce their conversion. Nor were they to be rewarded by satisfaction in the early career of their offspring. To remedy accumulated evils, the second Bank must use correctives which were resented and allow concessions which produced fresh mischief. These obstacles would have been overcome but for the fault of loose management in the central bank and worse abuses in some of its branches, added to which was the misfortune of postwar depression in 1818-19.

William Jones, having proved himself feckless in the Treasury, was made president of the bank. Not only was his hand on the helm weak but his itching fingers seized on a share of profits of directors speculating in bank stock. The state banks were the enemies of reform. Unregenerate, especially in the South, they wanted to continue to extend loans recklessly while they refused to redeem their notes in specie or to transfer to the Treasury government deposits held by them. How restore uniform value in the currency and collect public revenue? By degrees the bank accomplished these all-important ends in 1817, but this was at the cost of rendering its precarious resources vulnerable to raids of the willful state banks. In playing its enforced role of indulgent disciplinarian the second Bank of the United States violated the spirit if not the letter of its charter.

The end of the war brought false prosperity in excessive importations of English goods, rampant purchases of western lands, mounting prices due to swollen issues of state and national bank paper, and extravagant speculation in bank shares. The Bank of the United States lent on its own stock at 25 per cent above par; with the proceeds borrowers bought more stock and the process continued. Seeking to furnish a uniform currency, notes of the branches were redeemed at whatever branch they were presented. Since there was no check on these issues, the result was to drain the specie from the more prudent northern banks in favor of the infatuated southern and western ones. At the parent bank in Philadelphia the directors were grossly negligent in allowing inordinate borrowings. But at the Baltimore branch the president, his business partners, and James W. McCulloch (their clerk who was made cashier of the branch) practiced unabashed though long undetected fraud. The national directors, at length alarmed, called for curtailment of loans and payment of balances due. The scramble for specie caused widespread consternation. Numerous state banks failed, cursing the "monster" which had worked their ruin. Happy days had turned to horrid, and it was inevitable that the second Bank, readily blamed as chief miscreant, should find itself investigated by Congress (December-January 1818-19).

The report, declaring malfeasance on several grounds, was vigorously debated for ten days in February. These exchanges in Congress let us sense the highly charged atmosphere in which the Supreme Court must soon render a decision on the right of the bank to operate. James Johnson of Virginia led with his demand for repeal of the bank's charter. Issues were not clarified when the chairman of the investigating committee admitted that its report was carelessly worded. In no wise deterred, Johnson exclaimed that "this shaming institution" had no claim on the liberality of the nation. "No; justice hides her face; she wishes not to look at the black catalogue of iniquities which this institution presents; humanity would gladly drop the tear of oblivion on the sickening scene." Alas, that in the forty-third year of its age the nation should have produced "a monster of fraud and corruption without parallel." The charter was illegal in the first place; even so, it had been violated, and should now be rescinded outright. Another member from Virginia, since the national bank was degraded, represented the state banks as comparatively innocent. If these issued too much paper, it was at the behest of the government during the war. Then when they were preparing to resume specie payments, the newly chartered Bank of the United States pressed them for $7,000,000 of hard money; to prevent being stripped and ruined they were compelled to shut their vaults against the demand.

Lowndes of South Carolina took the floor to mitigate the blame heaped on the national bank. He had been a member of the investigating committee, but could not concur in its harshest conclusions. The national bank had tried to supply a dependable currency in its own issues and to support the credit of the state banks in order that their notes might be received by the government. These worthy objects impelled the national bank to go into full-scale operation prematurely. In doing so it failed to require its shareholders to pay in as much "real money" (gold and silver) as the bank charter stipulated. This was an error, though it was excusable because committed in a good cause. Another mistake of the Bank of the United States, however, Lowndes could not forgive. This was in making the notes of every branch payable at any other branch. The stronger branches, by this rule, were drained of their specie, while the weaker and less responsible branches were at liberty to issue notes in excessive amount without having these notes return upon them for redemption.

The result was that the parent bank and the branches in Boston and New York, which had specie and should have been able to lend freely, were prevented from doing so, for they must answer the demands of distant branches to the southward which went on discounting merrily, unchecked by their own slender resources. In this process much of the capital of the system found its way to areas with less legitimate need for it. Lowndes defended the bank against the repeated charge that directors had furnished credit to speculators to the neglect of merchants with better claims for accommodation. He reminded Congress that whatever the shortcomings of the bank in this or that particular, it had supplied for commerce and the public revenue a circulating medium both stable and uniform.

Purple Passages in Congress

Tyler of Virginia replied to Lowndes with florid oratory. He flayed the main bank at Philadelphia and the branch at Baltimore for lending unconscionable sums to speculators, running as high as $1,800,000 to a single borrower. As a consequence, credits to deserving small applicants had to be restricted, and the state banks in self-defense were obliged to follow suit. "Ruin and bankruptcy have been the inevitable effects. Sir, eighteen months ago we were prosperous and happy. What now is our situation? Gloom and despondence in our cities—usury stalking at large, and boasting of its illicit gains, while honesty and industry are covered with rags . . . and yet my friend from South Carolina gravely contends that this charter is not forfeited!" Bank abuses had lifted us to the heights, only in the aftermath to cast us into the depths. "The dreams of wealth visited our pillows. The vision was . . . enchanting. We fancied we held in our embraces youth, and beauty, and . . . purity. But the sun rose, and the cup of our joy was dashed from our lips. Instead of . . . the form of loveliness and virtue, we found ourselves in the embraces of an old and haggard witch, deformed in her features, corrupting by her example, and breathing around her ruin and misery." He was describing abuses of state banks in the previous period, but the national bank, heralded as the savior, had produced new mischief.

In his passion, Tyler damned "the banking system; a system not to be supported by . . . correct principles of political economy. A gross delusion" fit only "to corrupt the morals of society . . . which has made the husbandman spurn his cottage and introduced a spirit of luxury at variance with the simplicity of our institutions." The denunciations of this agrarian would have been fiercer had he known what was disclosed only later—the barefaced thievery of president and cashier at the Baltimore branch.

Louis McLane of Delaware, who was a consistent friend of the bank, and would later be secretary of the treasury, offset Tyler's rhetoric. He gave a calm review of the career of the bank to that point. Some of its actions, though not illegal, had been ill-judged, and individuals had been culpable (President Jones had resigned), but what was needed was reform of conduct, not revocation of the charter. Sergeant of Pennsylvania supported the bank in similar vein. Where errors of policy had been committed, it was in the effort to serve the public. If any suffered, it was the stockholders, who presumably did not need Congress to protect them. The debate wore on. Two Southerners, haters of the bank, closed the discussion. Pindall of Virginia condemned joint public and private enterprise. He found "something oppressive . . . painful, cruel, and almost horrid, in the very idea of a Government being a partner in trade," because the sovereign power was beyond the reach of municipal law. This was the classic *laissez-faire* revulsion against mercantilism. The treatises cited in the debate were Adam Smith's *Wealth of Nations* and "a book on political economy . . . published here, with high . . . commendations—the work of Mr. Tracy,"* both of which eschewed government interference in economic activity. The speaker evidently foresaw that the motion to cancel the bank's charter would be rejected, and that speculators would be covered by the cloak of governmental immunity.

David Walker of Kentucky was more precise in his foreboding. The "flaming zeal for sacred State rights" was about to "be smothered in bank paper . . . Have we not got reasons to believe, from the known complexion of a majority of the members of the United States Supreme Court, that that court will determine that the United States

---

* Count Destutt Tracy, A *Treatise on Political Economy* . . . translated from unpublished French original. Georgetown, D.C., published by Joseph Milligan, 1817 (actually 1818); the translation was revised by Thomas Jefferson.

Bank have a right to extend her branches over every individual state in the Union, and that the States have no right to prune them?" In this condition of helplessness he lashed out at the bank, "an engine of . . . stockjobbing . . . giving to money virtue's true reward . . . and . . . coupling the destiny of this fair Republic to a detested monarchy." His reference was to the many English stockholders in the bank, and to the specie supply which the bank had been able to secure only in England. Hatred of that country, renewed by the recent war, was fresh in mind. The bank was guilty of "binding in adamantine chains the blessed, innocent lambs of America to *accursed* . . . *European* tigers." He pronounced against "all banking systems," for they had "a direct tendency to depress the indigent . . . and add to wealth, affluence, power and domination . . ." In his flight the Kentucky orator forgot the extravagance of his own frontier constituents; they had misused state banks and the Lexington branch of the national bank in land speculation and unwarranted promotions.

At length, February 24, 1819, the motion was put to instruct the judiciary committee "to report a bill to repeal the . . . act to incorporate the subscribers to the Bank of the United States." It was decided in the negative, only 23 of some 155 in favor. Other proposals for putting down or disciplining the bank were similarly rejected in short order. This was in committee of the whole, and when its report upholding the bank came before the House proper it was overwhelmingly sustained, 121 to 30. The vote was largely on sectional lines; representatives from the northern states favored the bank, those from the South, West, and Southwest were opposed. The only restraint of the bank was an unexceptionable one penalizing bribery of officers. In these actions the Senate concurred.

The crisis of the bank in Congress, after its first two years of operation, had passed. But feeling against it ran high. Depression sharpened the resentments of debtors, including those whose speculations had been curbed. States' rights men, in alliance with state banks, were in revolt against central authority. Though it had been determined that Congress would not—or, in accordance with the Dartmouth College decision, could not—annul the charter of the bank, another hope of its enemies loomed. Southern and western states laid heavy taxes on branches of the national bank within their borders. These levies ran from $5000 annually in North Carolina, to $15,000 in Maryland, $50,000 in Tennessee and Ohio, and reached $60,000 in Kentucky. The constitutions of Indiana and Illinois contained outright prohibitions of banks chartered outside of these states.

McCulloch versus Maryland

How would these state laws fare at the hands of the judiciary? The test came in the case of the Baltimore branch, where mismanagement had been flagrant. Suit was brought in the name of James W. McCulloch, cashier of the branch and a principal miscreant, against the State of Maryland. (To anticipate a little, hardly had the Supreme Court given its decision when McCulloch, the president, and several directors were forced to reveal their malfeasances, two months later were compelled to quit their posts, and afterward were prosecuted for conspiracy to defraud the bank.) As was to be expected, the Baltimore County court decided for John James, the state treasurer, who sued McCulloch for refusal to pay the state tax. The Maryland Court of Appeals affirmed the action in the county court. The case came to the Supreme Court of the United States on writ of error.

If the Maryland tax was allowed to stand, the Baltimore branch (and every other branch of the national bank) would be destroyed, probably to the ruin of the parent bank also. If the supposed province of the national government could be so invaded, then the states were masters in the American system. The crucial question was: Is the central authority supreme within its area of action as described by the Constitution? If the answer was yes, this involved the further query: With what responsibilities is the federal government charged? This in turn raised a third problem. Are the powers delegated to Congress and the executive strictly confined, or are the words of the Constitution to be read so as to allow suitable scope of action?

This case was to decide between the policy of the Federalists, who wanted an effective national legislature and administration, and the preference of the Republicans for reserving latitude in the states. To which did the penumbra, or shadow-land, of power belong? Which force could legally extend itself? Where nation and state conflicted, which must prevail? *McCulloch v. Maryland* was not the first case that required the Supreme Court to judge between national rights and state rights. But it was the earliest to demonstrate that our written Constitution, however precise in its wording, is not a suit of steel armor, but is a garment allowing freedom of action to a growing body. It must leave room for unforeseen—indeed unforeseeable—needs. No set of constitution makers, however wise and patriotic, can bind the future. No specifications can be timeless. Number the articles and divide some into sections; guard the language; debate whether a clause should be set off by comma or semicolon, but, in the verdict of experience, all must prove relative to developing circumstance. Adjustments must be made with prudence, but the fidelity of legislators, executives, and judges is not to a document, but to the well-being of the society. What, then, is the difference, in long practice, between a written constitution such as that of the United States, and an unwritten fundamental law such as that of Britain? Among a disciplined, self-respecting people there is little to choose between the two forms. Does anyone suppose that the British subject is less free, less safe, governed by flexible tradition, than the American citizen, governed by a written text?

In the Supreme Court, Daniel Webster, who had recently won the Dartmouth College decision, opened for the plaintiff in error (i.e. the bank). The arguments for the constitutionality of the bank, said Webster, "were exhibited, with characteristic perspicacity and force, by the first Secretary of the Treasury in his report to the President of the United States." He repeated Hamilton's reasoning and went on to urge that Maryland's levy on the branch of the bank, a national agency, was illegal because the "power to tax involves . . . a power to destroy."

Joseph Hopkinson and Walter Jones, answering for Maryland, did what they could. The former forbore to assail Hamilton's argument as such; it may have been sound in 1791 but could not hold in 1819 "when so many facilities for money transactions abound"—that is, state banks to which he gave a better character than they deserved. Thus some powers of the Constitution were "fluctuating in character." A branch bank placed in a state by "a money-trading corporation" could not claim to be exempt from "the ordinary and equal taxation of property, as assessed in the states." (This was a strange description of a tax intended to be unequal.) Jones said flatly that the Constitution was not formed by the people; instead "It is . . . a compact between the states, and all the powers which are not expressly relinquished by it are reserved to the states."

The durable old Luther Martin (who for fifty years after imbibing Blackstone had steadily imbibed brandy) was attorney general of Maryland. He had quit the Constitutional Convention in disgust because the framers in his belief were exceeding their powers. Even so, he declared, those who made the document denied that Congress had authority to grant a charter of incorporation. He scouted the claim of implied powers. The Constitution left none to be inferred, but spelled out what the national government could do under each head. The result was that nothing further was permissible. Here Martin conveniently forgot what Hamilton had elaborately shown when he undermined the restrictive argument of Edmund Randolph years before. Randolph had unwisely undertaken to list the capacities of Congress. These, according to him, excluded any others. But Hamilton, with better knowledge and diligence, readily added to the list, using Randolph's own reasoning, and thus destroyed the argument.

William Pinkney's defense of the bank, longer than Webster's (he required three days for his address), had added force because he was a Marylander opposing the pretensions of his own state. "I never, in my whole life," Justice Story recorded, "heard a greater speech; it was worth a journey from Salem to hear it . . . He spoke like a great statesman and patriot . . . All the cobwebs of sophistry and metaphysics about State rights . . . he brushed away with a mighty besom." This praise was justified. Pinkney's grasp of the issues was as comprehensive and his reasoning was as prophetic as Marshall's. He distinguished vividly between the old Articles of Confederation in which the feeble central government acted only upon the sovereign states, and the Constitution, ordained by the people, and providing that the individual citizens were subject to the national government. He embraced the doctrine of implied powers, condemned the attempt of a state to interfere with the exercise of a federal function.

The arguments had taken nine days. During this time the capitol resounded with the pros and cons of nation against state, for in the first three days of the Court's hearing, Congress, above stairs, was at it hammer and tongs on the motion to revoke the bank's charter.

Marshall Decides for National Supremacy

Chief Justice John Marshall's opinion, delivered for the unanimous Court, has been called by his biographer Beveridge "his ablest and most carefully prepared exposition of the Constitution." The choice to be made, said Marshall, between "the conflicting powers of the government of the Union and of its members . . . may essentially influence the great operations of the government." His apprehension reflected the inflamed opposition of southern and western states so recently demonstrated in Congress. The issue "must be decided peacefully, or remain a source of hostile legislation, perhaps of hostility of a still more serious nature." Marshall, himself a Virginian, wanted, by judicial process, to lay at rest incipient civil war. Disunion was not a vain fear. Only five years earlier the Hartford Convention had threatened revolt by the New England states, and a decade later South Carolina was to nullify an act of the national authority.

As the long opinion was delivered within three days after argument closed, it is assumed that Marshall prepared most of it at his leisure at his home in Richmond the summer before. The contentions that were brought forward by both sides were familiar to him prior to the trial. The root question—whether we were a nation—was that to which Marshall's whole life was the affirmative answer. It is noteworthy that the issue of nationality versus dominance of sovereign states was not frankly submitted to the Supreme Court until the Constitution had been thirty years in operation. In influential quarters in the South and the North—in the Kentucky and Virginia resolutions of 1798-99, and in the movements for New England separation in 1804 and 1814—it was assumed that states might secede if they chose to do so; it was a matter of policy, no question of constitutional right. Probably Marshall was glad when the contest was presented, not in defiant threats of this or that section, but in arguments by able counsel before the highest judicial tribunal. Though mindful of the "awful responsibility" laid on him, he must have relished the opportunity, in solemn fashion, to declare the law before angry men took to muskets.

The Constitution, made by and for all the people, Marshall pronounced, was by its own declaration "the supreme law of the land, anything in the constitution or laws of any state notwithstanding." The bank was constitutional, under powers plainly implied as belonging to those expressly given. The Chief Justice repeated Hamilton's reasoning and illustrations establishing this conclusion, and almost his words in the famous declaration, "Let the end be legitimate, let it be within the scope of the constitution, and all means which are appropriate, which are plainly adapted to that end, which are not prohibited, but consist with the letter and spirit of the constitution, are constitutional." The degree of necessity was not to be inquired into by the Court, for that lay in the wisdom of the legislature.

Then Marshall entered on that portion of the decision which was new. The question was whether a state, exercising its otherwise sovereign powers of taxation within its borders, could by this means hamper or destroy an instrument of the national government? No, the inferior power must give way to the superior. It was fruitless to argue that the states must be trusted to be reasonable in taxing or otherwise regulating agencies of the central government. Would the people of one state entrust even their petty local affairs to the control of another state?

Therefore the Maryland law taxing the Baltimore branch of the Bank of the United States was "contrary to the constitution . . . and void." The decision of the state courts below was reversed and the Baltimore County Court was instructed to enter judgment not for John James, the Maryland treasurer, but for James W. McCulloch as cashier of the branch bank.

Marshall's decision in the *McCulloch* case drew voluble criticism from southern and western quarters, especially from those in Virginia devoted to state rights. More than validation of the United States Bank excited outcry. Until the War of 1812-14, America was under the influence of Europe, much in the way that astrologers say a person's life is under the sway of this or that planet. The second war with England accomplished our economic independence, as the Revolution had achieved our political independence. We now fastened our eyes on our own continental problems of national development. Central versus local power over banking, slavery, and internal improvements became the theme of controversy. Several forces enlarged the national role, gave opponents a sense of impending defeat, and made them shrill in protest. The recent war had been of course a national undertaking, and soon following came charter of the second Bank and enactment of a higher protective tariff in 1816. Population was growing, western territories were filling. Advocates of the "American system" planned interdependence of the states—an industrialized East and a "producing interior" supplying raw materials and foodstuffs. They wanted means of transport which required sponsorship by the central government. But the cotton gin of that Connecticut Yankee, Eli Whitney, had at length fastened the South to slavery. This institution was voracious. It ate up old lands and cried hungrily for new. The claims of slavery threatened fatal division of the country, economic, moral, and political. Feelings were embittered by the prevailing business depression.

The judiciary perforce became the focus of attention. Congress and the national executive were elected, and therefore were subject to citizens' control. But the judges of the federal courts were appointed, held office during good behavior, could not be displaced except by conviction on impeachment. The Supreme Court had the last word. It repeatedly declared that this was true, and illustrated its duty, or power, in its decisions. Therefore the Supreme Court, by dissenters, was looked upon with jealousy and fear. This resentment was keener because the justices did not rely upon statutes. When they chose to do so they canceled statutes not only of the states but of the national legislature.

The justices wrapped themselves in the Constitution itself. They proclaimed that they spoke for all.

Protests against the Supreme Court for the McCulloch and similar opinions came thick and fast in newspaper attacks, hostile pamphlets, resolutions of state legislatures, speeches and motions in Congress, and were voiced even in the truculent arguments of counsel before the bench.

Jefferson Riled by Marshall's Decisions

Hezekiah Niles in his *Register*—quite out of character as pleader for local autonomy—was the first in assault. He was followed by Spencer Roane, Virginia judge and Republican politician, in the Richmond *Enquirer*. Roane's thrusts, not only at the decision but at the Chief Justice for imposing his political bias on the other justices, stirred Marshall to tedious reply, under a pen name, in a Philadelphia Federalist paper. Jefferson was all along giving endorsement and encouragement to such champions of state rights as Roane. "The Judiciary branch," he wrote, "is the instrument which, working like gravity, without intermission, is to press us at last into one consolidated mass. Against this . . . no one . . . equally with judge Roane . . . possesses the power and the courage to make resistance; and to him I . . . have long looked, as our strongest bulwark." Jefferson went on to suggest, as Roane had done, that the states might be compelled to defend themselves by force. "If Congress fails to shield the States from dangers so palpable and imminent, the States must shield themselves, and meet the invader foot to foot." A remarkable sentiment in a former President of the Union!

When the Virginia legislature met, Roane prodded the members into a resolution condemning the Supreme Court for attempting to "change the whole character of the government." Virginia's attachment to her defiant resolutions of 1798 was reaffirmed. Virginia senators were instructed to work for an amendment of the Constitution to provide a super-Supreme Court to determine controversies between the national and state governments. This appeals tribunal would be free of the vices of the existing court because it would be appointed partly by central and partly by state authorities. This was only one of numerous proposals at this time for limiting the Supreme Court in reaching decisions hostile to pretensions of the states.

John Taylor of Caroline, who for more than thirty years had execrated every assertion of central power, rushed into print with a trio of tracts. *Construction Construed* was the first and most vehement against the Court and John Marshall particularly for preserving the Bank of the United States. The doctrine of national supremacy would sanctify the tariff and imperil slavery. He charged Marshall with holding that while national powers were limited, the means of executing these were unlimited. Taylor's inference was, "as ends may be made to beget means, so means may be made to beget ends, until the cohabitation shall rear a progeny of unconstitutional bastards, which were not begotten by the people." Taylor's explosions were violent even for Jefferson, who praised the book privately but declined to have his endorsement printed. He confided that "The Judiciary of the United States is the subtle corps of sappers . . . constantly working . . . to undermine the foundations of our confederated fabric."

However, rumblings of discontent at supposed invasion by the national government of areas of state prerogative did not deter Marshall from reasserting the supremacy of Congress where its laws were constitutional. Two famous cases followed *McCulloch v. Maryland* and belong in the same category—*Cohens v. Virginia* (6 Wheaton 264, 1821) and *Osborn v. Bank of the United States* (9 Wheaton 738, 1824).

P. J. and M. J. Cohen were fined in the mayor's (hustings) court of Norfolk, Virginia, for selling tickets in the National Lottery established by the City of Washington, D.C., to raise money for improvements in the national capital. The Cohens claimed that the law of Virginia forbidding such sale was unconstitutional since the lottery was operated by a corporation set up by Congress. They brought their appeal on writ of error from the Supreme Court of the United States to the local court of Norfolk. Counsel for Virginia (Senator James Barbour, who refused a large fee for his services) moved to dismiss the writ on broad grounds of state rights. A state was the defendant. No appeal could be taken from a state court to the Supreme Court. Anyhow, the judgment of the state court violated neither the Constitution nor any law of the United States. David B. Ogden of New York, and William Pinkney of Maryland, for the Cohens, disputed each of these points. No state was sovereign as against the Union. The authority of the Supreme Court covered all cases arising under the Constitution, laws, and treaties of the United States. The Cohens' case was of this description. The important argument, and decision of the Supreme Court, was on this question of the jurisdiction of the national over a state tribunal. Marshall upheld this authority. As the national power, within its range of duties, was supreme, so it must have its own courts to determine the legality of its legislation. Without this, each state, through state courts, could veto the enactments of Congress and we should have no effective government of the whole Union. The Chief Justice rebuked claims of some states and sections that they were superior to and could nullify national mandates. The body of the people who made the Constitution could unmake it. But no part of the people could cancel what all had decreed.

So much for that. On the merits of the punishment of the Cohens for breaking a Virginia law, the judgment of the local Norfolk court was confirmed. The Washington city ordinance for the lottery was intended to apply only to the District of Columbia, and gave the Cohens no authority to sell tickets in contravention of the law of a state. That is, the Cohens in fact were found to be in the wrong. But their right to contest the Virginia decision in the highest national court was vindicated.

The story in the *Osborn* case is quickly told. The principle involved was the same as that in the previous bank suit. While *McCulloch v. Maryland* was still on the carpet, the Ohio legislature directed the state auditor, Ralph Osborn, to demand of the branches of the United States Bank at Chillicothe and Cincinnati the payment of $50,000 tax each. If this was refused, the auditor's agent was to ransack the premises and seize everything of value. The Chillicothe branch got an injunction, from the United States District Court, staying Osborn's hand, but before the actual writ was served the state auditor's men loaded $100,000 in cash and securities in a wagon and made off toward the capital at Columbus. When the court papers reached them on the road they paid no attention and lodged the loot with the state treasurer. The district court ordered them to show cause why an attachment should not be issued against them for their disobedience to the injunction. The Ohio legislature defended its own action and the doings of its servants in a resolution blasting the presumption of the Supreme Court in the *McCulloch* case. Contempt for Marshall and his colleagues in sustaining the national power was mixed with concession. If the bank would abolish its branches in Ohio the state would refund the tax money.

The case dragged on, was argued twice by prominent counsel, including Henry Clay, Daniel Webster, and Robert Goodloe Harper. Meantime fulminations against the Supreme Court and its wicked role in championing national authority continued to reverberate. The decision in the *Cohens* case called out more state rights artillery. All made no difference. The Ohio law designed to destroy the branches of the Bank of the United States was declared null and void.

United States versus Nixon

This case involved the subpoena of special prosecutor Leon Jaworski addressed to federal district judge John J. Sirica for 64 tape recordings of White House conversations, on the ground that they constituted necessary evidence in the trial of six defendants for conspiracy in the Watergate cover-up case. Judge Sirica granted what was asked, subject to appeal; Mr. Jaworski, however, asked for immediate review by the Supreme Court, rather than waiting for appellate court action. The High Court agreed, because of imminence of the trial, and decision was handed down on July 23, 1974.

Decision was unanimous by the eight Justices taking part (Justice Rehnquist had disqualified himself because of previous service in the Department of Justice under John Mitchell, one of the defendants in the case). Written and read in court by Chief Justice Warren Burger, the decision answered three basic questions raised in argument.

First, could Mr. Jaworski, part of the executive branch, sue the President, its head? The Court ruled that, because of "unique authority and tenure" granted the special prosecutor by the attorney general, including the explicit power to contest in court presidential claims of executive privilege, the suit was valid.

Second, is the President subject to the Court? It had been argued that he was not, under the doctrine of separation of powers and a claim that presidential confidentiality was absolute. Here the Court sided with Mr. Jaworski, harking back to *Marbury v. Madison*, stating that "it is emphatically the province and duty of the judicial department to say what the law is." It added: "The judicial power of the United States vested in the Federal courts . . . can no more be shared with the Executive Branch than the Chief Executive, for example, can share with the Judiciary the veto power, or the Congress share with the Judiciary the power to override a Presidential veto."

Third, can presidential records be subpoenaed? The Court ruled that, although a limited executive privilege does exist, the needs of criminal prosecution must take precedence in the absence of any need to preserve military, diplomatic, or sensitive national security secrets.

The White House was ordered "forthwith" to turn over to Judge Sirica the material subpoenaed, he to review it for relevance to the Watergate cover-up trial. Subsequently, after several hours' delay in responding, it was announced that President Nixon would comply fully with the decision, and Judge Sirica took action forcing an agreement with the President's lawyers to produce the tapes promptly.

The basic importance of this decision was the declaration that neither separation of powers nor executive privilege was enough to stand in the way of providing evidence for a criminal trial. While the Court acknowledged some "constitutional underpinnings" for executive privilege, it refused to discuss the relevance of such claims to civil litigation or Congressional demand. Also refused was a ruling on the legality of a grand jury's having named the President as an "unindicted co-conspirator" in the case at issue, although a promise had been made to do so. This promise, the court said, had been "improvidently granted."

As is not unusual, the Supreme Court decided *U.S. v. Nixon* on deliberately narrow grounds, in this instance probably to achieve unanimity in a case of immediate and vital import to the nation.

II CIVIL RIGHTS

Dred Scott (1795?-1858) in the one-word description of him in the *Dictionary of American Biography* is set down as "slave." That is accurate, for he was the descendant of Africans imported and sold as slaves, and he was held in slavery almost all his life, and the Supreme Court of the United States declared he was a slave. But even more he was a symbol of the conflict between champions of free labor and forced labor, between democracy and privilege, between the progress of a varied economy and the sloth of single-crop agriculture. Dred Scott, by the same token, was the forecast of the bitterest civil war. Himself nobody, he became everybody. History, viewed in its sweep, is nameless. Dred Scott, until well along in his life, was called simply "Sam," as nearly anonymous as one could be. The humblest of mortals, by an accident he figures in the story of human frailty and striving.

In order to understand the events and passions that clustered about Dred Scott we must revert to an economic law, or at least a strong tendency which will surely operate unless deliberately checked and constantly corrected. This is the law of diminishing returns in the extractive industries that take from nature, such as agriculture, mining, forestry, and fishing. In these, for the same successive input of labor and capital you get a smaller and smaller result, because the resources of nature are limited and tend to become exhausted.

Slavery destroyed the soil. For this there were several reasons. Slaves could be compelled to work, but—with no reward in sight—they could not be compelled to think. Consequently their labor had to be applied to the most routine cultivation, to doing the same tasks over and over again. This meant they must be used to grow a single crop—tobacco or cotton or sugar cane. The same crop planted year after year depleted the land, for it continued to take out of the soil the same essential chemical elements. Further, slaves were not resourceful, nor ingenious (except in sparing themselves effort), would not conserve land or tools or work animals. Why should they be saving or show forethought? Their condition could not improve over the years, they could never have anything for themselves, they could not expect a better lot for their children. But most of all, slavery ruined the soil because labor was costly and land was cheap. It seemed to the master more economical to crop his acres ruthlessly until their yield was unprofitable and then take in virgin land, which was in its turn exhausted. Finally this produced a continuous migration. Sons or sometimes the planters themselves with their families and slaves moved southwestward to the unspoiled lands of Alabama, Mississippi, Louisiana, and Texas. After about 1830 slavery supported itself in the older tidewater districts only by sale of the surplus of field hands "down the river" to the Gulf states. But for this the slaves would have eaten themselves out of house and home; the masters, trying vainly to support them, would have been impoverished and obliged to free their slaves in self-defense.

Slavery as an institution was voracious for new lands, could not live without devouring millions of acres of untilled soil. As several observed the scene, "To confine slavery is to kill it." Hence the contest of owners to secure safety for their slave property in the territories, and, when these were organized as states, have them enter the Union recognizing the legality of slavery. Not only did the slave South require territorial expansion. The slave power needed to preserve a political parity with the free states. So, on one occasion after another, new states were created in pairs, one slave, the other free.

If Congress had prohibited slavery in a territory, it was settled by free workers and later would come in as a free state. Thus, as the rivalry became fiercer, the established principle and practice that Congress might dedicate a region to freedom came to be questioned by the land-hungry slave power. Could the people of a territory decide this matter for themselves? This was the issue concretely presented in the celebrated case of Dred Scott.

We need to list briefly the main events in this struggle which began benevolently and ended in bitter strife:

1787, the Northwest Ordinance of the Continental Congress. Among conditions laid down for states to be admitted from this region was that none should permit slavery.

1820, the Missouri Compromise. Maine was admitted as a free state, Missouri as a slave state, but all other territory in the Louisiana Purchase north of the line 36 degrees 30 minutes (the southern border of Missouri) was to be forever free. That is, Missouri thrust up into a region dedicated to free labor.

1847, Wilmot Proviso rejected. Wilmot and his friends in Congress had urged that lands to be acquired from Mexico at the end of the war then in progress should be closed to slavery. The purchase money was voted with no such condition attached.

1850, the Compromise of 1850 was embodied first in an omnibus bill, but later took form in five companion statutes. These admitted California as a free state; territorial governments were provided in Utah and New Mexico with liberty of the settlers to decide whether they wanted to be admitted later as slave or free states; the slave trade was abolished in the District of Columbia; the fugitive slave law was made more favorable to the masters; the Texas-United States boundary dispute was settled. This bundle of laws, giving something to each side, was the work of Henry Clay, and temporarily quieted the threat of secession by the slave states. Failure to prohibit slavery in Utah and New Mexico in effect repealed the Missouri Compromise of 1820, because Utah lay north of the line of 36 degrees 30 minutes in a region supposed to be preserved for free labor.

1854, Kansas-Nebraska Act. This provided for two territories and eventually states, west of Missouri and Iowa respectively. The settlers in these territories were given popular or "squatter" sovereignty, the right to form state constitutions allowing or forbidding slavery as they chose. To make assurance doubly sure (since Kansas and Nebraska were included in formerly free territory), the slave states insisted that this law explicitly repeal the Missouri Compromise. For five years the struggle between pro-slavery and free soil settlers (two territorial legislatures, raids, murders by John Brown and others) produced the scandal of "Bleeding Kansas."

The Dred Scott decision in the Supreme Court (19 Howard 393, 1857) is the next in this series of tests of strength between slavery and free labor forces.

Wanderings of Dred Scott, Geographical and Judicial

Dred Scott seems to have been born in Southampton County, Virginia. When we first know of him he was a slave, called Sam, owned jointly by Peter Blow, a planter of the county, and one Henry Moore. In 1819 Blow sold his large but probably unproductive place of 860 acres, and with his wife, five of his children, Sam, and doubtless other slaves, moved to northeastern Alabama near Huntsville. This was a region of rich soil, where the Blow tribe tarried for eleven years. They then pushed west and north to St. Louis, in Missouri, a state which, after disturbing controversy, had been admitted to the Union with a constitution allowing the holding of slaves. Here the Blows opened a boarding house and Sam was hired out as a roustabout on the river.

After two years the elder Blows died, and the administrator of the estate sold Sam to Dr. John Emerson of St. Louis for $500. Dr. Emerson was a civilian physician at the Jefferson Barracks near St. Louis, but was soon commissioned as assistant surgeon in the army (1832) and ordered to Fort Armstrong at Rock Island, Illinois. To this post in a free state Dr. Emerson took his slave (henceforth Dred Scott). After four years the surgeon and his slave transferred to Fort Snelling. This was on the west bank of the Mississippi at the junction of the Minnesota River—a part of the Louisiana Purchase in which by the Compromise of 1820 slavery was prohibited. Here Dr. Emerson bought Harriet, the slave of the Indian agent at the post, and Dred married her, having lost a previous wife by sale. Dr. Emerson soon returned to St. Louis and after a year or so the Scotts, who had been hired out at Snelling in the meantime, joined him. On the steamboat down the Mississippi, at a point north of the line 36-30, Eliza Scott was born. It may be that Dred now (1838) sued his master for his freedom, contending that he had gained his liberty when he was taken into territory where slavery was forbidden. But we hear no more of such an effort on his part for five years during which the Scotts seem to have remained principally in Missouri.

Dr. Emerson died in 1843, and soon afterward Dred offered to buy, on installments, his and his family's freedom. Dred had recently spent a while as servant to an army officer in the Southwest, had accumulated about $300, and doubtless this stirred his desire for independence. Mrs. Emerson refused Dred's offer, whereat he petitioned the Missouri Circuit Court at St. Louis for permission to bring suit for his freedom because he had been taken to Illinois and Wisconsin Territory. A similar petition was made for Harriet. Permission was granted, depositions were taken, witnesses for both sides were called. It is not known just how Dred came to go to law, whether on his own motion or induced to it by counsel with philanthropic or financial motives. Numbers of lawyers appeared for the Scotts as their various suits progressed. The later ones were free soil advocates encouraged by members of the

Blow family, to whose father Dred had belonged years before. During this period of the 'forties and 'fifties the issue of the extension of slavery into the territories was ever more heatedly debated. Since Dred's plea presented a concrete test of this question, he attracted prominent legal talent for and against him.

In the first suit, June 1847, the jury found for Mrs. Emerson. Dred's lawyers moved for a new trial, the court granted it, and in 1850 the Scott family, now including a second daughter, was declared free. This was on the ground that he had been taken into Illinois (free under the Northwest Ordinance of 1787) and into Wisconsin Territory, free under the Missouri Compromise. Opposing counsel argued in vain that the voluntary return of the Scotts to Missouri—if they had ever acquired freedom—gave them back to Dr. Emerson.

However, Mrs. Emerson appealed to the Missouri Supreme Court, which in 1852, with the chief justice dissenting, decided for Mrs. Emerson, ordering the decision of the Missouri Circuit Court reversed. The Scotts were slaves again. Dred's counsel had cited the fact that repeatedly Missouri courts had sanctioned the freedom of slaves because they had been transported to free territory. The majority decision fully admitted this precedent, but chose to depart from it because recently the slave power—Missouri being a slave state—had been ominously threatened. The opinion was: "Times now are not what they were when the former decisions . . . were made. Since then not only individuals but States have been possessed with a dark and fell spirit in relation to slavery . . . whose inevitable consequence must be the overthrow and destruction of our government." Thus the decision to return the Scotts to slavery was frankly a political one.

After this see-sawing in the state courts, the Scotts (or their friends) tried their fortunes in the federal Circuit Court in St. Louis (1853). Dred, as a citizen of Missouri, sued John F. A. Sanford (Mrs. Emerson's brother, now managing her affairs) as a citizen of New York. Sanford was sympathetic to Dred Scott and co-operated in the test case to establish his freedom and prevent the taking of more slaves to free territory. If Scott was not free he was not a citizen (of Missouri or any other state) and therefore could not sue. His lawyers paid no attention to this. Nor did the lawyers of Sanford, in objecting to the right of Scott to sue, declare that he was a slave. They simply claimed that Dred was "a negro of African descent, whose ancestors were of pure African blood, and who were brought into this country and sold as slaves." The court decided that Scott could sue, but the jury found that he was a slave, the property of Sanford.

His lawyers promptly took the case on writ of error to the Supreme

Court of the United States, found an able and sympathetic attorney for Dred in Washington—Montgomery Blair, who contributed his services—and money to pay court costs. The case was not reached until February 1856. The lawyers against Scott were Henry S. Geyer, senator from Missouri, and Reverdy Johnson of Maryland, who since the death of Daniel Webster was regarded as the most eloquent advocate at the bar. After three days of argument the justices were at odds on a procedural point but were substantially agreed that they would not decide whether the Missouri Compromise line, dividing slave from free territory, was constitutional. Judge Curtis, with a freedom in disclosing secrets of the judicial chamber not uncommon in that day, wrote this news to his uncle. Beside that, the presidential campaign was coming on—between Buchanan (Democratic), Frémont (Republican), and Fillmore (American party)—and the Court was willing to postpone pronouncement on the dangerous slavery issue until a new chief executive was chosen. According to order, the case was reargued at greater length in December 1856.

The judges did not confer for two months, until mid-February 1857. Most of them still felt that they should not meddle with the momentous query which divided the country: does Congress have power to forbid slavery in the territories? They preferred to take refuge in the subordinate decision that, whatever Dred's status had been while in Illinois and in Wisconsin Territory, he had returned to Missouri, there he was a slave by decision of the Missouri Supreme Court, and so he had had no right to sue in the federal Circuit Court from which the case came to the highest tribunal.

Court Forced To Face Slavery Issue

Mr. Justice Samuel Nelson, a New York Democrat, was assigned to write this opinion for the Court. But he had hardly set about it when Judge John McLean of Ohio and Judge Benjamin Curtis of Massachusetts, strong anti-slavery men, made known their intention to present dissenting opinions upholding the constitutionality of the Missouri Compromise. This would make the opinion of the majority conspicuous for what it omitted. So the majority reluctantly canceled the assignment to Judge Nelson, and asked Chief Justice Roger Brooke Taney to deliver the majority decision. This was accomplished only with maneuvering which, if known at the time, would have confirmed the charge of many, after the decision was rendered, that it was politically inspired. What happened was that Judge James M. Wayne, of Georgia, lined up the majority to deal with the substantive question. Anxious to have as many as possible in this group, Judge Catron, of Kentucky, appealed to the President-elect, Buchanan, who was to be inaugurated within a couple of weeks, to urge Judge Grier, from Pennsylvania, who was wavering, to join the majority. Evidently he did so, for Grier replied that he would concur with the Chief Justice, try to persuade others to do so, and that there would be at least six "who will decide the Compromise law of 1820 to be of *non-effect.*"

This is a disillusioning incident. Here is a justice discussing with the President-elect the policy of the Court in reaching a decision and asking him to influence a brother judge. Worse, from what we have of the correspondence, Buchanan complied. Then the judge to whom Buchanan appealed disclosed to Buchanan what the decision of the Court would be. The temple of justice seems to have been polluted. The Supreme Court had always claimed its independence of executive and legislative branches, but now judges were inviting what amounted to executive interference. Further, they informed Buchanan, so far as the Court was concerned, what he might say in his inaugural address, for the Court, they promised, would not give its opinion until two days later. Accordingly, Buchanan announced that slavery or no slavery in the territories would be speedily and finally settled in the Supreme Court, and that he, "in common with all good citizens," would cheerfully submit to this decision "whatever this may be." Actually, he knew in advance that the majority opinion would be: Congress had no authority to forbid slavery in the territories.

March 6 and 7, 1857, the judges read their opinions. With minor differences here and there, six concurred in holding that a Negro could not be a citizen of the United States, consequently could not sue in the federal courts; and further that Congress had no power to prohibit slavery in the territories. In this majority were Taney, Campbell, Catron, Daniel, Grier, and Wayne, all of them except Grier (Pennsylvania) from slave states. Judge Nelson stuck to the opinion he had prepared, declaring simply that Dred Scott was a slave because the law of Missouri said that. McLean and Curtis disagreed vigorously on all three of these positions.

Taney took two hours to read the decision of the Court. He was almost eighty years old, tall, thin, bent, his face exceedingly lined. A native and still a resident of Maryland, he had long since freed the slaves he inherited, but his sympathies were with the planter class in which he had been born. For years he was the faithful follower of Jackson, with whom he had co-operated to deprive the second Bank of the United States of government deposits. One feels, on reading his long, comprehensive opinion, that Taney had a mind-set in favor of the slave society. He wrote to his son-in-law while the Scott case was under consideration by the Court: "The South is doomed to sink to a state of inferiority, and the power of the North will be exercised to gratify their cupidity and their evil passions without the slightest regard to the principles of the Constitution . . . it is my deliberate opinion that the South is doomed, and that nothing but a firm united action, nearly unanimous in every state, can check northern insult and northern aggression." Professor Carl B. Swisher, a recent and sympathetic biographer of Taney but also a long-time student of our Constitution, has said of the opinion in the Dred Scott case:

First and foremost it is necessary to remember [Taney's] devotion to the South, of which he was a product, and his belief that, if the trend of events continued, the South was doomed . . . the North had outstripped the South in numbers, and it seemed . . . inevitable that the federal government should become a tool of the North, to which the South in an increasing degree would be compelled to submit. Such a condition had not been contemplated by the framers of the Constitution, and such domination of the South, in Taney's estimation, was unconstitutional. He preferred secession by force of arms to submission to it. His deepest fear seems to have been that when a northern political party directly assumed the reins of government the South would not act with sufficient assiduity to make rebellion effective.

We are to assume that the Dred Scott decision, reopening the territories to slavery, was to offer expansion for the southern way of life, rebuke assertive abolitionists, and do what was possible to redress the imbalance between the growth of the sections in economic and political power.

Do Justices Decide Past or Present?

It seems harsh to think that a man in Taney's exalted position, ancient too, with nothing more to look for in life, would be moved by prejudice. He surely believed that he was deciding in the public interest. John Marshall had the opposite inclination, to make the most of central government authority. Are we to say that Marshall was biased? Perhaps the only satisfactory judgment that may be passed on these two chief justices, one following the other, is that of history. As America developed, politically and economically, Marshall's choice to magnify national rather than state or local power proved an accurate forecast of events. Taney's approval of states' rights and the agricultural economy resting on slavery (and before that his opposition to central banking) misjudged the course this country was to take.

Taney had poor Dred Scott (which was to say some four million slaves) boxed in. Every avenue of escape to freedom was closed to him. This slamming of doors in Dred's face was based on a disparagement, a scorn of the Negro race. Taney, be it noted, did not declare this was his own view or that of the Court. Rather he was describing the mean estimate in which Negroes, as he believed, were held by the men who made the Declaration of Independence and the Constitution. Negroes, he found, "had for more than a century before been regarded as beings of an inferior order, and altogether unfit to associate with the white race, either in social or political relations; and so far inferior that they had no rights which the white man was bound to respect; and that the negro might justly and lawfully be reduced to slavery for his benefit . . . This opinion was at that time fixed and universal in the white race. It was regarded as an axiom in morals as well as in politics which no one thought of disputing . . ." In colonial times "no distinction . . . was made between the free negro or mulatto and the slave, but his stigma, of the deepest degradation, was fixed upon the whole race."

In this condemnation, which Taney supported with citations, he forgot notable exceptions to his rule. As early as 1683 Quakers of Germantown, Pennsylvania, had spoken out against slavery, a hundred years after that George Mason had described slavery as the curse of a country, and the first Congress under the new national government received an impressive petition, headed by Benjamin Franklin, for abolition. It is hard to escape the conviction that Taney shared, subconsciously perhaps, the notion of his ancestors, that the Negro was a creature to be despised and exploited. He would be disillusioned, could he have returned a hundred years after his Dred Scott decision, to see a score of African nations rising to independence.

Taney chose to decide this critical case in accordance with what he understood the framers of the Constitution meant by "people" and "citizens" of the United States. He refused to consult policies appropriate to his own time, but insisted on applying definitions of three-quarters of a century earlier, when American society was far simpler and when the tide of public opinion in this country and in Europe had not begun to run against the institution of slavery. Was this the wise interpretation of the premises of our society? Legalistically, it may have been accurate to seek to resurrect the conceptions of men who were fifty years in their graves. But a more serviceable handling of the fundamental law makes it subject to judicial amendment in accordance with the apparent needs of the nation.

One may say that the Supreme Court is obligated to hew to the line and apply the Constitution as its makers would presumably have applied it. If such decisions are not what two-thirds of the people of the states consider desirable, they may amend the Constitution. But eventual amendment, the result of widespread dissatisfaction or indignation, may result only after much harm has been suffered or a dreadful cataclysm (such as the Civil War) has befallen. Many decisions of the Supreme Court are not legal rulings in the narrow sense, but are truly guides for social policy. The people are likely to accept peaceably interpretations by the highest court which in fact preserve the Constitution as a living document with meaning for the progress of the nation.

The justices of the Supreme Court are in such cases law-givers. They differ from legislators because they take a longer view, are not swayed by temporary popular demand, try to hold in mind the enduring good of the community. They are protectors of the law in the true sense that they allow for prudent change. Someone said, "There is nothing so conservative as progress." We shall see that our Supreme Court justices, trained in the law as commonly practiced, many times have not been sufficiently alert to alteration in national habit and thought. They have often been bound by outmoded precedent instead of treating our heritage with a degree of flexibility.

Guns of Gettysburg

If Dred Scott, being admittedly "a negro, whose ancestors were imported into this country, and sold as slaves," could not be a citizen of the United States, the Circuit Court had no right to entertain his suit. That compelled the Supreme Court to dismiss the case. The Circuit Court, though allowing Scott to plead, had determined in the end that he was a slave. So Scott was out of court, and still the property of his master. Taney need have said no more. But two of the justices, McLean and Curtis, were going to dissent on the ground that, over and above any procedural matter, Scott had been taken into the Louisiana Territory where Congress had prohibited slavery, and was therefore free. Taney, for the majority of the Supreme Court, chose to refute this contention. To do so he had to go beyond the demands of Dred's case and hold the Missouri Compromise unconstitutional. Congress had power "to . . . make all needful rules and regulations respecting the territory . . . belonging to the United States." But, said Taney,

Congress had no right to declare that "slavery . . . shall be forever prohibited in all that part of the territory ceded by France" north of the 36-30 line and not included in Missouri.

Why? Because Congress, by the Fifth Amendment, was limited in its authority to regulate this territory. It could not deprive any person "of life, liberty, or property, without due process of law." "And," Taney concluded, "an act of Congress which deprives a citizen of the United States of his liberty or property, merely because he came himself or brought his property into a particular territory of the United States, and who had committed no offense against the laws, could hardly be dignified with the name of due process of law." The right to hold slaves was recognized in the Constitution. Slaves were not different from any other kind of property. Therefore "the act of Congress which prohibited a citizen from holding or owning property of this kind in the territory . . . mentioned, is not warranted by the Constitution, and is . . . void. . . ."

For good measure Taney pointed out that the status of slaves who had been taken to free states or supposedly free territory and who afterward returned to slave territory depended on the law of the state to which they had returned. Dred Scott and his family now resided in Missouri, the highest court of Missouri said they were slaves, and the Supreme Court of the United States accepted this verdict.

Of course the dissenters disputed all this reasoning. Slavery existed only by state law. Congress could prohibit slavery in a territory. The slave owner transferring to this territory, or to the free state of Illinois, could not bring his state law with him. The moment the slave was taken to free soil he became free. The Fifth Amendment did not apply. As to the decision of the Missouri Supreme Court that Dred was a slave when he returned there, this overthrew a practice of thirty years whereby slaves taken to free jurisdictions were free when they came back. The Missouri court had not disputed that this was the law. It had merely chosen, in Scott's case, to disregard the settled law. But the court could not abolish the law by construction. A statute of Missouri was required for this, and there had been no statute. Dred and his family were free when they went back to Missouri. Being free, Dred was a citizen. To be a citizen he did not have to be able to vote. Many citizens could not vote. He was not a foreigner, did not need to be naturalized to become a citizen. Dred, a free man (Negro or not) lived in a different state from the defendant, Sanford, and as a citizen of the United States he could sue in the federal courts.

We do not need to deal with the winding opinions of the justices who concurred with Taney. If any judicial disquisitions are forgotten, those are.

Dred Scott's case, taking it as the case of slavery versus freedom, could have been decided for freedom. The opinions of two dissenting judges show that. The fact was that most of the members of the Court sympathized with the slavery interest. They failed to consult the manifest wishes of three-quarters of the people of the country. They did not remember the grand object of American government, which was liberty. Possession (of slaves) proved to be nine points of the law. These judges were two generations removed from the constitutional fathers. The men who created the fundamental law could interpret it liberally. Those who inherited the written Constitution invested it with a textual authority. They fastened on words, quarrelled about definitions, did not feel themselves empowered to treat the document as adaptable. They became technical, legalistic. If we are to think the best of them, we may say that they did not realize what drove them in their tortuous reasoning. Men hold tenaciously to economic privilege, which makes law and morals in its own image. The Dred Scott decision illustrated what slave-holders of the South had long since discovered, that it is sweet to live by the sweat of another man's brow.

As for Dred, he and his family were freed by their owner when the case was over. Dred spent his remaining years as a porter in a St. Louis hotel.

Bread and Butter Basis of Life and Law

The Civil War was tragic proof of the failure of the Constitution to produce "a more perfect Union." "We, the people" of the preamble had been done away by willful seceding states in the historical sequel. Four years must be devoted to death and destruction before the national bond was restored, and after that a decade and more of bitter social strife before the healing process could commence. Too often the eventual result of the war is remembered with gratification, and the calamity of disruption is diminished if not forgotten. True, the Union was firmer afterward, as an arm or leg bone, knitted following a break, is stronger than ever. But the fact is that the effort of the constitutional fathers to set law above violence, after two generations of trial, was wretchedly disappointed.

The seeds of disunion were early planted. The beginning of dissent was in states' rights opposition to the adoption of the Constitution, notably in Massachusetts, Virginia, and New York. The document was only a decade old when this defection was declared in the Virginia and Kentucky resolutions of Madison and Jefferson. In these pronouncements states claimed the right to judge for themselves when the federal government had exceeded its delegated powers. Shortly afterward it was clear that this doctrine was not exclusive with the southern and western country. Influential New Englanders, after the Louisiana Purchase promised to magnify the power of slavery, conspired to swarm to themselves in a sectional confederacy and if possible incorporate some of the middle states in their design. This project was frustrated, but in another ten years it assumed more threatening form in the Hartford Convention of 1814 in the protest of the Northeast against the second war with England.

Then a slightly longer gap before South Carolina's attempted "nullification" of protective tariff acts of 1828 and 1832. We think of this as the work of John C. Calhoun, who pertinaciously elaborated on the contention of the Virginia and Kentucky resolutions. Then came ever more acute dissensions over the character of western expansion, temporarily calmed in the Compromise of 1850, inflamed again in aftermath of the Kansas-Nebraska Act, and running on to the Dred Scott decision, John Brown's raid, and the secession of the Confederate states.

These differences increasingly assumed, outwardly, political form, and were supported by juridical reasoning. One would suppose from the controversial essays and books, debates, and election campaign speeches that Americans were divided on high government principles. But this was the sublimation of disparities in economic life and institutions. These disparities were the solids which, treated with heat, gave off political vapors. The North was developing varied industry, commerce, finance, as well as agriculture with free labor, while the South clung to staple crops, produced by Negro slaves.

All that makes up a society, broadly its culture (economic interest, religion, law, education, politics) contributed to the sectional rift that became civil warfare. The different modes of getting a living were of chief importance. These determined institutions, which in turn controlled ideas and loyalties. If we are required to reduce to simplest terms the constitutional conflict over secession we must revert to the black man with the hoe and the white man at the lathe. This contrast, many will say, neglects more than it depicts. It is true that mind and heart, purpose and willingness to sacrifice for ideals become forces in themselves, and the noblest endeavors of mankind are identified with moral convictions. Still, when we seek to explain behavior and beliefs, we are sure to encounter modes of mastering the natural environment.

Be as comprehensive as we will, take into account as many complexities of a civilization as we know how, economic pursuits loom as fundamental. Recollection of these furnishes the best means of understanding constitutional pretensions, legal enactments, and court decisions that led to and resulted from the Civil War. Attempts have been made by historians, statesmen, philosophers, and poets to discount the humble springs of actions and ideas. Yet how otherwise explain the division of principles along Mason and Dixon's line? How else perceive the contest of North and South for allegiance of the West? Geography and climate seem to take command of the "higher life." In one environment thrives varied enterprise; in another, agricultural routine.

We may not disregard the prime part played by the institutions of free labor in one region and of slavery in the other. True, not all northern workers were able to be self-assertive or independent of exploitation. Nor were all who toiled in the South chattels on plantations, for scattered widely, on the uplands particularly, were small white farmers and those of other occupations with no stake in slavery. But we are concerned with principal interests, with main motives. If those who speak for a society—politicians, editors, educators, clergymen —are allied to a class, though this be a minority class in numbers, the desires they represent will be, for the time anyhow, dominant.

The Civil War had opposite effects, in all respects, upon North and South. In the former, war contracts, ampler money supply, rising prices, and the vehement demand for workers stimulated industry and all elements of the economy. Victory produced confidence which swept enterprise forward, especially in railroad construction, to the crisis of 1873. The North enjoyed a great press of business—so energetic, in fact, that it brought much corruption and waste. Features of the national economy with which the world is most familiar—large-scale production, corporate combination, expanding labor unions—took their rise from the Civil War. On the other hand, in the South, where most of the war was fought, the story was one of depletion both physical and moral. The South had few embryonic industries to be forced by public and private demand into flourishing development. The South's wage earners were few. After the blockade of southern ports became effective, the principal saleable product, cotton, could not be got out, and thus proved a poor dependence for borrowing at home or abroad. Public security issues and paper money, instead of acting as a tonic, raised prices to ruinous heights and became instruments of confiscation.

Motives in Reconstruction

After surrender, the economic outlook of the former Confederacy was sorrowful. An impressive lesson of economic history is the speed with which a country or a region recovers from war and sets new records of production, even though equipment and manpower have been reduced. Provided, however, its basic knowledge, skills, and institutions are unimpaired. But the South's labor system was destroyed, and it possessed little versatility, inventiveness, or science. It had not nourished freedom, so when spontaneity and resolve were demanded the South was bankrupt in more than credit. Rebuilding must be on new lines, for which the South of slavery was unprepared in experience or in desire. To make all worse, what, ironically, was called Reconstruction took the form of political tyranny, military rule, and vindictiveness and prevented the South from making an earlier start on social recovery. Pride is an enormous ingredient in progress, but it was the lot of the conquered Confederacy to be systematically humiliated for years. It is comparatively easy to rebuild fences, barns, cities, railroads, but the task of redesigning social institutions takes time, patience, and sympathy—not haste, hatred, violence, and confusion.

Before the war the North was cultivating industrial arts which directed talents into the private business sphere. The South, on the contrary, could and did devote more of its men of parts to public life. The consequence was that southern sway in national politics was resented but not checked until the rise of the Republican party. After the war, with ex-Confederates excluded from Congress, the victorious North was determined to hold the whip hand. This was more than national loyalty. In good part it was the unspoken aim to run the federal government in the interest of industry as against agriculture. The North was to have its innings. Of course this purpose would be defeated if Confederates were promptly forgiven for rebellion and welcomed back into national councils. They would now enjoy even fuller representation because all of the Negroes, and not three-fifths of the slaves as before, were to be counted for the apportionment.

On this issue of policy came a sharp division within the North. The pistol of John Wilkes Booth that killed President Lincoln killed in the same instant the prospect for an orderly, early return of the seceding South to the Union. Lincoln's wisdom, compassion, and command might have speeded and eased the process, allaying bitterness, encouraging reconciliation. But the wicked and stupid assassination of this foremost figure invited revenge on the South. How tempting was this excuse for punishment is evident in the suddenness with which the Radical Republicans, a minority in their own party, achieved control. They had distrusted Lincoln during the war, and they might have borne him down afterward in spite of his powerful national appeal to all classes in the North and to most in the South.

But his successor, Andrew Johnson, was easier game. He was not the commander in chief who won the war for the Union. He was a Southerner (Tennesseean) who had filled a loyal but minor role. Though sensible, a man of integrity and courage, he could not wear the mantle of Elijah. Fair-minded and likable, he lacked Lincoln's depth, magnetism, and mastery. His wish to continue Lincoln's conciliatory policy toward the South met antagonism and defeat at every turn. The Radicals' hostility to him was spurred by Edwin M. Stanton, the hold-over secretary of war, who had been suspicious of Lincoln and was scornful of Johnson. Johnson's unsuccessful effort to remove Stanton was the excuse for impeachment of the President by the House. He escaped conviction by a single vote of the Senate.

The rough handling of Johnson by his enemies was, by the same token, magnified in the treatment of the states lately in rebellion. The dominant Radical Republicans, resolved to prevent a fusion of Democrats north and south, chose to administer the former Confederate states as "conquered provinces." They were to be divided into military districts and governed by major generals under martial law. Extension of the Freedmen's Bureau—the federal agency for defense of rights and opportunities of ex-slaves—was passed over Johnson's veto. Negroes went to the polls protected by northern bayonets. Negroes entered southern legislatures in numbers which gave political control to northern adventurers ("carpetbaggers") and to "scalawags" (native Southerners who joined Republicans in the reconstruction program). This is a quick description which does violence to the honesty and ability of many, including freedmen so precipitately thrust into public responsibilities.

The economic motive of the inside clique of reconstructionists in Congress—to ensure the dominance of industrial capitalism in the national life—must not be emphasized to the neglect of other purposes. The desire to enforce social justice was often uppermost. Union spokesmen wanted to give freedmen the rights and opportunities so long denied them. It was inevitable that the means used in coercing the white South were harsh and sudden. But we cannot lose sight of ethical intentions, marred though they were by the spirit of retribution. Nor should we condemn attempts of Southerners at retaliation without remembering their long-time dread of slave revolts. The former Confederate states enacted "black codes" which severely limited Negroes' rights. The Ku Klux Klan and similar vigilantes were guilty of cruel excesses.

The pity was that the "war after the war," which could not be avoided under any circumstances, was so virulent and protracted. A dozen years were endured before the last troops occupying southern soil were withdrawn and self-government restored to all southern states. The difficult readjustment would have been aided had not the leaders to whom the white South was accustomed to look been discredited and immobilized by northern fears. Actually, this threw power to men of less experience and often of less principle, who became tools of reckless intrigue. The aftermath of war has never been favorable to right reason.

With this swift sketch of the situation, we are to see how the turmoil of the times was reflected in constitutional amendments, and in Supreme Court interpretation of these amendments and of accompanying legislation.

Narrow Meaning of Fourteenth Amendment

The Thirteenth, Fourteenth, and Fifteenth Amendments and acts to enforce them were products of the Civil War and Reconstruction. The Thirteenth Amendment formally ended slavery everywhere in the United States. This was followed, at the close of 1865, by the Civil Rights Act. It undid the Dred Scott decision by declaring that all persons born within the United States were citizens entitled to enjoy perfect equality. President Johnson vetoed the bill because he considered it unconstitutional and impolitic. It obtruded the central authority into management of relationships that belonged to the states. Thus it would rouse resentments bound to slow the process of peaceable reunion.

The law was passed over Johnson's veto. Then, to make sure that its protections to ex-slaves would go unquestioned, the Fourteenth Amendment was put together in the joint committee on Reconstruction. This steering committee was controlled by the Radical Republicans under the leadership of Thaddeus Stevens of Pennsylvania in the House and of Charles Sumner of Massachusetts in the Senate. The framers of the amendment were angered by the "black codes" of southern states, intended, with little disguise, to keep Negroes in subjection, economic and political.

Consequently the amendment was designed to make the national government—overriding the states—the keeper of the rights of individual citizens. The circumstances and legislative history of the amendment leave no doubt of this purpose. However, the first section was given a negative, not a positive wording, whereby hung a tale. After declaring that all persons born or naturalized in the United States "are citizens of the United States and of the state wherein they reside," it went on to prohibit state interference with citizen rights: "No state shall make or enforce any law which shall abridge the privileges or immunities of citizens of the United States; nor shall any state deprive any person of life, liberty, or property without due process of law; nor deny to any person within its jurisdiction the equal protection of the laws."

The idea was to make the Bill of Rights, which defended against invasion of personal liberties by the central government, applicable to the states as well. The famous phrases of this section of the Fourteenth Amendment, necessarily general in meaning, have led to more interpretation by the courts than other parts of the Constitution. This section particularly proved both a disappointment and a surprise. It did not accomplish what most people thought was its aim, and it did accomplish what few imagined was its intent. These developments will be explored below.

The second section would compel the states to give Negroes the vote for state and federal officers, or suffer a corresponding reduction in representation. This commandment was the darling of the Radical Reconstructionists because it was meant to ensure support by Negro votes necessary to carry their program into effect. The third section excluded "unreconstructed rebels" from state or federal office. No one who had violated his official oath to support the Constitution, by taking part in the Confederacy, could hold office again unless Congress removed his disability. The fourth section was a formality; it acknowledged the national debt incurred in the war and outlawed payment by nation or state of debts of the Confederacy. The last section gave Congress power to enforce the amendment by appropriate legislation.

The Fourteenth Amendment came into force in July 1868, but it was five years later before the Supreme Court construed it in the *Slaughterhouse Cases* (1873). In this interval the Court had retreated from its former practice and showed a tendency to uphold state instead of federal powers. This was a reaction against the stridency of the Radical Republicans in command of Congress. The majority of the judges believed that, determined to clinch the results of victory in the war, Congress had too far invaded the province of the states. This check, if deserved, was the proper constitutional function of the Supreme Court, but it raised an almighty howl not only from those who contended their rights were violated, but from political sponsors of the protective measures.

The Reconstruction legislature of Louisiana in 1869, ostensibly in the interest of sanitation and health, but doubtless induced also by bribery, passed a law requiring that livestock slaughtering for New Orleans and an extensive area around must be done in the plant of a single company in a location below the city. While, nominally, all butchers were to have access to this facility, in fact the regulation granted a monopoly. A thousand excluded butchers flourished their cleavers in protest, and were supported in their complaint by much of the local population. Their suits came to the Supreme Court on several contentions. The Louisiana law violated the Fourteenth Amendment by abridging their privileges and immunities as citizens of the United States, denied them the equal protection of the laws, and deprived them of their property without due process. If that was not enough, the statute subjected them to involuntary servitude as forbidden by the Thirteenth Amendment.

In a five-to-four decision the Supreme Court rejected their appeals (*Slaughterhouse Cases*, 16 Wallace 36, 1873). The amendment did not empower the federal government to define and enforce the rights of citizens of a state, but required only that privileges and immunities of citizens of the United States should not be abridged by a state. A line was drawn between national and state citizenship; a narrow construction was given to the former, and most of the relationships of life were thrown into the province of the state to control. Citizens of the United States, for instance, had the right to go to the seat of government, enter all ports, be protected on the high seas and in foreign countries. Fuming New Orleans butchers observed that these privileges would hardly be interfered with by the states anyhow. The state could settle the rights of its own citizens; the amendment commanded simply that whatever these immunities or limitations might be, they must apply equally to citizens of other states within that jurisdiction. If the federal government was to correct infractions of rights of citizens of a state, it would logically be put into the business of prescribing what those rights are. From censor it must turn legislator within the state. The effect would be "to fetter and degrade the State governments by subjecting them to the control of Congress, in the exercise of powers heretofore universally conceded to them." Such an interpretation of the amendment "radically changes the whole theory of the relations of the State and Federal governments to each other and of both these governments to the people." The conviction of the Court that "no such results were intended by the Congress" was reached without consulting legislative debates on the measure. In fact the lawmakers wanted national supervision of state action toward state citizens to be increased.

Police Power of States

The argument that the law giving slaughtering in New Orleans, for all practical purposes, to one firm deprived others (the plaintiffs) of their property without due process, was little stressed. The majority of the Court thought the regulation was within the police power of the state. The due process clause of the Fourteenth Amendment, some years later, was to be called into far greater service, especially in cases involving social legislation and civil liberties. Similarly, the Court guessed badly about the future of the provision that no state should "deny to any person within its jurisdiction the equal protection of the laws." The belief was that this clause was to preserve the rights of Negroes only. That was a natural assumption in the temper of the time, but actually this prohibition was later to apply to many minority groups.

Four judges, including Chief Justice Chase, dissented. The amendment in their view charged the national government with protecting fundamental rights of citizens against state trespass. These rights—to life, liberty, and pursuit of happiness—were not conferred by any government, but by nature, and it was the duty of all government to defend them. If the privileges and immunities covered in the amendment were those of citizens of the United States as such, the amendment had no purpose, for by the Constitution as it stood beforehand the state could not infringe those rights.

The press exclaimed over the opinion pro and con. The decision, if it could be confined to the facts in this case, seems to have excused a monopoly which, as the dissenters said, was a "flagrant and indefensible violation of the rights of many for the benefit of a few." However, later estimate generally approved the broad position that the federal government was not the keeper of the state conscience, that central and local jurisdictions had different duties toward citizens. More recently this complacent view has been abandoned, and the dissenting justices in the *Slaughterhouse* cases have been justified. It is demanded by the Supreme Court that certain national standards—such as equality of all citizens in educational opportunity—must be complied with by the states. The Court, as we shall see, has outgrown its own more restricted interpretation of discretion of the state in dealings with its own citizens.

Properly, protection of state citizens by the federal courts has its counterpart in national legislation, for example, grants in aid to backward communities to enable them to give acceptable services to their people. Unemployment compensation and social security, touching the most intimate welfare of state citizens, have proceeded from the federal authority, and further developments of similar character impend. Who can look back without a smile to the determination of the Supreme Court, promptly applying its principle in the *Slaughterhouse* cases, that Illinois did not violate the Fourteenth Amendment when it refused to a woman the right to practice law in the state courts? The judges justified the state on the basis of their own prejudices. Thus, "The paramount destiny and mission of woman are to fulfill the noble and benign offices of wife and mother . . . And the rules of civil society must be adapted to the general constitution of things . . ." Further, it was within the province of the state legislature to say what callings "shall receive the benefit of those energies and responsibilities, and that decision and firmness which are presumed to dominate in the sterner sex." This pronouncement of "a man-made world" was more dignified than the jeer of a newspaper at "A Chicago she-attorney," but the masculine self-satisfaction was the same.

Freedom Is Administration, Not Legislation

The Fifteenth Amendment (1870) was more specific than the Fourteenth. It prohibited interference by states with voting rights (of Negroes, was the intention), and empowered Congress to legislate to this end. The new amendment was provoked by the illegal means used in the southern states to keep ex-slaves from the polls. The mildest methods were those of election officials and legislatures that disqualified Negro citizens on one pretext or another of registration procedure. At the other extreme were cowardly, cruel raids by hooded, mounted white men (Ku Klux and others) on Negroes who in any way showed they meant to enjoy their new free status. If a Negro offered to vote or had a shotgun in his house he might be visited by night, terrorized, whipped, or murdered. The disgraceful story was told in detail in federal investigations.

But solemn amendments to the Constitution were hardly more than signals to erstwhile Confederates to keep the freedmen in their old condition of servility. Therefore Congress turned to enforcement statutes under which the military was employed. It was hard enough to police obstruction by angry southern communities, without decisions of federal courts that struck down prosecution of individual violators of the laws. Congress was authorized, the courts held, only to prohibit positive action by the states, and the states were blind to systematic crime that "kept the Negro in his place." State authorities were brought under federal control only in elections in which federal officials were chosen.

What was needed in the immensely difficult task of ushering millions of chattel slaves into the rights of men and citizens was enlightened, purposeful, patient administration by many kinds of agencies, national, state, and local. This want was supplied to some extent by the Freedmen's Bureau, commissioned to provide schools, land, and defend the civil rights of ex-slaves. But the Freedmen's Bureau had the disabilities inseparable from an emergency war measure. With much that was serviceable, its operations were frequently uninformed, dishonest, and inapplicable.

This disappointing, not to say tortured, history illustrated the fact that a constitution, or a statute for that matter, does not so much ensure desired social conduct as register what the community is prepared to live by. Law is a consequence more than it is a cause. Without the willingness, indeed the positive wish, of most of the people in an area to behave in a given fashion, putting words on parchment is premature and idle. The Constitution of the United States replaced the Articles of Confederation because the country became convinced that the old system was a failure and must be reformed in ways that had become manifest to the majority.

Reconstruction of the former Confederate states came to an end with President Grant's administration in 1877. Coercion could not continue indefinitely. The people of the North were weary of the effort, many were disgusted with it. The southern states were back in the Union, the troops were withdrawn from their soil. Their legislatures and officials were returned to their national and local responsibilities, which they interpreted much as they chose. The economic, not the political, purposes of the Radical Republicans in Congress in advancing the prospects of corporate capitalism had been achieved. Indeed, so swift had been the industrial and financial expansion that the North had its own troubles in the dismaying depression that followed the panic of 1873.

What the Civil War and Reconstruction liberated was business enterprise. The black man got his freedom, not from the Thirteenth, Fourteenth, and Fifteenth Amendments, but from the national economic progress in which the southern states, following Reconstruction, began to share. Poor white people of the South, who had been as much as the Negroes the victims of slavery, found new opportunities when factories came to the cotton fields. The "persons" protected by due process against state interference with their rights were "legal persons," the corporations. These were the surprise beneficiaries of the political and social revolution. They were guilty of their own excesses and oppressions, which through many years were sought to be corrected by labor and anti-trust legislation.

A century has passed since Reconstruction, and many of its guarantees of legal rights to Negroes have not yet been achieved. Only after World War I did progress quicken pace. The indispensable feature was invasion of the "Solid (Democratic) South" in national elections. Though civil rights legislation still encounters obstinate opposition in Congress, the Supreme Court does better, and gives the Constitution fresh application to our times.

III SOCIAL PATTERN

The Fourteenth Amendment was adopted in the aftermath of the Civil War to prevent the southern states from discriminating against the newly freed Negroes. Nobody at the time supposed that, years later, it would be invoked to protect large business enterprises against regulation in the public interest. Least of all was it imagined that the clause forbidding a state to deprive a citizen of life, liberty, or property "without due process of law" would become the means of exploiting workers. The fact was that between the Civil War and thirty or forty years later the economy of America had undergone a transformation. The war itself had given stimulus to industry, transportation, and finance. Employing the corporate form, business operated on a scale previously unknown. As a counterpart of this development, an undoubted working class appeared. This was a new phenomenon. Earlier the expectation (or fiction) was that any workman could raise himself to be the boss. Now workers themselves recognized—as John Mitchell, leader of the coal miners, declared—that nine-tenths of them would remain wage earners all of their lives. Consequently they organized in the centralized Knights of Labor and in loosely federated national craft unions. The social constitution of the country had altered. Unfortunately the justices of the Supreme Court had lagged behind. In applying the political Constitution they did not take account of changed circumstances.

The leading case of *Lochner v. New York* (198 U.S. 45, 1905) illustrates this failure of the judges to keep abreast. For twenty years the state legislatures, using their police power, had tried to protect workers against oppressive hours, unfair methods of wage payment, and factory conditions injurious to health. The state courts had invalidated many of these laws because they interfered with "liberty of contract," which was held to be a property right. The notion was that parties were free to make any agreement they chose, so long as it was not contrary to public policy, without restraint by law. But where one party was a powerful corporate employer and the other was the single worker, "liberty of contract" did not exist. One party could dictate terms to the other. The theory of individualism, of competition between units, of "every man for himself and the devil take the hindmost," was not tenable here. One party to the contract (the employer) though nominally an individual, possessed in fact collective power, controlling the capital, the means of production on which the worker was dependent for a livelihood. Adam Smith, the Scottish philosopher who proclaimed the sacredness of *laissez faire*, of letting economic forces take their own course, had been in his grave a hundred years, but the judges had not revised the lesson learned from him. They were oldish men, in the habit of venerating legal precedents and abstract principles. It would have been desirable had they put off their robes, descended from the bench, and, like a famous sultan, mingled in the market place.

In Lochner's case the state court convicted him (the employer) under the New York labor law which said that no employe should be "required or permitted to work in a . . . bakery . . . establishment more than sixty hours in one week, or more than ten hours in any one day. . ." Many bakeries, especially in New York City, were in sunless cellars where rules of sanitation were grossly violated. The legislature determined that if bakers labored in these places for excessive hours their own health, and consequently that of the public which consumed their product, was endangered.

Lochner appealed to the Supreme Court on the ground that his liberty under the due process clause of the Fourteenth Amendment had been infringed. The Court in a five to four decision held the New York statute unconstitutional. The state could use its police power to protect "the safety, health, morals, and general welfare of the public." But the law in question interfered with the freedom of the employer (and of the employe) to contract, while it could not be justified as a health measure. Said the Court:

There is no reasonable ground for interfering with the liberty of person or the right of free contract, in determining the hours of labor, in the occupation of a baker. There is no contention that bakers as a class are not equal in intelligence . . . to men in other trades . . . or that they are not able to assert their rights and care for themselves without the protecting arm of the state, interfering with their independence of judgment and action. They are in no sense wards of the state. . . The law must be upheld, if at all, as a law pertaining to the health of the individual engaged in the occupation of a baker. It does not affect any other portion of the public than those who are engaged in that occupation. Clean and wholesome bread does not depend upon whether the baker works but ten hours per day or only sixty hours a week. . . We think that there can be no fair doubt that the trade of a baker . . . is not an unhealthy one to that degree which would authorize the legislature to interfere with the right to labor, and with the right of free contract on the part of the individual, either as employer or as employee.

Warming to their theme, the majority justices continued:

It is unfortunately true that labor . . . in any department, may possibly carry with it the seeds of unhealthiness. But are all, on that account, at the mercy of legislative majorities? . . . In our large cities there are many buildings into which the sun penetrates for but a short time in each day. . . Upon the assumption of the validity of this act under review, it is not possible to say that an act, prohibiting lawyers' or bank clerks . . . from contracting to labor for their employers more than eight hours a day would be invalid . . . We do not believe in the soundness of the views which uphold this law. . . The act is not . . . a health law, but is an illegal interference with the rights of individuals . . . to make contracts regarding labor upon such terms as they may think best.

If ten hours were allowable, without peril to health, why not ten and a half, or eleven? The regulation was "unreasonable and entirely arbitrary."

Three justices (Harlan, White, and Day) in a dissenting opinion pointed to the familiar concern of all civilized peoples with hours of labor. (England had had statutes on the subject for almost a century.) Medical men agreed that certain limits could not be passed with impunity. All judges would admit that eighteen hours a day were excessive. It was a matter to be determined by factual inquiry. If the legislature fixed ten hours as the maximum, the Court must presume this provision was reasonable.

Work Bench versus Judicial Bench

It was plain that the majority was substituting its own belief for that of lawmakers chosen by the people to represent them. The statute had not been enacted without much evidence by physicians and others concerned with the public health to support it. If anyone was being arbitrary, it was the judges who, without particular knowledge, undertook to say that the conditions sought to be corrected were not dangerous to the workmen and to those who ate their bread. The question really turned on facts, not on opinion or precedent. This was realized later, as we shall see, but for the time being the Court was proceeding on an outworn doctrine of freedom of contract not sufficiently related to welfare.

This was the protest made by Mr. Justice Holmes in his famous dissent in the Lochner case. "This case," he objected, "is decided upon an economic theory which a large part of the country does not entertain." The majority of the people had a right to embody their opinions in law, and in consonance with this the Court had upheld "state constitutions and state laws [which] regulate life in many ways," though the judges, were they legislators, might think the compulsions extreme. Sunday laws and usury laws were ancient; those prohibiting lotteries, sales of stock on margin, or requiring vaccination and school attendance were recent. "The Fourteenth Amendment does not enact Mr. Herbert Spencer's Social Statics." (Spencer, who had died only a few years before, was an English philosopher who made a dogma of individualism.) "General propositions," Holmes continued, "do not decide concrete cases." It was fallacious to proceed on an abstract major premise. "Every opinion tends to become a law . . . the word 'liberty' in the Fourteenth Amendment is perverted when it is held to prevent the natural outcome of a dominant opinion" unless a reasonable man would condemn this result as out of harmony with traditions and law. Holmes implied that the New York statute could be viewed "as a first instalment of a general regulation of the hours of work."

In Lochner's case the Supreme Court found social legislation of a state repugnant to the national Constitution. In some subsequent decisions the Court was more liberal, but in the famous opinion in *Adkins v. Children's Hospital* (261 U.S. 525, 1923) the justices applied the due process clause (this time that in the Fifth Amendment) against a law of Congress. Several states, following efforts by social reformers, had passed laws providing for minimum wages for women and children, typically in employments where labor unions had not been organized, and where, consequently, the workers had no protection unless by statute. Courts had validated laws prescribing maximum hours, disregarding the earlier Lochner decision. Regulation of wages seemed to many to be more disputable, but legislatures had been convinced that women paid less than a living wage were endangered in their health and morals. Congress enacted such a law for the District of Columbia. A wage board, after hearings and other inquiry, set the minimum wage. It was in fact the least on which a woman could live in decency, independently of a family group. Nothing was allowed for savings, medical and dental care, and precious little for amusement.

A hospital refused to pay the prescribed minimum wage, and an elevator operator, who lost her job in the hospital in consequence, attacked the law because it took her property (violated her freedom of contract) without due process. On the decision hung the legality of state minimum wage laws already in operation and of others which were contemplated. We may not separate judgments of the Supreme Court from the temper of the times. In the wake of World War I the country was suffering a conservative reaction. Only two years before, depression had left millions with no employment. Employers were pushing an open shop (anti-union) drive. Organized workers rightly felt that their eager co-operation in the war effort was being badly rewarded. A recent attorney general of the United States had vigorously prosecuted not only those suspected of disloyalty, but many individuals and groups known to possess nothing more than liberal views on social and political questions.

Whatever these influences may have been, the Court (five to three, Brandeis not participating because his daughter had been a member of the wage board) held the law unconstitutional. Said the majority: "That the right to contract about one's affairs is a part of the liberty of the individual protected by [the due process clause of the Fifth Amendment] is settled by the decisions of this Court and is no longer open to question. . . In making . . . contracts [of employment], generally speaking, the parties have an equal right to obtain from each other the best terms they can as the result of private bargaining." Only exceptional circumstances could justify legislative abridgment of this individual liberty. No such excuse offered in this case. "It is simply and exclusively a price-fixing law, confined to adult women . . . who are legally as capable of contracting for themselves as men. It forbids two parties having lawful capacity . . . to freely contract with one another in respect of the price for which one shall render service to the other in a purely private employment. . ."

Economic Ruminations

The majority of justices were of opinion that the statute gave the board no guidance in fixing the minimum wage, nor could it furnish any standard. "The amount will depend upon a variety of circumstance: the individual temperament, habits of thrift, care, ability to buy necessaries intelligently, and whether the woman lives alone or with her family. . . The co-operative economies of the family group are not taken into account though . . . it is obvious that the individual expense will be less in the case of a member of the family than in the case of one living alone."

Here the Court was passing judgment on matters of which it was ignorant. Experience of economists, statisticians, social workers, nutritionists, and others had shown that it was practicable, on full investigation, to arrive at a budget of minimum expenses of a woman worker. The items to be included and their cost were not plucked out of the minds of members of the wage board, but resulted from inquiry into actual expenditures in a large number of cases, supplemented by determination of what was indispensable for living as a self-respecting member of the community. What was being set was the minimum, and it would take exceptional contrivance in a woman worker to do on less. The Court itself, in innumerable instances, was fond of taking as a guide what was "reasonable," and considered to "accord with the common understanding." But in this case the justices of the majority failed to apply this criterion. Before that time the fixing of minimum wages, sanctioned by statute, was familiar, reaching back hundreds of years in England. Since then methods have been perfected, and have been applied for the great proportion of workers in many countries, including the United States.

The judges were plainly in error in insisting that expenses of a woman worker living in a family group should enter into the computation. Since many women workers lived independently, the minimum wage must be sufficient, with strict economy, to support them, and this minimum must apply to all. Trying to make a distinction between those living in their families and those living alone would lead to endless complications and surely to injustice. The fact was that the pittance paid to a large number of women workers enabled their employers to be parasitic on fathers, husbands, brothers, or, actually, on the employers of these relatives. Well-defined industries and types of retail stores, paying less than a living wage, were leeches on the community. So far from demanding that a mere supplement to the family income should be respected by the wage board, the judges should have known that many women workers were supporting dependents, were heads of families.

Then the Court went blithely on to declare that "The relation between earnings and morals is not capable of standardization. It cannot be shown that well-paid women safeguard their morals more carefully than those who are poorly paid. Morality rests upon other considerations than wages . . . nor is there ground for distinction between women and men, for . . . if women require a minimum wage to preserve their morals men require it to preserve their honesty." The mere idea of a minimum wage for men, since become American law, was abhorrent to the Court.

The Court's economic lecture plunged deeper. "The feature of this statute, which perhaps more than any other, puts upon it the stamp of invalidity, is that it exacts from the employer an arbitrary payment for a purpose . . . having no causal connection with his business. . . The declared basis . . . is not the value of the service rendered, but the extraneous circumstance that the employee needs to get a prescribed sum of money to insure her subsistence, health and morals." The justices seemed to recognize, in the next instant, that whether the woman could live while she performed her work was hardly an "extraneous circumstance." So they quickly explained that "The ethical right of every worker, man or woman, to a living wage may be conceded." They applauded the abstract principle. More, they agreed in the efforts of labor unions to secure a living wage.

But they objected to requiring a living wage by statute because "it assumes that every employer is bound at all events to furnish it." A contract of employment was moral if "the amount to be paid and the service to be rendered . . . bear to each other some relation of just equivalence. . ." This the minimum wage statute "completely ignored." "Certainly the employer, by paying a fair equivalent for the service rendered, though not sufficient to support the employee, has neither caused nor contributed to her poverty." (It is difficult to see how "a fair equivalent for the service rendered" could fail to include enough for the worker to live on.) The judges went on in other inconsistencies and confusion which it is not necessary to follow. One was the assumption that it was easy to know what services were worth to an employer, but impossible to discover the amount necessary to support the worker.

Chief Justice Taft, in his dissent, thought it improper to reason, as the majority did, from the decision in the Lochner (New York bakers') case. For that had in effect been overruled when recently the Court approved an Oregon law limiting hours of labor of any worker in certain employments. And if hours could be regulated, why not wages? The two were reciprocals, one the multiplier, the other the multiplicand. Justice Holmes dissented on the same ground and because he assigned to the legislature—Congress in this case—the decision as to whether the requirement was for the public good.

The ruling was widely criticized, and minimum wage laws in some of the states continued in force in spite of it. The perceptive cartoonist, Rollin Kirby, in the New York *World* showed Justice Sutherland delivering the opinion of the Court to a woman worker, with the assurance, "This decision affirms your constitutional right to starve."

The Social View of Due Process of Law

The decision in the Adkins case fixed the doctrine of the Supreme Court for fourteen years, then it was reversed in holding valid the minimum wage law of the state of Washington which had been in force since 1913. The Court came tardily to retract its old position. In the meantime it had disallowed statutes of Arizona, Arkansas, and New York. When the Court did overrule the Adkins decision, the justices divided five to four. Enough had happened to reform the opinion of the majority. Business enterprise was no longer strident as in 1923, but had collapsed in the Great Depression of the 1930's. So far from maintaining that government must not intervene to protect workers, employers had themselves grasped at many forms of public assistance to maintain their prices, credit, and production. Two great labor unions, more than others—the Amalgamated Clothing Workers and the International Ladies' Garment Workers—under gifted leadership were eradicating sweatshops, which had been notorious in the needle trades. The Congress of Industrial Organizations was unionizing workers in occupations previously neglected, and stressed the power of masses of workers to improve their lot through use of their political strength. The New Deal of President Franklin Roosevelt had proclaimed the responsibility of government to promote social welfare. The Supreme Court had come directly under the President's attack for decisions which he held defeated progressive policies.

The case from the state of Washington was on all fours with the earlier one from the District of Columbia. Elsie Parrish, a chambermaid in a hotel, brought suit to recover the difference between the wages paid her by the hotel and the minimum wage fixed under the state law, the latter being $14.50 for a 48-hour week. The hotel company relied on the decision in the Adkins case which declared that a minimum wage law denied freedom of contract without sufficient cause. The want of "due process of law" now complained of was that stipulated in the Fourteenth Amendment, which was enjoined upon the states.

Chief Justice Hughes in delivering the opinion of the Court granted much more scope to the legislature in regulating the wage contract than had been allowed before. The former individualist interpretation was abandoned. "The liberty safeguarded," he affirmed, "is liberty in a social organization which requires the protection of law against the evils which menace the health, safety, morals and welfare of the people. Liberty under the Constitution is thus . . . subject to the restraints of due process, and regulation which is reasonable in relation to its subject and is adopted in the interests of the community is due process." Earlier expressions of the Court were cited, sustaining this principle. Certain persons were economically unable to insist on a fair contract of employment, and, in the interest of the public health, must be protected against themselves. The reasoning of the dissenting justices in the Adkins case was praised. There was no distinction in principle between setting maximum hours and minimum wages. Procedures of the wage commission were proper and fair. It was right that "sweating employers" should be compelled to yield "that part of their profits, which were wrung from the necessities of their employees." If employers paid less than a living wage the taxpayers must make up the difference. "The community is not bound to provide what is in effect a subsidy for unconscionable employers. The community may direct its law-making power to correct the abuse which springs from their selfish disregard of the public interest. . . Our conclusion is that the case of *Adkins v. Children's Hospital* . . . should be, and it is, overruled. The judgment of the supreme court of the state of Washington is affirmed."

Oliver Ellsworth, who was to become the second Chief Justice of the United States, in recommending the. Constitution for ratification, stressed the solution it offered for problems of national commerce. "The regulation of trade ever was and ever will be a national matter.

A single state in the American union cannot direct much less control it. This must be a work of the whole, and requires all the wisdom and force of the continent. . ." He referred particularly to foreign trade, but that between the states was at the time (1787) equally in need of supervision by a central government which the Constitution provided. Indeed, as we have seen earlier in this book, pestiferous trade discriminations of the states against each other principally prompted formation of the new national system.

In the first case to come before the Supreme Court under the commerce clause (*Gibbons v. Odgen, 9 Wheaton 1, 1824*), Chief Justice John Marshall gave a generous construction to the authority of Congress. His opinion alone carried great weight, but it was the more significant because he overruled another foremost jurist, Chancellor James Kent of New York. The power "to regulate commerce . . . among the several states," said Marshall, "like all others vested in Congress, is complete in itself, may be exercised to its utmost extent, and acknowledges no limitations other than are prescribed in the Constitution." And in another place, "The word 'among' means intermingled with. A thing which is among others is intermingled with them. Commerce among the states cannot stop at the external boundary line of each state, but may be introduced into the interior."

The police power has been defined as that "to pass laws . . . for the protection of the health, morals, safety, good order, and general welfare of the community." The Constitution does not give this authority, as such, to Congress. Under the Tenth Amendment it is reserved to the states. But, as our national life became more integrated, Congress felt obliged to correct social abuses. It used means to accomplish indirectly what it could not effect directly. The power to tax, to provide a postal service, and, most of all, to regulate commerce furnished the "constitutional pegs" on which to hang welfare laws. In the course of time, after varying experience, what were at first regarded as constitutional excuses have come to be accepted as thoroughly legitimate. The ends justify the means. We came to realize, says a knowing commentator, "that serious evils which menace the health, safety, and welfare of the nation are spread and even generated by our vast national system of transportation and communication, and by our continent-wide network of interstate markets. It was clear that interstate commerce could be used for the public injury as well as for the public welfare. The commerce clause makes Congress the guardian of interstate commerce—and the only guardian. It is therefore not only the right of Congress, but its clear duty, to see to it that the facilities of interstate commerce are not used by any one, in any manner, to do any kind of harm."*

Attempt To Regulate Child Labor through Commerce Clause

Cases discussed above concerned the police power of the states, at first given a narrow interpretation, and afterward much broadened. The next cases illustrate the same increased liberalism in the Supreme Court, but now with reference to the police power—if we may call it that—of Congress, exercised through authority to regulate interstate commerce, and to tax.

Hammer v. Dagenhart (247 U.S. 251, 1918) is historic for several reasons. Its subject was the ancient evil of child labor. Employment—mostly forced employment—of young children for excessive hours in factories and mines arose in Britain with the Industrial Revolution toward the end of the eighteenth century. With the exception of Negro slavery in America, the social record holds no more shocking page. Yet the persistent efforts of devoted men—Robert Owen, Richard Oastler, Lord Shaftesbury—during a full generation were needed to persuade Parliament to forbid the worst features of this practice. The children in British mills and mines were either orphans apprenticed by the poor-law guardians or were "free children"—a bitter term—equally compelled to their toil by the necessities of their parents. Long humanitarian protest and education finally defeated the cruelty of masters and lethargy of the public clinging to the shibboleth of let-alone in industrial affairs.

When the factory system developed in America, some fifty years later than in Britain, the abominations of child labor were repeated. The northern states were commencing to curb this wickedness when the cotton textile industry, shortly after the Civil War, began shifting to the South, where fresh excuses were found for coining children into profits. Spinning frames were built low to be operated by youngsters, sometimes under the age of ten years. The steel of these machines was not harder than the resistance of cotton manufacturers and their allies in the state legislatures to reform. Again champions of the children came forward—Owen Lovejoy, Edgar Gardner Murphy, A. J. McKelway—who soon discovered that they must direct their appeals to the American public generally and to Congress, since southern lawmakers responded feebly or not at all. They were encouraged by manufacturers

* Robert Eugene Cushman, Leading Constitutional Decisions (Appleton-Century-Crofts, Inc.), 10th edition, 1955, p. 333.

in areas where child labor was forbidden, for these were damaged in their business by the competition of southern mill men who employed the "cottontots."

In 1916 Congress acted. No products should be shipped in interstate commerce if the factory, or mine, within thirty days, had employed children under the age of fourteen, or allowed any children between the ages of fourteen and sixteen to work more than eight hours in a day, six days in a week, after 7 o'clock at night or before 6 in the morning. Two brothers, John and Reuben Dagenhart, were working in a cotton factory in Charlotte, North Carolina, in violation of the law. One was under fourteen, the other was between fourteen and sixteen but was working more than eight hours a day. An association of manufacturers persuaded the father of these boys to appeal to the federal courts. The law was attacked as unconstitutional for three reasons: 1. It was not a regulation of interstate commerce; 2. It transgressed the Tenth Amendment which reserves to the states all powers not delegated to Congress; 3. It conflicted with the Fifth Amendment forbidding the taking of life, liberty, or property without due process of law. Of course the manufacturers provided the lawyers and bore the expense of the suit. The boys and their parents were just pawns.

The courts had upheld prohibition by Congress of interstate transportation of lottery tickets, impure or misbranded foods and drugs, diseased cattle, narcotics, and prostitutes. But the federal district court and then the Supreme Court (five to four) drew a distinction between these injurious uses of commerce and the interstate shipment of child-made goods. The majority held that this statute was not a regulation of commerce, a control of the means by which commerce is carried on, but was directly the opposite, a prohibition of it. In other cases, where Congress banned movement in interstate commerce, it was because of the character of the articles and persons affected. The same power did not extend to "ordinary commodities." "The thing intended to be accomplished by this statute is the denial of the facilities of interstate commerce to those manufacturers in the States who employ children within the prohibited ages. The act in effect does not regulate transportation among the States, but aims to standardize the ages at which children may be employed in mining and manufacturing within the States. The goods shipped are themselves harmless. . . When offered for shipment, and before transportation begins, the labor of their production is over, and the mere fact that they were intended for interstate commerce transportation does not make their production subject to federal control under the commerce clause . . . the production of articles, intended for interstate commerce, is a matter of local regulation. . . ."

Nor was the Court more sympathetic to another argument of the government attorneys. It was that Congress could prevent unfair competition by closing interstate commerce to manufacturers in states permitting labor standards inferior to those of other states. The Court replied, "There is no power vested in Congress to require the States to exercise their police power so as to prevent possible unfair competition. Many causes may cooperate to give one State, by reason of local laws or conditions, an economic advantage over others." Manufacturers in states setting maximum hours and minimum wages for women might complain that their costs were higher as a result, but Congress could not be expected to relieve them. The Tenth Amendment reserved to the states authority to regulate conditions of local manufacture. The motives of Congress (to destroy child labor) might be commendable, the Court implied, but its method was wrong. It struck at the shipment of goods which were in themselves harmful to nobody, and it invaded the power of the states to regulate internal production. The Court was alarmed at the prospect opened by upholding this act. ". . . if Congress can thus regulate matters entrusted to local authority by prohibition of the movement of commodities in interstate commerce, all freedom of commerce will be at an end." The power of the states over local matters might be eliminated, "and thus our system of government be practically destroyed."

Justice Holmes in his earnest dissent, in which three others concurred, deplored the plea of states' rights as a shield for abuses which the conscience of the nation condemned.

It does not matter, whether the supposed evil precedes or follows the transportation. It is enough that, in the opinion of Congress, the transportation encourages the evil . . . if there is any matter upon which civilized countries have agreed,—far more unanimously than they have with regard to intoxicants . . . over which this country is now emotionally aroused,—it is the evil of premature and excessive child labor. I should have thought that if we were to introduce our own moral conceptions where, in my opinion, they do not belong, this was preeminently a case for upholding the exercise of all its powers by the United States. . . It is not for this Court to pronounce when prohibition is necessary to regulation . . . to say that it is permissible as against strong drink, but not as against the product of ruined lives. . . . The act does not meddle with anything belonging to the state. They may regulate their internal affairs and their domestic commerce as they like.

But when they seek to send their products across the state line they are no longer within their rights.

Restriction Through Taxing Power Invalid

Nothing daunted, Congress the next year (1919) tried to curb child labor by using its taxing power. This had been allowed by the Supreme Court in a variety of instances where it was obvious that Congress was regulating or penalizing instead of taxing. Cases were an import duty so high that it yielded no revenue, because it kept out the article taxed; a 10 per cent tax on state bank notes, intended to compel these banks to join the national banking system; a tax of 10 cents a pound on margarine colored to resemble butter; a prohibitive tax on opium. So Congress placed a 10 per cent tax on the net profits of factories, mines, and quarries employing children under the prohibited conditions, the same as those in the previous act which had been held unconstitutional. The law came before the Supreme Court in 1922 in *Bailey v. Drexel Furniture Co.* (259 U.S. 20).

Chief Justice Taft, delivering the majority opinion, said the case was like that of Dagenhart. Congress was again seeking, this time under the pretense of a tax, to trespass in the area of labor legislation which belonged to the states. In earlier decisions, to be sure, the Court had approved of taxes because Congress called them taxes, though plainly they were prohibitions. But in the other cases Congress had at least taxed a thing—a bank note, oleomargarine, opium. Here Congress was taxing the profits of an employer who pursued a forbidden course of action. This made the ostensible tax really a regulating, a punitive measure, not a revenue act. The regulation of child labor, now attempted by Congress, lay in the province of the states, and the Chief Justice could not permit such a "serious breach . . . in the ark of our covenant." If Congress was allowed "to enact a detailed measure of . . . regulation . . . and enforce it by a so-called tax upon departures from it," this would "completely wipe out the sovereignty of the states."

Here was a poser. Congress could not get rid of child labor because of decisions of the Court. The states that wanted to prohibit the evil were hampered by complaints of their employers that they could not meet competition from states that sanctioned child labor. The only solution seemed to be to recommend to the states an amendment to the Constitution which gave to Congress power "to limit, regulate, and prohibit the labor of persons under eighteen years of age." This was done in 1924. Of course if this explicit authority were granted and

Congress used it, the Supreme Court and the recalcitrant states could no longer stand in the way of effective reform. Opposition to the proposed amendment was clamorous and disingenuous. Every time-worn supplication was brought forward. The states knew best how to manage their internal affairs. Parents should be allowed to decide what to do with their children; what horrors would result if the authority of the family was supplanted by government! In states with no compulsory school attendance laws children excluded from factory discipline would "run wild in the gutters." Self-righteous elders descanted on the benefits of their own childhood work experience, which had helped them to become the physically robust, morally upright, and successful citizens now to be beheld.

Ratification of the amendment dragged. More states passed resolutions against it than ratified. Came a change with the Great Depression of the 1930's and New Deal measures to overcome mass unemployment or at least mitigate its hardships. When millions in the prime of life were desperate for want of jobs it was obviously senseless to depend on the labor of children. At the other end of the age scale efforts were made through the social security system to persuade older workers to retire on pensions and annuities. The codes under the National Industrial Recovery Act forbade employment of young persons below the age of sixteen. Ratifications stepped up, but eight more states were needed, by 1937, to bring the amendment into force. But the New Deal marched on. President Roosevelt in the spring of this year called on Congress "to take further action to extend the frontiers of social progress." The country under the Constitution was competent to remove the reproach of "one-third of our population . . . ill-nourished, ill-clad, and ill-housed." The national government must be able to establish maximum hours, minimum wages, and eliminate the menace of child labor. The chief executive praised Justice Holmes's dissent in the Dagenhart case, saying that though Holmes "spoke for a minority of the Supreme Court, he spoke for a majority of the American people." In supporting a bill for putting a ceiling on hours, and floor under wages, and banishing child labor, the attorney general called the child labor decision of twenty years before a "perversion of our Constitution" and had similar words for the Supreme Court's refusal, in 1923, to approve minimum wages for women.

The Fair Labor Standards Act of 1938 cut through old constitutional inhibitions. A fresh "recession" in the economy lent urgency to the reform. Workers in interstate commerce were to reach, gradually, a maximum of forty hours a week, a minimum of forty cents an hour, and none was to be employed under sixteen years of age or, unless approved by the Children's Bureau of the Department of Labor, under eighteen.

This sweeping statute came to the Supreme Court in 1941 (*United States v. Darby*, 321 U.S. 100, 1941) after a district court held it unconstitutional. The indictment charged that a lumber manufacturer in Georgia who shipped a substantial part of his product in interstate commerce paid less than the minimum wage, employed workmen more than the maximum hours without overtime pay, and neglected to keep the records prescribed in the law. The Court must decide two principal questions. First, did Congress have constitutional power to prohibit shipment in interstate commerce of lumber manufactured under forbidden conditions? Second, had it power to prohibit employment of workers in production for interstate commerce for lower wages and longer hours than those prescribed? This second question involved production within the state of Georgia. A subsidiary point was whether the employer must keep the stipulated records for all his workers. The Supreme Court was new and younger in personnel than when negative decisions, as in *Hammer v. Dagenhart* and *Adkins v. Children's Hospital*, were given two decades before. The justices shared the conviction of the public, received in the Great Depression, that only the national government could cope with economic problems national in scope. Country and court had learned an economic lesson, now to be applied in a judicial recital.

The Supreme Court unanimously affirmed all of the powers of Congress asserted in the Fair Labor Standards Act. Products and persons excluded from the facilities of interstate commerce need not be deleterious or cause immorality. The Dagenhart decision, which permitted child-made goods to move interstate because not in themselves harmful, was flatly reversed. Further, Congress, in its power to protect interstate commerce, could prescribe minimum conditions of production within a state where a substantial portion of the output was intended to be sold in other states. Where interstate commerce is affected, Congress had a police power like that of the states. "The obvious purpose of the act was not only to prevent the interstate transportation of the proscribed product, but to stop the initial step toward transportation, production with the purpose of so transporting it." The law was not to be disallowed on the ground (as previously held) that its real motive, under guise of exercise of the commerce power, was to compel observance of approved labor conditions. "The motive and purpose of a regulation of interstate commerce are matters for the legislative judgment upon the exercise of which the Constitution places no restriction and over which the courts are given no control." The Court quoted with approval its pronouncement many years before in the state bank note case, "The judicial cannot prescribe to the legislative department of the government limitations upon the exercise of its acknowledged power."

The Court continued: "Congress, having by the present act adopted the policy of excluding from interstate commerce all goods produced for the commerce which do not conform to the specified labor standards, it may choose the means reasonably adapted to the attainment of the permitted end, even though they involve the control of intrastate activities." States' rights did not include the right, by exploiting labor, to undercut better standards prevailing elsewhere. ". . . the evils aimed at by the act are the spread of substandard labor conditions, and the consequent dislocation of the commerce itself caused by . . . competition . . . through interstate commerce." The Tenth Amendment did not stand in the way, for the authority of Congress over interstate commerce was specifically delegated by the Constitution. Lastly, the requirement that the employer keep records of wages and hours was a reasonable means of enforcing the law.

Of course the ban on child labor was approved also. The proposed amendment to give this power to Congress was no longer needed. The Dagenhart brothers, by now men approaching the age of forty, gave a statement to the newspapers. They were sorry and ashamed that they had been the means of fastening child labor on themselves and so many others for so many years. All had been denied, in differing degrees, education, health, and opportunity. The Dagenhart boys were not responsible. They were too young when their case came up to see the consequences and object to being used for a melancholy purpose. Those who deserved blame were the organized cotton manufacturers who fought the law. They offended against these little ones, and deserve the millstone that hangs about their necks. And what of the five judges who ignored "the weightier matters of the law?" If only for their blindness we follow them with our reproaches.

Definition of a Direct Tax

To the question whether a federal income tax was constitutional, the Supreme Court first said yes (1881), fifteen years later reversed itself to answer no (1896), and this led to the Sixteenth Amendment (1913) which empowered Congress "to lay and collect taxes on incomes, from whatever source derived, without apportionment among the . . . States . . ." The confusion was rooted in both history and theory. In the Philadelphia Constitutional Convention the southern states feared they would be the victims of discriminatory taxation. Their property was principally in land and slaves. Their population was relatively sparse. Therefore they insisted that any national direct taxes, understood to rest on heads and acres, must "be laid . . . in Proportion to the Census . . ." This would prevent the northern states, with larger representation in Congress, but with less land and few or no slaves, from burdening the southern members of the Union. Massachusetts, for example, would not favor land and capitation taxes, because, with her large population, her citizens would suffer high rates. By the same token South Carolina and Georgia, thinly settled, would come off lightly.

"Duties, Imposts and Excises," on the other hand, need not be apportioned among the states according to population; it was enough if they were "uniform." These levies—chiefly on imports and domestic spirits—were indirect. Southerners, like others, could escape them by refusing to consume the articles taxed.

The distinction between direct and indirect taxes, which the Constitution commanded should be treated so differently, was not sharply drawn before or after the document went into effect. However, it was illustrated in the carriage tax, which Alexander Hamilton had long approved and which was enacted by Congress on his recommendation in 1794. The rate ran from $10 for a coach down to $1 for an open gig, kept for pleasure or hire, but farm vehicles and those for hauling com modities were exempt. Madison opposed the tax because in his view, though direct, it was not apportioned among the states according to population. Daniel Hylton of Virginia, politically inspired, brought a test case which reached the Supreme Court. Hamilton, who had left the Treasury a year earlier, was prevailed upon by the attorney general to defend the tax against distinguished counsel for Hylton.

In his long speech, with characteristic candor, Hamilton found no reliable partition between direct and indirect taxes. He regretted "that terms so . . . vague in so important a point are to be found in the Constitution." We need not repeat the conflicts of meaning which he explored. It was enough that "no construction ought to prevail . . . to defeat the . . . necessary authority of the government," and a duty on carriages was as much within the competence of Congress as a duty on lands or buildings. If the carriage tax was called direct, to be apportioned among the states according to population, the result must be absurd. For the owner in a state with few carriages but many people would pay dearly compared to the owner in another state where opposite conditions prevailed.

The justices agreed with Hamilton that the Constitution gave Congress power "over every species of taxable property, except exports." Hence the tax must be held to be a circuitous means "of reaching the revenue of individuals, who generally live according to their income." The carriage tax, so long as uniform, was legal. Incidentally, this was the first case (*Hylton v. the United States*, 3 Dallas 171, 1796) in which the Supreme Court passed upon the constitutionality of an act of Congress. Of more significance is the prescience of the first secretary of the treasury in claiming for Congress generous authority to derive federal revenue. Since his day the tax base, notably of the national government, has been transformed from that of tangible to intangible property, from things to income as the measure of fiscal capacity. The advice of a specialist in the field of his experience may not be lightly disregarded.

The income tax was first used in this country during the Civil War when extra revenue was imperative. The law of 1862 went into effect the next year. With the exemption of $600 (deemed necessary for living expenses) every person residing in the United States must pay 3 per cent on "the annual gains, profits or incomes . . . whether derived from any kind of property, rents, interest, dividends, salaries or from any profession, trade, employment or vocation . . . or from any source whatever," and to the extent that income exceeded $10,000 the rate was 5 per cent. Thus the personal income tax was progressive, though that on corporations was at the lower rate only. The law was several times amended; after the war the progressive feature was dropped, and the tax expired by limitation in 1872.

At its best the tax yielded one-quarter of the entire internal revenue. It was officially called an "income duty," as distinguished from a direct tax on land, which under the Constitution must be apportioned. Most in Congress acquiesced in this interpretation. No tax is popular, but this, out of patriotism, was paid with unexpected willingness. Until the war emergency was passed, the progressive character of the tax, contribution of citizens according to capacity, was not effectively questioned. Later men of means successfully complained that the tax bore on them unequally as a class. Then objections to the theory of the levy, its faulty and costly administration, and absence of further fiscal need led to its discontinuance.

No frank test of constitutionality of the income tax occurred until almost a decade after it expired, when in *Springer v. the United States* (102 U. S. 586, 1881) the Supreme Court upheld the law as not direct and therefore not requiring to be apportioned among the states. The earlier case of *Hylton v. the United States* (tax on carriages, declared to be indirect) was cited with approval.

National Income Tax Revived

The Civil War gave the decisive impetus to capitalism in the United States. In this development the Northeast, its economy already varied, got the head start in industry, commerce, and finance. The West long remained agricultural, where not semi-empty. The South, already backward from devotion to staple crops, made a slow recovery from war destruction. Naturally the have-not sections and classes (farmers and workers) repeatedly urged in Congress revival of the income tax. The deep depression following 1873 and the relapse in 1884 prepared the way for widespread protests against business combinations, exactions of railroads, and the concentrated money power. "Wall Street," which in the mouths of complaining Grangers, Knights of Labor, and Greenbackers symbolized exploitation, was the object of hatred. The tariff was blamed as the mother of monopoly and oppressive prices of consumer goods. The Sherman Anti-Trust Act sought to curb this evil, but in the same year, 1890, the McKinley Act carried protection to new heights. Many discontents blended in the Populist Party, while the Democrats were split between gold standard and free-silver factions.

This was the strained counterpoise of forces—economic, social, and political—when the panic of 1893 precipitated sharper conflict. Previous depression had produced grief, but this one hatched proposals for correction. One movement was angry but pathetically confused—the "army" of the unemployed led to Washington by "General" Coxey. Another was better based and eloquently pressed by William Jennings Bryan in his "sixteen-to-one" campaign. A third was more limited—the demand by President Cleveland, elected by traditionally free-trade Democrats, that the tariff be drastically reduced.

If import duties were to be cut in the Wilson tariff bill of 1893-94 it seemed to many fitting that the national revenue be compensated by tacking on an income tax. The amendment introduced by Benton McMillin of Tennessee had the additional motive of a thrust against the money-bags. Actually, the tariff was not seriously lowered, but the emotional backing of the income tax did not suffer. This project of laying the rich under contribution, though an afterthought, stole the legislative show. Said the House ways and means committee, "the burdens of government ought to be borne in proportion to the ability of each citizen who is protected by it. Yet . . . there are citizens of great wealth who, by our method of taxing what we must consume rather than what we have accumulated, pay little more to the support of government than is paid by the day laborer, who has nothing." An opposing congressman rejoined that the income tax "arbitrarily selects for confiscation the property of a limited class in this country . . . designates as its victims but eighty-five thousand out of sixty-five million." Senator Sherman was more excited. Two decades before he had approved an income tax, but now the Treasury did not need funds from this source. "In a republic like ours, where all men are equal, this attempt to array the rich against the poor or the poor against the rich is socialism, communism, devilism."

Another argument against the income tax was more ingenious but equally unavailing. The Democrats now urging this measure were forgetting their attachment to state rights. Income taxes properly belonged to the state governments, but, said Senator Hill of New York, "No such federal aggrandizement was ever projected" as this "insidious and deadly assault upon state rights, state powers, and state independence." Senator Hoar of Massachusetts similarly condemned this "drastic . . . assertion of national power against the state power, state interest, and state functions. . ."

The Wilson tariff, including the income tax, became law in 1894 without receiving President Cleveland's signature. The income tax resembled that of the Civil War except that the exemption was larger ($4000), the rate was lower (2 per cent), the interpretation of business expense to be deducted by corporations and other profit enterprises cut their contribution, and the tax was not progressive. The broad purpose of the law, to balance general property taxes and import duties, resting mainly on those of small means, with contributions from those with higher incomes, was timely. But vehement advocacy and swift adoption had left the measure mistaken in several principles, defective in administration, and downright contradictory in certain provisions.

These shortcomings might have been remedied subsequently had not opponents, defeated in Congress, promptly organized to kill the income tax in the courts. In March 1895, only two months after the law went into effect and before any payments were due, the test case of *Pollock v. Farmers' Loan and Trust Company* (157 U.S. 429, 1895) was argued before the Supreme bench. Ablest counsel prepared tomes, which all but staggered the judges, to invalidate the measure. The lawyers' industry in assembling arguments constitutional, economic, and historical was inspired, declared the attorney general, by "the immense pecuniary stake which is now played for, . . . so large that counsel fees and costs and printers' bills are mere bagatelles."

Since by statute "no suit for the purpose of restraining the assessment or collection of any tax shall be maintained in any court," Pollock sought to prevent the Farmers' Loan and Trust Company from voluntarily complying with the income tax law. He was a citizen of Massachusetts, the bank was in New York, Pollock's interest as a stockholder was material, the income tax was alleged to be unconstitutional, and for these reasons the suit in equity should be entertained by federal courts. The circuit court sustained the directors in their refusal to comply with the stockholder's demand, and dismissed Pollock's complaint. But, as a constitutional question was involved, the Supreme Court allowed appeal to it.

Income Tax Unconstitutional, 1895

Chief Justice Fuller in April 1895 delivered the opinion of a divided Court that the taxes on income from land and municipal bonds were unconstitutional. The justices were equal in number for and against other features of the act, so no opinion was expressed on these. The chief question not treated was whether taxes on income from personal property (investments in other than real estate) were unconstitutional. "We are unable to perceive any ground for the alleged distinction," said Fuller, between a tax on land and a tax on the income from land. "The name of the tax is unimportant. . . An annual tax upon the annual value of . . . real estate appears to us the same in substance as an annual tax on the real estate, which would be paid out of the rent or income." As the tax was not apportioned according to population or representation, it was invalid. Further, the federal government was powerless to tax the property or revenues of the states. A municipality was an instrumentality of a state. If the income from bonds of the municipality were taxed, this reduced the capacity of the municipality to borrow. Consequently the law was repugnant to the Constitution.

Justice Field wrote an opinion agreeing with the views expressed by Fuller, but went farther to declare "the whole law of 1894 . . . void." And he added with some heat, "If the provisions of the constitution can be set aside by an act of congress, where is the course of usurpation to end? The present assault upon capital is but the beginning . . . till our political contests will become a war of the poor against the rich."

Justice White entered a vigorous dissent because "the result of the opinion just announced is to overthrow a long and consistent line of decisions, and to deny to the legislative department of the government . . . a power conceded to it by universal consensus for 100 years, and which has been recognized by repeated adjudications of this court." He particularlized: ". . . the constitution has left congress untrammeled by any rule of apportionment as to indirect taxes,—imposts, duties, and excises. The opinions in the Hylton Case, so often approved and reiterated, the unanimous views of the text writers, all show that a tax on land, to be direct, must be an assessment of the land itself, either by quantity or valuation. Here there is no such assessment." However, he agreed that municipal bonds were exempt from federal taxation. Finally, White thrust at the majority decision because it overthrew previous ones on the taxing powers of Congress and so was "fraught with danger to the court, to each and every citizen, and to the republic." The Supreme Court should "preserve the benefits of consistent interpretation. . . Break down this belief in judicial continuity, and let it be felt that on great constitutional questions this court is to depart from the settled conclusions of its predecessors . . . and our constitution will . . . become a most dangerous instrument to the rights and liberties of the people." Also Justice Harlan disssented, on White's grounds, but found the court below correct in dismissing the suit out of hand. "Congress intended to forbid the issuing of any process that would interfere in any wise with the prompt collection of the taxes imposed," and the present attempt was a mere evasion of the statute.

Impressed by the significance of the case, the Court had it reargued and a month after the first pronouncement condemned the tax on income "from bonds, stocks, or other forms of personal property" as equally void with a tax on income from land. Both were levies on the property itself, and, being direct, must be apportioned among the states. Again Chief Justice Fuller delivered the opinion, now of five judges against four. He went back to the Hylton (carriage tax) case, which in accordance with Hamilton's reasoning had given to direct taxes limited meaning and correspondingly wider scope for duties on consumption. Appealing to Hamilton's writings, Fuller tried to make him contradict his advocacy of the carriage tax as indirect.

Fuller was on surer ground when he took comfort from the stand of Madison, in Congress and in his complaint to Jefferson, that the carriage tax was unconstitutional. Fuller's reliance on Madison was not shaken by the fact that Madison, as President, approved just such an act as he previously held to be invalid. The Chief Justice dismissed "the speculative views of political economists or revenue reformers" in favor of "the constitution, taken in its plain and obvious sense." The separation, in the Constitution, of direct and indirect taxes could not "be refined away by forced distinctions between that which gives value to property and the property itself."

Reasons for Approving Income Tax

Similarly, Fuller had no tolerance for the argument that a tax on income from real and personal property must be adjudged indirect because practically such a tax could not be apportioned. He believed it could be apportioned, simply allowing each state, by its own methods, to collect its quota of the national levy. If that would not work, then the Constitution could be amended. In any event, he rejected the view of White that adherence to former judgments, in the interest of consistency and stability, must be preferred to announcement of the deliberate conclusion on the case in hand, whatever that might be. At the end the majority opinion said all the income tax sections of the act were interconnected, and therefore parts otherwise innocent were invalid with the rest.

Justices Harlan, Brown, Jackson, and White all wrote dissenting opinions. Harlan's was long, painstaking, and delivered with such passion that at times he waggled his finger under the nose of the Chief Justice. (Social conflicts of the time are illustrated in the fact that Eugene V. Debs, leader of the Pullman strike, was denied the writ of habeas corpus in the decision rendered just before the Supreme Court knocked out the income tax.) Harlan underscored opinions in the Hylton case at the outset of the national government when all, court and counsel, had been concerned in constructing the Constitution. A telling argument, applicable to the later income tax, was used by Hamilton and repeated by Justice Chase, who said, "The constitution evidently contemplated no taxes as direct taxes, but only such as congress could lay in proportion to the census. The rule of apportionment is only to be adopted in such cases as where it can reasonably apply; and the subject must ever determine the application of the rule." And Justice Iredell put it crisply: "As all direct taxes must be apportioned, it is evident that the constitution contemplated none as direct but such as could be apportioned. If this [tax on carriages] cannot be apportioned, it is, therefore, not a direct tax, in the sense of the constitution."

Harlan cited the century of history in which Congress and courts had maintained "that duties on personal property were not direct taxes." The opinion of the majority did not respect the maxim of *stare decisis*, "the principle that decisions resting upon a particular interpretation of [the Constitution] should not be lightly disregarded." Harlan went on to declare, "it is certain that a departure by this court from a settled course of decisions on grave constitutional questions, under which vast transactions have occurred, and under which the government has been administered during great crises, will shake public confidence in the stability of the law." Precedent was all on his side, for "a tax on income derived from real property . . . until now has never been . . . regarded by any court as a direct tax on such property, within the meaning of the constitution." A tax on income from real estate could not be apportioned without gross injustice, for many lands yielded no income.

Harlan stigmatized the reversal of settled law, declaring "in view of former adjudications, beginning with the Hylton Case, and ending with the Springer Case, a decision now that a tax on income from real property can be laid and collected only by apportioning the same among the states on the basis of numbers may . . . be regarded as a judicial revolution that may sow the seeds of hate and distrust among the people of different sections of our common country." And he went on to charge that the decision of the majority "strikes at the very foundations of national authority . . . denies to the general government a power which . . . may become vital to the very existence . . . of the Union in a national emergency. . . It tends to re-establish that condition of helplessness in which congress found itself during the period of the . . . Confederation, when it was without authority, by laws operating directly upon individuals, to lay and collect . . . taxes. . ."

Without an amendment of the Constitution, the government could not command any part of income from real estate and other investments. He contrasted income from property—exempt—with income from labor of hand and brain, which was to be unfairly burdened. This might "provoke a contest . . . from which the American people would have been spared if the court had not overturned its former adjudications. . ." The only parts of the Wilson act that the majority left operative were tariffs which rested on "the great body of the . . . people who derive no rents from real estate, and who are not so fortunate as to own invested personal property, such as . . . bonds or stocks of corporations. . ." Justice Harlan was keenly conscious that the character and distribution of wealth and income in the country had radically altered. In this situation what was needed, fortunately, was not a new constitutional doctrine, but obedience to the old one. Yet the majority chose to overturn the familiar interpretation rather than recognize a new condition.

Consistency More Important Than Correctness?

Justice Brown in his dissent was emphatic for keeping the old rule, if for no other reason than that it was old. "There are a vast number of questions," he declared, "which it is more important should be settled in some way than that they should be settled right, and, once settled by the solemn adjudication of the court of last resort, the legislature and the people have a right to rely upon such settlement as forever fixing their rights. . . Even 'a century of error' may be less pregnant with evil to the state than a long-deferred discovery of the truth." Congress must not be obliged to recruit revenue in a crisis (a business depression) "in fear that important laws like this shall encounter the veto of this court through a change in its opinion. . ." And further, "Respect for the constitution will not be inspired by a narrow and technical construction which shall limit or impair the necessary powers of congress."

Justice Jackson put his objections briefly but boldly. The framers of the Constitution did not contemplate an income tax. It was a decade before England imposed her first income tax. This law was upheld though it taxed income from public securities which, by the loan acts, were to be "free of any tax or charge whatever." An income tax does not consider the source of income, but only the receipt of it. The majority decision flew in the face of the principle of taxation according to capacity, "relieving the citizens who have the greater ability, while the burdens of taxation are made to fall most . . . oppressively upon those having the least ability." He called the decision "the most disastrous blow ever struck at the constitutional power of Congress."

Equally severe was Justice White, who had dissented in the earlier hearing of the case. By holding incomes from effort—salaries, earnings of professional people, and wages—subject to the law, while exempting revenue from invested wealth, the decision "stultifies the constitution by making it an instrument of the most grievous wrong. . ." And to do this the majority overthrew "the decisions of this court, the opinions of the law writers and publicists, tradition, practice, and the settled policy of the government. . ."

Though several justices of the Supreme Court, in the Pollock decision of 1896, had observed that only a constitutional amendment would empower Congress to enact an income tax, this expedient was not used until seventeen years later. If the decision suddenly reversed long practice and ran counter to the fiscal tendency in democratic countries, why this delay? Several answers suggest themselves. The amendments in the wake of the Civil War, protecting rights of freedmen, were adopted promptly. But these were pressed by men who were managing the nation's life and they seemed necessary to ensure the results of a costly contest. These amendments were political in inspiration. The desire for an income tax amendment, by contrast, was antagonized by the powerful group of the wealthy, and it could not plead the benefit of a war emergency. The demand must come from the masses of common people; to the extent that they depended on the Democratic party this leadership was weakened by secession and by internal strife. Progress toward an income tax must be social and slow, not political and swift. Principal Republicans, President Theodore Roosevelt in 1906 and Taft two years later in his acceptance speech, hoped that a law could be devised that would win approval of the Supreme Court.

However, opposition to high duties in the pending Payne-Aldrich tariff and sentiment for a general income tax were companion cries. The Democratic platform of 1908 called for an amendment to authorize an income tax. Taft, when a few months in the Presidency, changed his tune and recommended submission of an amendment. Wording, with full latitude, had already been introduced in the Senate. In slightly different form this became the Sixteenth Amendment to the Constitution in February 1913. The same year, as part of the "New Freedom" program of President Woodrow Wilson, an income tax was enacted with low rates, graduated for personal incomes, and a flat percentage for corporate incomes. Three years later the law was unanimously upheld by the Supreme Court (*Brushaber v. Union Pacific Railroad Co.*, 240 U.S. 1, 1916). With increased rates the income tax was a significant source of revenue during World War I. Income taxes have been adopted by two-thirds of the states and by several hundred municipalities.

Impact of Great Depression

The economic depression of the 1930's was the longest and deepest in this country's history. As before when business broke down, the causes were many and varied. This collapse caught government and people unawares, for most had believed that the "New Economic Era" or "plateau of prosperity" of the 1920's would continue indefinitely. Premonitory signs of hesitation and weakness had been disregarded. President Calvin Coolidge's administration symbolized the seven good years of Joseph's Egypt. Coolidge ("Silent Cal" he was called) was a Vermonter who in his banking, legal, and political career in Massachusetts was known for business prudence and no foolishness in government. In the White House he was content to leave finance and industry to successful self-direction. Fortune was never kinder to any chief executive, for he left office in the spring of 1929, shortly before our national complacency was to be profoundly shocked.

He was succeeded by President Herbert Hoover, who as secretary of commerce was noted for his efforts to further business efficiency. Hoover had a world reputation as an engineer and, joining compassion to competence, he had been the chief American administrator of overseas relief following World War I. How could our future be in safer hands? Shortly before he entered office a distinguished assemblage of analysts published under Hoover's sponsorship a comprehensive survey of our business posture (*Recent Economic Changes*). Their forecast, with minor misgivings, was confident of continued prosperity.

The swan song of happy days was a soaring stock market. The country was shaken out of this delirium by the crash of security values in October 1929. For some months it was believed that this was no more than a sudden correction of extravagant speculation. It was called a chastisement, severe but salutary, from which we would quickly recover. We need not fear spread of the contagion. President Hoover assured that "underlying business is sound." Chief personages in government, finance, and industry predicted that "prosperity is just around the corner." They reiterated this hopeful slogan while the providential upturn receded. Meanwhile convincing signs of a general involvement multiplied—price decline, an epidemic of bank failures, mounting mass unemployment, stagnation in the construction industry, mortgage foreclosures, downturn in industrial production, especially of automobiles. As breadlines lengthened, the sad admission grew that the American economy was in profound trouble not to be wished away by cheery words from Washington. We reflected that the on-rushing 'twenties had concealed ominous lags in agriculture, coal mining, textiles; banks were steadily closing even then, and toward the end, more than a year before the stock market plunge, heavy construction was falling off. The American outlook was rendered gloomier when, following panic in private and public finance, industrial depression fastened on western Europe. Britain was forced off the gold standard, and the end of an historic era of reliance on that automatic regulator of credit and trade was at hand.

President Hoover at length confessed that this country was economically sick. He believed that the cure lay in patient suffering while nature took its course. We had run a fever in the heedless 'twenties, and now corrective chills were to be endured. This was the traditional policy of let-alone. Excessive action must be punished by reaction, inflation by liquidation. When we had sunk low enough recovery would emerge from natural causes. He was strengthened in his reluctance, or refusal, to muster the force of the central government for revival when he could point to "world-wide depression." America, unjustly, was gripped in a cosmic convulsion. But Hoover's stern therapy appealed less and less to farmers, business men, and to the millions of unemployed. Exhortation for local remedy brought faint response. Big industrialists, called to the White House, could not keep their promises of fresh investment. Community charity chests, temporarily supplied by the cry "help your neighbor," were as quickly emptied by extraordinary demands on their inadequate resources.

At length the President was compelled to apply government aids. A Federal Farm Board sought to remove surpluses of staple crops. A Reconstruction Finance Corporation loaned public money to banks, insurance companies, railroads, and other distressed enterprises. Lastly, some hundreds of millions of direct relief funds were made available. But these helps were too little and too late. The country was resolved on a change of leadership. In the presidential election of 1932 Hoover and his Republican party were defeated by the Democrats with Franklin D. Roosevelt as their champion.

Later inspection was to show that in many respects the depression had reached bottom in the summer of 1932, but signs of improvement were slight and slow in the painful interval after the old national administration was discredited and before the new dispensation was ushered in. The country waited, sullenly. Sullenly except for dismay at the stepped-up tempo of bank closings. The governors of one state after another had to decree "bank holidays" to prevent universal credit collapse. President Hoover blamed this acceleration of misfortune on the dangerous forecasts of Roosevelt, who was soon to succeed him. Roosevelt, he charged, had thrown a fright into the economy by threatening to take the country off the gold standard. Except for this, the beginnings of recovery would have been evident.

However this might be, most banks had been closed by the day Roosevelt was inaugurated, March 4, 1933. The economic heart of the country, for the moment, had stopped beating. The new President's address struck a new note, instilling courage. The warmth and courage of his words—"We have nothing to fear but fear itself"—gave the listening millions a mighty lift, the first surge of confidence they had felt in many a day. He promised to use all the resources of the national government to fight the depression just as he would have summoned them to defeat a foreign invader. His speech proved that economics is composed of more than debits and credits. Moral force may stir material forces.

Coercive Codes under National Industrial Recovery Act

Forthwith the President and his advisers of the "brain trust" set about the task of recovery by resolute use of executive and legislative authority. For the next hundred days laws and orders poured from Washington. They were not empty words. By an emergency provision the banks that were fit to operate were reopened. The safety of new deposits was guaranteed. The Agricultural Adjustment Act decreed destruction of impending additions to surpluses, and promised benefit payments to farmers who reduced their future plantings. Crop prices were to be raised to the point where farmers could again purchase industrial products as in normal times.

This active help to industry and commerce was surpassed by a comprehensive scheme dealing with this sector of the economy directly. The National Industrial Recovery Act, commonly referred to as National Recovery Administration (NRA), was the most comprehensive of these measures. It gave new liberty to business men to take joint action, among themselves and with government, to control production and prices. It provided stimulus for re-employment and for spreading employment. It furnished a charter of rights to labor unions, with which employers were required to bargain in good faith. It initiated plans for public works large and small. We are not concerned here with other features of the "New Deal" which followed fast—enormous expansion of credit agencies, relief, and soon the Tennessee Valley Authority and Social Security legislation.

Since the Schechter decision of the Supreme Court which we are to describe, arose from the NRA, we must explain the "codes of fair competition" which were a characteristic innovation in that act. Business men for decades had been struggling to combine to eliminate or to restrain competition. Their principal motive was private profit, but much that was beneficial to investors, consumers, workers, and the economy generally could result from their efforts, as well as some consequences that were anti-social and alarming. But the federal government, for more than forty years—ever since the Sherman Anti-trust Act of 1890—had tried to thwart and punish these attempts. Government policing of business had been only partially successful, mainly because of economies inherent in large-scale, planned production and sales. Much business consolidation, as in mergers and growth of giant corporations, was legal; more agreements to limit production and hold up prices by numerous devices were furtive and sub rosa.

But now, with industrial output at half of capacity, and with some thirteen millions of unemployed, the national government invited enterprisers to co-operate and to improve operation in their many areas of industry and trade. It was impossible to deal with an industry unless it was organized in a trade association or otherwise. If organized, the members of the group dared not agree on measures to regulate output, trade practices, and prices, so long as the anti-combination (Sherman, Clayton, and Trade Commission) statutes were in effect. Therefore the government promised to suspend these laws in the emergency, and business men thus freed to combine must as a quid pro quo respect the right of workers to bargain collectively.

Representatives of many sectors of industry and commerce were haled to Washington and invited to formulate "codes of fair competition" for government of themselves and their fellows. These codes were syndicalist or cartel-like sets of rules which had the object of restoring prosperity and employment in the different areas of enterprise. "Fair competition" really meant reduced competition, penalizing price cutters, wage cutters, and those giving special services and privileges to favored customers. Hearings were held to allow all objectors to a proposed code to express their dissent, though in fact consumers received little protection. When the code was at length approved by the President of the United States it became law, and all in the covered group were bound to conform to it on pain of being fined for infractions. More than 575 such codes were put into effect.

One of these codes governed the business of slaughter and sale of live poultry in New York City and its environs. Practically all the chickens brought to New York City came from New Jersey and other states. The Schechter Poultry Corporation, with two establishments in Brooklyn, was covered by the code. The corporation sold the chickens, alive or slaughtered, to butchers and other retail dealers for local consumption. That is, after once entering New York City, the poultry never went to another state.

"Sick Chicken" Test Case

The code authority (the officers elected to supervise operation of the rules) brought suit against the Schechter corporation on many counts for code violations. For one thing, Schechter refused to observe the rule that a retailer must accept a half-coop or whole coop just as it came, without selecting particular birds. This meant that "unfit" chickens were left on the wholesaler's hands, and Schechter was accused of selling a "sick" chicken. Also the firm paid less than code wages and worked their slaughterers more than the maximum hours permitted.

In both federal district and circuit courts, NIRA (government) won, but Schechter continued to appeal and the case was decided by the Supreme Court in October 1934. Only two points were involved. Since NIRA rested on the power of Congress to regulate interstate commerce, a question was whether the live poultry industry of New York City, which was the subject of the code, was in the stream of or affected interstate commerce. The other doubt concerned the delegation of legislative power to the President, who by approving the code gave it the force of law.

The Supreme Court, in a unanimous decision (*Schechter v. United States*, 295 U.S. 495, 1935) read by Chief Justice Charles Evans Hughes, determined that interstate commerce had ceased when the poultry came to rest in New York City, for the birds were then sold for final consumption. Had they been merely processed in New York and then shipped to other states, the business would have been a part of interstate commerce. Was interstate commerce affected by practices in the local New York industry? The lawyers for NIRA had successfully contended in the courts below that interstate commerce would be impeded by forbidden forms of competition in New York City. The shipment of the poultry into New York City and the handling and conditions of sale there were intimately connected.

But the Court said this was at best an indirect effect. The industry was local and any correction of behavior of the Schechter corporation came within the police power of New York state, not of the federal government. To be embraced under national authority the effect must be direct. For example, the failure of a railroad that carried both intrastate and interstate shipments to use safety appliances would come under federal jurisdiction. The negligence of a railroad employe in

intrastate hauls which might result in the injury of an employe in interstate carriage would be another case of direct effect. Said the Court,
"If the commerce clause were construed to reach all . . . transactions
which could be said to have an indirect effect upon interstate commerce, the federal authority would embrace practically all the activities
of the people and the authority of the State over its domestic concerns
would exist only by sufferance of the federal government."

NIRA had urged that the crisis of depression justified Congress in
deputing to the President broad powers for the rehabilitation of industry and commerce. It was allowable for him to approve a code of
conduct designed to achieve this purpose. "But," the Chief Justice
pointed out, "the statutory plan is not simply one for voluntary effort.
It does not seek merely to endow voluntary trade or industrial associations or groups with privileges or immunities. It involves the coercive
exercise of the law-making power . . . If valid [the codes] place all
persons within their reach under the obligation of positive law, binding equally those who assent and those who do not assent. Violations
of the provisions of the codes are punishable as crimes."

The Court declared that Congress had only set forth the objects of
rehabilitation and expansion of trade and industry, but had not been
sufficiently specific in directing how the power delegated to the President was to be exercised by him. Congress could not resign its legislative function, handing over to the President "an unfettered discretion
to make whatever laws he thinks may be needed . . ." The statute
"Instead of prescribing rules of conduct . . . authorizes the making of
codes to prescribe them." It would be legal, if Congress laid down
guide-lines, to assign to an administrative agency, through the President, subordinate judgment in the application of rules to particular
situations. But the act as it stood conferred entirely too much liberty,
and was unconstitutional.

This decision, May 27, 1935, destroyed the code-making section, and
that was the heart of NIRA. The remainder of the law lingered only
until the end of that year.

President Franklin Roosevelt's Resentment

President Franklin D. Roosevelt was exasperated by this and a dozen
other decisions of the Supreme Court that knocked out lesser recovery
agencies of the New Deal. In February 1937 he sent to Congress a
message and accompanying bill to reorganize the federal judiciary. It
permitted the increase of judges of the Supreme Court from nine to a

maximum of fifteen, provided fifty more judges for lower federal courts, and directed reform of Court procedure to hasten consideration of constitutional cases. At first the President pretended that his proposals, especially providing additional judges for the Supreme Court, had the purpose of relieving the bench from an excessive burden of cases. But the public and otherwise friendly persons in official life were not deceived, and pronounced Roosevelt's scheme one for "packing the Court."

Senator Burton K. Wheeler, an ardent New Dealer, led the fight on the bill, which was further discredited when Chief Justice Hughes announced that the Supreme Court needed no additional members, and was abreast of its work. Roosevelt was forced personally to take charge of defending his measure. He publicly inveighed against the "personal economic predilection" of majority members of the Court. In a "fireside chat" over a national radio hookup he charged that the decisions of the Court had "cast doubts on the ability of the elected Congress to protect us against catastrophe by meeting squarely our modern social and economic conditions." The purpose of the bill was to restore the balance between the branches of government, since the judges had arrogated to themselves too much authority and were undoing the will of the people as committed to the legislature and executive.

This was an illustration of how even the most responsible man, in a crisis, could lose sight of the safeguards in our constitutional system. The Supreme Court had been less impressed than were Congress and the executive with permission given by the national emergency to expand constitutional powers. But that was the function of the Court, to move with deliberation, to refuse to sanction what the judges regarded as dangerous departures from tried restraints on popular demands. Of course all was a matter of more or less, of the exercise of discretion. With the wisdom of hindsight we must feel that where the choice was between rule of the Constitution and apparent claims of the moment, conservation of principles must be preferred. The codes, had they been continued and expanded, would have presented to private business interests excessive power over the economic life of the country, with too few checks from public bodies chosen by the people.

As it happened, the President was not obliged to press his ineligible proposal far. The Court in the spring of 1937 approved significant New Deal innovations, as in the Wagner Labor Relations Act and the Social Security law. With deaths and retirements among the justices, Roosevelt was able to name seven new members of the Court, including Stanley Reed, who had defended NIRA. As a counterweight, the

1938 congressional elections reduced the Democratic majorities, which had the effect of moderating further New Deal legislation. But soon World War II broke out in Europe, and huge orders placed in America for munitions and other materials served as no peacetime expedients had done to herald the end of the Great Depression.

Policies in Race Relations

The Civil Rights Act of 1875 forbade discrimination by state action against Negroes in inns, public conveyances, theaters, and other places licensed to serve those who could pay the charges. The law had been more honored in the breach than the observance. Often the offenders were individuals or private groups—or those contriving to appear as private—without any agency of the state. In significant respects the state itself was guilty, but violations of civil rights of Negroes went unredressed. In former slave states more especially, the effort, official and unofficial, was to repress the Negroes in every department of life.

Motives of the whites were several. Negroes must be prevented from competing as producers, where opportunities of work were insufficient. The misfortune was that the whites who felt themselves most threatened by Negroes were common laborers or those in any jobs requiring little skill, or small tenant farmers. The whites who were in closest economic contact with Negroes were those with the least education, least resources, fewest means of improving their own lot. Whites of higher competence and standard of living—business men, lawyers, doctors, preachers, teachers—who were best fitted to understand the Negroes' needs, did not have constant intimate touch with Negroes of similar training and abilities. They moved in different spheres. Consequently, race relations were left to be determined largely by the ignorant and the fearful of both groups.

The poor white people of the South, having little economic superiority to Negroes of the same class, clung fiercely to the claim of racial superiority. The result was to deny to the Negro, wherever possible, social equality. The poor whites, to satisfy their pride, must feel themselves better than somebody. So their jealousy was directed against the Negroes, and they demanded distinctions where there were precious few differences. Hence segregation—in schools, churches, buses, trains, employment, living quarters in cities and often even in country neighborhoods. One who has not lived long in the South, indeed who did not grow up there and share from his earliest consciousness the ways of the people, cannot appreciate how sharp was the social separation of the races. Where physical contact was closest, white superiority, para-doxically, was most emphasized, often by subtle means that an out-sider would not detect but that were perfectly understood by both Negroes and whites. Whites in the same cotton row or railroad gang with Negroes were addressed as "Mister," while the Negroes were spoken to as "Joe" or "Sam." Much of the inveterate, all-pervasive dis-crimination is told in the incident of a Negro-back-country farmer who was stopped by a policeman at the approach to a Mississippi River bridge because he drove his mule through a traffic light when red. His explanation was, "I saw all the white folks going through on green and I thought the red was for me."

The determination of the whites of the lowest economic and social groups to preserve their superiority to Negroes by any means, however artificial, was powerfully and unworthily encouraged by unprincipled politicians appealing for white votes. The regular device of demagogues, big and little, was to pose as friends of the whites against the blacks. They would picture their white opponents for office as favoring the pre-tensions of Negroes. Thus racial suspicions of whites were constantly being aggravated into hatreds. Old wounds were reopened and freshly inflamed.

To make the situation worse, many Negro leaders, instead of asserting the rights of their people, found their bread buttered on the side of toadying to the whites who imposed discriminations. These conspicu-ously humble ones, bootlickers, "Uncle Toms" (from the amenable character in Mrs. Stowe's novel), were patronized as displaying the patterns of behavior which all Negroes should imitate. Besides, many Negroes with too much self-respect to stoop to such fawning conscien-tiously believed that the progress of southern Negroes would benefit most from making haste slowly, objecting to little, taking the easiest ways to gains, however slight, here, there, and elsewhere. Their sub-mission to injustice was unwilling, but their protests were selective and tactful.

White Southerners who genuinely wished the Negroes well and wanted to see them advance in opportunity and achievement were most apt to approve of and co-operate with Negro leaders who practiced the patience just described. The well-meaning organizations of influential white persons, co-operating with Negroes and often embracing Ne-groes in their membership, were and are numerous. These regard them-selves as responsible and sufficiently advanced. As a group they re-gretted or condemned efforts of whites, or of whites and Negroes jointly, and surely of Negroes alone, to press for legal rights of the minority.

346 of THE CONSTITUTION

Anything like economic radicalism—say advocacy inspired by principles of socialism or communism—was not only discountenanced but actively feared and fought.

The policy of those of both races who considered themselves most enlightened and responsible was to seek unobtrusive, piecemeal betterment for Negroes and mutual understanding of Negroes and whites. They constantly pointed with satisfaction to progress made since the days of slavery and begged that this gratifying history not be interrupted, or perhaps reversed, by demanding too much too fast. They listed advances of Negroes in schooling, in earnings, in admission to new employments, in property ownership, in the exercise of the suffrage here and there, in occasional appointments to public office, and the achievements of individuals in business and the professions. If one asked, how long will it take to realize equality of rights, the answer was disappointing. The prospect was that good will must be combined with forbearance into the indefinite future. Few expected that guarantees of the Constitution would be enjoyed by Negroes, or by certain other minority racial groups, in the lifetime of living persons.

The programs of these moderate groups rarely contemplated desegregation in schools, housing, or places of recreation. Education and inculcation of moral conduct were relied upon as the most certain means of betterment; but schools and churches were segregated. Educators and clergymen of both races who might be looked to for the maximum of tolerance were themselves practicing segregation—the whites actively, the Negroes more passively. So these leaders were convicted out of their own mouths. This disability attached not only to the administrators of primary and secondary schools, and to pastors of congregations, but to college and university presidents and the highest policy-making church functionaries and governing bodies. Thus the moderates fought—where legal rights of Negroes were concerned—with broken lances.

The foregoing characterization of racial opinion and purpose in the South, where most of the Negroes were concentrated, is necessarily rough, and it does injustice to many individuals and organizations. Much that is more courageous or hopeful could be recited with truth. But generally speaking, cultural inhibitions, ingrained habits political, economic, and social, got in the way of assertion of legal claims. "We are not ready for that," or "by premature demands you harm those you are trying to help," were oft-heard remonstrances of the cautious. From honest motives they sought to discredit those who went beyond them, even though what was proposed was unmistakably proclaimed in the Constitution, in theory the fundamental law of the nation.

"Separate but Equal"

Demands to apply the Constitution to racial rights, which flamed in Civil War and Reconstruction and then subsided into circumspect, selective advance, stirred from time to time in late years of the nineteenth century and early in the twentieth. We may not even touch upon the many evidences except for revival of the effort to end discrimination in public conveyances. Here the Supreme Court for half a century blocked progress, not only in this specific field but in desegregation of the races in use of public facilities generally. The controlling case was *Plessy v. Ferguson* (163 U.S. 537), decided in 1896. The Court, one justice dissenting, upheld the constitutionality of a law of Louisiana requiring railroads to furnish "separate but equal" accommodations to white and Negro passengers. The act was attacked on the ground that it violated the Fourteenth Amendment, which forbids a state to make or enforce a law which abridges the privileges or immunities of citizens, deprives any person of life, liberty, or property without due process, or denies to any person within its jurisdiction the equal protection of the laws. The Court said the object of the amendment was to enforce "absolute equality of the two races before the law, but in the nature of things it could not have been intended to abolish distinctions based upon color, or to enforce social, as distinguished from political equality, or a commingling of the two races upon terms unsatisfactory to either."

This last was gratuitous, as it was not established that Negroes, except from fear of mistreatment, would object to sharing common facilities. Then the Court went on to a more unwarranted assumption: "Laws . . . requiring . . . separation [of the races] in places where they are liable to be brought into contact do not necessarily imply the inferiority of either race to the other . . ." Such compulsory separation had "been generally, if not universally, recognized as within the competency of the state legislatures in the exercise of their police power. The most common instance of this is connected with the establishment of separate schools for white and colored children." Segregation had state court approval in Massachusetts, and in "acts of Congress requiring separate schools for colored children in the District of Columbia." Such a regulation by Louisiana was permissible if only it was reasonable. In exercising its discretion the state could be guided by "the established usages, customs and traditions of the people . . . with a view to the public peace and good order." That is, what was demanded (actually by the white people) was legal.

The judges, as though to assure themselves of the accuracy of their contention that the mere fact of segregation was not demeaning to the Negroes, returned to their assertion. "We consider the underlying fallacy of the plaintiff's argument to consist in the assumption that the enforced separation of the two races stamps the colored race with a badge of inferiority. If this be so, it is not by reason of anything found in the act, but solely because the colored race chooses to put that construction upon it." Furthermore, social prejudices might not be "overcome by legislation," and the decision of a New York court was quoted to support this position. The Supreme Court went on with its own wisdom: "Legislation is powerless to eradicate social instincts or to abolish distinctions based upon physical differences. . . . If one race be inferior to the other socially, the Constitution of the United States cannot put them upon the same plane." The Court was in deep water when it talked about "racial instincts" which, if such exist, psychologists and anthropologists have found to vary widely under different circumstances.

Mr. Justice Harlan, dissenting, swept aside these rationalizations. "Our Constitution," he declared, "is color-blind, and neither knows nor tolerates classes among citizens. In respect of civil rights, all citizens are equal before the law . . . the judgment this day rendered will, in time, prove to be quite as pernicious as the decision . . . in the Dred Scott Case."

Whatever the effects of the "separate but equal" doctrine on race relations, states and local communities obeyed the court sanction of separate facilities with alacrity, while disregarding the condition that the facilities provided to the Negroes be equal. The justices had swept dirt under the rug. Anybody the least wise, not black-robed, not perched on a high bench, could have told their honors that where prejudice was approved prejudice would behave like prejudice. Railway carriages, wash-rooms, waiting-rooms, quarters in boats, and particularly schools "For Colored" were as a rule distinctly inferior to those reserved for white people—inferior physically, inferior in upkeep. This had to be the fact where Negro patrons were fewer than white patrons. The space allotted was smaller, and if there was little demand on the part of Negroes (who met such shabby treatment), there might be no service at all available. Sleeping car berths and use of dining cars were denied to Negroes, except servants traveling with white employers. A Negro

wishing to study law or medicine in his own state was refused entrance
to the appropriate institution supported by tax funds, though often
the state, if the applicant persisted, would offer to pay his expenses, or
maybe just his tuition, in another state where segregation was not practiced. It is not possible financially or educationally to set up a separate
professional or graduate school for a few Negro students.

Every part of the population should have proper facilities in travel,
housing, and recreation, but enjoyment of the best schools available in
the community is of main importance to a group which has lacked
training and needs to advance in competence. An elaborate survey of
public schools in the South, published during World War I, showed
the shocking disparity in per capita expenditure for Negro pupils and
for whites. The result was that schools for Negroes had poor buildings and equipment, short terms, teachers who lacked education themselves. In states with little public revenue it is difficult to support one
school system, and impossible to have two systems of decent quality.
Consequently, the schools for Negroes suffered most, but those for
whites were also of low standards. This meant an inferior start in life
for all southern children.

Demand for Legal Rights

The social-work, cultivate-good-will, always-be-tactful approach to removal of discriminations against Negroes was supplemented and then
superseded by frank, persistent demand that Negroes should enjoy
equal benefit of the laws. The organization most active in claiming
citizenship rights, the National Association for the Advancement of
Colored People, was founded and led by Negroes, but with the cordial
assistance of white friends. The NAACP considered that the time had
come when patience was no longer a virtue. During the Great Depression of the 1930's public welfare on an enormous scale supplanted inadequate private charity. In the general economic collapse, government necessarily made itself responsible for the fundamentals of life
for a great part of the population—food, employment, housing, old age
dependency, and, to an increasing degree, health. These essentials
were supplied not by the states, which early proved unequal to the task
financially and otherwise, but by the national government.

This meant that services were more nearly equal for all groups than
had been the case when states were free to practice discrimination.
Local and state governments were incapable of meeting even the relief
problems of the depression, let alone measures for inducing recovery

and reform. Thus local and state authority was relatively discredited, and national resources were the only rescue. The Great Depression produced a revolution in the scope and purpose of the national government, ushering in what was called, with gratitude or suspicion, the welfare state. *Laissez faire*, the doctrine that every man should take care of himself in a perfectly competitive economy, faded when it was demonstrated that the most industrious were faced by starvation when the system of private business failed. The economy became manifestly mixed, public and private, and economic and social planning were no longer frightening words.

Then came the Second World War, during and after which America preached democracy to the world and was eager to support its principles with generous grants for development of backward peoples. How could Negroes in the United States do other than proclaim at home, we are a backward people and demand for ourselves the democracy and progress which our country is bestowing in distant lands. And government and the public had to agree, if only because our professions of democracy, as against Nazi and Soviet dictatorship, sounded hollow while we were allowing systematic public discrimination against millions of American citizens.

Court cases were brought to correct discrimination against Negro plaintiffs, especially in education, but also in transportation, public housing, and use of public recreational facilities.

The first progress was forced admission of a few Negro students to professional and graduate departments of state universities in the South, after token attempts to provide separate training for Negroes in these fields had been disallowed by the Supreme Court. But the real break came in 1954 with the unanimous decision of the Supreme Court that segregation of Negroes in elementary public schools was in itself discriminatory, even if the schools provided for Negroes were equal in all respects to those reserved for whites. Never since the Civil War and Rconstruction had the Constitution been so brought to the relief of the Negro minority. The 1954 decision had a superior impact because it came in a period of domestic peace and did not issue from aroused public passion.

The Court gave a consolidated opinion on four cases reaching it from the states of Kansas, South Carolina, Virginia, and Delaware. All involved the legal question whether Negro children denied admission to schools confined to white children were deprived of equal protection of the laws under the Fourteenth Amendment. In three of the cases federal district courts had refused relief to the plaintiffs (the legal representatives of the Negro children) on the "separate but equal" doctrine announced more than a half-century earlier by the Supreme Court in the *Plessy v. Ferguson* decision.

Segregation in Itself Is Discrimination

The Supreme Court now, in *Brown v. Board of Education of Topeka* (347 U.S. 483, 1954), speaking through Chief Justice Warren, repudiated the older finding. The judgment was reached only after the cases had been argued in 1952 and reargued in 1954. After exhaustive inquiry into the circumstances surrounding adoption of the Fourteenth Amendment in 1868, the Court could not determine how the amendment was intended at that time to apply to public education. Further, said the Court, the Negro and white schools involved in these cases "have been equalized, or are being equalized, with respect to buildings, curricula, qualifications and salaries of teachers, and other 'tangible' factors. Our decision, therefore, cannot turn on merely a comparison of these tangible factors . . . We must look instead to the effect of segregation itself on public education."

The Court then dwelt on the paramount function of public education in present-day American life. "Compulsory school attendance laws and the great expenditures for education both demonstrate our recognition of the importance of education in our democratic society. It is required in the performance of our most basic public responsibilities . . . It is the very foundation of good citizenship. Today it is a principal instrument in awakening the child to cultural values . . . and in helping him to adjust normally to his environment. In these days, it is doubtful that any child may reasonably be expected to succeed in life if he is denied the opportunity of an education. Such an opportunity, where the state has undertaken to provide it, is a right which must be made available to all on equal terms."

Then the Court came to the nub of the matter. "Does segregation of children in public schools solely on the basis of race, even though the physical facilities and other 'tangible' factors may be equal, deprive the children of the minority group of equal educational opportunities? We believe that it does."

The Court reflected that in other recent cases involving higher education it had disallowed segregation because of itself it condemned students of the minority group to inferior training. Such educational and psychological considerations, the Court continued, "apply with added force to children in grade and high schools. To separate them from others of similar age and qualifications solely because of their race generates a feeling of inferiority as to their status in the community that may affect their hearts and minds in a way unlikely ever to be undone." The decision quoted with approval a finding in the Kansas case by the court below, even though that court felt compelled to rule against the Negro plaintiffs on the "separate but equal" precedent: ". . . the policy of separating the races is usually interpreted as denoting the inferiority of the Negro group. A sense of inferiority affects the motivation of a child to learn." The highest court explicitly rejected the complacent declaration of the same court in the Plessy case that if Negroes felt demeaned by segregation it was only because they chose to put that construction on the practice. "Separate educational facilities are inherently unequal" and the Negro children were held to be deprived thereby "of the equal protection of the laws guaranteed by the Fourteenth Amendment."

Segregation in the public schools was thus declared unconstitutional. The next question, of greater complexity, was how most wisely to grant relief to the plaintiffs and to others in similar situation. To define the law is one thing, but to apply it, in many states and localities under varying conditions, is another. The Court ordered reargument on the appropriate method of enforcement of the decision. The conclusion was to remand the cases to the lower federal courts which should ensure that the schools be desegregated "with all deliberate speed."

This policy recognized that the problem of readjustment could best be solved in the districts affected, and that this process would take time. But not endless time, not be subject to indefinite and disingenuous postponement. The compulsion of law was urgent but reasonable. As someone phrased the direction of the Supreme Court to school authorities, it was, "Go slow, but go!"

Experience with response to the Court's decision was what might be expected. In an increasing number of states and communities desegregation was accomplished promptly and smoothly, partly because much preparatory work had been done by the Southern Regional Council, composed of white and Negro citizens devoted to this object. In others, notoriously, Little Rock, Arkansas, and Oxford, Mississippi, the President of the United States was obliged to call out troops to protect a token number of Negro students who entered former "white" schools. In several states "White Citizens' Councils," got up for the purpose, opposed the decision with propaganda and sometimes with violence.

The Supreme Court ban on segregation in public schools marked the beginning of a new phase in the progress of American democracy. It promised the legal removal of racial barriers in many other areas of our society. The process of accelerated change must test the talents of all the people in the arts of living together. Desegregation was difficult, but integration is more vexing. This endeavor will try the capacity of the national community for tolerance, discipline, and orderly advance. The reliable guide in this enterprise will be, as hitherto, the Constitution of the United States.

Dominance of Rural Representation

On March 26, 1962, the Court handed down a controversial decision of far-reaching implications in a Tennessee case (*Baker v. Carr*, 369 U.S. 186) involving apportionment of the state legislature. The background for this case was the malapportionment of state legislatures, resulting in a general gross overrepresentation of rural and small-town voters at the expense of large cities and their suburbs. Since the resulting unrepresentative state legislatures have the responsibility for carving out Congressional districts in their states, this rural dominance is reflected in Congress also.

In the twenty-five years preceding the *Baker v. Carr* decision, the dimensions of the problem had increased greatly. In twenty-seven states there had been no redistricting for at least twenty-five years (in Vermont, not since 1793). It was estimated that in 44 states a majority in the state legislature could be elected by less than 40 per cent of the population. In some states these percentages were substantially less; 25 per cent of the voters in Alabama could elect a majority in either legislative house, while in Florida the state senate could be controlled by 12 per cent of the electorate, the house by 15 per cent. Nation-wide, it was estimated that the discrepancies in representation worked out at two to one in favor of rural and small-town voters, on the average, and a study by University of Florida political scientists showed that between 1937 and 1955 the malapportionment worsened in three-fourths of the states.

Prior to 1962 the Court had avoided many opportunities to rule on apportionment cases, for discretionary reasons. Justice Frankfurter, one of the Court's most consistent foes of this sort of intervention, said in a 1946 case (*Colegrove v. Green*, Illinois), "It is hostile to a democratic system to involve the judiciary in the politics of the people."

Baker v. Carr, brought by a group of city voters in Tennessee, claimed denial of the guarantee of the Fourteenth Amendment to "equal protection of the laws," because since 1901 the Tennessee legislature had refused to reapportion seats in that body, despite a provision of the state constitution requiring reapportionment after every decennial census. The Court was asked to declare the 1901 reapportionment unconstitutional, to forbid the holding of further elections under it, and to order the state to conduct an election either at large, or by equitably apportioned districts as determined by the 1960 census. The decision in the case, however, was based on the narrowest possible grounds, holding only that Tennessee citizens have the right to challenge the apportionment of their state legislature in the federal courts, returning the matter to the district court which had earlier refused to take jurisdiction. Justice Brennan's majority decision (6-2) said that "we have no cause at this stage to doubt the District Court will be able to fashion relief if violations of constitutional rights are found . . . it is improper now to consider what remedy would be most appropriate if appellants prevail at the trial." Neither the alleged violation of the Fourteenth Amendment nor the proposed remedial action was decided by the Court. Justice Frankfurter's dissenting opinion reflected clearly his misgivings; he said the decision was a "massive repudiation of the experience of our whole past," and asserted "destructively novel judicial power." He believed that the lack of a clear basis for relief would "catapult the lower courts" into a "mathematical quagmire," and that "litigation begun so speculatively today will outlast the life of the youngest member sitting on this court."

There was no clue in the Court's decision as to what it would consider a constitutional apportionment. The case brought by Tennessee voters was clear-cut. Not only had the state legislature refused for more than sixty years to do what the state's constitution plainly required; the state courts had also refused to intervene, and Tennessee had no provision for referendum or initiative. The only possible redress lay in the federal courts. The decision in *Baker v. Carr*, however, opened the floodgates to litigation from other states, in which conditions varied widely. Among the questions posed were these: how gross would malapportionment have to be for the federal courts to take jurisdiction? Suppose a state constitution provided for initiative or referendum, giving voters there a possible means of securing reapportionment? What if a state's constitution included a legislature in which one house was based on population and the other on geographic units—a "little federal system?"

One thing seemed clear. Since the federal system is deliberately fashioned to be a system of balanced and unequal representation, the courts

were unlikely to hold that representation in the state legislatures must
be based on districts having precisely equal numbers of voters. The majority of the Court had indicated that what it wanted was some *rational*
system, not precise equality of representation.

Following *Baker v. Carr*, apportionment suits were pending or expected to be filed in no fewer than twenty-seven states, with the likelihood that more would follow. One reason for the haste in filing suits
was the imminence of the 1962 Congressional elections, and the hope
that some remedial action could be had before they were held.

On April 14, 1962, a federal court in Alabama gave the state legislature until July to accomplish a satisfactory reapportionment, saying
also that the court would act if the legislature did not. On July 25
the same court rejected reapportionment plans made at a special session of the legislature, and ordered into immediate effect a plan of
its own. In accepting an alternative plan made by the legislature for
the state senate, the court indicated that it considered this only a step
toward a satisfactory proposal, since it left rural areas greatly overrepre-
sented. The court would act further to break the rural stranglehold if
necessary.

Georgia has had a "county unit" system of election, under which
each of the state's 159 counties was assigned from 2 to 6 votes, although county populations in 1962 varied from about 1800 to nearly
half a million. The candidate polling the highest number of votes got
all the county's votes, and a majority of the county units made him the
winner in a state-wide election. Under this system, it was routine for a
majority of the units to go to candidates polling a minority of the popular vote. Under repeated fire earlier, the unit system was attacked anew
following *Baker v. Carr*. A three-man federal court enjoined its use in
the primary and November elections of 1962, and separately decided
that current apportionment of the Georgia legislature constituted "invidious discrimination" against urban voters, and was "irrational and
arbitrary." The legislature was ordered to reapportion at least one house
according to population before January 1963, threatening action by
the court if compliance were not forthcoming.

A case involving the Georgia system as applied to state-wide elections
was appealed to the Supreme Court, and decided by it on March 18,
1963 (*Gray et al. v. Sanders*, 112 October Term, 1962). Decision for
the majority was delivered by Justice Douglas, Justice Harlan being the
sole dissenter. Noting the extreme inequalities of the system (one vote
in Echols County having the same influence as 99 votes in Fulton
County, containing the city of Atlanta), the majority disagreed with

the district court's willingness to be satisfied with a mere modification of the unit system, and rejected an analogy to the federal electoral college. The Court held that Georgia must, once the geographic unit had been determined, allow equal weight to each vote cast within it, and might not continue a system which, in counting votes, weighted rural votes more heavily.

Together with a subsequent case decided on appeal from Maryland, *Gray v. Sanders* has the effect of requiring "one man, one vote" as the prime criterion in districting state legislatures. *Reynolds v. Sims* (377 U.S. 533, 1964) decided a more determined support of the federal analogy, since Maryland judicial authorities upheld the constitutionality of apportioning one house of the state legislature on a geographic base, so long as the other was based on population. Speaking for the Court, Chief Justice Warren said:

We hold that, as a basic constitutional standard, the Equal Protection Clause requires that the seats in both houses of a bicameral state legislature must be apportioned on a population basis. We . . . find the federal analogy inapposite and irrelevant to state legislative districting schemes. Attempted reliance on the federal analogy appears often to be little more than an after-the-fact rationalization offered in defense of maladjusted state apportionment arrangements. . . .

The system of representation in the two Houses of the Federal Congress is . . . conceived only as compromise and concession indispensable to the establishment of our federal republic. . . .

The Court's opinion allowed for some flexibility:

. . . we mean that the Equal Protection Clause requires that a State make an honest and good faith effort to construct districts . . . as nearly of equal population as is practicable. We realize that it is a practical impossibility to arrange legislative districts so that each one has an identical number of residents, or citizens, or voters. . . . For the present, we deem it expedient not to attempt to spell out any precise constitutional tests. What is marginally permissible is one State may be unsatisfactory in another . . . [The decision] does not mean that States cannot adopt some reasonable plan for periodic revision of their apportionment schemes.

This lack of precision, however necessary, has had the effect of keeping the reapportionment controversy alive in the states, particularly when the one man, one vote standard is applied by extending it to Congressional districts. It can be said, however, that the political trend, beginning with *Baker v. Carr*, has been away from over-representation of rural areas and toward more equitable representation of cities and suburbs. The effect on political parties, and on liberal-conservative influence, is not at all clear.

Decisions on Legality of Abortions

The decision, in January 1973, which substantially invalidated the anti-abortion laws existing in most of the states (44) was that in *Roe et al. v. Wade, District Attorney of Dallas County* (410 U.S., 113, 959). The opinion of the Court, delivered by Justice Blackmun, had the concurrence of six of his brethren; Justices White and Rehnquist dissented.

Jane Roe (the name was fictitious) was a pregnant single woman; in her federal action she sought a declaratory judgment that the Texas criminal abortion statutes were unconstitutional, and an injunction restraining the defendant from enforcing the statutes. Jane Roe wanted but could not get in Texas a legal abortion because her life did not appear to be threatened by continuation of her pregnancy; she could not afford to travel to another constituency where she might receive a legal abortion. She claimed that the Texas statutes were vague and abridged her personal privacy protected by the First, Fourth, Fifth, Ninth, and Fourteenth Amendments. Actually her pregnancy came to term before the appellate process was complete.

As the right of a woman to obtain a legal abortion though her health or life was not in danger had been an increasingly controversial issue, Justice Blackmun's opinion explored the question in its legal, medical, and theological history. He thought it doubtful whether abortion was ever firmly established as a common law crime even with respect to the destruction of a "quick fetus." The first English statute, 1803, made abortion of a quick fetus a capital crime and prescribed lesser penalties for abortion before quickening. In the United States only after the Civil War did legislation begin to replace the common law. Most statutes dealt severely with abortion after quickening, more leniently with abortion earlier. The laws exempted abortions judged necessary to preserve the mother's life. By the end of the nineteen-fifties the distinction between pre-quickening and post-quickening tended to disappear, and the laws became more severe. However, in most recent years a third of the states adopted less stringent statutes, and the objections of the American Medical Association tended to be relaxed. The more liberal attitude reflected the fact that abortion, previously dangerous, under proper conditions had become no more hazardous than childbirth.

The Constitution does not explicitly mention the right of privacy, but the Supreme Court has recognized that certain "zones of privacy" exist as penumbras of the Bill of Rights (see the discussion of the birth control case, *Griswold v. Connecticut*, above). The Court said:

The right of privacy . . . is broad enough to encompass a woman's decision whether or not to terminate her pregnancy . . . Maternity, or additional offspring may force upon the woman a distressful life and future. Psychological harm may be imminent. Mental and physical health may be taxed by child care. There is also the distress, for all concerned, associated with the unwanted child, and there is the problem of bringing a child into a family already unable, psychologically and otherwise, to care for it.

The stigma of unwed motherhood may be involved. "All these are factors the woman and her responsible physician necessarily will consider in consultation."

However, a woman's right to an abortion is not absolute. The state has an interest in maintaining medical standards, in guarding health, and in protecting potential life.

In this case Jane Roe claimed the unlimited right of abortion. The state claimed the right of protecting prenatal life, from and after conception. The Supreme Court did not agree fully with either position. At this point a surprise bit of legal humor entered. If the fetus is a person within the meaning of the Fourteenth Amendment, then Jane Roe's case collapsed, for the fetus's right to life is specifically guaranteed by the amendment! However, the Court asserted that no allusion to "person" in the Constitution applies prenatally; "person" in the Fourteenth Amendment does not include the unborn.

Since those trained in medicine, philosophy, and theology cannot agree on when life begins, the Court would not speculate on the question. The medical profession tended to favor a point of time when the fetus becomes viable, potentially able to live outside the womb, albeit with artificial aid. Usually this point was placed at seven months (28 weeks), though it might occur as early as 24 weeks.

The state's compelling interest in the health of the mother, however, begins earlier, in the light of present medical knowledge "at approximately the end of the first trimester . . . from and after this point, a State may regulate the abortion procedure to the extent that the regulation reasonably relates to the preservation and protection of maternal health." Before that abortion is free of interference by the state.

The state's compelling interest in prenatal life begins at the point of viable life. The state may proscribe abortion after that period except to protect the life and health of the mother. The state may forbid abortion by any other than a qualified physician and may define "qualified physician." The Court determined that a statute like that of Texas which excepts from criminality only saving of the mother's life, without regard to stage of pregnancy, and without recognition of other interests involved, is violative of the due process clause of the Fourteenth Amendment. Hence the Texas statute must fall.

So the decision applied to three stages of pregnancy. In the first three months an abortion depends on the judgment of physician and patient. In the second three months the state may regulate abortion procedure to protect the mother's health. In the third three months the state, in protecting potential life, may forbid abortion except where necessary for sake of the health and life of the mother.

Chief Justice Burger, concurring, pointed out that the Court rejected any claim that the Constitution requires abortion on demand. The Court said, "For the stage prior approximately to the end of the first trimester, the abortion decision and its effectuation must be left to the medical judgment of the pregnant woman's attendant physician."

Justice Rehnquist in his dissent seemed to rely on a technical objection. At the time of filing her complaint Jane Roe, for all the Court knew, may have been in the last three months of pregnancy, when the Texas statute and the present decision of the Supreme Court would apply. In other words, the Court was deciding an hypothetical lawsuit, departed from the principle that it should never "formulate a rule of constitutional law broader than is required by the precise facts to which it is to apply."

The Texas decision struck down criminal abortion statutes in a majority of the states. On the same day a similar decision was rendered in *Doe et al. v. Bolton, Attorney General of Georgia.*

Prior to these decisions Texas and thirty other states barred abortion unless the mother's life was in danger. Georgia and fourteen others permitted abortion if to save the mother's life or where the fetus was likely to be deformed or the pregnancy resulted from rape. Only the states of New York, Alaska, Hawaii, and Washington met the new Supreme Court decision. The Roman Catholic clergy opposed the decision, liberal organizations of women applauded it. Dr. Alan F. Guttmacher, president of the Planned Parenthood Federation of America, while welcoming the judgment, deplored the three months' limit on unregulated abortion. He observed that this was a hardship on the young and poor who most often need an abortion after the twelfth week, and that furthermore genetic defects in a fetus may not be apparent until late.

Private Rights to Means of Birth Control

An eighty-year-old Connecticut law, revised as late as 1958, punished any person who used a contraceptive device or materials by a fine of not less than $50 or 60 days to a year in jail, or both. Any accessory who aided and abetted in the use of contraceptives was similarly condemned. In 1965 in *Griswold et al. v. Connecticut* (381 U.S. 479) the executive director and the medical director of the Planned Parenthood League of the state had been found guilty as accessories and fined $100 each. They had given contraceptive advice to married persons only; the medical director, a licensed physician, had examined the wife and supplied her with a device or material intended to prevent conception. They appealed to the U.S. Supreme Court against the decision of the highest court of Connecticut.

In a 7 to 2 decision the Connecticut statute was held to be in violation of the First Amendment of the United States Constitution. Justice Douglas delivered the opinion of the Court. ". . . the State may not consistently with the spirit of the First Amendment, contract the spectrum of available knowledge. The right of freedom of speech and press includes not only the right to utter or print, but the right to distribute, the right to receive, the right to read and freedom of inquiry, and the right to teach . . . These are proper peripheral rights." In dwelling on the rights which followed from the amendment the Court employed reasoning similar to that of Hamilton in relying on implied powers of the federal government, except that in the birth control case the reference was to implied protections of the individual against governmental interference.

The First Amendment confers peripheral rights, it "has a penumbra where privacy is protected from governmental intrusion." And again, "specific guarantees in the Bill of Rights have penumbras, formed by emanations from those guarantees that help to give them life and substance. Various guarantees create zones of privacy." So the judgment of the Supreme Court was that the Connecticut court below was reversed.

Justice Goldberg was joined by Chief Justice Warren and Justice Brennan in a concurring opinion. Goldberg stressed the application of the Ninth Amendment ("The enumeration in the Constitution, of certain rights, shall not be construed to deny or disparage others retained by the people.") He insisted that "the concept of liberty . . . embraces the right of marital privacy though that right is not mentioned explicitly in the Constitution."

Justice Harlan concurred in the judgment striking down the Connecticut statute, but could not join in the Court's opinion which rested on "radiations" from the provisions of the Bill of Rights. Similarly, Justice White agreed with the judgment, but for his own reasons. He observed that though in the state's view the law operated against all forms of promiscuous or illicit sexual relationships, in fact sales of contraceptives had long occurred and only infrequently been challenged.

Justices Black and Stewart dissented. They both thought the Connecticut statute offensive, silly, or, it was suggested, asinine. Black thought the state prohibition might have been overruled if the appellants had only given advice, but they assisted by a medical examination and the furnishing of the physical means of preventing conception. The majority in talking of the "right of privacy" substituted other words "for those the Framers used." He liked his privacy as much as any man, "but I am nevertheless compelled to admit that government has a right to invalidate it unless prohibited by some specific constitutional provision." He believed the majority voided the Connecticut law because they considered that the legislature had acted unwisely. But courts must not substitute their social and economic beliefs for the judgment of legislative bodies "which are elected to pass laws." Black would affirm the decision of the state court because "Connecticut's law as applied here is not forbidden by any provision of the Federal Constitution as that Constitution was written."

Justice Stewart was even more antagonistic to the state statute, but he would not overturn it on the reasoning of the majority, which stretched the Bill of Rights. ". . . to say that the Ninth Amendment has anything to do with the case is to turn somersaults with history." The law should be taken off the books by the people, using their constitutional rights to appeal to their legislature. Actually the Connecticut House of Representatives had recently repealed the statute, and, whatever the Senate might have done, it was relieved of the necessity by the decision of the Supreme Court.

Ebb and Flow of Court Opinion

In conclusion we may offer an outline of changes in interpretation of the Constitution by the Supreme Court. We must limit ourselves to fairly distinct periods or phases. Omitting detail always means neglecting shadings and the progress of the Court has been less jerky and spasmodic than our short summary reveals. Further, we caution that the Court's decision in each case has been based, as a rule, on a particular set of facts justifying or requiring in the opinion of the high tribunal the conclusion reached. Frequently, to be sure, judgment on a specific question has been used to declare a broad principal or policy. Also, *obiter dicta*—observations in passing, not necessary to the decision in hand—have indicated the trend of the Court's thought. Finally, dissenting views, for the historical record, modify in one way and another the positions taken by the majority of the justices. Though these features need to be stated they do not interfere with the accuracy of our compressed narrative.

A river conforms its course to the landscape through which it flows. It does not charge up hill, but seeks the valleys. So the Court has meandered through its sociological terrain, avoiding the ridges and following the open lowlands of prevailing public opinion. Not always, for just as a river will sometimes cut a new channel, so the Court at times has run counter to economic and political developments and preferences of most of the people of the country. It is not surprising that the Court reflects public sentiment. It is significant that only four chief justices had judicial training before ascending the highest bench. Aside from legal practice, the experience of most had been political, as senators, congressmen, governors, cabinet ministers, or diplomats. The chief justice has not always swayed his brethren, but as has been shown repeatedly he is in position to exercise dominant influence. We are often reminded that the judges are not wisdom incarnate, but are men subject to the urges of their environment. The best they can do is be faithful to their oath of office, spokesmen of the general good as they understand it, deliberate, not excited, in their cogitations and pronouncements. The Constitution encourages their independence, with life tenure and sufficient salary.

The Court began its work in 1790 but did not become a force in American life until a decade later. John Jay, the first chief justice, failed to appreciate the role the Court could play in our government. He found his duties onerous, their scope uninviting; he resigned to become governor of New York and later refused to return to the bench at President John Adams's urging. Chief Justice Oliver Ellsworth also left little impress. Vitality was injected with the appointment of John Marshall in 1801, at just the juncture to give opportunity to his commanding purpose. The Federalists in a dozen years had set the national government going prosperously, but were obliged to yield the Presidency to Jefferson, whose Republicans controlled Congress. Marshall rose to the challenge to preserve the claims of the central government against resurgent champions of the states. It was the function of the Supreme Court to declare what was the law of the land. The Court would strike down a statute of Congress (as in *Marbury v. Madison*) or of a state (*McCulloch v. Maryland*) if in conflict with the Constitution.

Marshall subordinated state authority. A far-reaching example was his decision (Dartmouth College case) that a private charter granted by a state was a contract which the state legislature might not thereafter violate. The result, unforeseen at the time, was to give freedom to corporate enterprise which became the powerful means of capitalist development. This was in accord with Federalist policy for building the national economy by fostering business initiative. The Marshall Court was creative in asserting the implied powers of the central government under the Constitution. Before Marshall's long sway ended, reaction had set in. The states demanded more authority. This was inevitable if American democracy, economic and political, was to mature. But Marshall had given a primacy to the national government which, though later disputed and obscured, was never lost as tenet in our constitutional system.

Chief Justice Taney's reign over the Supreme Court of twenty-eight years (1836-64) was less than Marshall's and was never as complete or consistent as that of his predecessor. The westward expansion of the period entailed penalties. Canal and railroad construction and fevered land speculation, accelerated by means of depreciated notes of state banks, received a rude check in the major economic depression commencing in 1837. This produced confusion that embittered developing conflict between the slave South and the industrial North. The two cultures might have continued longer glaring across Mason and Dixon's line had not both sections been determined to control the vast new areas opened beyond the Mississippi, stretching all the way to the Pacific. To Southerners extension of their economy to the territories was the condition of survival, for slave agriculture must possess new lands and new legislatures or perish.

The torturing question was whether the national government, or the state governments, would determine the policies in American growth. Taney and his Court, with exceptions, were in the camp of the states. The crisis came in the Dred Scott decision of 1857. Taney, speaking for the Court, divided 7 to 2, proclaimed that the nation could not forbid the territorial expansion of slavery.

The North was outraged and determined not to abide by the decision. Distinguished students of our constitutional history, reviewing the baleful pronouncement, have felt that the Court trespassed beyond its judicial function.* The Court should have limited its opinion to narrow ground, leaving the momentous issue of the future of slavery to be resolved by political processes. Certainly in this instance the decision was reversed by civil war and amendments to the Constitution. But one may hold that the error of the Court was not that it attempted to settle a controversy in which the people were deeply divided, but that it favored the side that was doomed by economic and moral forces. Are there areas of conflict in American public life which must be reserved for political settlement, exempt from judicial intervention? May not political adjustment be aided by guidance of the highest tribunal? Almost a century later, in the related but less crucial case concerning segregation of Negro children in public schools, the Supreme Court refused to follow a previous temporizing decision and commanded a clear-cut policy for the American people.

Effects on Court Decisions of Civil War

The Supreme Court having been massively defied in the Dred Scott case, it is not remarkable that it was held in low esteem during the Civil War and for a dozen years following. War brings forward action branches of the government—the President as commander in chief and Congress as munitioner and policy-maker. Taney died in 1864, and five appointees of President Lincoln, including Chief Justice Salmon P. Chase, changed the political complexion of the Court to be unquestionably loyal. This was to small avail in restoring the Court's prestige or self-confidence. After the war the justices saw the Reconstruction Congress charging ahead, sponsoring constitutional amendments to ensure freedmen's rights, and policing recently rebel states with the military. Repeatedly besought to pass on the legality of Reconstruction measures, the Court found discretion to be the better part of valor, and effaced itself in decisions that avoided application of the Constitution.

Ironically, at a time when the national will would seem to be peculiarly dominant, the aggressiveness of Congress inclined the majority of the Court to protect authority of the states. Typically (almost spitefully) the Court held that "privileges or immunities of citizens of the United States," which the Fourteenth Amendment forbade any state to abridge, did not belong to citizens in their daily local concerns. Not only did this forced interpretation leave defenseless Negroes who were the solicitude of the amendment, but it sanctioned state action

* For example, Carl B. Swisher, *The Supreme Court in Modern Role* (1958) pp. 145-8.

that invaded rights of white citizens as well. The *Slaughterhouse* cases enlarged state police powers in a fashion which prophetic dissenting justices considered scandalous. In progressive reaction from the license given to states to regulate business, the Court, down to the Great Depression of the 1930's, went far in the opposite direction. The judges read the "due process" provision of the Fourteenth Amendment to excuse private (increasingly corporate) enterprise from restraints in the public interest. As we have seen, in 1881 the Court approved a national income tax. Then when such a law was enacted in 1894 men of wealth screamed with pain. They proclaimed that taxing incomes heralded the march of predatory socialism or worse. The Supreme Court responded much as a tuning fork will vibrate when the critical note is sounded on a piano. Promptly the justices declared the tax was unconstitutional (*Pollock v. Farmers' Loan and Trust Company*, 1895).

Burgeoning business combinations threatened the public welfare, but the Court at first applied the Sherman Anti-Trust Act of 1890 not against industrial consolidations but against labor unions. "Yellow dog" contracts—engagements of employes not to join unions—were not to be forbidden by Congress under the commerce power. Nor could control of commerce, or the federal taxing power, prevent the evils of child labor.

Property Is Less Important than People

But strident free enterprise, which had so long found friends in the Court, collapsed in 1929. Thereafter business was obliged to receive from the federal government both relief and correction. For a few frustrating years the Supreme Court lingered in the belief of President Hoover that, with patience, the depression would cure itself. The justices met the emergency New Deal measures of President Franklin Roosevelt with a dozen adverse decisions. The laws to cope with the dire distress of business, workers, and farmers (National Industrial Recovery Act and Agricultural Adjustment Act) were knocked out as unconstitutional. The Court's repugnance to governmental intervention in the economy was not reserved for President and Congress alone, for a New York minimum wage law for women and children was struck down in 1936. The Court was acting, as Justice Holmes had said a generation earlier, "upon an economic theory which a large part of the country does not entertain." In the calamity of depression, with fourteen million jobless, the voters demanded rescue by positive authority and contrivance of government. The states had exhausted their inadequate resources. Only national powers, freely and promptly extended, could help. No outworn notion of let-alone could be allowed to compete with hunger and hopelessness.

President Franklin Roosevelt proposed a reorganization of the Court to secure its co-operation with Congress and the chief executive. The plan was rejected, but its purpose was accomplished. The Court itself had learned that property rights were less precious than human rights. The President's angry assault aided this conversion, and his new appointees to the bench clinched the result.

Beginning in the spring of 1937 the Court executed an about-face and approved every New Deal measure that came before it. The majority no longer contended that "The meaning of the Constitution does not change with the ebb and flow of economic events." Instead, "The Constitution . . . speaks of liberty and prohibits the deprivation of liberty without due process of law . . . the liberty safeguarded is liberty in a social organization which requires the protection of law against the evils which menace the health, safety, morals and welfare of the people."

Problems of American Democracy

World War II helped produce opposite results in two fields of civil rights. The war effort mingled Negro and white citizens in industry as well as the armed forces and shifted large numbers, in and out of uniform, from their accustomed localities to other regions of the country. After victory the United States emerged as main defender of democracy in the world, and strove to advance the economies of backward peoples in the hope that they would embrace democratic forms of government. As a result of these several forces, discrimination in the United States against certain minority groups, mainly Negroes, in voting, schooling, housing, employment, transportation, recreation and similar fields came under renewed and more vehement attack.

Contrasted with this liberal development in race relations were restrictions on freedom of speech, assemblage, and press, inspired by fear of subversion. The Soviet Union, our ally in the fighting war, appeared as our dangerous enemy in the "cold war" of ideologies that followed. The Bill of Rights was dishonored by the zeal and procedures of congressional committees and administrative boards probing and punishing actions, associations, and opinions alleged to imperil our national security. Chief inquisitor was Senator Joseph R. McCarthy of Wisconsin until he was censured by the Senate for his unwarranted charges and methods.

The Supreme Court's interpretation of the Constitution to forbid discrimination against Negroes and members of other minorities went far to correct, in law at least, long-standing wrongs. Earlier judgments had compelled the admission of Negroes to publicly supported professional schools previously reserved for whites. But the key decision was that of 1954 opening public elementary and high schools to Negro children. The Court held that segregation was in itself detrimental, psychologically, to educational development of the Negro pupils and thus denied them the equal protection of the laws guaranteed by the Fourteenth Amendment. The circumspect directions of the Court for enforcement have been abused, and decisions in the Court term ending in June 1963 demanded a speeding of desegregation. Following the public school cases, desegregation has been ordered in one activity and facility after another.

In passing on accusations of disloyalty under various enactments since World War II the Court's record is mixed. The more significant cases have involved construction of the First Amendment protection to freedom of speech. Defendants have regularly relied on the expression employed by Justice Holmes in the unanimous opinion of the Court in *Schenck v. United States* in 1919. The test, he said, is "whether the words used are used in such circumstances and are of such a nature as to create a clear and present danger that they will bring about the substantive evils that Congress has a right to prevent. It is a question of proximity and degree." The "clear and present danger" benchmark, inevitably, has been treated by different judges as movable depending, as Holmes allowed, on how clear and how present the forbidden consequence is estimated to be. Few have considered the right of free speech to be unqualified. More have felt that freedom of thought or belief is protected absolutely.

The Court sustained the provision of the Taft-Hartley Act of 1947 that a union forfeits the benefits of the earlier Labor Relations Act unless its officers take oath denying Communist party or similar connections. The status of the Communist party as such was at issue in the bitterly contested case of *Dennis v. United States* (1951). Conviction of eleven principal party leaders under the Smith Act of 1940 was upheld, 6 to 2. Potentially more important than the jailing of the petitioners was finding the Smith Act constitutional. That law forbade conspiracy to teach or advocate overthrow of the government by force, or organization of a group committed to such advocacy. The main contention of the convicted leaders was that merely teaching and organizing did not portend a "clear and present danger," but were lawful under the First Amendment. Justices Douglas and Black in dissenting from the majority, took this view, and the latter hoped that "in calmer times, when present . . . passions . . . subside, this . . . Court will restore the First Amendment liberties to the high preferred place where they belong in a free society." His optimism seemed to be rewarded six years later when the Court, much altered in personnel, refused to approve the conviction of minor Communist party leaders.

Passing over some less liberal positions of the Court, we end with the 6 to 1 decision in *Watkins v. United States*, 1957. Watkins, a union leader, had been convicted of contempt of Congress because he refused to testify before the House Committee on Un-American Activities against former associates who, unlike himself, had been members of the Communist party. He declined to be an informer. The majority reversed Watkins's conviction. "Un-American activities" was a term too vague to accord with due process under the Fifth Amendment. Chief Justice Warren took occasion to uphold First Amendment protections against abridgment of freedom of speech, press, religion, political belief, and association. He struck at an habitual abuse of the committee's power: "We have no doubt," he declared, "that there is no congressional power to expose for the sake of exposure."

A movement expressing opposition to current tendencies of the Court, may be mentioned as a footnote. A "package" of three proposed constitutional amendments was started by the route (never before used successfully) of approval by two-thirds of the state legislatures, which would require Congress to call a constitutional convention to consider them. If this body approved, ratification by three-fourths of the states would then be necessary.

The first of these propositions would leave the matter of apportionment specifically in the hands of the states, with federal courts forbidden to hear such cases; the second would permit amendment of the Constitution by action of three-fourths of the states, with no participation by federal government necessary; the third would set up a "Court of the Union," consisting of the chief justices in the fifty states, to pass finally on constitutional decisions of the Supreme Court.

In the first stages of this campaign, a number of states approved at least one of these proposals, with little or no debate. (Senator Paul Douglas of Illinois referred to them as "the silent amendments.") This was possible partly because the movement was begun during the news blackout in New York in the winter of 1962-3. After resumption of publication, the *New York Times* began to give the matter publicity, and other voices were also raised in opposition. Chief Justice Warren, without formally taking a position in opposition, appealed to the bar to give leadership in full public debate.

Momentum went out of this movement as opposition took form, partly because the proposals were subtly racist. They seem unlikely to be revived. Their effect in sum would have been to alter our constitutional system out of recognizable shape; restoring power to the states in such large measure would reverse the trend of nearly 185 years of constitutional development.

We have seen that the Constitution through 185 years has been many things to men of different minds. The hide-bound conservative has found in it support for his hostility to change. Those far to the left have believed that the Constitution authorizes their proposals. Between these extremes persons and groups of varying views have thought the fundamental law competent to their wishes.

This flexibility or mutability is a main merit of the document. It is couched in terms at once general and meaningful. A result of compromises, of give and take between contending interests and opinions, it is yet inspired by the resolve to furnish the American people a vehicle for permanence and progress. The Founding Fathers were prophets in projecting the future of the nation. They did not pretend to foresee particular turns of events, or to prescribe solutions for problems that would inevitably arise from expansion of population and geographic area and development of new modes of life. They did better; they provided the means of preserving balance during forward motion. We may say that the wisdom of the Constitution is physiological, just as the bone structure, heart, lungs, and other organs of the infant are equal later to meeting the demands of the mature body.

The expressions "strict construction" and "liberal interpretation" witness the adaptability of the instrument. "Equal protection of the laws" is a principle, not a program or blueprint. "Due process of law" is elastic in denotation. Besides such formal phrases in the Constitution, implied powers are capable of narrower or wider scope. The sense ascribed to provisions of the Constitution is commonly a question of degree, not of dogma.

Some have thought that it would have been preferable to reverse the emphasis of the Constitution. Instead of reserving to the states all authority not conferred on the central government, the functions of the states might have been defined and remaining powers be assigned for national exercise. Historically this would not have been possible.

For the states, though at best only semi-sovereign in fact, considered they were agreeing to bestow certain capacities on the national instruments they were creating. This is a chancy description of what happened. Many at the time and since would maintain that the Constitution was not a compact between the states but sprang from the will of the whole people. In any event, the course of experience has shifted more and more duties and options to national organs. With growing interdependence of sections, states, and localities, the mandate is apt to lie with the government that represents all of us.

SELECTED LIST OF BOOKS ON THE CONSTITUTION

Barrett, Edward L., Jr., and Paul W. Bruton, *Constitutional Law, Cases and Materials*, Mineola, N.Y., 1973.

Beard, Charles A., *An Economic Interpretation of the Constitution of the United States*, New York, 1937.

Benton, Thomas H., *Abridgment of Debates of Congress, 1789-1856*, 16 vols., reprint of 1857 ed., New York, 1970.

Berger, Raoul, *Impeachment: The Constitutional Problem*, Cambridge, Mass., 1973.

———, *Executive Privilege: A Constitutional Myth*, Cambridge, Mass., 1974.

Beveridge, Albert, *The Life of John Marshall*, Boston, 4 vols. in 2, 1929.

Brown, Robert E., *Charles Beard and the Constitution*, New York, 1965.

The Constitution of the United States of America, Analysis and Interpretation of Cases . . . Lester S. Jason, supervising ed., Washington, 1973.

Corwin, Edward S., *The Constitution and What It Means Today*, revised 13th ed., Princeton, 1973.

———, *Court over Constitution: A Study of Judicial Review as an Instrument of Popular Government*, Princeton, 1938.

Cushman, Robert E., ed., *Leading Constitutional Decisions*, 14th ed., New York, 1971.

Documents Illustrative of the Formation of the Union of American States, Washington, 1927.

Elliott, Jonathan, ed., *The Debates in the Several State Conventions on the Adoption of the Federal Constitution*, Washington, 2d. ed., 5 vols., 1936.

Farrand, Max, ed., *The Records of the Federal Convention of 1787*, New Haven, 4 vols., 1966.

The Federalist, edited with introduction and notes by Jacob E. Cooke, Middletown, Ct., 1961.

Furman, Charles, ed., *American Constitutional Decisions*, New York, 1950.

Garraty, John A., *Quarrels That Have Shaped the Constitution*, New York, 1964.

372 A BIOGRAPHY OF THE CONSTITUTION

Jensen, Merrill, *The Articles of Confederation*, Madison, 1948.

Kauper, Paul G., ed., *Constitutional Law: Cases and Materials*, Boston, 1972.

Konvitz, Milton R., *Bill of Rights Reader* . . . New York, 1954.

Mason, Alpheus T., *The Supreme Court from Taft to Warren*, Baton Rouge, 1968.

McDonald, Forrest, *We the People: the Economic Origins of the Constitution*, Chicago, 1958.

Mitchell, Broadus, *Alexander Hamilton*, New York, 2 vols., 1957, 1962.

———, *Depression Decade* . . . New York, 1969.

Peirce, Neal R., *The People's President* . . . New York, 1968.

Pritchett, Charles H., *The American Constitution*, New York, 1968.

Rutland, Robert A., *The Birth of the Bill of Rights*, 1776-1791, Chapel Hill, 1955.

Schwartz, Bernard, *Constitutional Law: A Textbook*, New York, 1972.

Swisher, Carl B., *American Constitutional Development*, Boston, 2d. ed., 1954.

———, *The Supreme Court in Modern Role*, New York, revised ed., 1965.

———, *Roger B. Taney*, Hamden, Ct., 1961.

Van Doren, Carl C., *The Great Rehearsal*, New York, 1948.

Warren, Charles, *The Supreme Court in United States History*, Boston, 2 vols., 1960.

THE CONSTITUTION OF
THE UNITED STATES

We the people of the United States, in Order to form a more perfect Union, establish Justice, insure domestic Tranquility, provide for the common defence, promote the general Welfare, and secure the Blessings of Liberty to ourselves and our Posterity, do ordain and establish this Constitution for the United States of America.

ARTICLE I

SECTION 1. All legislative Powers herein granted shall be vested in a Congress of the United States, which shall consist of a Senate and House of Representatives.

SECTION 2. The House of Representatives shall be composed of Members chosen every second Year by the People of the several States, and the Electors in each State shall have the Qualifications requisite for Electors of the most numerous Branch of the State Legislature.

No Person shall be a Representative who shall not have attained to the Age of twenty-five Years, and been seven Years a Citizen of the United States, and who shall not, when elected, be an Inhabitant of that State in which he shall be chosen.

Representatives and direct Taxes shall be apportioned among the several States which may be included within this Union, according to their respective Numbers, *which shall be determined by adding to the whole Number of free Persons, including those bound to Service for a Term of Years,*[1] and excluding Indians not taxed, *three fifths of all other Persons.*[2] The actual Enumeration shall be made within three

[1] Altered by the Fourteenth Amendment.
[2] Rescinded by the Fourteenth Amendment.

Years after the first Meeting of the Congress of the United States, and within every subsequent Term of ten Years, in such Manner as they shall by Law direct. The Number of Representatives shall not exceed one for every thirty Thousand, but each State shall have at Least one Representative; *and until such enumeration shall be made, the State of New Hampshire shall be entitled to chuse three, Massachusetts eight, Rhode-Island and Providence Plantations one, Connecticut five, New-York six, New Jersey four, Pennsylvania eight, Delaware one, Maryland six, Virginia ten, North Carolina five, South Carolina five, and Georgia three.*[3]

When vacancies happen in the Representation from any State, the Executive Authority thereof shall issue Writs of Election to fill such Vacancies.

The House of Representatives shall chuse their Speaker and other Officers; and shall have the sole Power of Impeachment.

SECTION 3. The Senate of the United States shall be composed of two Senators from each State, *chosen by the Legislature thereof,*[4] for six Years; and each Senator shall have one Vote.

Immediately after they shall be assembled in Consequence of the first Election, they shall be divided as equally as may be into three Classes. The Seats of the Senators of the first Class shall be vacated at the Expiration of the second Year, of the second Class at the Expiration of the fourth Year, and of the third Class at the Expiration of the sixth Year, so that one third may be chosen every second Year; *and if Vacancies happen by Resignation, or otherwise, during the Recess of the Legislature of any State, the Executive thereof may make temporary Appointments until the next Meeting of the Legislature, which shall then fill such Vacancies.*[5]

No Person shall be a Senator who shall not have attained to the Age of thirty Years, and been nine Years a Citizen of the United States, and who shall not, when elected, be an Inhabitant of that State for which he shall be chosen.

The Vice President of the United States shall be President of the Senate, but shall have no Vote, unless they be equally divided.

The Senate shall chuse their other Officers, and also a President pro tempore, in the Absence of the Vice President, or when he shall exercise the Office of the President of the United States.

The Senate shall have the sole Power to try all Impeachments. When sitting for the Purpose, they shall be on Oath or Affirmation. When the President of the United States is tried, the Chief Justice shall preside:

[3] Temporary provision.
[4] Modified by the Seventeenth Amendment.
[5] Modified by the Seventeenth Amendment.

And no Person shall be convicted without the Concurrence of two thirds of the Members present.

Judgment in Cases of Impeachment shall not extend further than to removal from Office, and disqualification to hold and enjoy any Office or honor, Trust or Profit under the United States: but the Party convicted shall nevertheless be liable and subject to Indictment, Trial, Judgment and Punishment, according to Law.

SECTION 4. The Times, Places and Manner of holding Elections for Senators and Representatives, shall be prescribed in each State by the Legislature thereof, but the Congress may at any time by Law make or alter such Regulations, except as to the Places of chusing Senators.

The Congress shall assemble at least once in every year, and such Meeting shall be on the first Monday in December, unless they shall by Law appoint a different day.[6]

SECTION 5. Each House shall be the Judge of the Elections, Returns and Qualifications of its own Members, and a Majority of each shall constitute a Quorum to do Business; but a smaller Number may adjourn from day to day, and may be authorized to compel the Attendance of absent Members, in such manner, and under such Penalties as each House may provide.

Each House may determine the Rules of its Proceedings, punish its Members for disorderly Behaviour, and, with the Concurrence of two thirds, expel a Member.

Each House shall keep a Journal of its Proceedings, and from time to time publish the same, excepting such Parts as may in their Judgment require Secrecy; and the Yeas and Nays of the Members of either House on any question shall, at the Desire of one fifth of those Present, be entered on the Journal.

Neither House, during the Session of Congress, shall, without the Consent of the other, adjourn for more than three days, nor to any other Place than that in which the two Houses shall be sitting.

SECTION 6. The Senators and Representatives shall receive a Compensation for their Services, to be ascertained by Law, and paid out of the Treasury of the United States. They shall in all Cases, except Treason, Felony and Breach of the Peace, be privileged from Arrest during their Attendance at the Session of their respective Houses, and in going to and returning from the same; and for any Speech or Debate in either House, they shall not be questioned in any other Place.

No Senator or Representative shall, during the Time for which he was elected, be appointed to any civil Office under the Authority of the

[6] Superseded by the Twentieth Amendment.

United States, which shall have been created, or the Emoluments whereof shall have been increased during such time; and no Person holding any Office under the United States, shall be a Member of either House during his Continuance in Office.

Section 7. All Bills for raising Revenue shall originate in the House of Representatives; but the Senate may propose or concur with Amendments as on other Bills.

Every Bill which shall have passed the House of Representatives and the Senate shall, before it becomes a Law, be presented to the President of the United States; If he approve he shall sign it, but if not he shall return it, with his Objections to that House in which it shall have originated, who shall enter the Objections at large on their Journal, and proceed to reconsider it. If after such Reconsideration two thirds of that House shall agree to pass the Bill, it shall be sent, together with the Objections, to the other House, by which it shall likewise be reconsidered, and if approved by two thirds of that House, it shall become a Law. But in all such Cases the Votes of both Houses shall be determined by yeas and Nays, and the Names of the Persons voting for and against the Bill shall be entered on the Journal of each House respectively. If any Bill shall not be returned by the President within ten Days (Sundays excepted) after it shall have been presented to him, the Same shall be a Law, in like Manner as if he had signed it, unless the Congress by their Adjournment prevent its Return, in which Case it shall not be a Law.

Every Order, Resolution or Vote to which the Concurrence of the Senate and House of Representatives may be necessary (except on a question of Adjournment) shall be presented to the President of the United States; and before the Same shall take Effect, shall be approved by him, or being disapproved by him, shall be repassed by two thirds of the Senate and House of Representatives, according to the Rules and Limitations prescribed in the Case of a Bill.

Section 8. The Congress shall have Power To lay and collect Taxes, Duties, Imposts and Excises, to pay the Debts and provide for the common Defence and general Welfare of the United States; but all Duties, Imposts and Excises shall be uniform throughout the United States;

To borrow Money on the credit of the United States;

Te regulate Commerce with foreign Nations, and among the several States, and with the Indian Tribes;

To establish an uniform Rule of Naturalization, and uniform Laws on the subject of Bankruptcies throughout the United States;

To coin Money, regulate the Value thereof, and of foreign Coin, and fix the Standard of Weights and Measures;

To provide for the Punishment of counterfeiting the Securities and current Coin of the United States;

To establish Post Offices and post Roads;

To promote the Progress of Science and useful Arts, by securing for limited Times to Authors and Inventors the exclusive Right to their respective Writings and Discoveries;

To constitute Tribunals inferior to the supreme Court;

To define and punish Piracies and Felonies committed on the high Seas, and Offences against the Law of Nations;

To declare War, grant Letters of Marque and Reprisal, and make Rules concerning Captures on Land and Water;

To raise and support Armies, but no Appropriation of Money to that Use shall be for a longer Term than two Years;

To provide and maintain a Navy;

To make Rules for the Government and Regulation of the land and naval Forces;

To provide for calling forth the Militia to execute the Laws of the Union, suppress Insurrection and repel Invasions;

To provide for organizing, arming, and discipling, the Militia, and for governing such Part of them as may be employed in the Service of the United States, reserving to the States respectively, the Appointment of the Officers, and the Authority of training the Militia according to the discipline prescribed by Congress;

To exercise exclusive Legislation in all Cases whatsoever, over such District (not exceeding ten Miles square) as may, by Cession of particular States, and the Acceptance of Congress, become the Seat of the Government of the United States, and to exercise like Authority over all Places purchased by the Consent of the Legislature of the State in which the Same shall be, for the Erection of Forts, Magazines, Arsenals, dock-Yards, and other needful Buildings;—And

To make all Laws which shall be necessary and proper for carrying into Execution the foregoing Powers, and all other Powers vested by this Constitution in the Government of the United States, or in any Department or Office thereof.

SECTION 9. *The Migration or Importation of such Persons as any of the States now existing shall think proper to admit, shall be prohibited by the Congress prior to the Year one thousand eight hundred and eight, but a Tax or duty may be imposed on such Importation, not exceeding ten dollars for each Person.*[7]

The Privilege of the Writ of Habeas Corpus shall not be suspended, unless when in Cases of Rebellion or Invasion the public Safety may require it.

[7] Temporary provision.

No Bill of Attainder or ex post facto Law shall be passed.

No Capitation, or other direct, Tax shall be laid, unless in Proportion to the Census or Enumeration herein before directed to be taken.

No tax or Duty shall be laid on Articles exported from any State.

No Preference shall be given by any Regulation of Commerce or Revenue to the Ports of one State over those of another; nor shall Vessels bound to, or from, one State, be obliged to enter, clear, or pay Duties in another.

No Money shall be drawn from the Treasury, but in Consequence of Appropriations made by Law, and a regular Statement and Account of the Receipts and Expenditures of all public Money shall be published from time to time.

No Title of Nobility shall be granted by the United States: And no Person holding any Office of Profit or Trust under them, shall, without the Consent of the Congress, accept of any present, Emolument, Office, or Title, of any kind whatever, from any King, Prince, or foreign State.

SECTION 10. No State shall enter into any Treaty, Alliance, or Confederation; grant Letters of Marque and Reprisal; coin Money; emit Bills of Credit; make any Thing but gold and silver Coin a Tender in Payment of Debts; pass any Bill of Attainder, ex post facto Law, or Law impairing the Obligation of Contracts, or grant any Title of Nobility.

No State shall, without the Consent of the Congress, lay any Imposts or Duties on Imports or Exports, except what may be absolutely necessary for executing its inspection Laws: and the net Produce of all Duties and Imposts, laid by any State on Imports or Exports, shall be for the Use of the Treasury of the United States; and all such Laws shall be subject to the Revision and Controul of the Congress.

No State shall, without the Consent of Congress, lay any Duty of Tonnage, keep troops, or Ships of War in time of Peace, enter into any Agreement or Compact with another State, or with a foreign Power, or engage in War, unless actually invaded, or in such imminent Danger as will not admit of delay.

ARTICLE II

SECTION 1. The Executive Power shall be vested in a President of the United States of America. *He shall hold his Office during the Term of four Years*,[8] and, together with the Vice President, chosen for the same Term, be elected, as follows:

Each State shall appoint, in such Manner as the Legislature thereof

[8] Modified by the Twenty-second Amendment.

may direct, a Number of Electors, equal to the whole Number of Senators and Representatives to which the State may be entitled in the Congress: but no Senator or Representative, or Person holding an Office of Trust or Profit under the United States, shall be appointed an Elector.

The Electors shall meet in their respective States, and vote by Ballot for two persons, of whom one at least shall not be an Inhabitant of the same State with themselves. And they shall make a List of all the Persons voted for, and of the Number of Votes for each; which List they shall sign and certify, and transmit sealed to the Seat of the Government of the United States, directed to the President of the Senate. The President of the Senate shall, in the Presence of the Senate and House of Representatives, open all the Certificates, and the Votes shall then be counted. The Person having the greatest Number of Votes shall be the President, if such Number be a Majority of the whole Number of Electors appointed; and if there be more than one who have such Majority, and have an equal Number of Votes, then the House of Representatives shall immediately chuse by Ballot one of them for President; and if no Person have a Majority, then from the five highest on the List the said House shall in like Manner chuse the President. But in chusing the President, the Votes shall be taken by States, the Representation from each State having one Vote; A quorum for this Purpose shall consist of a Member or Members from two thirds of the States, and a Majority of all the States shall be necessary to a Choice. In every Case, after the Choice of the President, the Person having the greatest Number of Votes of the Electors shall be the Vice President. But if there should remain two or more who have equal Votes, the Senate shall chuse from them by Ballot the Vice President.[9]

The Congress may determine the Time of chusing the Electors, and the Day on which they shall give their Votes; which Day shall be the same throughout the United States.

No Person except a natural born Citizen, or a Citizen of the United States, at the time of the Adoption of the Constitution, shall be eligible to the Office of President, neither shall any Person be eligible to that Office who shall not have attained to the Age of thirty-five Years, and been fourteen Years a Resident within the United States.

In Case of the Removal of the President from Office, or of his Death, Resignation, or Inability to discharge the Powers and Duties of the said Office, the Same shall devolve on the Vice President, and the Congress may by Law provide for the Case of Removal, Death, Resignation or Inability, both of the President and Vice President, declaring what Officer shall then act as President, and such Officer shall

[9] Superseded by the Twelfth Amendment.

act accordingly, until the Disability be removed, or a President shall be elected.

The President shall, at stated Times, receive for his Services, a Compensation, which shall neither be encreased nor diminished during the Period for which he shall have been elected, and he shall not receive within that Period any other Emolument from the United States, or any of them.

Before he enter on the Execution of his Office, he shall take the following Oath or Affirmation:—"I do solemnly swear (or affirm) that I will faithfully execute the Office of President of the United States, and will to the best of my Ability, preserve, protect and defend the Constitution of the United States."

SECTION 2. The President shall be Commander in Chief of the Army and Navy of the United States, and of the Militia of the several states, when called into the actual Service of the United States; he may require the Opinion, in writing, of the principal Officer in each of the executive Departments, upon any Subject relating to the Duties of their respective Offices, and he shall have Power to grant Reprieves and Pardons for Offences against the United States, except in Cases of Impeachment.

He shall have Power, by and with the Advice and Consent of the Senate, to make Treaties, provided two thirds of the Senators present concur; and he shall nominate, and by and with the Advice and Consent of the Senate, shall appoint Ambassadors, other public Ministers and Consuls, Judges of the supreme Court, and all other Officers of the United States, whose Appointments are not herein otherwise provided for, and which shall be established by Law; but the Congress may by Law vest the Appointment of such inferior Officers, as they think proper, in the President alone, in the Courts of Law, or in the Heads of Departments.

The President shall have Power to fill up all Vacancies that may happen during the Recess of the Senate, by granting Commissions which shall expire at the End of their next Session.

SECTION 3. He shall from time to time give to the Congress Information of the State of the Union, and recommend to their Consideration such Measures as he shall judge necessary and expedient; he may, on extraordinary Occasions, convene both Houses, or either of them, and in Case of Disagreement between them, with Respect to the Time of Adjournment, he may adjourn them to such Time as he shall think proper; he shall receive Ambassadors and other public Ministers; he shall take Care that the Laws be faithfully executed, and shall Commission all the Officers of the United States.

SECTION 4. The President, Vice President and all civil Officers of the United States, shall be removed from Office on Impeachment for, and Conviction of, Treason, Bribery, or other high Crimes and Misdemeanors.

ARTICLE III

SECTION 1. The judicial Power of the United States, shall be vested in one supreme Court, and in such inferior Courts as the Congress may from time to time ordain and establish. The Judges, both of the supreme and inferior courts, shall hold their Offices during good Behaviour, and shall, at stated Times, receive for their Services, a Compensation, which shall not be diminished during their Continuance in Office.

SECTION 2. The judicial Power shall extend to all Cases, in Law and Equity, arising under this Constitution, the Laws of the United States, and Treaties made, or which shall be made, under their Authority;—to all Cases affecting Ambassadors, other public Ministers and Consuls;—to all Cases of admiralty and maritime Jurisdiction:—to Controversies to which the United States shall be a Party;—to Controversies between two or more States;—*between a State and Citizens of another State*;[10]—between Citizens of different States,—between Citizens of the same State claiming Lands under Grants of different States, and *between a State, or the Citizens thereof, and foreign States, Citizens or Subjects*.[10]

In all Cases affecting Ambassadors, other public Ministers and Consuls, and those in which a State shall be Party, the supreme Court shall have original Jurisdiction. In all the other Cases before mentioned, the supreme Court shall have appellate Jurisdiction, both as to Law and Fact, with such Exceptions, and under such Regulations as the Congress shall make.

The Trial of all Crimes, except in Cases of Impeachment, shall be by Jury; and such Trial shall be held in the State where the said Crimes shall have been committed; but when not committed within any State, the Trial shall be at such Place or Places as the Congress may by Law have directed.

SECTION 3. Treason against the United States, shall consist only in levying War against them, or in adhering to their Enemies, giving them Aid and Comfort. No Person shall be convicted of Treason unless on the Testimony of two Witnesses to the same overt Act, or on Confession in open Court.

[10] Restricted by the Eleventh Amendment.

The Congress shall have Power to declare the Punishment of Treason, but no Attainder of Treason shall work Corruption of Blood, or Forfeiture except during the Life of the Person attainted.

ARTICLE IV

SECTION 1. Full Faith and Credit shall be given in each State to the public Acts, Records, and judicial Proceedings of every other State. And the Congress may by general Laws prescribe the Manner in which such Acts, Records and Proceedings shall be proved, and the Effect thereof.

SECTION 2. *The Citizens of each State shall be entitled to all Privileges and Immunities of Citizens in the several States.*[11]

A Person charged in any State with Treason, Felony, or other Crime, who shall flee from Justice, and be found in another State, shall on Demand of the executive Authority of the State from which he fled, be delivered up, to be removed to the State having jurisdiction of the Crime.

No Person held to Service or Labour in one State, under the Laws thereof, escaping into another, shall, in Consequence of any Law or Regulation therein, be discharged from such Service or Labour, but shall be delivered up on Claim of the Party to whom such Service or Labour may be due.[12]

SECTION 3. New States may be admitted by the Congress into this Union; but no new State shall be formed or erected within the Jurisdiction of any other State; nor any State be formed by the Junction of two or more States, or Parts of States, without the Consent of the Legislatures of the States concerned as well as of the Congress.

The Congress shall have Power to dispose of and make all needful Rules and Regulations respecting the Territory or other Property belonging to the United States; and nothing in this Constitution shall be so construed as to Prejudice any Claims of the United States, or of any particular State.

SECTION 4. The United States shall guarantee to every State in this Union a Republican Form of Government, and shall protect each of them against Invasion; and on Application of the Legislature, or of the Executive (when the Legislature cannot be convened) against domestic Violence.

11 Made more explicit by the Fourteenth Amendment.
12 Superseded by the Thirteenth Amendment in so far as pertaining to slaves.

ARTICLE V

The Congress, whenever two thirds of both Houses shall deem it necessary, shall propose Amendments to this Constitution, or, on the Application of the Legislatures of two thirds of the several States, shall call a Convention for proposing Amendments, which, in either Case, shall be valid to all Intents and Purposes, as Part of this Constitution, when ratified by the Legislatures of three fourths of the several States, or by Conventions in three fourths thereof, as the one or the other Mode of Ratification may be proposed by the Congress; *Provided that no Amendment which may be made prior to the Year One thousand eight hundred and eight shall in any Manner affect the first and fourth Clauses in the Ninth Section of the first Article;*[13] and that no State, without its Consent, shall be deprived of its equal Suffrage in the Senate.

ARTICLE VI

All Debts contracted and Engagements entered into, before the Adoption of this Constitution, shall be as valid against the United States under this Constitution, as under the Confederation.[14]

This Constitution, and the Laws of the United States which shall be made in Pursuance thereof; and all Treaties made, or which shall be made, under the Authority of the United States, shall be the supreme Law of the Land; and the Judges in every State shall be bound thereby, any Thing in the Constitution or Laws of any State to the Contrary notwithstanding.

The Senators and Representatives before mentioned, and the Members of the several State Legislatures, and all executive and judicial Officers, both of the United States and of the several States, shall be bound by Oath or Affirmation, to support this Constitution; but no religious Test shall ever be required as a Qualification to any Office or public Trust under the United States.

ARTICLE VII

The Ratification of the Conventions of nine States, shall be sufficient for the Establishment of this Constitution between the States so ratifying the Same.

Done in Convention by the Unanimous Consent of the States present the Seventeenth Day of September in the Year of our Lord one thou-

[13] Temporary clause.
[14] Extended by the Fourteenth Amendment.

sand seven hundred and Eighty seven and of the Independence of the United States of America the Twelfth. In witness whereof We have hereunto subscribed our Names,

G° WASHINGTON–Prest
and deputy from Virginia

New Hampshire	John Langdon Nicholas Gilman		Geo: Read Gunning Bedford jun
Massachusetts	Nathaniel Gorham Rufus King	Delaware	John Dickinson Richard Bassett Jaco: Broom
Connecticut	Wm Saml Johnson Roger Sherman		James McHenry
New York	Alexander Hamilton	Maryland	Dan of St Thos Jenifer Danl Carroll
New Jersey	Wil: Livingston David A. Brearley. Wm Paterson. Jona: Dayton	Virginia	John Blair– James Madison Jr.
		North Carolina	Wm Blount Richd Dobbs Spaight. Hu Williamson
Pennsylvania	B Franklin Thomas Mifflin Robt Morris Geo. Clymer Thos FitzSimons Jared Ingersoll James Wilson Gouv Morris	South Carolina	J. Rutledge Charles Cotesworth Pinckney Charles Pinckney Pierce Butler.
		Georgia	William Few Abr Baldwin

AMENDMENTS TO THE CONSTITUTION

Articles in addition to, and Amendment of the Constitution of the United States of America, proposed by Congress, and ratified by the Legislatures of the several States, pursuant to the fifth Article of the original Constitution.

ARTICLE I

[The First Ten Articles Proposed 25 September 1789; Declared in Force 15 December 1791]

Congress shall make no law respecting an establishment of religion, or prohibiting the free exercise thereof; or abridging the freedom of speech, or of the press; or the right of the people peaceably to assemble, and to petition the Government for a redress of grievances.

ARTICLE II

A well regulated Militia, being necessary to the security of a free State, the right of the people to keep and bear Arms, shall not be infringed.

ARTICLE III

No Soldier shall, in time of peace be quartered in any house, without the consent of the Owner, nor in time of war, but in a manner to be prescribed by law.

ARTICLE IV

The right of the people to be secure in their persons, houses, papers, and effects, against unreasonable searches and seizures, shall not be violated, and no Warrants shall issue, but upon probable cause, supported by Oath or affirmation, and particularly describing the place to be searched, and the persons or things to be seized.

ARTICLE V

No person shall be held to answer for a capital, or otherwise infamous crime, unless on a presentment or indictment of a Grand Jury, except in cases arising in the land or naval forces, or in the Militia, when in actual service in time of War or public danger; nor shall any person be subject for the same offence to be twice put in jeopardy of life or limb; nor shall be compelled in any criminal case to be a witness against himself, nor be deprived of life, liberty, or property, without due process of law; nor shall private property be taken for public use, without just compensation.

ARTICLE VI

In all criminal prosecutions, the accused shall enjoy the right to a speedy and public trial, by an impartial jury of the State and district wherein the crime shall have been committed, which district shall have been previously ascertained by law, and to be informed of the nature and cause of the accusation; to be confronted with the witnesses against him; to have compulsory process for obtaining witnesses in his favor, and to have the Assistance of Counsel for his defence.

ARTICLE VII

In Suits at common law, where the value in controversy shall exceed twenty dollars, the right of trial by jury shall be preserved, and no fact tried by a jury, shall be otherwise re-examined in any Court of the United States, than according to the rules of the common law.

ARTICLE VIII

Excessive bail shall not be required, nor excessive fines imposed, nor cruel and unusual punishments inflicted.

ARTICLE IX

The enumeration in the Constitution, of certain rights, shall not be construed to deny or disparage others retained by the people.

ARTICLE X

The powers not delegated to the United States by the Constitution, nor prohibited by it to the States, are reserved to the States respectively, or to the people. [The first ten amendments went into effect November 3, 1791.]

ARTICLE XI

[Proposed 5 September 1794; Declared Ratified 8 January 1798]
The Judicial power of the United States shall not be construed to extend to any suit in law or equity, commenced or prosecuted against one of the United States by Citizens of another State, or by Citizens or Subjects of any Foreign State.

ARTICLE XII

[Proposed 12 December 1803; Declared Ratified 25 September 1804]
The Electors shall meet in their respective states and vote by ballot for President and Vice-President, one of whom, at least, shall not be an inhabitant of the same state with themselves; they shall name in their ballots the person voted for as President, and in distinct ballots the person voted for as Vice-President, and they shall make distinct lists of all persons voted for as President, and of all persons voted for as Vice-President, and of the number of votes for each, which lists they shall sign and certify, and transmit sealed to the seat of the government of the United States, directed to the President of the Senate;—The President of the Senate shall, in presence of the Senate and House of Representatives, open all the certificates and the votes shall then be counted;—The person having the greatest number of votes for the President, shall be the President, if such number be a majority of the whole

number of Electors appointed; and if no person have such majority, then from the persons having the highest numbers not exceeding three on the list of those voted for as President, the House of Representatives shall choose immediately, by ballot, the President. But in choosing the President, the votes shall be taken by states, the representation from each state having one vote, a quorum for this purpose shall consist of a member or members from two-thirds of the states, and a majority of all the states shall be necessary to a choice. And if the House of Representatives shall not choose a President whenever the right of choice shall devolve upon them, before the *fourth day of March*[15] next following, then the Vice-President shall act as President, as in the case of the death or other constitutional disability of the President.—The Person having the greatest number of votes as Vice-President, shall be the Vice-President, if such number be a majority of the whole number of Electors appointed, and if no person have a majority, then from the two highest numbers on the list, the Senate shall choose the Vice-President; a quorum for the purpose shall consist of two-thirds of the whole number of Senators, and a majority of the whole number shall be necessary to a choice. But no person constitutionally ineligible to the office of President shall be eligible to that of Vice-President of the United States.

ARTICLE XIII

[Proposed 1 February 1865; Declared Ratified 18 December 1865]
SECTION 1. Neither slavery nor involuntary servitude, except as a punishment for crime whereof the party shall have been duly convicted, shall exist within the United States, or any place subject to their jurisdiction.

SECTION 2. Congress shall have power to enforce this article by appropriate legislation.

ARTICLE XIV

[Proposed 16 June 1866; Declared Ratified 28 July 1868]
SECTION 1. All persons born or naturalized in the United States, and subject to the jurisdiction thereof, are citizens of the United States and of the State wherein they reside. No State shall make or enforce any law which shall abridge the privileges or immunities of citizens of the United States; nor shall any State deprive any person of life, liberty, or property, without due process of law; nor deny to any person within its jurisdiction the equal protection of the laws.

15 Superseded by the Twentieth Amendment.

SECTION 2. Representatives shall be apportioned among the several States according to their respective numbers, counting the whole number of persons in each State, excluding Indians not taxed. But when the right to vote at any election for the choice of electors for President and Vice-President of the United States, Representatives in Congress, the Executive and Judicial officers of a State, or the members of the Legislature thereof, is denied to any of the male inhabitants of such State, being twenty-one years of age, and citizens of the United States, or in any way abridged, except for participation in rebellion, or other crime, the basis of representation therein shall be reduced in the proportion which the number of such male citizens shall bear to the whole number of male citizens twenty-one years of age in such State.

SECTION 3. No person shall be a Senator or Representative in Congress, or elector of President and Vice-President, or hold any office, civil or military, under the United States, or under any State, who, having previously taken an oath, as a member of Congress, or as an officer of the United States, or as a member of any State legislature, or as an executive or judicial officer of any State, to support the Constitution of the United States, shall have engaged in insurrection or rebellion against the same, or given aid or comfort to the enemies thereof. But Congress may by a vote of two-thirds of each House, remove such disability.

SECTION 4. The validity of the public debt of the United States, authorized by law, including debts incurred for payment of pensions and bounties for services in suppressing insurrection or rebellion, shall not be questioned. But neither the United States nor any State shall assume or pay any debt or obligation incurred in aid of insurrection or rebellion against the United States, or any claim for the loss or emancipation of any slave; but all such debts, obligations and claims shall be held illegal and void.

SECTION 5. The Congress shall have power to enforce, by appropriate legislation, the provision of this article.

ARTICLE XV

[Proposed 27 February 1869; Declared Ratified 30 March 1870]
SECTION 1. The right of citizens of the United States to vote shall not be denied or abridged by the United States or by any State on account of race, color, or previous condition of servitude—

SECTION 2. The Congress shall have power to enforce this article by appropriate legislation.—

ARTICLE XVI

[Proposed 12 July 1909; Declared Ratified 25 February 1913]
The Congress shall have power to lay and collect taxes on incomes, from whatever source derived, without apportionment among the several States, and without regard to any census or enumeration.

ARTICLE XVII

[Proposed 16 May 1912; Declared Ratified 31 May 1913]
The Senate of the United States shall be composed of two Senators from each State, elected by the people thereof, for six years; and each Senator shall have one vote. The electors in each State shall have the qualifications requisite for electors of the most numerous branch of the State legislatures.

When vacancies happen in the representation of any State in the Senate, the executive authority of such State shall issue writs of election to fill such vacancies: *Provided*, That the legislature of any State may empower the executive thereof to make temporary appointments until the people fill the vacancies by election as the legislature may direct.

This amendment shall not be so construed as to affect the election or term of any Senator chosen before it becomes valid as part of the Constitution.

ARTICLE XVIII

[Proposed 3 December 1917; Declared Ratified 29 January 1919]
SECTION 1. *After one year from the ratification of this article the manufacture, sale, or transportation of intoxicating liquors within, the importation thereof into, or the exportation thereof from the United States and all territory subject to the jurisdiction thereof for beverage purposes is hereby prohibited.*

SECTION 2. *The Congress and the several States shall have concurrent power to enforce this article by appropriate legislation.*

SECTION 3. *This article shall be inoperative unless it shall have been ratified as an amendment to the Constitution by the legislatures of the several States, as provided in the Constitution, within seven years from the date of the submission thereof to the States by the Congress.*[16]

[16] Rescinded by the Twenty-first Amendment.

ARTICLE XIX

[Proposed 19 May 1919; Declared Ratified 26 August 1920]
The right of citizens of the United States to vote shall not be denied or abridged by the United States or by any State on account of sex.

The Congress shall have power by appropriate legislation to enforce the Provisions of this article.

ARTICLE XX

[Proposed 3 March 1932; Declared Ratified 6 February 1933]
SECTION 1. The terms of the President and Vice-President shall end at noon on the twentieth day of January, and the terms of Senators and Representatives at noon on the third day of January, of the years in which such terms would have ended if this article had not been ratified; and the terms of their successors shall then begin.

SECTION 2. The Congress shall assemble at least once in every year, and such meeting shall begin at noon on the third day of January, unless they shall by law appoint a different day.

SECTION 3. If, at the time fixed for the beginning of the term of the President, the President-elect shall have died, the Vice-President-elect shall become President. If a President shall not have been chosen before the time fixed for the beginning of his term, or if the President-elect shall have failed to qualify, then the Vice-President-elect shall act as President until a President shall have qualified; and the Congress may by law provide for the case wherein neither a President-elect not a Vice-President-elect shall have qualified, declaring who shall then act as President, or the manner in which one who is to act shall be selected, and such person shall act accordingly until a President or Vice-President shall have qualified.

SECTION 4. The Congress may by law provide for the case of the death of any of the persons from whom the House of Representatives may choose a President whenever the right of choice shall have devolved upon them, and for the case of the death of any of the persons from whom the Senate may choose a Vice-President whenever the right of choice shall have devolved upon them.

SECTION 5. SECTIONS 1 and 2 shall take effect on the 15th day of October following the ratification of this article.

SECTION 6. This article shall be inoperative unless it shall have been ratified as an amendment to the Constitution by the legislatures of three-fourths of the several States within seven years from the date of its submission.

ARTICLE XXI

[Proposed 20 February 1933; Declared Ratified 5 December 1933]
SECTION 1. The eighteenth article of amendment to the Constitution of the United States is hereby repealed.

SECTION 2. The transportation or importation into any State, Territory, or possession of the United States for delivery or use therein of intoxicating liquors, in violation of the laws thereof, is hereby prohibited.

SECTION 3. This article shall be inoperative unless it shall have been ratified as an amendment to the Constitution by conventions in the several States, as provided in the Constitution, within seven years from the date of the submission thereof to the States by the Congress.

ARTICLE XXII

[Proposed 24 March 1947; Declared Ratified 1 March 1951]
SECTION 1. No person shall be elected to the office of the President more than twice, and no person who has held the office of President, or acted as President, for more than two years of a term to which some other person was elected President shall be elected to the office of the President more than once. But this Article shall not apply to any person holding the office of President when this Article was proposed by Congress, and shall not prevent any person who may be holding the office of President, or acting as President, during the term within which this Article becomes operative from holding the office of President or acting as President during the remainder of such term.

SECTION 2. The article shall be inoperative unless it shall have been ratified as an amendment to the Constitution by the legislatures of three-fourths of the several States within seven years from the date of its submission to the States by the Congress.

ARTICLE XXIII

[Proposed 16 June 1960; Declared Ratified 3 April 1961]
SECTION 1. The District constituting the seat of Government of the United States shall appoint in such manner as the Congress may direct:

A number of electors of President and Vice-President equal to the whole number of Senators and Representatives in Congress to which the District would be entitled if it were a State, but in no event more than the least populous State; they shall be in addition to those appointed by the States, but they shall be considered, for the purposes of the election of President and Vice President, to be electors appointed by a State; and they shall meet in the District and perform such duties as provided by the twelfth article of amendment.

SECTION 2. The Congress shall have power to enforce this article by appropriate legislation.

ARTICLE XXIV

[Proposed 27 August 1962; Declared Ratified 4 February 1964]
SECTION 1. The right of citizens of the United States to vote in any primary or other election for President or Vice President, or for Senator or Representative in Congress, shall not be denied or abridged by the United States or any State by reason of failure to pay any poll tax or other tax.

SECTION 2. The Congress shall have power to enforce this article by appropriate legislation.

ARTICLE XXV

[Proposed 6 July, 1965; Declared Ratified 23 February 1967]
SECTION 1. In case of the removal of the President from office or of his death or resignation, the Vice President shall become President.

SECTION 2. Whenever there is a vacancy in the office of the Vice President, the President shall nominate a Vice President who shall take office upon confirmation by a majority vote of both houses of Congress.

SECTION 3. Whenever the President transmits to the President pro tempore of the Senate and the Speaker of the House of Representatives his written declaration that he is unable to discharge the powers and duties of his office, and until he transmits to them a written declaration to the contrary, such powers and duties shall be discharged by the Vice President as Acting President.

SECTION 4. Whenever the Vice President and a majority of either the principal officers of the executive departments or of such other body as Congress may by law provide, transmit to the President pro tempore of the Senate and the Speaker of the House of Representatives their written declaration that the President is unable to discharge the powers and duties of his office, the Vice President shall immediately assume the powers and duties of the office as Acting President.

Thereafter, when the President transmits to the President pro tempore of the Senate and the Speaker of the House of Representatives his written declaration that no disability exists, he shall assume the powers and duties of his office unless the Vice President and a majority of either the principal officers of the executive departments or of such other body as Congress may by law provide, transmit within four days to the President pro tempore of the Senate and the Speaker of the House of Representatives their written declaration that the President is unable to discharge the powers and duties of his office. Thereupon Congress shall decide the issue, assembling within forty-eight hours for that purpose if not in session. If the Congress, within twenty-one days after receipt of the latter written declaration, or, if Congress is not in session, within twenty-one days after Congress is required to assemble, determines by two-thirds vote of both houses that the President is unable to discharge the powers and duties of his office, the Vice President shall continue to discharge the same as Acting President; otherwise, the President shall resume the powers and duties of his office.

ARTICLE XXVI
[Proposed 23 March 1971; Declared Ratified 5 July 1971]
SECTION 1. The right of citizens of the United States, who are 18 years of age or older, to vote shall not be denied or abridged by the United States or any state on account of age.

SECTION 2. The Congress shall have the power to enforce this article by appropriate legislation.

ARTICLE XXVII
[Proposed 22 March 1972; Declared Ratified ———*]
SECTION 1. Equality of rights under the law shall not be denied or abridged by the United States or by any State on account of sex.

SECTION 2. The Congress shall have the power to enforce, by appropriate legislation, the provisions of this article.

SECTION 3. This admendment shall take effect two years after the date of ratification.

* As of January 1974 lacked six states of ratification.

INDEX

Abortion decisions, 357-59

Adams, John, 20, 21, 24, 26, 29, 43, 214, 238, 246

Adams, John Quincy, 52

Adams, Samuel, 20, 25, 40-42, 130; attitude toward Constitution, 145 ff

Alexandria, Va., 15

Alien and Sedition acts, 43, 204

Ames, Fisher, 137, 138, 144, 200, 203

Annapolis Convention, 15, 16 ff, 25, 44

Antifederalists, 39, 96, 135

Apportionment of representation, 353-57

Army, 103, 142

Assumption of state debts, 42, 103, 104, 110

Atkins v. Children's Hospital, 313 ff, 365

Baldwin, Abraham, 62

Bank of U.S., 8, 34, 39, 42, 123, 269, ff

Beard, Charles A., 47-50, 148, 159-60

Bedford, Gunning, his threat on behalf of small states, 68-69, 70

Benson, Egbert, 16, 17, 84, 204, 209

Bill of Rights, 42, 103-4, 112, 121, 123, 132, 144-45, 146, 166, 171, 173, 193 ff, 305, 366; how incorporate in Constitution, 199, 208

Birth control decision, 360-61

Blackstone, William, 22, 28

Boston, 41; massacre, 26

Bowdoin, James, 14, 26, 141

Brackenridge, H. H., 131

British Constitution, xiii, 60, 198-99, 242

Brown, Robert E., 49

Burke, Aedanus, 203, 209

Burr, Aaron, 37, 45, 238, 255

Butler, Benjamin, 90

Butler, Pierce, 71, 105, 109

Calhoun, John C., 23, 273, 300

Canada, 136

Carroll, Charles of Carrollton, 36, 46

Carroll, Daniel, 123-24

Charles River bridge, 266 ff

Chase, Samuel, 36, 37, 252 ff

Chesapeake Bay, 15

Chisholm v. Georgia, 212

Christy, Howard Chandler, 51

Civil rights, 304 ff, 344 ff; voting act of 1964, 234